D1453768

ROYAL HISTORICAL SOCIETY

STUDIES IN HISTORY

New Series

HENRY VIII,
THE LEAGUE OF SCHMALKALDEN
AND THE ENGLISH REFORMATION

HENRY VIII,
THE LEAGUE OF SCHMALKALDEN
AND THE ENGLISH REFORMATION

Rory McEntegart

THE ROYAL HISTORICAL SOCIETY
THE BOYDELL PRESS

DA
339
. M34
2002

First published 2002

A Royal Historical Society publication
Published by The Boydell Press
an imprint of Boydell & Brewer Ltd
PO Box 9, Woodbridge, Suffolk IP12 3DF, UK
and of Boydell & Brewer Inc.
PO Box 41026, Rochester, NY 14604–4126, USA
website: www.boydell.co.uk

ISBN 0 86193 255 2

ISSN 0269–2244

A catalogue record for this book is available
from the British Library

Library of Congress Cataloging-in-Publication Data
McEntegart, Rory.
   Henry VIII, the league of Schmalkalden, and the English Reformation/
Rory McEntegart.
   p. cm. – (Royal Historical Society studies in history. New series,
ISSN 0269–2244 ; v. 25)
   Includes bibliographical references and index.
   ISBN 0–86193–255–2 (alk. paper)
   1. Great Britain – Foreign relations – 1509–1547.   2. Henry VIII, King
of England, 1491–1547.   3. Great Britain – Foreign relations. – Germany.
4. Germany – Foreign relations – Great Britain.   5. Germany – Foreign
relations – 1517–1648.   6. Schmalkaldic League, 1530–1547.
7. Reformation – England.   I. Title: Henry the Eighth, the league of
Schmalkalden, and the English Reformation.   II. Title.   III. Series.
DA339.M36 2002
274.2'06 – dc21   2001056098

This book is printed on acid-free paper

Printed in Great Britain by
St Edmundsbury Press Ltd, Bury St Edmunds, suffolk

Contents

FOR MY FATHER

Acknowledgements

This book grew out of a London University PhD thesis; my thanks are due to my supervisor, David Starkey, for his advice, guidance and kindness through my years as a doctoral student and beyond. I also wish to thank Diarmaid MacCulloch, both for his general encouragement of my research and for his particular suggestion that I seek to have this book published by the Royal Historical Society. In turning the thesis into a book I have benefited greatly from the rigorous historical criticism of Steven Gunn and the keen editorial eye of Christine Linehan.

Finally, I wish to thank my family; my parents and my children, and especially my wife for her long and unfailing support.

Rory McEntegart
Bray, Co. Wicklow 2001

Abbreviations

BayHSt	Bayerisches Hauptstaatsarchiv, Munich
BL	British Library, London
Bo	*Die Beschlüsse der oberdeutschen schmalkaldischen Städtetage, 1530–1536*, ed. E. Fabian, Tübingen 1959–60
BwP	*Briefwechsel Landgraf Philipps des Grossmüthigen von Hessen mit Bucer*, ed. M. Lenz, Leipzig 1880–7
CCCC	Corpus Christi College, Cambridge
CR	*Corpus reformatorum*, ed. C. G. Bretschneider, Halle 1834–60
DNB	*Dictionary of national biography*
DWA	*Die Wittenberger Artikel von 1536*, ed. G. Mentz, Leipzig 1905
EHR	*English Historical Review*
HJ	*Historical Journal*
HStMar	Hessisches Staatsarchiv, Marburg
LP	*Letters and papers, foreign and domestic, of the reign of Henry VIII, 1509–47*, ed. J. S. Brewer, J. Gairdner and R. H. Brodie, London 1862–1910
PC	*Politische Correspondenz der Stadt Strassburg im Zeitalter der Reformation*, ed. H. Virck and O. Winckelmann, Strassburg 1892–8
PRO	Public Record Office, London
SchmBa	*Die schmalkaldischen Bundesabschiede, 1530–1536*, ed. E. Fabian, Tübingen 1958
SpCal	*Calendar of state papers, Spanish*, ed. G. Bergenroth, P. de Gayangos and M. A. S. Hume, London 1862–95
StP	*State papers, published under the authority of His Majesty's Commission, of Henry VIII*, London 1830–52
TStWei	Thüringisches Staatsarchiv, Weimar
WABr	*Weimarer Ausgabe der Werke D.M. Luthers, Abteilung Briefe*, Weimar 1930–48

Note on the Text

All Latin and German quotations are translated into English in the text (well-known phrases excepted). Translation policy is to reflect the spirit rather than the letter of the original. In all cases the original is supplied in full in the footnote.

For manuscript quotations, original spellings have been retained; English punctuation and abbreviations have been modernised.

Arabic numerals refer to page numbers in all cases except citations from *Letters and papers*: here the arabic numerals refer to the document number and, if followed by a roman numeral, to its part.

Introduction

Revisionism has transformed early modern historiography.[1] Today there are few fields of historical research whose comfortable certainties have resisted the relentless labours of revisionist scholarship. Nevertheless, there remain some historiographical backwaters where the grand systems of history stand unchallenged. One of these is the historiography of diplomatic relations during the Reformation. Here, inevitability and determinism still reign supreme. Scholars continue to accept and observe the tenets laid down long ago by James Anthony Froude:

> those who believe that human actions obey the laws of natural causation, might find their philosophy confirmed by the conduct of the great powers of Europe during the early years of the Reformation. With a regularity uniform as that on which we calculate in the application of mechanical forces, the same combinations were attended with identical effects; and given the relations between France and Spain, between Spain and Germany, between England and either of the three, the political situation of all Western Christendom could be estimated with as much certainty as the figure and dimensions of a triangle from the length of one of its sides and the inclination of two of its angles. When England was making advances towards the Lutherans, we are sure that France and Spain were in conjunction under the Papacy, and were menacing the Reformation. When such advances had been pushed forward into prominence, and there was a likelihood of a Protestant league, the Emperor was compelled to neutralize the danger by concessions to the German Diet, or by an affectation of a desire for a reconciliation with Henry, to which Henry was always ready to listen. Then Henry would look coldly on the Protestants, and the Protestants on him. Then Charles could afford again to lay the curb on Francis. Then Francis would again storm and threaten, till passion broke into war. War brought its usual consequences of mutual injury, disaster, and exhaustion; and then the pope would interfere, and peace would, and the same round would repeat itself. Statesmen and kings made, as they imagined, their fine strokes of policy. A wisdom other than theirs condemned them to tread again and again the same ineffectual circle.[2]

---

1 For a discussion of what the word 'revisionism' means to early modern English historians and a summary of the historiography see, for example, C. Haigh, 'The recent historiography of the English Reformation', *HJ* xxv (1982), 995–1007, and G. Redworth, 'Whatever happened to the English Reformation?', *History Today* xxxvii (Oct. 1987), 29–36. See also the opening essay in C. Russell, *Unrevolutionary England, 1603–1642*, London 1990.
2 J. A. Froude, *History of England from the fall of Wolsey to the defeat of the Spanish armada*, London 1870–5, iii. 269–70.

One could forgive and forget all this if Froude's analysis had become nothing more than an historiographical museum-piece, a curiosity from the dim and distant nineteenth century, that age of the great scheme-makers. What makes it less easy to bear is that Froude and his triangles, far from being historiographical artifacts, hold the field in the analysis of foreign policy to this day, and nowhere more so than where relations between England and the League of Schmalkalden are concerned.[3] Here, England and the League remain simple components in the Froudean mechanic. When Charles and Francis are together, Henry inclines towards the League; as soon as they fall out, Henry moves away from the Germans. In all this there is only political calculation; religion does not enter the frame. When Henry makes religious intimations to the Schmalkaldeners, he is being disingenuous, for he has no genuine interest in their religion; his intimations are simply enticements, designed to keep the Germans interested during times of diplomatic necessity. It is all very simple: diplomacy by trigonometrical tables.

Thus, Friedrich Prüser, the first historian of Anglo-Schmalkaldic relations, writes that Henry was interested in negotiations with the League only during those periods when

> the king knew of no other means of aid against the political constellation which endangered him. . . . As soon, however, as the slightest improvement in the foreign situation was noticeable, Henry, only too happy to give his inborn inconstancy free rein, would uniformly lose his taste for a closer connection with the Germans. If he let himself negotiate further with them, this was done simply with a view to retaining the possibility of an alliance for any future eventualities. The Schmalkaldeners were regarded by him simply as an expedient in case of the most critical emergency.[4]

As for the theological discussions which took place between England and the League, Henry, whose 'nature was in the first instance political',[5] saw these purely as 'points of contact for political purposes'.[6] The other main German commentator on Anglo-German relations, Philipp Lange, also argues that Henry only inclined towards the Germans when it was politically necessary,

---

[3] More recently, however, there have been signs of change. See, for example, S. Doran, *England and Europe in the sixteenth century*, London 1999, 88–101, and S. Doran and G. Richardson (eds), *Tudor foreign policy*, London forthcoming.

[4] '[D]er König kein anderes Hilfsmittel gegen eine ihm gefährliche politische Konstellation mehr wusste. . . . Sobald sich aber die geringste Erleichterung der aussenpolitischen Lage bemerkbar machte, verlor Heinrich VIII, der nur allzugern seinem angeborenen Wankelmut freien Lauf liess, regelmässig den Sinn für eine nähere Verbindung mit den Deutschen. Wenn er weiterhin noch mit ihnen unterhandeln liess, so geschah es nur in der Absicht, sich Anknüpfungsmöglichkeiten für alle Notfälle der Zukunft zu bewahren. Die Schmalkaldener waren ihm also nur ein für die äusserste Not berechneter Behelf': F. Prüser, *England und die Schmalkaldener, 1535–40*, Leipzig 1929, 277–8.

[5] '[W]ar in erster Linie eine politische Natur': ibid. 29.

[6] 'Berührungspunkte für politische Zwecke': ibid. 30.

and gives no credence to the sincerity of the religious approaches which were made to the League.[7]

These interpretations stand on well-worn ground. 'The suggestion', wrote James Gairdner at the beginning of the twentieth century, 'of a union with the German Protestants on matters of the faith was intended for nothing but a lure from the first. . . . Henry let the Lutherans alone whenever he thought he could do without them.'[8] Or, according to A. F. Pollard, 'Henry would have no hesitation in throwing over the German princes when once he saw his way to a renewal of friendship with Charles. He would welcome, even more, a relief from the necessity of paying attention to German divines . . . a union with the Protestants could never for Henry be more than a *mariage de convenance*.'[9] More recent interpretations have followed similar lines. 'That the king changed his attitude to the German reformers', writes Gordon Rupp of Henry's decision to approach the Germans after his campaign against Luther during the 1520s, 'was entirely due to political considerations, and not to any kindling sympathy with evangelical doctrine.'[10] R. B. Wernham, the leading English historian of Tudor foreign policy, similarly regards Henry's approaches to the Germans as a series of essentially duplicitous calculations: 'the better to encourage them', he writes of the king's intentions when sending an embassy to the League in the mid-1530s, 'the envoys might even hold out some hope of Henry's accepting the Augsburg Confession and suggest the opening of negotiations in London about this'.[11] But Henry was simply playing the Germans along as part of his diplomatic balancing act. He had no intention of a genuine doctrinal exchange with them. As soon as the temporary difficulties had passed he would abandon the Germans; and indeed before long 'a chain of events had begun to unfold which seemed to justify Henry's confidence', and 'for a season these Protestant approaches made small headway'.[12] This picture, of a king fixed from the outset in his determination to avoid any long-term political involvement with the League and using religion simply as an artifice to achieve diplomatic ends, has survived

---

7 P. Lange, 'Die englisch-deutschen Beziehungen 1531 bis 1535 mit besonderer Berücksichtigung der Politik Philipps von Hessen', unpubl. DPhil. diss. Marburg 1924. See also the short article, H.-U. Delius, 'Königlicher Supremat oder evangelische Reformation der Kirche: Heinrich VIII. von England und die Wittenberger, 1531–1540', *Wissenshaftliche Zeitschrift der Ernst-Moritz-Arndt-Universität Greifswald, gesellschafts- und sprachwissenschaftliche Reihe* xx (1971), 283–91. Although the title suggests a perspective which would take a fuller view of the relevance of religious questions to Anglo-Schmalkaldic relations, the article is in fact little more than a summary of Prüser's views, as expressed in *England und die Schmalkaldener*.
8 J. Gairdner, *Lollardy and the Reformation in England*, London 1908–13, ii. 176–7.
9 A. F. Pollard, *Henry VIII*, London 1902, 386, 388.
10 E. G. Rupp, *Studies in the making of the English Protestant tradition*, Cambridge 1947, 91.
11 R. B. Wernham, *Before the armada: the growth of English foreign policy, 1485–1588*, London 1966, 132.
12 Ibid. 133.

unscathed and unquestioned up to recent times. Glyn Redworth, for example, writes that

> there were numerous contacts between English and Lutheran divines when invasion threatened in the 1530s. Though we tend to forget that no agreement on a radical doctrinal statement was forthcoming (the king had not intended one), the flurry of activity nonetheless produced by such conferences achieved Henry's aim of creating the veneer of an anti-Roman front in the face of the military threat posed by papal supporters.[32]

It has been fashionable to supplement the Henrician duplicity thesis by way of reference to the influence of the king's minister, Thomas Cromwell. This view has it that if Henry on occasion got closer to the Lutherans than he had intended, then the reason lies with the pro-German advocacy of Cromwell. The founding father of this school was the influential R. B. Merriman. From Wolsey's ministry Henry

> had learned that England's best security lay in maintaining a position of neutrality between Charles and Francis, and in balancing one against the other, while all disputes between them were encouraged under cover of offers of mediation. It was along these lines that Henry had determined to guide the foreign affairs of England.[14]

But Cromwell 'overestimated the danger of a foreign invasion',[15] and

> after successfully cooperating with Henry for seven years on the basis of maintaining strict neutrality between France and Spain, and of encouraging all disputes between them, he abandoned the wise policy of his master in favour of an alliance in Germany which, in one form or another, had been under consideration on several occasions before, but which had been abandoned every time as unnecessary.[16]

Sir Geoffrey Elton, in this respect at least, adheres closely to Merriman's interpretation. Throughout his ministry, Cromwell 'overestimated the danger from abroad and therefore overvalued an alliance with foreign Lutherans'.[17] The king, however,

> seems to have understood the essential safety of England's isolated position. Cromwell was always much too inclined to practise the directness and thoroughness of his methods in the field of foreign affairs which required delays, waiting, and opportunism; he was temperamentally a worse foreign minister than the king.[18]

13 Redworth, 'English Reformation', 36.
14 R. B. Merriman, *Life and letters of Thomas Cromwell*, Oxford 1902, i. 214.
15 Ibid.
16 Ibid. i. 214–15.
17 G. R. Elton, *England under the Tudors*, 2nd edn, London 1974, 151.
18 Ibid. 152.

Thus, when England was closely involved with the League, it was a result of a divergence in policy between the king and minister: the League 'was Protestant and therefore suspect to Henry VIII. By the same token it was attractive to Cromwell, fatally so, as the event proved'.[19] A. G. Dickens follows the same lines. While the inexperienced Cromwell searched for alliances in Germany, Henry was happier 'to seek a position of friendly neutrality' between Charles and Francis.[20] The naval historian James Williamson takes a similar view. Henry was

> a master of diplomacy, greater than his tutor Wolsey, because less arrogant and with a finer sense of realities and a better judgement of the characters of those with whom he had to deal. Cromwell was inferior both in knowledge and judgement of foreign affairs. Henry kept the decisions in his own hands, but allowed Cromwell some scope in negotiating with the German Protestants, mainly because such negotiations would be easier to disavow if carried on by the minister rather than by the king in person.[21]

Still, 'it is fairly certain' that Henry 'never relished the tentative negotiations with the Lutherans and the small encouragement given to the English Protestants under Cromwell'.[22]

What of the Schmalkaldeners? Where do they fit into this system? Most historians prefer to ignore the possibility that the Germans had any thoughts at all, but when reference is made to the League it is usual to argue that they were guided and even blinded by religious motives. 'These Schmalkaldeners were good Protestants', writes Prüser, 'but they were very bad politicians';[23] and indeed all historians have contrasted the overriding religiosity of the Germans with the calculated politicking of Henry.[24] This put the Germans at a certain disadvantage in their dealings with Henry: 'the naive credulity of the Schmalkaldeners took no occasion to doubt the honesty of the English efforts', laments Prüser of Henry's approaches during the mid-1530s.[25] But the Schmalkaldeners' piety did at least save them from being used ceaselessly for the king's political purposes. Whether it is Dickens speaking of Schmalkaldic reservations about the king 'since they took their religion seriously and

---

19 Idem, *Reform and Reformation*, London 1977, 184.
20 A. G. Dickens, *Thomas Cromwell and the English Reformation*, London 1959, 153.
21 J. A. Williamson, *The Tudor age*, London 1964, 158–9.
22 Ibid., 162.
23 'Gute Protestanten waren diese Schmalkaldener, aber sehr schlechte Politiker': Prüser, *England und die Schmalkaldener*, 284–5.
24 This is especially true of some American Lutheran scholarship. See, in particular, N. S. Tjernagel, *Henry VIII and the Lutherans*, St Louis 1965, and H. E. Jacobs, *The Lutheran movement in England*, Philadelphia 1891.
25 'Die naive Gutgläubigkeit der Schmalkaldener nahm keine Veranlassung, an der Ehrlichkeit der englischen Bestrebungen zu zweifeln': Prüser, *England und die Schmalkaldener*, 28.

doubted Henry',[26] or the great seventeenth-century German historian Seckendorf noting German suspicion of Henry because they saw that 'the king did not take religion seriously, but used it only as a disguise',[27] the message is much the same: the spiritual contrast between the pious Protestants and the crafty king was bound to cause them eventually to lose patience with him. As Prüser puts it, 'all negotiations with an England, which let only political considerations prevail, and whose church development was entirely dependent on the political world situation and personal whim, must, from the beginning, fail'.[28]

The historiography of Anglo-Schmalkaldic relations seems therefore to have been dominated by a deterministic outlook, by an inevitability thesis as systematic and unyielding as that propounded by Froude in the nineteenth century. Today, as then, it is accepted that Henry never seriously intended to enter into an alliance with the Schmalkaldic League; rather, he made a succession of finely calculated, disingenuous approaches to it in order to balance the temporary formation of anti-English alliances by the other powers of Europe. The king's balanced diplomatic manoeuverings were only upset when influential counsellors such as Cromwell pushed him away from his favoured position of non-alignment. Similarly, Henry never had a genuine interest in discussing with, or importing from, the Schmalkaldic League the theological principles upon which it was based; those theological conferences which did take place were permitted simply for reasons of political expediency, either in response to pressure from such men as Cromwell, or as bait to draw the Schmalkaldeners towards England during times of need. As for the Germans, they were innocent pawns in the grand Henrician scheme; only their strong sense of religious piety caused them finally to reject the king's political manipulations.

In this study I offer a different interpretation. I argue that for most of the period of Anglo-Schmalkaldic negotiation Henry was, in fact, genuinely interested in close religious and political contact with the League. Though he was certainly encouraged in that direction by his evangelical advisers (who saw that their interests could be advanced by a close relationship with the League), he had a strong and sincere interest of his own in the League's religious and political principles; indeed, the king's pre-existing, independent interest in the League was the *sine qua non* of the prominent place which Anglo-Schmalkaldic relations would occupy in English domestic politics. I have found no evidence of a consistently applied royal plan of approaching

---

[26] Dickens, *Thomas Cromwell and the English Reformation*, 155.

[27] '[S]ie sahen, dass der König mit keinem Ernst die Religion meyne, sondern selbige nur zum Deckmantel gebrauchen wolle': V. L. von Seckendorf, *Historie des Lutherthums*, trans. E. Frick, Leipzig 1714, 1463.

[28] '[M]ussten alle Verhandlungen mit einem England, das nur politische Rücksichten walten liess, dessen kirchliche Entwicklung dazu völlig von politischer Weltlage und persönlicher Laune abhängig war, von Anfang an scheitern': Prüser, *England und die Schmalkaldener*, 282–3.

the Germans only in times of necessity and retreating from them as soon as the external situation improved. Equally, I have found no basis for the notion that England was guided by political precepts and the League by religious ones; both sides indulged in roughly equal amounts of religious pontification and political calculation in their relations with each other. Yet my research does not only suggest that previous work on Anglo-Schmalkaldic relations is misconceived. It also suggests that the real story is more important. One of the central problems with the received view of Anglo-Schmalkaldic diplomacy is that it reduces relations between England and the League to the level of an irrelevancy, to little more than a series of deceptions and counter-deceptions between the leading statesmen of Europe. The evidence uncovered in the course of this study, however, suggests that there is a great deal of highly relevant and hitherto unrealised religious and political history bound up with diplomacy between England and the League. This 'new' history not only casts Anglo-Schmalkaldic relations in a fresh light, it also illumines more generally a number of other questions of wider historical concern, especially during the 1530s.

If one wishes to write new history it helps to have new sources; in this respect I have been fortunate. My six working archives have been the Public Record Office and the British Library in London (for the bulk of the English state papers), the Hessian State Archives in Marburg (for the records of the Landgrave Philip of Hesse, one of the two leaders of the Schmalkaldic League), the Thuringian State Archives in Weimar (for the records of the League's other leader, the duke of Saxony), the Parker Library of Corpus Christi College, Cambridge (for a small number of papers given by Archbishop Parker to the college which are relevant to the 1538 Anglo-Schmalkaldic theological discussions in London) and the Bavarian State Archives in Munich (for a few papers which shed some light on the English embassies to Germany of the early 1530s). I have augmented this store of primary evidence with a range of printed sources, including the well-known English calendars and source collections,[29] the main German state publications,[30] private publications[31] and those publications which have recorded the relevant letters and papers of the leading German theologians;[32] I have also combed the contemporary English and German histories and chronicles for additional material.[33] Certainly, all these manuscript and printed source

---

29 LP; StP; SpCal; J. Strype, *Ecclesiastical memorials, relating chiefly to religion, and the Reformation of it, and the emergencies of the Church of England, under King Henry VIII, King Edward VI, and Queen Mary I*, Oxford 1822; G. Burnet, *History of the Reformation of the Church of England*, ed. N. Pocock, Oxford 1865; Merriman, *Life and letters of Thomas Cromwell*.
30 PC; BwP.
31 DWA; Bo; SchmBa; Prüser, *England und die Schmalkaldener*, 293–342.
32 WABr; CR.
33 Those with relevant material include J. Foxe, *Acts and monuments*, ed. G. Townsend, London 1843–9; C. Wriothesley, *A chronicle of England during the reigns of the Tudors, from*

collections have been excavated to some degree or other before now, but I think I am the first student of this subject to have used them all in combination. Even Friedrich Prüser, the most important writer on Anglo-Schmalkaldic relations, limited his archival work to Marburg, and I suspect this limitation served to distort the vision of what is in most respects a model of historical scholarship and intelligence; in particular, I cannot help but feel that Prüser would have given greater weight to the relevance of religious questions to Anglo-Schmalkaldic relations had he seen the hundreds of folios concerned with theology which lie in the archives of London, Cambridge and Weimar. Quite apart from anything else, then, advantages of evidence have given this study a headstart on other histories: the fact that I have had access to a considerably improved body of evidence has been of the first importance in allowing me to tell anew the story of Anglo-Schmalkaldic relations.

In so doing I have deliberately sought to concentrate on those issues which seemed to be of the most historiographical significance and have explored them as fully as possible. This has been in preference to giving a superficial survey of every facet of Anglo-Schmalkaldic relations covered by the vast range of evidence. I have therefore tended to neglect the German Reformation in favour of its English counterpart; not, of course, because I consider the German Reformation intrinsically less important, but because Anglo-Schmalkaldic relations had a greater influence on English than on German history. This is not to say that there is no German history in what follows, for there is a great deal, but only that as a matter of conscious choice I have let the balance tip to the English side. I have also left administrative, institutional and financial questions largely untouched; again, not because I considered them necessarily less important in themselves, but because I found that they shed little light on the religious and political issues which are the focus of this study.

The finished work seeks to demonstrate that it was religion rather than great power politics which dominated the course of Anglo-Schmalkaldic relations. Instead of the areligious calculations of the Froudean mechanic, this study holds that it was the very Protestantism of the League that played the major part in arousing and sustaining English interest in a foreign policy in Protestant Germany. Certainly, wider diplomatic considerations had their place. But the key dynamic of Anglo-Schmalkaldic relations was the faith. In developing this interpretation, a number of wider historical questions are considered, particularly in England during the first decade of the Reformation. An appraisal of the relevance of Anglo-Schmalkaldic relations to

1485 to 1559: by Charles Wriothesley, ed. W. D. Hamilton, London 1875; F. Mykonius, Historia reformationis, Leipzig 1718; J. Sleidan, A famouse cronicle of oure time, called Sleidanes commentaries, concerning the state of religion and common wealth, during the raigne of the Emperour Charles the Fift, trans. J. Daye, London 1560, and The general history of the Reformation of the Church, trans. E. Bohun, London 1689.

English domestic affairs allows for a reinterpretation of two major events, the passing of the Act of Six Articles and the fall of Thomas Cromwell. An examination of the king's interest in relations with the League offers an opportunity to assess his religious beliefs during the second half of the reign. An analysis of the motives behind Thomas Cromwell's consistent advocacy of closer relations with the League clears the way for a consideration of the nature and influence of his religious convictions, and an evaluation of the historical significance of his ministry. Finally, an investigation of the influence of English political relations on Anglo-Schmalkaldic diplomacy provides the basis for a discussion of the nature, motivations and historical importance of elite political groupings, or factions, during the Henrician Reformation.

Such topics as these are underpinned by the chief concern of the work: to illustrate the character and significance of the inter-relationship between religion and politics during the Henrician Reformation. During the Reformation religion came to be indistinguishable from politics. In ending the *de facto* division between Roman Church and English State, the Reformation effectively transferred all religious debate to the political arena. Essentially, this examination of Anglo-Schmalkaldic relations provides a case study of how the politicisation of religion affected the conduct and nature of politics. In so doing, it moves away from the thematic lines of many of the modern histories of the Henrician Reformation, with their sharply drawn distinctions between political and religious history, and back towards a more fully integrated account of the sort presented by traditional historians, such as John Foxe and Gilbert Burnet. It is my belief that in modern times the religiosity of Reformation politics has been underemphasised; if this study should serve in some small way to restore religion to the foreground of the political history of the English Reformation, I shall be satisfied.

1

The Emergence of Anglo-Schmalkaldic Relations, 1531–1534

Anglo-German relations, February 1531–July 1533

To most observers in the 1520s England and Protestant Germany would have seemed unlikely diplomatic partners. After all, in the decade which followed Martin Luther's posting of the ninety-five theses Henry VIII had been at the forefront of those attacking the reformer and his religious ideas. In 1521 Henry had published the explicitly anti-Lutheran *Assertio septem sacramentorum*. Apart from earning for the king the papal title 'Defender of the Faith', this tract had set the scene for a brisk trade in insult and invective between him and Luther for much of the rest of the decade.[1] As with so many other things, however, the collapse of Henry's marriage to Catherine of Aragon triggered a change in his views. It both brought him into conflict with the two greatest enemies of Lutheranism, the pope and the emperor, and it gradually led him to regard the Protestants with a greater degree of sympathy than he had previously found possible.[2] By 1531 the change in the king's views was clear; he was now not only disillusioned with Clement and Charles, but also had a more favourable attitude to those Germans who had themselves more than a decade before challenged the pope's supremacy and stood up to defend their principles before the emperor.

For their part, the German Protestants were likewise more inclined to regard their former antagonist positively from the early 1530s. Partly this was due to the king's growing disenchantment with the papacy and Charles V. But it was also because of their own particular difficulties which had come to a head in 1530. In the summer of that year Charles V had summoned an imperial diet to Augsburg, intending to resolve once and for all the religious problems which had developed over the previous decade. The hope had been that at Augsburg the Protestants would explain their religious position to

---

[1]   The row between Henry and Luther during the 1520s is discussed in P. Smith, 'Luther and Henry VIII', *EHR* xxv (1910), 658–65; E. Doernberg, *Henry VIII and Luther*, London 1961, 1–69; Tjernagel, *Henry VIII and the Lutherans*, 3–33. See also R. A. W. Rex, 'The English campaign against Luther in the 1520s', *Transactions of the Royal Historical Society* 5th ser. xxxix (1989), 85–106.
[2]   On the change in Henry's attitude towards Lutheranism see J. J. Scarisbrick, *Henry VIII*, London 1968, 246–8.

Charles and establish with him and his theologians a mutually acceptable settlement.[3] Philip Melanchthon was given the task of writing for the imperial party a statement of the Protestant faith. He presented a conciliatory tract, the *Confessio augustana*, consisting of twenty-one articles of Protestant doctrine: on God (the creed), natural depravity, the son of God, justification, the ministry of the Church, new obedience, the Church, the nature of the Church, baptism, the lord's supper, confession, repentance, the use of the sacraments, church orders, religious ceremonies, civil affairs, Christ's return to judgement, free will, the cause of sin, good works and the invocation of saints. The response of Charles's theologians, the *Confutatio*, was not accommodating. Ignoring much of what Melanchthon had written, it concentrated instead on a number of areas of disagreement, including communion, clerical marriage and the mass. Melanchthon's reply to this, the *Apologia*, enumerated and discussed the seven abuses which he considered the most important areas of dispute: communion in one kind only, the celibacy of the clergy, the mass, confession, diversity of meats, monastic vows and the power of the Church. Two significant points about the discussions at Augsburg should be stressed. First, though it is convenient to refer to Melanchthon's two tracts by the single name – the Confession of Augsburg – their actual separateness should not be forgotten.[4] In analysing the Anglo-Schmalkaldic theological discussions which took place during the second half of the 1530s, it will be interesting to note that while the Confession was generally acceptable to Henry VIII, the doctrine contained in the Apology was not. Second, the very wide acceptance of the Confession of Augsburg among Protestants and the general European currency which it gained through the printing press gave to both the author and the work an authority in Protestant theology. Before very long, acceptance of the Confession of Augsburg would come to be regarded as coterminous with being a Protestant. Moreover, where alternatives to Roman doctrine were concerned, the Confession of Augsburg would become the foremost source; for any potentate who was erecting an alternative Christian faith to that of Rome, recourse to the work and its author would be essential. These matters, however, lay some way ahead; for the moment, the main significance of the Confession of Augsburg was that it confirmed and threw into sharp relief the religious differences between the Roman Church and the Protestants. In the wake of the Diet of Augsburg, Charles V renewed calls for

---

3   The following survey compresses a huge literature on the difficulties facing the German Protestants during the 1520s and early 1530s. For a detailed account of the events in the years immediately preceding the Diet of Augsburg see E. Fabian, *Die Entstehung des Schmalkaldischen Bundes und seiner Verfassung*, Tübingen 1962, 18–137. A good short survey of the League's history is T. A. Brady's 'Phases and strategies of the Schmalkaldic League: a perspective after 450 years', *Archiv für Reformationsgeschichte* lxxiv (1983), 162–80 (for the League's early history see especially pp. 162–3, 166–8).

4   In this book the *Confessio augustana* will be referred to as the 'Confession', and the *Apologia* as the 'Apology'; the two together will be referred to as the 'Confession of Augsburg'. In quotations, however, the writer's terminology will be followed precisely.

the Protestants to return to the Roman Church or suffer the consequences. The Protestant response was to meet in the Thuringian town of Schmalkalden in late 1530 to discuss a collective security alliance; on 27 February 1531 a treaty was concluded which brought into being a defensive military alliance of Protestant princes and cities under the dual leadership of the duke of Saxony and the landgrave of Hesse: the League of Schmalkalden.[5]

At its inaugural meetings the League discussed the desirability of approaching both Henry VIII and Francis I of France for help in the event of an imperial attack. As a result, in late February 1531, minor ambassadors were sent with letters to England and France. That to the king of England drew no immediate response; it was only after further missives from the League in June and a round of Anglo-French consultations that Henry finally took the decision to despatch an ambassador to the Holy Roman Empire. In August he sent William Paget, the bishop of Winchester's servant, to Germany with instructions to discuss the possibility of English support for the new focus of German opposition to the Habsburgs, the movement to revoke the election of Charles V's brother Ferdinand as king of the Romans, or emperor elect. It should be emphasised that at this stage the king's interest was in diplomacy with both sides of Germany's confessional divide; Paget's embassy went to both Catholic and Protestant Germany and had no brief for seeking a common religious policy with the Protestants: it was a German, rather than a Schmalkaldic, embassy.[6] Paget's efforts, together with those of a French ambassador, one Gervasius Wain, met with some success. In late 1531 embassies were despatched from Catholic Bavaria and Protestant Hesse, Saxony and Lüneburg to England and France in order to seek support from the kings for the campaign to revoke Ferdinand's election. When the German ambassador to England arrived at the court, however, he found himself unable to make much headway with the king. Henry was prepared to talk about resistance to the Habsburgs in Germany, but he was not prepared to give any specific undertaking to involve himself in the sort of forthright diplomatic activity which the Germans were proposing. A willingness to engage in diplomatic discussion with the Germans, but not action, is characteristic of Henry's policy in 1531 and 1532. It is probably best explained by reference to the general caution and hesitancy which dominated English counsels in these

---

5 For the discussions at Schmalkalden in late 1530 and early 1531 see Fabian, *Entstehung des Schmalkaldischen Bundes*, 151–83.

6 This is an important distinction. In 'The making of religious policy, 1533–1546: Henry VIII and the search for the middle way', *HJ* xli (1998), 343, G. W. Bernard points to Anglo-German contacts in the late 1520s and early 1530s, and argues that 'it is by no means the case ... that the pursuit of a German alliance began when Cromwell became the king's chief minister'. That is true, but it rather misses the point for it fails to distinguish between the bi-confessional Anglo-German contacts of the late 1520s and early 1530s (on the divorce) and the exclusively Protestant Anglo-Schmalkaldic relations that developed from 1533–4.

years as Henry sought to find a way through the difficulties of his great matter while still keeping the path open to a restoration of his former good relations with the papacy and the Habsburgs. It would seem likely that during the fraught, uncertain, early years of the divorce, Henry – while happy to see the emperor and pope preoccupied with whatever troubles he might be able to foment for them from afar – did not want to run the risk of an irrevocable break by pursuing an overtly provocative diplomatic policy. Thus, during 1532, Henry stood back and allowed Francis to take the lead in subverting Habsburg designs in Germany. Although Thomas Cranmer tended the king's affairs in the empire during his time as imperial ambassador from January to November 1532 and William Paget returned to Germany during the summer to build on Cranmer's work, the abiding impression remains that Henry's main interest was to exhort anti-Habsburg machinations in Catholic and Protestant Germany from the sidelines, without any thoroughgoing involvement on his own part.[7]

England's new German policy, July 1533–May 1534

In 1533 this all changed. At the beginning of the year Henry rejected Catherine for good and married Anne Boleyn.[8] In parliament he widened the breach with Rome which the legislation of 1532 had opened by introducing the Act in Restraint of Appeals. Then, during the session of 1534, he confirmed England's separation from Rome by introducing the landmark legislation of the Henrician Reformation, the Act of Supremacy.[9] As England drifted further away from the old Roman and imperial allegiances, it became less necessary to avoid offending Charles or to leave open a way back to Rome. The divorce and growing split with Rome also witnessed the rise to power of the man whose influence on England's German policy in the years ahead would be second only to that of the king himself, Thomas Cromwell. Cromwell had emerged from the wreck of Thomas Wolsey's ministry. In the aftermath of Wolsey's demise he remained in the shadows of government as a relatively anonymous member of the council. During these years, however, he built up a small yet powerful following of other ex-Wolseians in the privy chamber. Moreover, where others had dithered he showed a willingness and ability to deal with the seemingly insoluble problems of the divorce. Before long, Anne Boleyn realised that Cromwell was the man most likely to bring

---

[7] For a more detailed narrative of the diplomatic moves outlined in this paragraph see Rory McEntegart, 'England and the League of Schmalkalden, 1531–1547: faction, foreign policy and the English Reformation', unpubl. PhD diss. London 1992, 33–54.
[8] The traditional date for the marriage is 25 January 1533. For the possibility of a ceremony in November 1532 see D. MacCulloch, *Thomas Cranmer: a life*, New Haven 1996, 637–8.
[9] J. A. Guy, *Tudor England*, Oxford 1988, 131–6.

her success in her quest to become Henry's queen. Soon her entourage and Cromwell's followers were working in unison. In 1532 Cromwell's fortunes began to soar. The crucial opportunity was supplied in May of that year by Stephen Gardiner's badly misjudged opposition to anti-papal legislation, that is to the Supplication against the Ordinaries. Had Gardiner played his hand more adroitly, he might well have been promoted as Warham's successor to the archbishopric of Canterbury, and become the unchallenged successor to Wolsey as the king's minister. As it was, he had the secretaryship taken from him and was banished from his position of influence close to the king.[10] In Gardiner's absence, Cromwell took the reins of power. During the remainder of 1532 he championed the divorce with increasing vigour, and cemented his and his followers' relationship with the Boleyn entourage. When Henry married Anne in early 1533 Cromwell's place in the new regime was assured: he was now the king's minister and the leader of the dominant political grouping.[11]

In July 1533 Henry received word that the pope was threatening to excommunicate him. In the weeks that followed it was decided that a new approach, more energetic than hitherto countenanced, should be made to the German princes. Embassies would be despatched to Germany to request resident ambassador status at the courts of the two most powerful centres of resistance to the Habsburgs at the time, Catholic Bavaria and Protestant Saxony.[12] It is reasonable to see in this mission the first signs of an interest in Anglo-German affairs on the part of Thomas Cromwell. Certainly, Cromwell would dominate the correspondence with the ambassadors, and, as if to confirm his special interest, the embassy would be led by two men of reformed views from his own service, Stephen Vaughan and Christopher Mont. Vaughan need hardly be mentioned here: he would soon show himself unsuited to diplomatic work in Germany and would not be used again by Cromwell for this purpose. Mont, however, was rather different. Born and raised in Cologne, he probably first came into contact with Cromwell through mutual trade and business interests in the Low Countries. He appears to have entered Cromwell's service about 1530 or 1531; in October 1531 he received English denization.[13] Perhaps the earliest task Mont performed for Cromwell was to translate certain books out of German into English, apparently to help

---

10 G. Redworth, *In defence of the Church Catholic: the life of Stephen Gardiner*, Oxford 1990, 30–47.
11 This account generally follows D. R. Starkey, 'Intimacy and innovation: the rise of the privy chamber, 1485–1547', in D. R. Starkey (ed.), *The English court: from the Wars of the Roses to the Civil War*, London 1987, 108–9, and *The reign of Henry VIII: personalities and politics*, London 1985, 105–7.
12 There are no extant instructions for the embassy, but the letters and papers associated with it show that its central purpose was to create English ambassadorial posts in Saxony and Bavaria. See, for example, PRO, SP 1/78, fos 192–3 [*LP* vi. 1079].
13 *LP* v. 506.i.

Cromwell build up his knowledge of German matters.[14] Mont was a convinced Protestant and would soon establish himself as Cromwell's chief agent for Anglo-Schmalkaldic affairs: he would be assigned to every one of the seven English embassies which were sent to the League between 1533 and 1540.

The two ambassadors and their servants set out on 28 July. Held up by bad weather as they made their way to Nuremberg by way of Calais and Antwerp, they did not arrive at the imperial city until 22 August.[15] After a short stay there together they split up. Mont went into southern Germany, while Vaughan struck out for Saxony. From the beginning Vaughan was unhappy. He wrote to Cromwell in late August, voicing the familiar lamentations of the anglophone abroad: the 'lacke of the tonge muche cumberithe me',[16] he complained, adding that 'the superfluous drynkyng wyll muche more trouble me',[17] and that 'I loste muche money in the chanyge of my money whiche puttogether maketh me have letle money in my purse.'[18] For all his difficulties, he did manage to find his way to Torgau, where he was able to deliver to Duke John Frederick of Saxony the king's letter requesting resident ambassador status.[19] He later rode with the duke's court to Weimar, where on 5 September he was given a written response. John Frederick turned down the request on the grounds that he feared that such an unprecedented move would incur the displeasure of Charles. In response to a complaint from Henry that neither John Frederick nor the other German princes had sent an ambassador to England since the death of his father, the young duke said simply that the princes had not had anything new to relate.[20] This response, to a thoroughly demoralised Vaughan, seems to have been the last straw, and without any further delay he set off for home. He decided not to deliver his remaining letters, to Philip of Hesse and Duke Ernst of Lüneburg, explaining to Cromwell that after John Frederick's unenthusiastic response there was little chance that the other princes would be more accommodating.[21] Mont was rather happier in his work, although he had no greater substantial success than Vaughan. After Nuremberg, he went, by way of Augsburg, to the court of the Bavarian dukes in Munich, arriving on 7 September. Mont was no more able than Vaughan to have Henry's suggestion that he remain as an

14 E. Hildebrandt, 'Christopher Mont, Anglo-German diplomat', *Sixteenth Century Journal* xv (1984), 283–4. The content of the books is not known.
15 PRO, SP 1/78, fos 57–8 [*LP* vi. 917], 192–3 [*LP* vi. 1040]; *LP* vi. 918. They were met and their lodgings arranged in Nuremberg by Laurence Staber, the king's resident agent there.
16 PRO, SP 1/78, fo. 192 [*LP* vi. 1040].
17 Ibid.
18 PRO, SP 1/78, fo. 193 [*LP* vi. 1040].
19 PRO, SP 1/78, fos 192–3 [*LP* vi. 1040]; SP 1/79, fo. 29 [*LP* vi. 1082].
20 PRO, SP 1/79, fos 25–6 [*LP* vi. 1079]; TStWei, Reg. H. 76, fo. 29 (Latin draft, Weimar, 5 Sept. 1533).
21 PRO, SP 1/79, fos 27–8 [*StP* vii. 501–4; *LP* vi. 1081], 29 [*LP* vi. 1082]; BL, MS Cotton Vitellius B.xxi, fos 101–2 [*LP* vi. 1083].

ambassador accepted. Although Philip of Hesse recommended that the Bavarians accept Henry's offer, the dukes decided to refuse Mont any possibility of an extended stay. No reason for this was given, but fear of the Habsburgs is the most likely explanation.[22]

In spite of the failed embassies, English interest in developing a diplomatic policy in Germany continued to grow during the second half of 1533. Around October Cromwell directed Christopher Mont to collect intelligence on Germany and on the attitude of the Germans to the English realm.[23] As the year approached its end, discussions were in train at the highest levels of English government on renewed diplomatic efforts in the Holy Roman Empire. These culminated in a meeting of the king's council on 2 December at which one of the items under consideration was a proposal for the despatch of ambassadors to Germany.[24] The initial draft memorandum of the discussions proposed to send ambassadors into 'the parties of Germany to practise and conclude with the prynces and potentates of Germany'; it then proceeded to name, in respective order, the princes, Hanse cities and imperial free cities the ambassadors might visit.[25] At the second drafting stage Thomas Cromwell's hand appeared to provide a first indication of his involvement in proceedings.[26] Under his supervision the sequence of points from the first draft was re-ordered, and he embarked upon a series of corrections and additions. To the point touching the dispatch to the German princes he added the name of 'duke ffrederyke' (of Brandenburg) and superscripted that the ambassadors should seek to conclude 'som leyge or amyte' with them.[27] Further on in the same item he added 'and also to Inserche of [what] Inclynacyon the sayd prynces and potenttattes be of';[28] he made an identical addition to the next point, on a mission to the Hanse cities.[29] The final memorandum followed the order of the second draft and incorporated all Cromwell's corrections.[30] It was written in the hand of Ralph Sadler, then Cromwell's clerk:[31]

14. Item, certen discrete and grave persons to be appoynted to repaire into the parties of Germany, to practise and conclude some lege or amytee with the prynces and potentates of Germany, that is to sey: the king of Pole, king John of Hungary, the duke of Saxony, the dukes of Bavyere, duke Frederyk, the

---

22 HStMar, PA 1452, fos 74–5; PA 2556, fos 47–8.

23 PRO, SP 1/80, fo. 55 [*LP* vi. 1374].

24 This council meeting is the subject of detailed analysis in G. R. Elton's *The Tudor revolution in government: administrative changes in the reign of Henry VIII*, Cambridge 1953, 361–7. For a contrasting interpretation see G. W. Bernard, 'Elton's Cromwell', *History* lxxxiii (1998), 594.

25 PRO, SP 1/80, fos 172v–3 [*LP* vi. 1487.iii].

26 PRO, SP 6/3, fos 88–92 [*LP* vi. 1487.iii]; Elton, *Tudor revolution*, 363.

27 PRO, SP 6/3, fo. 90v [*LP* vi. 1487.iii].

28 Ibid.

29 Ibid.

30 BL, MS Cott. Cleopatra E.vi, vol. 2, fos 325–8 [*LP* vi. 1487.i; *StP* i/1, 411–14].

31 Elton, *Tudor revolution*, 363.

landegrave van Hesse, the bisshop of Magons, the bishop of Trevers, the bisshop of Coleyn and other the potentates of Germany and also to ensearche of what inclynacion the saide prynces and potentates be of, towardes the king and this realme.

15. Item, like practise to be made and practised with the Cytees of Lubeke, Danske, Hamburgh, Bromeswyke and all other the steddes of the Haunse Tutonyk, and to enserche, of what inclynacion they be towardes the king and this realme.

16. Item, lyke practise to be made and practised with the Citees of Norimbergh and Aughsbrough.[32]

The quantity of Cromwell's handwriting on the papers produced by this meeting may well be a significant indicator of his role in the council's decision-making process.[33] Nevertheless, Cromwell was now, as he always would be, the king's servant. Though he might be guiding policy, he certainly was not making it: the king remained the final arbiter. In the margin of the final memorandum Cromwell wrote beside point 14 that the matter was one standing in 'the kynges arbytrement',[34] and beside point 15 he noted 'to know when of the kyng'.[35] Thus Cromwell went to the king to seek his approval of the council's proposals. The results of these discussions were then recorded in a final decision entitled 'Acta in Concilio domini Regis, ijdo Decembris'.[36] Henry agreed to the proposal to send ambassadors to Germany, requiring only that a letter first be written to his ambassador in France, Sir John Wallop, directing him to inform the French king of his plans.[37]

Before this happened there was a fundamental shift in policy. The original council resolution had been to send ambassadors to both Catholic and Protestant Germany, thus following the pattern established in 1531 of engaging in diplomacy with both sides of the German confessional divide.

---

[32] BL, MS Cott. Cleo. E.vi, vol. 2, fos 327v–8 [LP vi. 1487.i; StP i/1, 413–14].

[33] Elton, Tudor revolution, 363. See, however, Bernard, 'Elton's Cromwell', 594, for the argument that Cromwell may just as well have been 'writing down what the king, or someone else, had said'. Bernard's point is important: Cromwell's writing on council or office memoranda does not allow for any larger conclusions as to his foreign policy preferences unless it can be linked to independent external evidence. It is to be hoped that some such evidence will emerge in the remainder of this work.

[34] BL, MS Cott. Cleo. E.vi, vol. 2, fo. 327v [LP vi. 1487.i; StP i/1, 413].

[35] BL, MS Cott. Cleo. E.vi, vol. 2, fo. 328 [LP vi. 1487.i; StP i/1, 414].

[36] BL, MS Cott. Cleo. E.vi, vol. 2, fo. 329 [LP vi. 1486; StP i/1, 414–15]. Elton, Tudor revolution, 365–6, argues that the final decision on the council proposals was taken by the council alone under Cromwell's supervision, saying that this 'strengthens the possibility of Cromwell's sole parentage'. Although I agree that Cromwell played a substantial role in the proceedings, on the basis of the language of this document (noting, for example, at three points that 'the kynges highnes hath apoynted'), I prefer to imagine a situation in which Cromwell, probably alone, but possibly in the company of other councillors, first went to the king to discuss the proposals which the council had made, and then returned to record the final resolutions on this document.

[37] BL, MS Cott. Cleo. E.vi, vol. 2, fo. 329 [LP vi. 1486; StP i/1, 415].

Now, however, the proposed embassy began to be shaped in such a way as effectively to limit its scope of operation: it was decided specifically to seek the advice and help only of those Germans who themselves were opposed to the Roman Church. The letter to Wallop was drafted in late 1533 by Cromwell's clerk Wriothesley, and corrected by Cromwell himself.[38] Wallop was to explain that 'whereas we have nowe perfite advertisement and knowledge of the popes endured herte and moost obstinate and ungodlie entente purpose and disposicion towardes us and our reaulme',[39] it is thought good

> to acquire and geete oother newe freendes and so conioyne ourself in amitie with them as maye be to thincrease and advauncement of our strengith and power and the more confusion of our adversaries we be mynded by the deliberate advise of our said Counsaill to sende nowe incontinentely som of our trusty servaunts . . . unto the princes of Germanye.[40]

Though a full list of both the Catholic and the Protestant German princes and cities named in the 2 December council meeting followed, the remaining passages suggested that the embassy was now effectively being targeted only at those Germans who were opposed to Rome. It was noted that Henry had decided to abolish Roman power, and that the Germans would be sought for 'thair advysis and assistens to concurre with us in the defence of our moost iuste and lawful cause and the revenging of so hiegh displeasour and injurie doon unto us by the pope', and 'tassist us in the callyng and congregatyng of a generall counsaile'.[41] The instructions which were prepared for the ambassadors confirmed the shift from a bi-confessional alliance to one exclusively with those Germans opposed to the papacy.[42] The ambassadors were directed to stress that Henry had decided to 'reduce the said popes powers'.[43] To this end, the Germans were to be requested 'to give unto his highnes thair assistence and best advise howe he shall procede to the accomplishement of his desired purposes'.[44] They should advise Henry of anything touching the common weal or abuses 'whiche in thair opynyon shalbe thought mete to be reformed and redressed', in which case they would find Henry ready to

---

38 PRO, SP 6/3, fos 66–72 [*LP* vi. 1491; *StP* vii. 524–6].

39 PRO, SP 6/3, fo. 66 [*LP* vi. 1491; *StP* vii. 524].

40 PRO, SP 6/3, fo. 67 [*LP* vi. 1491; *StP* vii. 525].

41 PRO, SP 6/3, fo. 69–v [*LP* vi. 1491; *StP* vii. 526].

42 PRO, SP 1/82, fos 20–31 [*LP* vii. 21.i] (draft of instructions for Heath and Mont), 32–9 [*LP* vii. 21.ii] (inferior draft of instructions for Heath and Mont); BL, MS Cott. Vit. B.xiv, fos 61–9 [*LP* vii. 148] (draft of instructions for Paget).

43 PRO, SP 1/82, fos 29v [*LP* vii. 21.i] (draft of instructions for Heath and Mont), 37v [*LP* vii. 21.ii] (inferior draft of instructions for Heath and Mont). This passage does not appear in Paget's instructions because of damage to the manuscript by fire. The quoted matter in this and the following two footnotes is taken from the first folio reference.

44 PRO, SP 1/82, fos 30 [*LP* vii. 21.i] (draft of instructions for Heath and Mont), 38 [*LP* vii. 21.ii] (inferior draft of instructions for Heath and Mont); BL, MS Cott. Vit. B.xiv, fo. 69 [*LP* vii. 148] (draft of instructions for Paget).

support just causes.[45] The instructions also dealt with one additional topic which had previously only been briefly mentioned, but now was outlined in extensive detail: the ambassadors were to seek the support of the Germans on the divorce, particularly should it be the subject of debate at any future general council.[46] Finally it was emphasised again that all this was only to be taken up with those Germans who stood in opposition to Rome:

> for asmuch as it is doubtfull of what minde, intencion and purpose the said princes be, or at least some of them, that is to witte whither they be soo dedicated to the popes devocion that there is noo likelihood of any good success touching the kinges purposes. . . . [the ambassadors should seek to] in[sea]rche, inquire and knowe the disposicion and inclinacion of the said princes, and of every of them severally. And so thereafter accordinge to their wisdoms and discrescions to deliver or retaine the kings said letters with declaracion or without declaracion of their said chardge.[47]

The effective narrowing of the mission's terms of reference may in part be explained by the worsening European situation. As Henry's difficulties with the papacy deepened, his choice of alliance partners necessarily became restricted to those willing to support him against Rome. But there were probably additional reasons for the mounting interest in Protestant Germany; and these were not merely the result of foreign policy pragmatism. Certainly, when the English ambassadors arrived in Germany early in the following year, they would suggest that this was so.[48] A Schmalkaldic diet at Nuremberg in May 1534 would note that the recently arrived English ambassadors had explained that the embassy had, '*though unknown to the king* [my italics], been promoted and effected by some of the realm's distinguished councillors and people, who are of the opinion and hope that the League will prepare and despatch there an embassy with articles etc'.[49] With the despatch of a Protestant embassy to England,

---

45 PRO, SP 1/82, fos 30v [*LP* vii. 21.i] (draft of instructions for Heath and Mont), 38v [*LP* vii. 21.ii] (inferior draft of instructions for Heath and Mont); BL, MS Cott. Vit. B.xiv, fo. 69 [*LP* vii. 148] (draft of instructions for Paget).

46 PRO, SP 1/82, fos 21–9 [*LP* vii. 21.i] (draft of instructions for Heath and Mont), 33–7 [*LP* vii. 21.ii] (inferior draft of instructions for Heath and Mont); BL, MS Cott. Vit. B.xiv, fos 63–8v [*LP* vii. 148] (draft of instructions for Paget). The background to the Anglo-German divorce discussions will be discussed in chapter 2.

47 BL, MS Cott. Vit. B.xiv, fo. 69v [*LP* vii. 148] (draft of instructions for Paget).

48 What follows is based on HStMar, PA 409, fos 17–27; TStWei, Reg. H. 91, fos 73–80 [*SchmBa* ii. 45–52]. This important evidence is not mentioned by either Lange, 'Englisch-deutschen Beziehungen', or Prüser, *England und die Schmalkaldener*.

49 '[D]urch etliche furtreffliche des reichs Engellandt rethen und ingesessen, doch unvermerckt des kunigs, gefurdert und angestiftet sein mochte, der meinung und hofnung, das die evangelische stende solten hinwider ein potschaft mit artikeln an den konig ausmachen und abfertigen etc': HStMar, PA 409, fo. 23–v; TStWei, Reg. H. 91, fo. 77 [*SchmBa* ii. 49–50].

the English councillors and distinguished people *who favour the gospel* [my italics] and have requested such an embassy will have greater cause to prompt the king, so that through this means, which the Almighty in his grace has now miraculously set forth, the gospel might be brought into England, and from a persecutor will be made a lover of the word of God.[50]

Moreover, even

if it does not immediately achieve anything useful with the king, it may still assist the advancement of God's glory in the land and among the king's people, particularly those who are around him; and through this the king will be made aware of our doctrine and belief.[51]

Is this evidence admissable? After all, to reveal information apparently without the king's knowledge was well-known ambassadorial practice. The idea was that it would suggest to the listener that the ambassador was not parroting instructions, but speaking from the heart; through the impression of sincerity thus created, the information would gain greater force and perhaps also help the ambassador to enter more fully into the confidence of his hosts. However, in such circumstances there would usually be specific directions in an ambassador's instructions. There was even a stock phrase for the practice: the envoy would be instructed 'to reveal [the relevant information] as of yourself'. For this mission to Germany there are three extant sets of instructions. They are detailed, covering every aspect of the ambassadors' despatch. They are long, more than fifty folio sides in all. In none of them is there any suggestion that the ambassadors should pass on ostensibly confidential or privileged information. It would appear, then, that the information from England discussed at the Schmalkaldic diet in May 1534 might be taken at face value. But if so, what does it mean? Certainly, it would appear from the records of the diet that a group of leading English politicians had agitated for the despatch of these ambassadors to Germany; they had given the ambassadors secret instructions to inform the Protestants of this and to ask for a return embassy to be sent to England – but why? Perhaps it would be best to start with personalities: with the composition of that anonymous, group of 'distinguished councillors and people' to which the diet referred.

Of this group, one name immediately suggests itself, that of Thomas

---

[50] '[D]amit also die engelische rethe und furtreffenliche die, so des evangelii begirig und solche legation gefurdert, desto mher ursach und fug haben mochten, dem konig inczusagen, ob durch solch mittel, wie dan der almechtig sein gnade zu zceiten wunderbarlich aufgehen lasset, das evangelium mochte in Engelandt gepracht und aus einem verfolger ein liebhaber des wort gots gemacht werden': HStMar, PA 409, fo. 23v; TStWei, Reg. H. 91, fo. 77 [*SchmBa* ii. 50].

[51] 'Wo es dan gleich bei dem konig nit nutz schaffen wurde, mochte es dannoch bei der landschaft und den seinen, sonderlich die umb inen sein, zu ehr Gottes furderlich und darczu dinstlich sein, das dannoch der kunig unsere lher, glawbens und des berichtet wurde': HStMar, PA 409, fos 23v–4; TStWei, Reg. H. 91, fo. 77r–v [*SchmBa* ii. 50].

Cromwell. Since the despatch of Mont and Vaughan in 1533 the minister had shown a close interest in things German. He had been an active participant in the council discussions of 2 December, in the subsequent consultations with Henry and in the communications with Wallop. Cromwell's involvement in formulating the official instructions was also manifest. Although the extant drafts were written in various clerical hands, a remembrance from early 1534 shows that Cromwell intended 'to devise instructions for them that shalbe sent into Germany', with the minister adding in his own hand, 'and to cause them with the letters to be signed'.[52] Just as Cromwell had been the dominant influence in proposing, discussing with the king and instructing the embassy to Germany, so he took charge of all other aspects of its despatch. He wrote to Thomas Cranmer, requesting that he send to Henry one Nicholas Heath, whom 'the kynges highnes entendeth to send into the parties of Germany in Ambassade to treate ther with the princes of Germany'.[53] Though Heath might seem an unusual appointment on an embassy to Protestant Germany given his consistent defence of orthodoxy in the reigns of Edward, Mary and Elizabeth, in the 1530s he was one of Cromwell's circle and seems to have been partial to evangelical ideas; certainly, in 1536 he would favourably impress Philip Melanchthon with his religious views.[54] The other ambassadors were also Cromwellian appointments: his own servant Christopher Mont; William Paget, who had been drifting away from his former patron the disgraced Stephen Gardiner and was about to come under Cromwell's formal control as clerk of the signet;[55] and Thomas Legh, who would be employed as one of Cromwell's most notorious commissioners for the dissolution.[56] Cromwell also took charge of financing and organising the travel documents for these ambassadors. A remembrance in his own hand reminded him 'to know what dyettes the kyng wyll gyve Mr Dr lee, Mr hethe and pagett. Item, to cause theyr pasporttes to be assigned'.[57] The subsequent warrant to pay their diets, signed at the head by Henry, was addressed to 'our trustie and right welbiloved Counsellour Thomas Crumwell, Master and Thresurer of our Juells'.[58] Any of this evidence on its own would not be sufficient to incriminate Cromwell; taken together, however, the weight and consistency of the materials pointing to Cromwell's involvement in all aspects of the embassy's despatch and his close ties with its personnel is enough to suggest that he was the leading member of that group of 'English councillors and distinguished people' with a particular interest in

---

[52] BL, MS Cott. Titus B.i, fo. 428v [LP vii. 48.ii]. A verbally identical copy of this draft remembrance, in an anonymous clerical hand, is at fo. 427 [LP vii. 48.i].

[53] BL, MS Harleian 6148, fo. 81 [LP vii. 19].

[54] Elton, Reform and Reformation, 184–5; LP x. 447–8.

[55] Elton, Tudor revolution, 261–2, 439.

[56] Legh would be criticised specifically by the pilgrims of 1536: Scarisbrick, Henry VIII, 340.

[57] BL, MS Cott. Tit. B.i, fo. 430 [LP vii. 52].

[58] PRO, SP 1/82, fo. 149 [LP vii. 137].

the German Protestants of the Schmalkaldic League. His associates were, no doubt, men in his own service such as Mont. But they probably also included others of significance in their own right: new men who had risen within the Boleyn–Cromwell axis in recent times, such as the king's almoner Edward Foxe, or Thomas Cranmer, who upon his return from his ambassadorial posting at the imperial court had been appointed archbishop of Canterbury in early 1533.

If these were the personalities, it remains to consider why they should have wanted to contact the Schmalkaldic League secretly with a request to send an embassy to England. It would be reasonable to assume that they were held together principally by a shared interest in the new religious ideas which had begun to gain a foothold in England: as the Schmalkaldic diet at Nuremberg noted, they were men who 'favour the gospel' or were, to use the conventional generic term, evangelicals.[59] In the light of this, a working hypothesis might be proposed to explain why they made their approach to the German Protestants. By the end of 1533 it was becoming obvious that the Reformation legislation had created an opportunity to introduce substantial religious reform to England. Before long the question would arise of what direction the emerging English Church would take in the absence of Roman authority. No English individual or group could make an outspoken and vigorous case for a Protestant Reformation of the Church. It would be much too dangerous. Those involved would be vulnerable to a charge of religious radicalism and even heresy. But the German Protestants could try. They would not be in danger and nor, moreover, would those Englishmen in favour of reform. If the Germans could be persuaded to send an embassy to England to discuss theology with the king the initiative would be dressed in diplomatic clothing; it would be perfectly respectable and above board. There would be open discussion around the king on the merits of Lutheran reform without fear of the stake. And if these discussions were successful, a religious and political alliance between England and the Schmalkaldic League might follow which in turn would lay the basis for introducing into England a programme of Protestant reform. These possibilities are intriguing, but need not be pushed too far at this stage. More evidence will be required before it is possible to see the diplomacy of 1533 and 1534 as part of a larger pattern of religiously motivated, pro-Schmalkaldic advocacy by a group of evangelicals under Thomas Cromwell's leadership. Still, the hypothesis should be noted. For there will be more evidence to follow: and as that material accumulates it will become clear that in the proposals for, and preparation of, the embassy to Germany in late 1533 it is reasonable to detect the first signs of activity of an elite pressure group led by Thomas Cromwell, which favours the Gospel and believes that

---

[59] For the utility of the term see D. MacCulloch, 'Henry VIII and the reform of the Church', in D. MacCulloch (ed.), *The reign of Henry VIII: politics, policy and piety*, London 1995, 168–9.

the development of links with the Schmalkaldic League will lend weight to the reformist cause in England.

Preparations for the ambassadors' despatch to Germany went on into the new year. In order to cover the whole of Germany, it was decided that they should operate separately. Heath was directed to meet Mont in Bavaria and from there move into central and upper Germany. Paget was to go to the king of Poland and the duke of Prussia. Legh was make his way into northern Germany and Denmark. They left in early February 1534, but in spite of the lengthy preparations, things appear to have gone awry almost from the beginning.[60] Mont and Heath failed to meet up at Munich, Mont having already left for Hesse. Heath decided to continue on his own from the Bavarian dukes to the Count Palatine Frederick, to Augsburg and Nuremberg. Before long, however, he had to report to Cromwell that the response was not as good as had been hoped.[61] His apparent lack of success seems to have been shared by Mont and Paget. The only significant reaction was elicited by Legh, whose efforts in northern Germany led to the arrival in England in mid-June of delegations from Hamburg and Lübeck.[62] Yet even these showed themselves reluctant to speak on the issues which the English ambassador had raised. Rather, they were interested in gaining Henry's support on the question of the disputed succession to the Danish throne.[63] The general lack of success with which the ambassadors met was, in fact, largely due to circumstances beyond their control: they had arrived just as a major military campaign in Germany to restore duke Ulrich to the duchy of Württemberg, from which he had been exiled in 1520, was about to begin. The whole of Germany was preoccupied with this and had little time to discuss the sort of diplomatic complications that Henry's ambassadors were proposing. A good example of this is the reponse of Philip of Hesse to the arrival at his court of Nicholas Heath.[64] Writing to Henry on 26 March 1534, Philip passed over the messages brought by Heath, and instead concentrated on his own current preoccupations, suggesting that Henry send a trusted person to the German princes 'who knows the king's disposition well and has sufficient powers to negotiate and close on the matter [ie. the Württemberg restoration], which will conduce to our common good and welfare'.[65] However, Philip said that this man would have to appear in Germany by 20 April. This did not give Henry enough time to prepare an embassy; in the event, his sole contribution to the restoration of

60 *LP* vii. 152.
61 *LP* vii. 395.
62 *LP* vii. 871.
63 *LP* vii. 926.
64 Heath brought a letter from Henry to Philip dated 20 January 1534: HStMar, PA 1799, fo. 48.
65 '[W]elcher das königliche gemüt vollkommen wisse und genugsam gewalt hat zu handeln und zu schliessen die ding, so unser beider gemeiner nutz und fruchtbarkeit antreffen': ibid. fos 50–1.

Ulrich would be 50,000 crowns, paid by diverting his French pension to the Germans.[66]

Just as the official diplomacy in Germany failed, so the secret intimations directed by Cromwell and his evangelical friends to the League of Schmalkalden also came to nothing. Even though the Nuremberg diet of May 1534 discussed and showed an interest in helping to promote the Gospel in England, this was not followed up.[67] In the months that followed the delicacy of the peace negotiations with the Habsburgs in the wake of the Württemberg restoration were probably responsible for the continuing lack of response in Germany to official and unofficial contacts. Indeed, during the remainder of 1534 the Germans would cease diplomatic contacts not only with England, but also with France.[68] Nevertheless, Henry had begun to show an interest in those Germans who shared his opposition to Rome, while a group of English evangelicals under Thomas Cromwell's leadership had made its presence felt and its enthusiasm for closer relations with the League known in Germany. The first concrete signs of a purely Protestant aspect to relations between England and Germany had started to emerge. The stage was now set for the development of specifically Anglo-Schmalkaldic relations.

66 This had been agreed with Francis earlier in the year: PRO, SP 6/3, fo. 69r–v [LP vi. 1491; StP vii. 526].

67 Wernham, Before the armada, 129, contends that the 1534 negotiations collapsed because 'Henry was not prepared to make any concessions that might cast doubt upon his Catholic orthodoxy.' However, doctrinal concessions were not being asked of him in 1533–4, and, as the May 1534 Nuremberg diet shows, far from rejecting Henry on religious grounds, the League was actually keen to approach him with a view to pushing him further in the direction of reform. (This also casts doubt on the suggestion in Merriman, Life and letters of Thomas Cromwell, i. 220, that the negotiations were not successful because the Lutherans were probably 'suspicious of the genuineness of Henry's Protestantism'.)

68 The silence accorded Henry was probably even more firmly entrenched during 1534 as he involved himself increasingly with the revolutionary democrats of Lübeck and the adventurer Jürgen Wullenweber against the newly installed King Christian III of Denmark (formerly the Lutheran duke of Holstein). Although English involvement would fizzle out by year's end, Henry's meddling in northern Germany probably caused the League to distance itself from him during the remainder of 1534. On the background to this subject see G. Waitz, Lübeck unter Jürgen Wullenwever und die Europäische Politik, Berlin 1855–6, ii. passim; iii. 166–247; C. F. Wurm, Die politischen Beziehungen Heinrichs VIII. zu Markus Meyer und Jürgen Wullenwever, Hamburg 1852.

2

Bishop Foxe's Embassy
to the Schmalkaldic League, 1535–1536

Preparations, September 1534–October 1535

In 1535 the supporters of Anglo-Schmalkaldic relations found that the European situation favoured their cause. The previous year Alexander Farnese had succeeded to the throne of St Peter as Paul III. Unlike his predecessor, Clement VII, Paul was enthusiastic about the imperial idea of solving Europe's religious problems by way of a general council of the Church. Henry and the German Protestants shared a deep suspicion of such a council. It was not the principle they objected to. Both Henry and the German Protestants had appealed on several occasions in the past to the arbitration of a general council. However, they wanted an independent and free council at a neutral location, not one in territories favourable to the papacy at which the agenda would be that of the Roman Church, and at which the papacy would be judge and jury. Henry and the German Protestants did not believe that a council under the direction of the papacy could have any other purpose than to attack them and to shore up the power of Rome. Henry feared condemnation of his divorce and the measures he had taken to establish an independent English Church. The Germans feared that they would be confirmed as wilful heretics and that a coalition would be formed to suppress their religious innovations. Together they could strive to hinder the summoning of a general council. If this did not work, and they were compelled to attend, they could support each other to prevent the general council from passing judgement against them.[1]

Early in 1535 English anxieties about a general council reached crisis proportions with the news that Francis I had invited Philip Melanchthon to come to France to discuss a religious peace. During 1534 Francis, hoping to settle the religious schism as a prelude to forming an anti-Habsburg coalition,

---

[1] This analysis of the reasons for Henry's growing interest in the League is only partly accepted by, for example, Lange, 'Englisch-deutschen Beziehungen', 246–7; Prüser, *England und die Schmalkaldener*, 22–3; Merriman, *Life and letters of Thomas Cromwell*, i. 226–8; Elton, *England under the Tudors*, 151–2. These see fear of Charles as the principal reason for his overtures to the Germans in 1535. Though obviously Charles was always a major consideration in Henry's diplomatic thinking, I believe (like Wernham, *Before the armada*, 132) that in the first instance his approaches had far more to do with an interest in seeking a common Anglo-Schmalkaldic line on a general council.

had attempted to begin through Melanchthon a process of reconciliation between the Roman and Protestant Churches.[2] Francis's stock with the Germans had plunged dramatically following the Affair of the Placards in October 1534 and the ensuing persecution of French evangelicals, but in early 1535 he began to make overtures to Melanchthon again, asking him to come to Paris to dispute with the theologians at the Sorbonne, either in the name of the League or on his own account.[3] News of these invitations seems to have reached England around March.[4] Fearing a Franco-German agreement which would leave Henry isolated in Europe, discussions began on the question of sending an embassy to the continent for the purpose of diverting Melanchthon from France to England.

Once again Thomas Cromwell was at the forefront of the planning process. A remembrance in his hand, which can be dated to about March, recorded his intention to see 'what the kyng myndyth ffor sendyng into germanye'.[5] Another, written in June (in an anonymous hand but with additions by Cromwell which show that the memorandum was his), noted 'Remembrances at my next goyng to the courte . . . to remember the sending into Almayne and also Doctor Barnes'.[6] The reference to Robert Barnes, England's foremost Lutheran and a friend of Cromwell, suggests that Cromwell had begun to envisage a role for him in connection with the forthcoming embassy. What that role would be emerged soon after. On 8 July Henry signed a letter of credence at Windsor (where, at the beginning of the summer progress, the court and council were) which authorised Robert Barnes to go to Germany to seek to arrange for Philip Melanchthon to come to England.[7]

Final discussions on this embassy ensued between Henry and the council. In the middle of July Cromwell was called away to London; plans were therefore conveyed to him by a letter from the progress dated 19 July at Langley from two leading councillors, Lord Rochford and the duke of Norfolk. It had been decided that two embassies should be sent, the main one led by Robert Barnes and Dereck Holt, the other by Christopher Mont and Simon Heynes. Barnes and Holt were to be sent to Germany. They would provide Melanchthon with information on the extent of the persecution of Protestants in France, and use this and other persuasions to divert him to England. If they arrived in Germany to find that Melanchthon had already left for France, Holt was to return to England with this news. Barnes meanwhile would approach some of the German princes. He would encourage them in

2 R. J. Knecht, *Francis I*, Cambridge 1982, 232–3.
3 Ibid. 390–3.
4 See, for example, *LP* viii. 429.
5 BL, MS Cott. Tit. B.i, fo. 424v [*LP* viii. 475].
6 BL, MS Cott. Tit. B.i, fo. 475 [*LP* viii. 892].
7 Barnes's letter of credence to John Frederick, signed by Henry and sealed at Windsor on 8 July: TStWei, Reg. H. 105, fo. 2 [*CR* ii. 939n.].

their opposition to Rome, pledge Henry's support and warn them not to entrust their affairs to Francis. Melanchthon would then be intercepted in France by Mont and Heynes, who would attempt to bring him to England as quickly as possible.[8]

Soon after receiving this letter Cromwell left London and on 23 July rejoined the court at Winchcombe.[9] In spite of his involvement at this time with the visitation and his distance from London, Cromwell remained heavily involved in the arrangements for the despatch of the embassies. In his own hand he noted 'what I shall gyve to doctor Barnes at his goyng ffor Melancton. Item, how I have spokyn with doctor Barnes, and that he is redye to goo and dowtyth not to bryng with hym the persons he shall goo ffor and of his oppynyon touching the leage Swebyk [that is, the Schmalkaldic League – Cromwell appears to have been confusing the name with the virtually defunct Swabian League, which had been a model for the organisation of the League of Schmalkalden]';[10] 'To send fforthe doctor Barnys';[11] 'to despache doctor Barnys with his letters and other wrytings'.[12] As it became clear that it would not be practicable to commute between the progress and London during the last third of July, he sent his financial agent, John Gostwick, the signet and gave him responsibility for issuing to the ambassadors the necessary diet money and papers. Up to the despatch of the last ambassador on 1 August (Barnes was the first to leave on 26 July), Cromwell and Gostwick engaged in an almost daily correspondence concerning preparations.[13]

Under Cromwell's supervision the ambassadors' instructions were expanded considerably and received closer definition. They also gained in the process a tone which suggests the influence of Cromwell's evangelical interests. For Robert Barnes's actions in Germany show that he was instructed on substantially more than the simple directions from Rochford and Norfolk to seek out Melanchthon, and (if he had already gone into France) to enter into discussions with the princes. Barnes was now also specifically instructed to announce that a major English embassy would be despatched shortly to the Schmalkaldic League. Its purpose would be to engage in a comprehensive Anglo-Schmalkaldic religious conference and to discuss whether Henry might be allowed to join the League.

There is no precise evidence as to who gave Barnes these expanded instructions between 19 July, the date of the letter from Norfolk and Rochford and his departure on 26 July. Nor is there any documentation which

---

8   BL, MS Cott. Cleo. E.vi, vol. 2, fos 337–8 [LP viii. 1062].

9   From Winchcombe Cromwell would proceed to use the progress as a vehicle for the early stages of the visitation: D. R. Starkey and S. Wabuda, 'Acton Court and the progress of 1535', in D. R. Starkey (ed.), Henry VIII: a European court in England, London 1991, 118.

10 BL, MS Cott. Tit. B.i, fo. 476 [LP viii. 1061].

11 PRO, SP 1/94, fo. 110 [LP viii. 1063].

12 PRO, SP 1/94, fo. 121 [LP viii. 1077].

13 PRO, SP 1/94, fos 150–1 [LP viii. 1109], 193–4 [LP viii. 1078], 223–4 [LP viii. 1123], 247–8 [LP viii. 1148].

shows who was responsible for the idea of sending a major embassy to Germany to enter into comprehensive religious and political negotiations with the Schmalkaldic League. But, as with the embassy of 1534, the signs point to Cromwell. It was his remembrances, after all, which on three occasions mentioned preparing Barnes, and Gostwick wrote to Cromwell on 21 July of having delivered a particular letter from Cromwell to Barnes, which may possibly have contained special instructions: 'I have delyvred to doctor Barons *youre letter* [my italics] and the other foure letters.'[14] Moreover, once Barnes reached Germany his actions and correspondence would suggest familiarity with, and adherence to, a plan of action devised and set in train by Cromwell. This is not to suggest that Cromwell was acting without the king's knowledge or against his interests. Henry must certainly have known of the plans to send a major religious and political embassy to the League which emerged between 19 and 26 July, and in the light of England's isolated position at this time no doubt welcomed them. Rather, as with the pro-Schmalkaldic advocacy proposed in the previous chapter, it is suggested that Cromwell saw a particular advantage in the king's German policy and acted on it; that it was he who, when he rejoined the court, proposed and gained the king's blessing to go further than the Rochford–Norfolk letter, and that he persuaded the king that Barnes's embassy should be but the first step in initiating a major religious and political exchange with the League of Schmalkalden.

Barnes arrived in Wittenberg in early September,[15] and quickly entered into discussions with his many friends there. By 12 September he had been able to persuade Martin Luther, Justas Jonas, Caspar Cruciger and John Bugenhagen to write jointly to John Frederick, requesting that he grant Barnes an audience and that Melanchthon be allowed to travel to England.[16] On 21 September Barnes was received at Jena by John Frederick[17] whose response shows that the Englishman raised three points: that Henry intended to send an embassy to discuss religious matters with the Wittenberg divines, that he requested the despatch of Philip Melanchthon to England, and that

---

[14] PRO, SP 1/94, fo. 122 [*LP* viii. 1078].

[15] *WABr* vii. 250–2.

[16] The text is in Luther's hand and signed by him, together with Jonas, Cruciger and Bugenhagen: TStWei, Reg. H. 105, fos 5–6 [*WABr* vii. 266–7]. After talking with Barnes, Luther wrote optimistically to the Saxon chancellor, Gregor Brück, the same day, that 'the king is offering to take on the gospel and to give himself to our princes' league and to let our apology go forth in his kingdom' ('der Konig sich erbeut, das Evangelion anzunehmen und in unser Fursten Bundnis sich zu begeben und unser Apologia in seinem Konigreich zu gehen lassen': *WABr* vii. 268). He was of course referring to what Barnes had told him the evangelicals hoped would be the result of Anglo-Schmalkaldic relations, rather than the actual state of affairs in England, which was not yet quite so advanced.

[17] Barnes had arrived at Jena on 18 September. Brück had arranged the audience with John Frederick: *WABr* vii. 270; *CR* ii. 938–9.

he wished to join the Schmalkaldic League.[18] John Frederick replied to each of these points in turn. To the first he said that he would direct the doctors of the university to prepare for theological discussions with the forthcoming English embassy. To the second, he explained that a decision on Melanchthon would have to be deferred until the divines had gathered at Wittenberg. To the third, he noted that Henry's entry to the League could not be decided by him alone but only by all the members together. He promised to put the matter to them at the first opportunity.[19]

On 27 September Barnes left Jena and returned to Wittenberg.[20] On 6 October he wrote to Cromwell from there, informing him of his progress.[21] Things looked promising:

> I have byn here with the elector and with hys [theologians] and have proposed suche thynges as ware commytty[d unto me. Your] h[onourable] goodnesse shal persayve be myne oration had to [the elector that (]thanke god) I have optayned al my petitions as your h[onourable] M[astership will] understand by the electors ansuer wyche I send yow als[o]. . . . And as for locum in federe the elector was very glad of in so much that streyt ways he wrot owt for a congregation of al them that be in federe to be had on S. Nycolas day next [that is, 6 December]. And his counsel ys that the kynges imbassaturs shuld be ther with the king's g[race's] leters for dyvers causys, lest that other men shuld thynke that he wold take al the honore to hym selfe and so myght cause a gruge and also he myght speke frelyer in the kyngs cause yf the matter ware proposyd by us and not by hym. He intendeth very ernestly on owr pryncys syde and doutyth not but al thynges shal come to passe as your g[racious] prynse wyl haue yt. And as for hys ful consent we haue yt, as your h[onourable] M[astership] shal perseyve by hys ansuere.[22]

As far as Melanchthon was concerned, Barnes reported that although he had been able to prevent his despatch to France, John Frederick had been reluctant to agree to his going to England and that the 'sayng gothe here that the elector wyl not let hym departe'.[23] Nevertheless, Barnes concluded that otherwise 'al thyng is brought to passe that my prynse hath recuyryd of me'.

---

18 TStWei, Reg. H. 76, fos 35–9 (Latin copy), 40–2 (German trans.) [CR ii. 940–3; LP ix. 390]. The citations that follow are from the printed version in CR.
19 Ibid.
20 WABr vii. 282. The next day John Frederick wrote a short and colourless courtesy letter to the king, commending Barnes, thanking Henry for the embassy and declaring his pleasure at Henry's piety: TStWei, Reg. H. 105, fos 24–5 [CR ii. 943–4].
21 BL, MS Cott. Vit. B.xxi, fos 120–1 [LP ix. 543]. The manuscript is damaged by fire. I have used the insertions and spellings proposed in P. Smith, 'Englishmen at Wittenberg', EHR xxxvi (1921), 430–2.
22 BL, MS Cott. Vit. B.xxi, fo. 120 [LP ix. 543].
23 Ibid. At around the same time Mont and Heynes were also writing from their embassy to France that it was unlikely that Melanchthon would go to the French king: see, for example, LP ix. 521, 541, 543. In September Mont was sent on from France to Germany to assist Barnes: LP ix. 209, 300.

He urged that a follow-up embassy be sent as soon as possible and closed with the fraternal farewell, 'Your mastership knowyth my fayth. Thus Jesus kepe yow in honore and vertu. Amen.'[24]

The progress and activities of the major English embassy which followed shortly afterwards can be divided into four, roughly chronological, phases. The first phase began with the departure of the embassy for Germany in mid-October and ended with a round of negotiations on an Anglo-Schmalkaldic alliance at Schmalkalden over Christmas. The second took place in Wittenberg from early January to the middle of February, and was concerned with an examination of Henry's divorce. The third, also at Wittenberg, ran from mid-February until the end of March, as discussions shifted to Lutheran doctrine and the possibility of an Anglo-Schmalkaldic theological agreement. The fourth phase began with the conclusion in early April of the theological discussions in Wittenberg and continued until September; this phase was taken up with deciding whether or not the League should send a return embassy to England for further consultations.

Alliance discussions, October–December 1535

Even before Barnes had officially announced the embassy preparations had begun. In July 1535, the task of representing the king in Germany had been given to Edward Foxe. Foxe had first made his mark in Wolsey's service. Though no explicit evidence of his doctrinal beliefs appears, his first independent moves during the late 1520s and thereafter associated him strongly with the reformist movement: he figured prominently in the negotiations for the divorce in Rome, he worked with Cranmer in compiling a source book justifying the divorce on historical grounds[25] and in 1534 published a book in defence of Henrician caesaropapism.[26] Small wonder then that the imperial ambassador, Eustace Chapuys, lumped him together with Cromwell and Cranmer as 'among the most perfect Lutherans in the world'.[27] By 1535 his polished diplomatic work and impeccable credentials as a supporter of the divorce and the supremacy had raised him to a high station. Then, on 19 September, in a move which may have been timed to increase his prestige as

---

24 BL, MS Cott. Vit. B.xxi, fo. 121 [LP ix. 543].
25 This book, the *Collectanea satis copiosa*, was presented to Henry by Foxe and Cranmer in 1531. It not only justified the divorce, but went on to argue for the separateness of the English Church on historical grounds. For its content and influence on the king see G. Nicholson, 'The Act of Appeals and the English Reformation', in C. Cross, D. Loades and J. J. Scarisbrick (eds), *Law and government under the Tudors*, Cambridge 1988, 25–8.
26 This was the *De vera differentia regiae potestatis et ecclesiae*. See Guy, *Tudor England*, 375.
27 *DNB*.

leader of the embassy, he was promoted to the bishopric of Hereford in a cer-emony at Winchester Cathedral attended by Henry and Anne Boleyn.[28]

Foxe had indeed been picked out as the leader of the embassy even before Barnes had left for Germany. As Barnes's letter to Cromwell of 6 October demonstrates, he and Foxe had been together during the summer to discuss strategies for the forthcoming negotiations in Germany. In his letter Barnes asked Cromwell

> t[o] geve M. Almener [that is, Foxe: Barnes obviously did not know of his recent promotion from king's almoner to bishop of Hereford] hys articles, that he and I mae agre, fo[r] we must propose more artycles here than wone, ne videam[ur] tantum querere nostra. I dyd tel M. Almener my menyng.[29]

He also noted that 'I desyre your h[onourable] M[astership] that Master almener mae come shortly, and none other but he, for in the handlyng of thos artycles that he shal bryng hyth al to gether the stablessyng of al christendome, and the stoppyng of al owre aduersaryse mouthes, and I know no man so fyt to do thes thynges as he.'[30] Barnes had little cause for concern: the combination of Foxe's evangelical inclinations, his associations with Cranmer, his diplomatic and theological expertise, and his high office made him a perfect choice as the man to lead the first major ambassadorial exchange between England and the League.[31]

The earliest signs that Foxe was preparing to go to Germany, aside from his discussions with Barnes, are to be found in early August, when a letter-writer noted that he was presently staying at Lambeth, where he was engaged in discussions with Thomas Cranmer. Their purpose was not noted, but it would seem reasonable to suppose that Foxe was preparing for the theological contests which awaited him in Germany.[32] During August and September,

---

[28] Starkey and Wabuda, 'Acton Court and the progress of 1535', 118. The ceremony, which also saw the promotion of Latimer to the bishopric of Worcester, may be seen as the climax of the reforming royal progress of 1535.

[29] BL, MS Cott. Vit. B.xxi, fo. 120 [LP ix. 543].

[30] BL, MS Cott. Vit. B.xxi, fo. 120v [LP ix. 543].

[31] There were, of course, degrees of Protestantism. Though Foxe's actions during 1535–8 identify him with the evangelical cause, he was not as doctrinally extreme as, say, Barnes. 'I am in a gret love with him', Barnes would confide in Cromwell a couple of months later, 'by cause he hathe usyd hym selfe so honorably, thowh he and I do not a gre in omnibus articulis religionis, but I trust at length so to use hym that ther shalbe no gret varyans, for he ys gentyl and mae a byde al maner of honest communication, wherfor I dout not but to drawe hym at length to me thorough goddes grace': BL, MS Cott. Vit. B.xxi, fo. 123v [LP ix. 1030]). This is partly quoted in L. B. Smith, *Tudor prelates and politics, 1536–1558*, Princeton 1953, 150–2, as evidence that Foxe was, in fact, a religious conservative and that had he lived longer 'he would have taken up his position alongside his friend Stephen Gardiner when it became apparent that religious reform was leading to social revolution' (p. 152). Apart from the abundant evidence for Foxe's evangelical leanings, Smith ignores the possibility that he could be less extreme in religion than Barnes (who was, after all, a dyed-in-the-wool Lutheran) yet still be a supporter of religious reform.

[32] LP ix. 29, 65.

Foxe's assistants were appointed. Nicholas Heath, who had been to Germany the previous year, was named as his deputy, while Mont and Barnes were directed to meet up with the embassy in Germany.

Once again, Cromwell's papers point to his involvement in the arrangements for the embassy's despatch. In his own hand, he reminded himself to prepare 'ffor the despache of my lord of herefforde'.[33] Elsewhere, he saw to financial matters, providing '298 l. 13 s. 4 d. to my lord of Hefforde', and '300 crowns ffor Melanckton'.[34] Otherwise he looked after administrative matters in general, noting in his own hand,

> ffor my lorde of hereffordes dispache. ffyrst letters to be assigned to all the prynces. A generall letter of Recomendacyon to all prynces under the brode Seale. A comyscyon generall to the duke of Sax. A letter to Mr Tuke ffor moneye. For money for Master Hethe and Master Barns. Item to know whether he shall have anye other comyscon to the residue of the prynces of germanye.[35]

Foxe's instructions were drafted by Cromwell's clerk Thomas Wriothesley.[36] They show that Henry's anxieties about a general council, which had caused the approach to Philip Melanchthon in the first place, remained a principal concern. Instructions on how Foxe should negotiate a common policy on this matter comprised about a third of the document's thirteen folios. Foxe was directed to propose that only an impartial general council should be countenanced and that England and the League should adopt a common strategy for any such council. He was also to seek the support of the Germans on the divorce and to explain and defend the recent executions of Thomas More and John Fisher. For the purpose of dealing with consequent questions concerning the subject's duty to obey the king, Foxe was to refer to the recent publication with which Stephen Gardiner had begun to ingratiate himself once more into the king's favour, the *De vera obedientia*: 'for the saide

---

[33] PRO, E 36/143, fo. 69 [*LP* ix. 498 i].

[34] BL, MS Cott. Tit. B.i, fo. 432v [*LP* ix. 219]. The original roman numerals in this citation have been converted to arabic.

[35] BL, MS Cott. Tit. B.i, fo. 421v [*LP* ix. 498.iii]. Apart from the three remembrances in Cromwell's hand, there were a number of other papers associated with the despatch of Foxe's embassy: *LP* ix. 212 (letter from Foxe, 31 Aug., arranging for his affairs while in Germany), 213.i–iii (drafts of Foxe's instructions from late August to early September in the hand of Cromwell's clerk Wriothesley), 213.iv–v (remembrances in anonymous clerical hands), 217 (dockets of financial warrants from August for the embassy), 218 (remembrance for payment of diets), 498.ii (remembrance in anonymous clerical hand); CR ii. 947–8 (letter from Henry to Melanchthon, 1 Oct.).

[36] PRO, SP 1/96, fos 12–25 [*LP* ix. 213.i]. Fragments of two other drafts are also in Wriothesley's hand: PRO, SP 1/96, fos 26–7 [*LP* ix. 213.ii], 28–9 [*LP* ix. 213.iii]. What may well be an earlier draft is so mutilated by fire as to be of little use: BL, MS Cott. Vit. B.xiii, fos 237–8 [*LP* ix. 499].

bishoppes better riping in answering herunto ther is delyvered unto hym also an answer lately made by the bishop of Wynchester'.[37]

Clearly, Henry was concerned that his increasingly radical actions in the 1530s were in danger of making him a pariah in Europe, and did not want to alienate that other prime European outcast, the Schmalkaldic League. Nevertheless, even for the sake of continued Schmalkaldic friendship he was not going to enter the evangelical league until he was sure of what it stood for. The instructions therefore showed some caution: 'in cace the sayd Duke or any other shal require that the kinges maiestie entre in fedus evangelicum', Foxe was to say that it would first be necessary for the king to be sent a proposal for entry to such a league. If these proposals were theologically agreeable and contained 'noon articles of defense and maytenance but such as his highnes conveniently ought and maye maynteyne', the League would then be invited to send ambassadors to England to discuss the remaining details with Henry.[38]

It should be noted that diplomatic approaches were also in hand in France and Scotland at about the same time. Indeed, one of Cromwell's remembrances was divided into three parts, respectively preparing embassies to France, Scotland and Germany,[39] and some of the financial arrangements for the embassies to Germany and France even appeared on the same bundle of dockets.[40] Moreover, the main draft of Foxe's instructions said that he should explain the purpose of his embassy to any French ambassador he might meet in Germany who himself was forthcoming.[41] Similarly, the instructions for the French ambassador, Stephen Gardiner, written by Wriothesley and signed at the head by the king, directed him to 'declare unto the said Frenche king the cause of the sending of the bisshop of hereford to the duke of Saxe and other'.[42] It was explained that Foxe had been sent to explain Henry's proceedings against the pope, who, having slandered Henry to Francis, would 'of lightlyhood spitt out his venom ells where moche moer plentifully'.[43] It is clear that the approaches to the Schmalkaldeners were part of a broader diplomatic effort to establish a series of anti-imperial and anti-papal alliances. Each of these had its own characteristics. That in Germany, for example, was

---

37 PRO, SP 1/96, fo. 25v [LP ix. 213.i]. A remembrance for the embassy's despatch noted a number of source books which were to be taken to Germany. These included 'The byshopp of Winchesters boke de obedientia', an unspecified book by Cranmer and Melanchthon's *Loci communes*: BL, MS Cott. Tit. B.i, fo. 458 [LP ix. 213.v].
38 PRO, SP 1/96, fo. 23 [LP ix. 213.i].
39 BL, MS Cott. Tit. B.i, fo. 421 [LP ix. 498.iii].
40 PRO, SP 1/99, fos 93 [LP ix. 878.i], 96 [LP ix. 878.iv].
41 PRO, SP 1/96, fos 23v–4 [LP ix. 213.i]. Though one of the early drafts of Foxe's instructions directed him to warn the Germans of French intentions at a general council (PRO, SP 1/96, fo. 28v [LP ix. 213.iii]), there was probably still a little anxiety at Francis's interest in bringing a general council to pass.
42 BL, MS Add. 25114, fo. 97v [LP ix. 443].
43 BL, MS Add. 25114, fo. 98 [LP ix. 443].

centred upon religious unity and opposition to the general council, while that in France sought to encourage a French campaign in northern Italy. They were also independent of each other: efforts to conclude an alliance in Germany would continue long after Francis had invaded northern Italy in April 1536. Thus the idea that the approach to the Germans in 1535 was simply a dependent movement in some mechanical, greater European diplomatic scheme should be resisted. Though the Schmalkaldic diplomacy may properly be regarded as an aspect of England's wider foreign policy, from the outset it had its own unique background, interests and aims.

Shortly after Barnes's arrival in Wittenberg in September, John Frederick was told that a major English embassy would be arriving soon. On 13 September he wrote to the governor of Saxony that an 'English embassy appears to be on the way'. He ordered the governor to make preparations for receiving and waylaying the embassy at Wittenberg, and then, after John Frederick had been informed of its arrival, conducting it to him.[44] At the same time he wrote to his chancellor, Gregor Brück, in Wittenberg, asking for his assistance in receiving the embassy, and noting that since he had heard that it would give its oration in Latin, he would require the services of a good Latinist such as Melanchthon or Spalatin.[45] Finally, towards the end of September he wrote to Luther, Jonas, Bugenhagen, Melanchthon and Cruciger, saying that Henry 'is sending a considerable embassy here, which will have a friendly discussion and colloquy, and negotiate some articles with you our theologians'.[46] He directed the divines to prepare to receive and confer with the ambassadors in Wittenberg or, if plague was still rampant there, in Torgau. Referring to a forthcoming journey to Austria to meet King Ferdinand, however, he stressed that they were under no circumstances to enter into any final agreement with the ambassadors until his return to Germany in December.[47]

Meanwhile, in England, final preparations were in hand. Although Foxe received his instructions around the end of August, his departure had to be delayed while his consecration as bishop of Hereford was being arranged. Then he became ill and it was not until the middle of October that he was

---

[44] 'Engellandische potschafft uff dem wege sein soll': TStWei, Reg. H. 105, fo. 7 [WABr vii. 281–2]. The governor acknowledged this letter and undertook to prepare for the embassy on 17 September: TStWei, Reg. H. 105, fos 12–14.

[45] TStWei, Reg. H. 105, fos 8–9 [CR ii. 938–9; WABr vii. 270]. The editors of WABr vii. 269–70, are confused about the particular embassy to which this reference alludes, and mistakenly assume that the letter concerns Christopher Mont's transfer from France to Germany in September. The preparations are, of course, far too elaborate for a minor agent like Mont (and it is doubtful that at this time his despatch to Germany was even known); the correspondence concerns Foxe's forthcoming embassy.

[46] '[E]ine stattliche Botschaft hernacher schicken, welche sich mit Euch als unsern Theologen von etzlichen Artikeln unterreden und freundliche Gespräch und Colloquia halten wurde': WABr vii. 283.

[47] WABr vii. 281–4.

well enough for the embassy finally to set off.[48] The ambassadors appeared in Germany the following month. On 28 November they were received at Erfurt by Wolfgang von Anhalt,[49] and were handed a letter dated 17 November from John Frederick which emphasised the determination of the princes to remain true to their religious principles as enshrined in the Confession of Augsburg. The duke had sent with the letter copies of recent papal proposals to go to a general council, and noted his disagreement with the assertion made in them that only the pope has the right to summon a council. He thanked Henry for his offers of assistance and commended 'to him the cause of the confederates'.[50]

In the first week of December John Frederick returned to Germany. On the 6th of the month he wrote a number of letters concerned with arrangements for the English embassy. He wrote to his vice-chancellor, Franz Burchard, informing him of his intention to meet the embassy in Weimar. He said that as far as he knew the ambassadors had not yet had the planned discussions with the Wittenberg theologians, and that he had now decided to direct Luther and Barnes to Jena (where Melanchthon was presently residing) to prepare for talks.[51] Accordingly, the duke wrote to Martin Luther that he should begin preparations in Jena for a theological conference there between the English ambassadors and the German divines.[52] He directed Barnes to accompany Luther.[53] He also ordered the governor of Saxony to provide Luther and Barnes with horses, supplies and all other things necessary for their expeditious despatch.[54] Finally, John Frederick wrote to the Weimar council, and ordered it to prepare for his arrival and for an audience which he intended to grant the English embassy.[55]

John Frederick arrived in Weimar on 8 December. He immediately sent for the English embassy to make the short journey from Erfurt to meet him. It arrived at Weimar the following day. According to their own account, the ambassadors were well entertained upon their arrival, and had three conferences with the duke, in which they tried to 'dissiphre [decypher]'[56] the Germans without revealing the full extent of their own instructions. After three days with John Frederick in Weimar they had received 'certen answer unto suche overtures as they hadde made'.[57] In accordance with John Freder-

---

[48] *LP* ix. 401, 563.
[49] BL, MS Cott. Vit. B.xxi, fo. 179 (contemporary abstract of the ambassadors' letters) [*LP* ix. 1018]: the ambassadors 'cam to Erford the xxviijth day of November where they were met by the prince of Henallt'.
[50] *LP* ix. 834 [*CR* ii. 968–72].
[51] TStWei, Reg. H. 105, fos 27–30.
[52] TStWei, Reg. H. 105, fos 32–3 [*CR* ii. 1007; *WABr* vii. 332–4; *LP* ix. 928].
[53] TStWei, Reg. H. 105, fos 34–5.
[54] Ibid. fo. 31.
[55] Ibid. fo. 26.
[56] BL, MS Cott. Vit. B.xxi, fo. 179 [*LP* ix. 1018].
[57] Ibid.

ick's discussions with Barnes in September, the ambassadors were then directed to negotiate with the League at a diet in Schmalkalden, which had convened on 6 December. The ambassadors departed with the duke for the diet on 12 December, arriving in Schmalkalden the following day.[58]

On 15 December the ambassadors entered into 'a secret and friendly discussion' with the Saxon chancellor and vice-chancellor, Gregor Brück and Franz Burchard respectively.[59] According to the German record of that meeting, the English ambassadors made five main points: Henry wanted an embassy to be sent to England to discuss theology; though Henry did not object to the principle of a general council, he insisted that it must be held in a safe place, that the papacy must not be its arbitrator, and that England and the League must be agreed on doctrine before attending; under any other circumstances a general council should not be attended; Henry was inclined to join the Schmalkaldic League; and, finally, he was not going to restore the pope's authority.[60] Nine days later, Foxe addressed the full diet of the Schmalkaldic League in similar terms. He emphasised the efficacy of a religious concord between England and the League, warned against the duplicity of the pope, and cautioned against any ill-considered involvement in a general council.[61] In response, the League's delegates returned the next day with a schedule containing thirteen articles, which set out the grounds upon which an Anglo-Schmalkaldic common policy might be based and the conditions for Henry's possible admission to the League. These required that Henry promote the Gospel and faith as set out in the Confession of Augsburg and defend it at any future general council. The king and princes were to act as one in deciding whether or not to participate in a general council, in ignoring its decrees if they did not take part and in rejecting the authority of the pope in any matter. Henry was to be appointed defender of the League and, like all members, to make a financial contribution to its security according to means; for Henry, the contribution was set at 100,000 crowns to be paid upon admission to the League (to be stored in Germany and only to be used for defensive purposes), with an undertaking to supply a further 200,000 crowns if it became necessary. Neither Henry nor the princes were to supply aid that might be used against the other. The petition closed with a

---

[58] BL, MS Cott. Vit. B.xxi, fos 179–80 [LP ix. 1018] (contemporary abstract: 'Theffect of my [lord of Hereford, Doctor] Heth and Doctor Bar[nes letters] to Mr Secretarie'). The duke's date of arrival in Schmalkalden is confirmed by the Strassburg delegates' account in PC ii. 315. John Frederick mentioned his meeting with the English ambassadors at Weimar as one of the reasons (his meeting with Ferdinand was the other) for his delayed arrival in Schmalkalden for the diet which had opened on 6 December: PC ii. 315.
[59] '[E]inem heimlichen und freundlichen Gespräch': CR ii. 1008. The Strassburg account mentions only that on 15 December the English embassy's address was heard, and that the League asked for time to consider it: PC ii. 318.
[60] TStWei, Reg. H. 105, fos 38–41 (Latin copy of English address), 36–7 (German paraphrase); HStMar, PA 443, fos 1–2 (German paraphrase) [CR ii. 1007–9; LP ix. 979].
[61] HStMar, PA 443, fos 33–8 [CR ii. 1028–32; LP ix. 1014].

request that Foxe convey Henry's answer to the articles as soon as possible. The League would respond to this by sending ambassadors to reach agreement on the theological questions.[62]

With the presentation of the League's articles to the embassy, the English ambassadors' part in the diet came to a close.[63] Shortly after Christmas they despatched the articles to Henry for consideration. They then packed their bags, prepared their company of twelve horses, and rode back down the mountains from Schmalkalden, ready for the next round of discussions early in the new year.

Divorce discussions, January–February 1536

On 6 December John Frederick had made plans for a theological conference between the English ambassadors and a group of Lutheran divines. The original location, Jena, was for some reason changed: on 28 December Barnes wrote to Cromwell from Gotha that the embassy was 'goy[ng to] Wyttenbergh'.[64] On 31 December the governor of Saxony wrote to John Frederick that he had met the English ambassadors at Düben and in accordance with his instructions was accompanying them to Wittenberg.[65] Thus, on the first day of 1536, the English ambassadors rode into the birthplace of the Reformation. They were lodged in the guesthouse of one Christian Goldschmied, and at John Frederick's command were allocated fifty hares, two oxen, some cutlets of venison, a cask of wine and two barrels of Torgau beer.[66] They had, however, little time to relax with these comforts, they were soon plunged into intense theological discussions which occupied them for the next three months.

Initially, discussions were concerned with the divorce. This, of course, had been one of Henry's central preoccupations since the late 1520s. It had caused the break with Rome, the repudiation of the Habsburgs, and the establishment of an independent English Church. It had also been an early point

---

62 TStWei, Reg. H. 105, fos 42–5 (German draft), 46–52 (Latin draft, partly in Melanchthon's hand), 53–8 (German draft), 59–62 (Latin draft), 64–6 (good Latin copy); HStMar, PA 443, fos 3–4 (German draft, barely legible), 5–6 (Latin draft), 7–12 (Latin copy), 13–15 (Latin copy), 17–24 (German draft), 25–32 (German trans. of final copy), 39–42 (Latin copy) [CR ii. 1032–6]; PRO, SP 1/99, fos 159–61 (English trans. in Wriothesley's hand) [LP ix. 1016.i], 162–5 (independent English trans.) [LP ix. 1016.ii]; BL, MS Cott. Cleo. E. vi, vol. 2, fos 304–5 (independent English trans.) [LP ix. 1016.iv].

63 Except, that is, for some awkward moments when Henry was asked to support Christian III of Denmark against the town of Lübeck (until recently he had been supporting the Lübeckers): PRO, SP 1/99, fo. 149 (signed letter on behalf of Christian III from John Frederick and Philip to to Henry) [LP ix. 1008]: LP ix. 1019. Papers on these discussions are in HStMar, PA 443, fos 43–4, 45–6.

64 BL, MS Cott. Vit. B.xxi, fo. 123 [LP ix. 1030].

65 WABr vii. 333.

66 Ibid.

of contact between England and Protestant Germany. Before considering the discussions which took place at Wittenberg in early 1536, therefore, it would be helpful to turn the clock back and look at the development of the contacts on this issue.[67]

The divorce controversy provided the ground for the first English attempts to establish a common theological position with the German Protestants. It was in mid-1531 that Anglo-German discussions concerned with the divorce began. About this time, just as the English campaign to seek approval of the divorce from Europe's universities seemed to be coming to a close, it was decided to make an effort to gain scholarly support from continental Protestants. Sheer desperation probably played the greatest part in the decision to seek the approbation of the heterodox theologians of Germany and Switzerland. Europe's orthodox universities had been largely unwilling to help Henry on the divorce. At least the Protestants could be counted on to deny the pope's authority in the matter and they might well have no desire to provide support for the woman whose nephew Charles V had been so unsympathetic to their own cause. Moreover, Henry had been asked for political support by the Protestants of the Schmalkaldic League at the beginning of 1531; surely they at least would be amenable to a similar approach from the English king.

The first moves were made in Switzerland through the Zwinglian reformer Simon Grynaeus. Between leaving a post at Heidelberg University in 1529 and taking up the chair vacated by Erasmus at Basel in 1531, Grynaeus had spent some time in England, 'to search for old books, and to print them'. There, at Henry's prompting, he had entered into discussions on the divorce with 'three or four of the principal doctors'. During these conversations he appears to have made a good impression on the king. At the close of the discussions he was given a sum of money as an inducement to canvass his colleagues as to their views on the divorce.[68] He proceeded to do this upon his arrival in Basel at the end of July, writing to Bucer, Melanchthon, Oecolampadius, Zwingli, Phrygio and perhaps to Calvin also. Grynaeus and the Swiss theologians soon agreed that Henry's marriage to Catherine was invalid and that she should be put away forthwith. Bucer and Melanchthon, however, the two German theologians of the Schmalkaldic League, saw the matter differently.[69]

---

67 It will also be useful to provide a review of the main Schmalkaldic writings on the divorce. The only major analysis of the contemporary treatises to date 'concentrates almost exclusively on the debate within England': V. M. Murphy, 'The debate over Henry VIII's first divorce: an analysis of the contemporary treatises', unpubl. PhD diss. Cambridge 1984, p. vii. For a fuller discussion of the divorce controversy as a whole and the literature it produced see also her 'The literature and propaganda of Henry VIII's first divorce', in MacCulloch, *Reign of Henry VIII*, 135–58; Scarisbrick, *Henry VIII*, 163–240; MacCulloch, *Cranmer*, 41–114; H. A. Kelly, *The matrimonial trials of Henry VIII*, Stanford, CA 1976; G. Bedouelle and P. Le Gal (eds), *Le 'Divorce' du roi Henry VIII*, Geneva 1987.
68 *LP* v. 287.
69 W. W. Rockwell, *Die Doppelehe des Landgrafen Philipp von Hessen*, Marburg 1904, 205–7;

Bucer's original judgement is not extant. Nevertheless, correspondence between Grynaeus and Bucer shows that the Strassburger stood against the divorce on the grounds that God had shown in Deuteronomy[70] that the prohibition in Leviticus[71] cited by Henry could be dispensed: that the law against marrying a dead brother's wife 'did no more bind Christians than the other ceremonial or judiciary precepts; and that to marry in some of these degrees was no more a sin than it was a sin in the disciples to pluck ears of corn on the sabbath day'.[72] Grynaeus was unhappy with Bucer's judgement, and in the following months begged him to reconsider. However Bucer would not change his mind. On 31 December 1531 he sent Grynaeus his final word on the matter. In a letter signed by his fellow Strassburgers Hedio, Capito and Zell he upheld the dispensing power of Deuteronomy and argued that Jewish law was applicable to Christians.[73]

For his part, Melanchthon immediately began writing a judgement, which he finished on 23 August 1531 at Wittenberg.[74] At the same time (and in the same town), Martin Luther also began writing an opinion. His reason for doing so was different from Melanchthon's. Unlike Melanchthon, he had been contacted directly from England with a request for an opinion on the divorce. Around the same time as Grynaeus returned to Switzerland, the English had made an independent approach to Protestant Germany. The man chosen for the task was Robert Barnes.[75] Barnes went first to Marburg to ask for Philip of Hesse's help. The landgrave obliged by directing the university which he had recently founded in the town to prepare an opinion on the divorce. However this did not bring the desired result. On 12 October the university found against the divorce, basing its judgement on the standard argument that Deuteronomy allowed a man to marry his dead brother's wife, and that God forbade divorce.[76] In spite of this setback, Philip did his best to help Barnes. Sometime after the Englishman had set off for Saxony to seek support in Wittenberg he wrote to Luther and the Saxon chancellor Brück that as much support as possible should be given to Henry, 'since much now depends on this man for the progress of the Gospel, as you know, and it is to be hoped that if he finds approbation from our Church in this matter, we shall without doubt win him for our lord Christ'.[77] However Philip's second

H. Eells, *Martin Bucer*, New Haven 1931, 122–6; P. Smith, 'German opinion of the divorce of Henry VIII', *EHR* xxvii (1912), 671–81; Burnet, *History of the Reformation*, i. 160–1.
[70] All references to Deuteronomy in this section apply specifically to Deut. xxv.5.
[71] All references to Leviticus in this section apply specifically to Lev. xx.21.
[72] Burnet, *History of the Reformation*, i. 160; Eells, *Bucer*, 122.
[73] Eells, *Bucer*, 125–6; Rockwell, *Doppelehe Philipps von Hessen*, 206–7.
[74] CR ii. 520–7.
[75] Smith, 'German opinion', 675, confuses Paget's diplomatic mission of around the same time with Barnes's divorce mission.
[76] HStMar, PA 1799, fos 8–15.
[77] 'Wann nun an diesem man der furderung des euangelii, wi ir wisst, etwas gelegen und guter hoffnung, so er deshalben bey unserer kirchen mit Gott zufall haben, wurden wir den one zweivel unserm heupt Christo gewinnen': *WABr* vi. 198.

attempt at helping Barnes was as ill-starred as the first: his letter arrived some time after Luther had provided Barnes with a judgement and so could not influence the outcome.

Upon his arrival at Wittenberg in August, Barnes went directly to Martin Luther who provided him with a judgement dated 3 September. Luther later wrote another version of this judgement from memory for the purpose of informing Philip of Hesse of his decision.[78] The coincidence of the dates and place of Melanchthon's and Luther's judgements strongly suggests that there was some consultation between the two on their respective decisions.[79] Nevertheless, the two pieces show substantial divergence in argumentation and style, so the extent of direct collaboration in writing up the opinions was probably limited. Be that as it may, the two theologians came essentially to the same conclusion. They argued that Deuteronomy was universally applicable and had precedence over the prohibition against marrying a dead brother's wife in Leviticus cited by Henry, which they characterised as merely a Jewish ceremonial law and thus open to dispensation by the papacy. The only way out they saw for Henry was the unusual step of bigamy, a course of action which Philip of Hesse would later take as a means of solving his own marital difficulties, but one which the prudish king almost certainly never took seriously. Melanchthon's judgement was sent directly to Grynaeus. Upon reading it he had the idea of sending it back to Wittenberg with the favourable opinions of Zwingli and the other Swiss theologians, hoping that they might have the effect of changing Melanchthon's mind. Bucer, however, warned him that this would only aggravate the current Zürich–Wittenberg discord. After further consideration Grynaeus reluctantly agreed to send the judgement to England.[80] Luther's opinion was probably taken back to England by Barnes personally.

Though Henry's reaction to the judgements of the German Protestants is not known, they cannot have been anything other than disappointing for him, refusing as they did to give even the slightest credence to any of his arguments for the divorce. It is not surprising, therefore, that no further embassies were sent from England to Germany exclusively for the purpose of obtaining support for the divorce. Nevertheless, the subject was not completely dropped: the ambassadors of early 1534 were instructed at some length on how they should raise the divorce question. And even though they were unable to elicit any response at all from the Germans, when it came to despatching Foxe's embassy to the Schmalkaldic League in 1535 the divorce once again figured among the ambassadors' papers.

Foxe's instructions dealt only briefly with the matter: it was probably

---

[78] WABr vi. 175–88. These are the only two extant versions of Luther's opinion. See also the English translation and commentary in Doernberg, Henry VIII and Luther.
[79] See the commentary in WABr vi. 175–7.
[80] Eells, Bucer, 124–5. Eells again mistakenly assumes that Luther's opinion was sent to Grynaeus with Melanchthon's and thence to England.

thought unnecessary to provide one as expert as he with any detail on how to argue. Instead the few directions which did appear were only concerned with explaining to Foxe the strategies he should employ. He was only to raise the divorce if the Germans seemed receptive, 'not making the determination of the kinges matier as any principal cause of his cumyng, but only in noting the craftye handeling of the bishop of Rome, by the waye to speke of yt', and only 'yf he perceave them to saver yt and inclinable to condescend to thapprobacion therof note that as oon article among other to be agreed upon'.[81]

As things turned out such circuitousness was unnecessary: the Germans showed themselves perfectly happy to enter into open discussions with the English on the divorce.[82] Without hesitation they made the appropriate arrangements for a disputation, which began at Wittenberg soon after the English ambassadors arrived there. The array of German theologians which assembled at Wittenberg in early January 1536 was formidable. In the chair was Martin Luther. He was supported by John Bugenhagen, Justus Jonas and Caspar Cruciger. Philip Melanchthon joined the party a couple of weeks later.[83] The English, however, were not overawed by this impressive line-up. Indeed, as the discussions developed they proved to be very formidable disputants; so much so that before long the Lutherans were beginning to reconsider their previously uncompromising position.

Luther at first remained completely sure of himself. He told John Frederick on 11 January that 'my previous judgement will stand', though he would listen to and converse gently with the English, lest they think 'we Germans were of stone and wood'.[84] By 19 January, however, the first faint signs of doubt were beginning to creep in. He wrote to the chancellor of Mansfeld that 'I must excuse the king's person, and yet still cannot approve the matter.'[85] A week later he was frustrated, grumbling to John Frederick that 'I have seen through much greater matters in four weeks, yet they want to spend twelve years on this one issue.'[86] But slowly, the tenacity of the English was paying off. By February, the Lutherans were beginning to relent.

---

81 PRO, SP 1/96, fo. 20 [LP ix. 213.i].

82 When Barnes first mentioned that the divorce might be a subject for discussion, Luther immediately commented that he would be very interested to hear what it was that continued to make the English so certain about the case: WABr vii. 268.

83 At the insistence of the English, who no doubt valued him for his reputation as a conciliator, John Frederick agreed to despatch Melanchthon from the university at Jena only after seeking Luther's opinion on 9 January, and receiving his approbation two days later: CR iii. 10–1; WABr vii. 340–3; Prüser, England und die Schmalkaldener, 41.

84 '[M]ein voriger sentenz sol auch bleiben ... wir Deudschen weren stein und holtz': WABr vii. 342.

85 '[I]ch des konigs Person fast entschuldigen muss, und doch die Sache nicht billigen kann': WABr vii. 349. In this letter Luther also referred, with regret, to the recent news of the death of Catherine, saying that only the Wittenberg theologians had stood by her.

86 'Ich hab wohl grossere Sachen und viel in vier Wochen ausgericht, und sie wohl zwölf Jahr in dieser einigen Sache zanken': WABr vii. 353–4.

The English were applying greatest pressure on the question of the relevance of Mosaic law to Christians, and it is this that no doubt explains Luther's growing indecision and annoyance during January. Before long, however, the frustration he and his colleagues felt was giving way to an acknowledgement that there were some merits in the English case. This was achieved with the help and influence of Andreas Osiander, an expert in Old Testament and Talmudic law and their contemporary Christian relevance.[87] As early as 1532 Osiander had written on incestuous marriage, and his book *De matrimonio incestuo* had been banned by the city council in his native Nuremberg, allegedly on the grounds that it supported the case of the English king and might therefore anger the emperor.[88] During the negotiations with the English ambassadors in early 1536, Luther and Melanchthon sought Osiander's views on marriage between a man and his dead brother's wife. In a letter from Nuremberg sent in the first week of February, Osiander gave his judgement. When it arrived in Wittenberg, it soon became clear that it amounted to a complete vindication of the English argument that Leviticus is a natural law and Deuteronomy a ceremonial law. The view which Melanchthon and Luther had mocked in 1531 was now given undeniable respectability and authority in Osiander's hands. Osiander's judgement demonstrated that the relevance of Deuteronomy to contemporary Christians had been greatly overrated by Melanchthon and Luther. It stood Melanchthon's and Luther's judgements on their heads, stating unequivocally that Leviticus was an unalterable natural law (and equally so, whether in the case of a dead or a living brother's wife), whereas the Levirate practice sanctioned in Deuteronomy was not applicable to Christians.[89]

The short judgement given to Foxe at Wittenberg in March 1536 showed the advances which the English embassy had made with Osiander's help and the ground which Melanchthon and Luther had conceded since 1531: 'for it is clear and no one can deny, that the Levitical law enshrined in Leviticus xviii. 20, prohibits the taking of a brother's wife etc.; and also that it is a divine, natural and moral law, and comprehends both a dead and living brother's wife, and that against this law no contradictory law may be made or cited'.[90] The judgement went on to acknowledge that this had been the

---

87 The suggestion that Osiander supported Henry's case because of his relationship with Cranmer's wife (in, for example, Scarisbrick, *Henry VIII*, 401) is probably mistaken; Osiander's position pre-dates Cranmer's marriage.

88 Rockwell, *Doppelehe Philipps von Hessen*, 220; cf. *LP* xiii/1, 140.

89 Osiander's judgement, and the correspondence concerning it, is in *WABr* vii. 359–62. For Osiander's background, his views and this judgement see W. Möller, *Andreas Osiander: Leben und ausgewählte Schriften*, Elberfeld 1870, 154–6, 190–6; Rockwell, *Doppelehe Philipps von Hessen*, 220–2; Prüser, *England und die Schmalkaldener*, 46–9.

90 '[N]am hoc manifestum est et negare nemo potest, quod lex Levit. tradita Levit. XVIII. 20 prohibet ducere fratris uxorem etc. sed divina, naturalis et moralis lex est intelligenda tam de vivi quam de mortui fratris uxore, et quod contra hanc legem nulla contraria lex fieri aut constitui possit': Burnet, *History of the Reformation*, iv. 145 [CR ii. 528].

accepted view in the decrees of the early councils and the patristic writings, and that in their own Church they would not allow or dispense for such a marriage.[91]

But, in spite of this major concession, a stumbling block remained. Henry's case was complicated by the fact that he had actually gone through with his first marriage. In the letter to the English king containing their decision the Germans said that they would need more time to consider this question of Henry's pre-contract to Catherine before they could give him a final judgement.[92] It is interesting that a subsequent draft of this judgement shows that at some later stage the German theologians did reach a decision on the problem of Henry's pre-contract which amounted to a rejection of his case. Once married, it claimed, 'the bond of marriage is stronger than the other law concerning a brother's wife'.[93] Nevertheless, the letter sent to Henry did not include this decision. He was given a letter accepting the precedence of Leviticus over Deuteronomy, but mere indecision on the question of pre-contract.[94] The king was sufficiently stimulated by the German response to direct his theologians in England to begin work immediately on a reply, and sufficiently satisfied to insist that a condition of his joining the League would be that the Germans must 'defend thopinions of the Reverand fathers Dr Martyn, Justas Jonas, Cruciger, Pomeran [ie. Bugenhagen], and Melanchton in the cawse of his graces mariage'.[95]

Thus, the final position on the divorce which emerged from the Wittenberg discussions was a curious one: the king thought that the Lutheran theologians agreed with the divorce, while they were equally sure that they did not. As if to confirm the final German position, in the remaining discussions of 1536 it would be unanimously agreed by the League members that for theological and political reasons they must not become involved in Henry's divorce. However, this remaining disagreement on the divorce was not to be a significant obstacle to continued Anglo-Schmalkaldic relations. The deaths during 1536 of both Catherine of Aragon and Anne Boleyn greatly reduced the international significance of the divorce and had the effect of removing it completely from the agenda in discussions between England and the League. After 1536 it did not feature again in Anglo-Schmalkaldic theological discussions which would be henceforth dominated by theology itself, by efforts to reach a common understanding and agreement on the doctrine of the faith.

---

91 Ibid.

92 Ibid.

93 '[S]o ist das Band der Ehe stärker denn das andre Gesetz von des Bruders Weibe': CR ii. 529.

94 The full text of draft is at CR ii. 528–9.

95 BL, MS Cott. Cleo. E.vi, vol. 2, fo. 308 [LP x. 457]. The evidence that Henry immediately directed his theologians to reply to the Germans comes from the imperial ambassador (Chapuys's speculation that the Germans had come down against the king's great matter may be discounted in the light of the quote above): SpCal v/2, 43 [LP x. 601].

Theological discussions, February–April 1536

A principal reason for sending Foxe's embassy to Germany was that it would allow for an Anglo-Schmalkaldic discussion of Protestant doctrine. There has already been occasion to suggest why the English evangelicals wanted these discussions to take place. But what of Henry? Why was it that he favoured doctrinal discussions with the League?

In part, his interest was purely practical: at some time in the future Henry and the Protestants might have to defend their respective religious innovations at a general council. If a general council not directly under papal jurisdiction were summoned, Henry and the League would in all probability be compelled to attend; in such a case it would be advisable for them first to have established a common position on the theological issues to which they might have to answer. And of course there was the question of establishing an Anglo-Schmalkaldic alliance, which would be much more effective if it included an agreement on religious matters. The practical side of the king's interest in the League's theology may be seen in Stephen Gardiner's instructions to France. These, signed by the king, noted that Foxe's embassy had 'also in comission to knowe their astate in religion, to thintent that upon communication and deliberation of the truth an unytie in christes religion might be established, wherin the kinges highnes wil by all wayes and meanes employe al his labour, study, travail and diligence'.[96] Such Christian unity would help England and the League resist their opponents more effectively. As Foxe's instructions noted, by 'the kinges hieghnes and they conferring together thair causes, matiers and procedinges and either allowing and approving the doing of thoder so farre as maye stand with the trouth of the gospel they shalbe somoche the stronger to withstande the adversaries'.[97]

However, the advantages which Henry saw in theological discussions with the League went further than a purely practical concern with establishing a common Anglo-Schmalkaldic front against the upholders of Roman orthodoxy. Henry also had an interest in the League's theology for its own sake, an interest which was tied up with the development of the English Church in the 1530s. If the dominant religious theme during the first half of the 1530s is the destruction of an established religious order, then the corresponding one for the second half must be the quest to raise a new order in its place. During the first half of the 1530s Henry had supervised the severing of England's theological moorings. As a result, by the middle of the decade his kingdom was spiritually adrift. The supreme head had abolished many of Rome's old certainties, but had not replaced them with any of his own. With the rejection of Rome Henry had lost that which he had long taken for granted: a definite faith to defend. As a result, during the mid-1530s Henry determined to halt endless diversification and to establish a definitive statement of the

96 BL, MS Add. 25114, fo. 98 [*LP* ix. 443].
97 PRO, SP 1/96, fo. 19v [*LP* ix. 213.i].

English faith. As early as 1534 he complained to Cranmer that in spite of the repeated councils summoned to promote unity in religion 'there swarmeth abrode a nombre of indiscreate personnes whiche being neyther furnished with wisdom, lernyng nor judgement be nevertheles auctorised to preache and permytted to blowe abrode their foly'.[98] Henry instructed Cranmer and his prelates to take greater care with the choice of preachers, 'to thintent our people may be educate, fedde and inrished with holsom fode'.[99] Though there is no talk here of the need for a definitive statement of the faith to guide the clergy and people, it may be seen that Henry was not far from considering such a measure. By August 1534 he was closer still with a document headed 'how the false heresyes which the bysshop of rome hath tought the people shuld be brought out of theyr conscences and hertes'.[100] This directed the archbishop of Canterbury to summon a council of bishops and doctors, and have them sign their decision on each of the articles contained in the 'boke of the charge'.[101] Nothing more is known of what became of this conference or the mysterious 'boke of the charge', but it is clear that Henry was beginning to push his theologians towards establishing a codification of the English faith.

In this Henry could use the advice of those European Christians who had themselves formulated a theological code to replace that of the Roman Church. It was Philip Melanchthon's European-wide reputation as the moderate face of Protestantism, as the conciliatory author of the Confession of Augsburg, that led to his being asked twice in 1534 to come to England,[102] and to his being approached by Robert Barnes early in 1535.[103] It was also one of the reasons why he was sought later in the year, and explains the deep interest Henry showed in consulting with him during the remainder of the decade.[104] There is also the example of those ambassadors who came from Hamburg and Lübeck to England in 1534 to discuss the succession to the Danish throne: they soon found that Henry regarded contacts with Germany as affording the opportunity to discuss German theology. Chapuys reported in December 1534 that the ambassadors had been put into conference with the king's bishops, to discuss 'the sacrifice of the mass, and whether faith alone without works is sufficient for our salvation'.[105]

As the only significant alternative to Rome as a centre of western Christian theological expertise, Wittenberg could provide Henry with advice that would complement that provided by his own theologians. One of the main

---

[98] PRO, SP 6/2, fo. 126v [*LP* vii. 750].
[99] PRO, SP 6/2, fo. 127v [*LP* vii. 750].
[100] PRO, SP 1/85, fo. 99v [*LP* vii. 1043].
[101] PRO, SP 1/85, fos 99v–100 [*LP* vii. 1043].
[102] *LP* vii. 1147.
[103] There is very little evidence for this mission; Melanchthon simply wrote to Henry, telling him that, as requested, he had commented on the articles Barnes had brought him: *LP* viii. 384–5.
[104] Henry's subsequent interest in Melanchthon is examined below.
[105] *LP* viii. 1432.

reasons why Foxe was sent to Germany was Henry's wish to tap this consultative source. Foxe's instructions provide evidence of this. Foxe was directed to tell the League's princes that Henry wanted the embassy 'to conferre, consulte and devyse with them in certain other thinges wherin his maiestie myndyng to procede according to the veray trueth of the gospel hath thought good to knowe thair advise and counsaille'.[106] The Germans were to be told that Henry intended to put his kingdom's Church in order, bringing a true understanding of religion 'to the knowlege of his people and subgiettes entending also so further and further to procede therin as his grace by good consultacion shal perceave maye tend and perteyne to the augmentacion of the glorye of god and the true knowleage of his word'.[107] The League should know that Henry would not 'without good advisement and mature deliberacion, consultacion also and conference with his frendes go in any parte beyonde the sayd trueth'.[108] He wished 'to be adcertayned in what poyntes and articles the lerned men there be so constantely and assuredly resolved as by no persuasion of may they canne be tourned from the same'.[109] Thus he wanted the Germans to 'entretayne in conferences and conversations the sayd byshop so frendlye and familierly concerning the matiers aforsayd'.[110] And so, when the time came for Foxe to speak to the League at Schmalkalden in December, he declared that Henry wished to be 'informed as to the state of religion, and receive advice as to what to reform in England in matters relating to faith and religion'.[111] Henry did not see these theological consultations as a one-off affair, beginning and ending with Foxe's visit to Germany. Rather, Foxe's embassy was conceived as but the first stage in the consultative process. The bishop was directed to 'note unto them that being in England soo many gret lerned men and not inferior to any parte of Christendom it shalbe necessary for the said duke and the princes confedrate to send thither to the kinges hignes'.[112] And in his address to the League in December, Foxe declared that 'the king, being devoted to the Gospel, is desirous of receiving an embassy from the princes and states of Germany'.[113]

One crucial feature of Henry's attitude to these discussions must be emphasised. He did not intend to accept without question a Lutheran confession of the faith. Consultation with the League to help him establish an English formulary of the faith was one thing; unqualified acceptance of the Confession of Augsburg was quite another. This was something which the League would find difficult to accept, but it should be noted that from the beginning Henry was quite open about it: although he wished to talk about

---

106 PRO, SP 1/96, fo. 13v [*LP* ix. 213.i].
107 PRO, SP 1/96, fo. 14v [*LP* ix. 213.i].
108 Ibid.
109 PRO, SP 1/96, fo. 15 [*LP* ix. 213.i].
110 Ibid.
111 *LP* ix. 979.
112 PRO, SP 1/96, fo. 23 [*LP* ix. 213.i].
113 *LP* ix. 979.

theology with the Germans, he had no intention of accepting out of hand their version of the faith. Edward Foxe was clearly instructed on this point: if the League should require that Henry 'receave thole confession of Germanye word for word as it is imprinted', he should say that Henry would accept it only when he had received an embassy from the League and 'shal have seen and perused tharticles of the said leage and shal perceyve that there is in it conteyned noon other articles but such as may be agreable with the gospel wherof thesaid leage is named'.[114] In March 1536 Henry directed the ambassadors to make a declaration to the League which stressed even more strongly his unwillingness simply to accept without question whatever the Germans considered to be the essentials of the faith and his insistence on a compromising approach:

> forasmoch as his majestie desireth moch that his bishops and lerned men might agree with thairs But seen that it cannot be oneles certain thinges in thair confession and Apologie shuld by thair familiar conferences mitigate, his grace therfor wold the orators and som excellent lerned man with them shuld be sent hither to confere, talke, treate and commone upon the same.[115]

It is, therefore, difficult to argue that Henry was seeking to deceive the Germans in the theological discussions, that 'the suggestion of a union with the German Protestants on matters of faith was intended for nothing but a lure from the first'.[116] Had Henry regarded the offer of religious discussions purely as bait for political purposes it is unlikely that he would have explicitly pointed out that the League must be prepared to compromise its religious principles, a statement which could only make the Germans politically less amenable. Had Henry been seeking to lead the Germans on it would clearly have been more sensible to leave the question of compromise out altogether, and simply allow the discussions to drag on. That the king did otherwise suggests that he was being neither crafty nor artful; rather that he had a genuine interest in consultations with the League on theology, and, far from being disingenuous, was from the first, as he would be throughout the 1530s, candid with the view that in these consultations he would expect moderation and concessions from the Germans.

Henry, then, did not consider religion simply to be a function or an instrument of foreign policy. During the second half of the reign Henry was a theological seeker. He may or may not have been very good at theology, but that is

---

114 PRO, SP 1/96, fo. 23 [LP ix. 213.i].

115 BL, MS Cott. Cleo. E.vi, vol. 2, fo. 307v [Burnet, *History of the Reformation*, vi. 160; LP x. 457].

116 Gairdner, *Lollardy and the Reformation*, ii. 176–7. See also, for example, Prüser, *England und die Schmalkaldener*, 63; Doernberg, *Henry VIII and Luther*, 97–8; Redworth, 'English Reformation', 36. This evidence may also cast doubt on the view that in 1536 Henry informed the Germans that in establishing his own Reformation 'he could manage the task without foreign help' and that he 'maintained this posture during the years of negotiations with the Lutherans': A. G. Dickens, *The English Reformation*, London 1964, 244.

not the point. What is important is that he cared. It would be well to resist the sort of popular view of the king characterised by the assertion of Lacey Baldwin Smith that 'if there is one thing that historians do know about Henry's mind, it is that he regarded religion, at least in its doctrinal and institutional sense, as an instrument of foreign policy, and that he was quite willing to cut his theological cloak to suit the diplomatic fashions of the moment'.[117] On the contrary, when Henry made religious intimations to the League he was not playing a diplomatic game, but pursuing a sincere interest in the new religious ideas which the events of the early 1530s had awakened in him.[118] Far from being a regrettable diplomatic necessity, the theological aspect to Anglo-Schmalkaldic relations was one of the principal reasons for the interest which Henry showed in the League.

The king's desire for consultation on the direction of his newly established Church transformed English politics. Had Henry been sure about the detail of the theology of the Church of England there would have been no room for debate. However, his uncertainty and consequent desire to seek a variety of views from across the non-Roman religious spectrum effectively inaugurated a contest to dominate the flow of advice he received: for just as there were evangelicals encouraging the king to go further with reform, so there were religious conservatives – men like Stephen Gardiner and Bishop Cuthbert Tunstall of Durham – who wanted him to retrench. During the middle years of the decade the contest for the king's ear began to develop into what may properly be called faction politics. 'Faction', like 'evangelical' or 'conservative', is a convenient generic term, used by historians to describe political contestation during the reign of Henry VIII: factions were small, elite groups within the inner governmental ring, made up of the key politicians, their servants and their immediate associates, all seeking to influence the king. This study follows the moderate interpretative approach to faction set out by Eric Ives, which sees factions as amorphous, fluid arrangements, flourishing in Henrician political culture largely as a result of the king's singular managerial style, yet always subject to the overarching context of the king's will. The terrain for factional contest was always set, and often manipulated, by the king and his pre-existing policy preferences: though evangelicals and conservatives might perceive a variety of potential gains and losses in Anglo-Schmalkaldic diplomacy, the only reason that such potential factional advan-

---

117 L. B. Smith, 'Henry VIII and the Protestant triumph', *American Historical Review* lxxi (1965–6), 1257.
118 A similar argument to this, though more broadly based, is advanced by Diarmaid MacCulloch, 'The religion of Henry VIII', in Starkey, *European court*, 160–2. See also his 'Henry VIII and the reform of the Church', 159–80. For the sincerity of Henry's religious convictions and policy and a stress on his complete independence see Bernard, 'Making of religious policy', 321–49.

tage or disadvantage existed at all was that the king had decreed his interest in relations with the Germans in the first place.[119]

In themselves faction politics were nothing new.[120] But in one fundamental respect the faction politics of the 1530s were different from anything that had gone before: they were based on differences in religious belief. It was because of this that of all England's foreign policy involvements during the middle and later 1530s, relations with the Schmalkaldic League were the most relevant to English faction politics. Certainly, France might have had some significance in English religious matters during the early 1530s insofar as she provided a possible conduit back to Rome. But by the mid-1530s things had changed. Following the Reformation legislation and the executions of More and Fisher, the question was no longer whether there should be an independent Church of England, but what form that institution should take and what doctrine it should profess. Because the Catholic powers had nothing new to say or offer on this matter, they would be less relevant to the faction politics of the middle and late 1530s. Because the king was interested in the theological alternative practised in Protestant Germany, however, the Schmalkaldic League would be highly relevant.

The evidence of 1533–5 suggests that a group of evangelicals under Thomas Cromwell was the first to perceive the possible relevance of Anglo-Schmalkaldic relations to English domestic politics. In spite of Henry's unwillingness to accept without reservation a Protestant confession, the very fact of his interest in discussing theology with the Germans represented a great opportunity. Though Henry was unsure as to the extent or direction of theological change in England, discussions with the German Protestants would allow the English supporters of reform to bring the king into contact with the doctrinal cutting edge of Lutheranism. If that contact proceeded well, political and religious union with the League could follow. From there the evangelicals might be able to persuade the king to move further and further away from Rome and ever closer to their goal of a full doctrinal reformation of the Church. But what of the conservatives? Did Henry's interest in consulting the League on theology spell the end for their

---

[119] E. W. Ives, 'Henry VIII: the political perspective', in MacCulloch, *Reign of Henry VIII*, 29–31. A factional interpretation of Henrician politics has dominated the historiography of the reign from Foxe's *Acts and monuments* to the present day. George Bernard has contested this in a number of articles that see factions, if they existed at all, as following the king. His views are usefully set out in his 'Making of religious policy', 321–49, and 'Elton's Cromwell', 587–607. For support for Bernard's position see R. J. Warnicke, *The marrying of Anne of Cleves: royal protocol in early modern England*, Cambridge 2000, 189–95; for a summary of the debate and an argument for the middle ground between 'the king's men and the factionalists', see S. J. Gunn, 'The structures of politics in early Tudor England', *Transactions of the Royal Historical Society* 6th ser. v (1995), 59–90.

[120] 'Competition to secure the ear of a ruler has characterised personal monarchies from ancient times to twentieth-century dictatorships and even the "courts" around the leaders of democratic parties': Ives, 'Henry VIII: the political perspective', 30.

cause? Not necessarily, although the conservatives' position by 1535 was increasingly beleaguered. The problem for the upholders of orthodoxy was that they had no well defined non-Roman theological standard to which they could rally. As a group they were diffuse, in the wake of the reforming wave of the first half of the decade lacking confidence, cohesion and coherence. Moreover, whenever they advised caution in introducing reform they faced the danger of being branded papists or disloyal, as Stephen Gardiner had found to his cost in 1532.[121] However, Henry had not demonstrated a desire to adopt the full text of the Confession of Augsburg: acceptance of a foreign code would implicitly question his position as supreme head of the English Church. For the conservatives, then, opposition to the doctrinal innovations which Anglo-Schmalkaldic relations threatened to introduce would need to be based on an emphasis on the king's, rather than the League's, authority in spiritual affairs and seek to encourage Henry's innate theological caution and hesitancy.

Paradoxically, the League gave the conservatives an excellent opportunity to strengthen their hand. As immovable as the Roman Church in the certitude with which they held to their religious opinions, the Protestants had little time for the consultative approach to theological negotiations which Henry envisaged. An early sign of this was to be seen in the first and second articles of the proposals which the League presented to Foxe on Christmas Day 1535. These demanded that Henry adopt Protestant doctrine as expressed in the Confession of Augsburg and defend it at any future general council.[122] Although the first article admitted that some things might by common consent be modified, from the beginning the terms of reference were those of German Protestantism, and in the negotiations which followed the League refused to shift from the principles enshrined in the Confession of Augsburg. Though this was fine for the Protestants' own internal purposes, it was an attitude which risked alienating a king who had come to consider himself the supreme arbiter in English theological affairs. It might also open the door to those English conservatives who recognised that their best chance of success lay not only in encouraging Henry's latent theological hesitancy, but in demonstrating to the king that German Protestantism was every bit as domineering and sceptical of his theological authority as Roman Catholicism.

It is not clear exactly when the 1536 discussions on the divorce ended and those on Protestant doctrine began, and indeed it is unlikely that there was any precise break. During January, for example, the divorce discussions were briefly halted for a debate in the town university on the private mass,[123] and

---

121 A similar point is made in S. Brigden, *London and the Reformation*, Oxford 1989, 277, and Smith, *Prelates and politics*, 159–72.
122 PRO, SP 1/99, fos 159 [*LP* ix. 1016.i], 162 [*LP* ix. 1016.ii]; BL, MS Cott. Cleo. E.vi, vol. 2, fo. 304 [*LP* ix. 1016.iv].
123 This debate is dealt with at pp. 55–7 below, where the March negotiations on the private mass are discussed.

occasional conversations on the divorce may well have continued through March. Nevertheless, it is probable that some time in mid-February doctrine began to dominate meetings between the English ambassadors and the Wittenberg theologians.

The discussions divide into two stages, the first on the thirteen articles of doctrine from the Confession, and the second on the four articles of doctrine from the Apology. The records of all seventeen articles in their manuscript form help illustrate the distinction. Although a German translation of all seventeen articles which was prepared for John Frederick (because he had little Latin) does not distinguish between the first thirteen articles and the final four,[124] the two surviving Latin working copies from the discussions demonstrate it clearly. In one of the copies the four articles are in a different hand and are bound separately from the other thirteen,[125] while in the other copy the hand is the same throughout but again the four articles are separately bound.[126] The principal source for the discussions was, not surprisingly, the Confession of Augsburg, although use was also made of more recent doctrinal statements in Melanchthon's *Loci communes*. There is no evidence to suggest that any of the English doctrinal papers which the embassy had brought with them to Germany were used.

The first stage of the discussions proceeded quickly and smoothly. Melanchthon wrote in the second week of March that all was going well. The ambassadors did not seem averse to evangelical doctrine and certain articles were being drawn up. Although he had his suspicions of Foxe, whom he found haughty and unfriendly, he had great praise for Nicholas Heath, whom he judged favourable to the new learning.[127] It was probably a week or so after the writing of this letter that the results of the first stage of the discussions began to be committed to paper.

On the centrepiece of Lutheranism, the doctrine of grace, the articles were most expansive. As in the Confession (article xii), repentance was explained as the first part of grace. The article provided a lengthy explanation of how repentance should be made, demonstrating the importance of genuine contrition and shame at sin. The connection between repentance and the second part of grace, justification, was then described and a conventional

---

124 TStWei, Reg. H. 106, fos 15–40v. This translation, together with a Latin version, was sent to the duke by Gregor Brück on 15 April: Reg. H. 105, fo. 158v. The translation was the work of Franz Burchard, who was in Wittenberg throughout the Anglo-Schmalkaldic discussions: Luther wrote to John Frederick on 28 March that Burchard had 'verdeudscht' all the articles for the duke: WABr vii. 383. See also DWA, 1.

125 TStWei, Reg. H. 106, fos 41–7v (the thirteen articles based on the Confession), 49–55 (the four articles from the Apology, on the private mass, communion in both kinds, priestly marriage and monastic vows; in a different hand and in a separate binding).

126 TStWei, Reg. N. 736, fos 1–10 (the thirteen articles based on the Confession), 11–17 (the four from the Apology, on private mass, communion in both kinds, priestly marriage, and monastic vows; in same hand as fos 1–10, but in a separate binding).

127 LP x. 447–8.

Lutheran exposition of justification developed: the sinner's merits or works cannot absolve sin; only by putting forward the merit of Christ and having faith in the promise of mercy which was made through his death can justification be achieved.[128] The longest of all the articles was that concerned with the third part of grace: good works. This no doubt reflected the fact that the Lutherans had long suffered criticism from those who accused them of prohibiting or downgrading the worth of good works, and that they were sensitive to this misunderstanding; the longest article of the Confession had also dealt with good works. It was explained that although good works were not the payment for eternal life, it was necessary to produce fruit in accordance with true repentance. As in the *Loci communes*, it was urged that the Church expound the doctrine of good works under five heads: it should teach the sort of works which are required; how good works come about; how they please God; which works are mortal sins and result in the loss of grace; and how important good works are.[129] In spite of the painstaking attention given to explaining the doctrine of good works, there were obscurities. In the section on how good works come about it was stated that 'faith itself is the finest work', an ambiguity which, if not strictly untrue, Luther had maintained should be avoided in the interests of clarity.[130] In the section on the importance of works, possible confusion was thrown on the relationship between justification and works by a biblical citation: 'You see that a person is justified by what he does and not by faith alone.'[131] Although the text went on to explain that this was simply meant to illustrate the interdependence of faith and works — that after the first the second must follow — the passage clashed with the well-known Lutheran view that man is 'justified by faith alone'.

Both elements of penance were discussed in a single article.[132] In keeping with the Confession (article xi), it was affirmed that confession should be kept in the Church, because of the importance of retaining the rich consolation it offered. Moreover, in confession it was possible to examine the faith of those confessing and counsel and instruct them appropriately. The usual Lutheran admonition was added: the Roman sacrament is impossible to perform because it demands an enumeration of all sins. The more controversial discussion of confession which had figured in the Apology (describing the circumstances in which it was an abuse, an issue which would cause such

128 TStWei, Reg. H. 106, fos 42–3v (good Latin copy), 18–22 (German trans.); Reg. N. 736, fos 2v–4v (mutilated Latin copy) [*DWA*, 24–33].
129 TStWei, Reg. H. 106, fos 44–6v (good Latin copy), 21v–7 (German trans.); Reg. N. 736, fos 5–8v (mutilated Latin copy) [*DWA*, 32–47].
130 Tjernagel, *Henry VIII and the Lutherans*, 263.
131 James ii.24. In the German, this was rendered as 'Der mensch wird durch die werk gerecht, nicht durch den glauben alleine': TStWei, Reg. H. 106, fos 46v (good Latin copy), 26 (German trans.); Reg. N. 736, fo. 8v (mutilated Latin copy) [*DWA*, 44–5].
132 TStWei, Reg. H. 106, fos 46v–7v (good Latin copy), 27v–9 (German trans.); Reg. N. 736, fos 9–10 (mutilated Latin copy) [*DWA*, 47–53].

heated debate between the Schmalkaldic party and the conservative English bishops in 1538), was not included in the Wittenberg articles. Moving on to the second element of penance, satisfaction, the article insisted that the practice was a tradition, not scriptural, and should not be thought of as a means to salvation; Christ's death alone was the oblation by which eternal death is remitted. An interesting distinction, already discussed in *Loci communes*, was developed between the remission of eternal damnation and the remission of those temporal punishments with which God often visits man: the first required observance of the process described in the doctrine of grace for remission to be achieved, but the second could be achieved by merit, and this should be emphasised in the Church as an incentive to perform good works.

A number of articles dealt with aspects of the two sacraments recognised by the Lutherans, holy communion and baptism. The article on the eucharist followed closely the formulation in the Confession (article x). The uncompromising affirmation of the real presence could have given no cause for disagreement.[133] Baptism's sacramental nature was affirmed in the article on original sin. The presence of original sin in all men was asserted, and it was explained that it could only be remitted by baptism.[134] In a further article, the Pelagians, who denied original sin, and the Anabaptists, who claimed that only adults could be baptised, were roundly condemned. Infants and adults who had not been baptised should receive the sacrament forthwith; it must be administered by the ministry and not be repeated.[135] The two articles on baptism leant heavily on the Confession (articles ii and ix), which also (article xiii) provided the basis for an article declaring that the sacraments were both marks of Christianity and the means through which God works and puts his grace into man. During their use true repentance and faith must be present in the recipient; it was not enough merely to perform the rite without these.[136] A further article on the sacraments again borrowed directly from the Confession (articles viii and xiv) in asserting that no one should teach or administer the sacraments unless called by those empowered to admit men to the ministry. Nevertheless, sacraments have a power which derives from Christ and are just as efficacious when administered by wicked persons; the word and the sacraments may be received from the wicked and still have their full effect.[137]

The remaining articles seem not to have detained the disputants very long. The article on civil affairs confirmed the separation between the spiritual and

---

133 TStWei, Reg. H. 106, fos 48v (good Latin copy), 27–v (German trans.); Reg. N. 736, fos 8v–9 (mutilated Latin copy) [*DWA*, 48–9].
134 TStWei, Reg. H. 106, fos 41–v (good Latin copy), 16v (German trans.); Reg. N. 736, fos 16v–17 (mutilated Latin copy) [*DWA*, 20–3].
135 TStWei, Reg. H. 106, fos 41v–2 (good Latin copy), 17–18 (German trans.); Reg. N. 736, fos 1v–2v (mutilated Latin copy) [*DWA*, 22–5].
136 TStWei, Reg. H. 106, fos 47v (good Latin copy, but only containing a fragment of this article), 29–v (German trans. with the full version) [*DWA*, 52–5].
137 TStWei, Reg. H. 106, fos 29v–30 (German trans.) [*DWA*, 55].

temporal spheres; the former confirms the latter, and is duty bound to obey it as a God-given creation. Only if rulers command sinful actions should Christians independently follow God. Holding to the text of the Confession (article xvi), it was asserted that it was no sin to hold civil offices, as the Anabaptists had claimed.[138] On ceremonies, it was agreed that the Church had the right to establish feast days, rites and so on. However, ceremonies are not necessary for salvation and they may be omitted; though it is better to retain traditional usages, those which claim to bring salvation should not be observed. It was asserted that ceremonies need not be uniform in all places: diversity of rites was acceptable so long as the Gospel, sacraments and peaceful co-existence were uniformly observed.[139] These articles also made extensive use of the Confession (articles vii and xv). The article on images took a moderate view: they have a didactic use which makes it worth retaining them. But they must not be worshipped or regarded as a means of reaching God.[140] The article on saints' days enunciated three reasons for their retention: saints are worthwhile examples of how God remits sin; they provide examples of faith and virtue for men to follow; and the meritorious works depicted in them ought to be praised. But their examples should only be observed: they must not be elevated so that they are invoked or used as mediators to God; there was no authority for this in Scripture and only Christ could fill this role.[141] Probably the least contentious article was the Creed. This asserted that all is to be believed, taught and defended that is in the Bible and the three symbols: in the Apostles', Nicene and Athanasian Creeds. These must be retained in their original form, for the articles of faith they posited were absolutely necessary for salvation and all who held otherwise were idolatrous. Those sects which had contradicted them were enumerated and condemned.[142]

The first part of the discussions appears to have concluded amicably about mid-March; soon after, the second part of the discussions commenced. Before these conversations had progressed far, however, there were problems. The disputants rapidly isolated four articles of doctrine from the Apology as areas of serious difference: private masses, communion in both kinds, priestly marriage and monastic vows.

The first of these had been picked out as a contentious issue almost from the time of the ambassadors' arrival in Germany. During their initial meetings with the Germans in November 1535 the English made it known that they wished to discuss private masses with the Wittenberg theologians. Martin Luther decided to deal with the matter by way of a preliminary public

138 TStWei, Reg. H. 106, fo. 31 (German trans.) [DWA, 57].
139 TStWei, Reg. H. 106, fos 30–1 (German trans.) [DWA, 56–7].
140 TStWei, Reg. H. 106, fos 39v–40v (German trans.) [DWA, 78–9].
141 TStWei, Reg. H. 106, fos 38v–9v (German trans.) [DWA, 77–8].
142 TStWei, Reg. H. 106, fos 41 (good Latin copy), 16 (German trans.); Reg. N. 736, fo. 1 (mutilated Latin copy) [DWA, 18–20].

disputation. From October 1535 he was engaged in preparing theses for the event.[143] The disputation eventually took place on 29 January at Wittenberg University in front of an audience which included the entire roll-call of faculty and students. Martin Luther not only prepared the propositions, but also took the chair and the role of respondent, fielding a range of objections from the floor.[144] The usefulness of the text of the disputation is limited by the fact that the objections put to Luther were all standard papal arguments, proposed, it would seem, for the purpose of setting him up to demolish Roman doctrine and expound that of the Protestants. Also, only one minor contribution to the debate can be specifically attributed to the English ambassadors.[145] Still, the fact that the disputation took place at the express request of the English ambassadors suggests an official concern over the fate which Protestant doctrine would imply for private masses in the English Church.

For the Germans too the question of private masses was very important, and a brief look at the article which they wished the English ambassadors to accept will explain why. In a sense the name of this article – private masses – was a misnomer, for it actually dealt with three distinct issues. First, there was the question of the private mass itself: the Roman idea that the sacrament could be celebrated on behalf of people, living or dead, who were not present at the mass, and that the performance of this rite would bring remission of their sins. The article claimed that this was a human invention, which tarnished a celebration instituted by Christ and obscured the doctrine of grace; private masses therefore ought to be abrogated. This was a deeply important question for the Lutherans. It was, after all, the idea that a man could apply to God on behalf of another which had prompted Luther to post his ninety-five theses in October 1517. The whole indulgence controversy had stemmed from Luther's conviction that the private mass was a Roman corruption; after the doctrine of grace, the abolition of private masses was arguably the most important point on the Lutheran agenda. Failure to reach agreement on this point would make theological unity between England and the League far less likely. The second issue upon which the article on the private mass touched was the Roman notion that the mass involved the offering of a sacrifice to God; rather, it was claimed that the mass should be seen as a thanksgiving and exercising of faith for the one and only sacrifice performed by Christ. The third issue was the need for public and corporate worship; Christ desired that all men pray and worship together, and this

---

[143] Prüser, England und die Schmalkaldener, 54.
[144] Luther mentioned the preparations for this disputation in a letter to Burchard of 25 Jan. 1536: WABr vii. 352–3. Entitled Disputatio contra privatam missam re. Patris D.M.L. anno 1536 mense Januarii in praesentia legatorum regis Angliae habita, the disputation is printed in P. Drews, Disputationen in den Jahren 1535–1545 an der Universität Wittenberg gehalten, Göttingen 1895, i. 68–89.
[145] Foxe offered a citation from Romans xi.4 ('I have reserved to myself seven thousand men, who have not bowed the knee to the image of Baal'), which Luther approved: Smith, 'Englishmen at Wittenberg', 425.

public custom should be valued for the encouragement and instruction it gives the people.[146]

The three remaining articles did not occupy so much of the ambassadors' time, but they were also the cause of problems. The article on communion in both kinds presented as an axiom the principle that both the bread and the wine should be given to the laity, with little in the way of supporting arguments. Christ meant the sacrament to be offered in both kinds; the ancient Church adhered to this practice; the prohibition on both kinds was mere human tradition and contrary to the practice instituted by Christ: the laity should therefore be allowed the sacrament in both kinds.[147]

On the marriage of priests, it was acknowledged that celibacy was admirable in a priest, and might in some respects be advantageous to the priest's vocation. But, the Wittenberg divines claimed, the law against priests' marrying was a human law, and those unsuited to celibacy should be allowed to marry. This was the ancient practice in the Church, and the contemporary Greek Orthodox and German Churches permitted priests to marry. After all, they argued, one priest can marry and be pure, just as another can remain celibate and be impure. Moreover, divine law had created marriage for those who were incontinent and this in itself must overturn any papal prohibition on the marriage of priests.[148]

As with the article on priestly marriage, a certain advantage in maintaining monastic vows was accepted. Those who entered a monastery could be trained and learn much about religion, and for this reason alone monasteries and colleges should be retained. But superstitious practices and beliefs should be abolished, especially the belief that vows bring salvation; vows taken in this or other godless beliefs were not binding. It was also asserted that the life of chastity was not suitable for everyone and that those who wish to rescind their vows and live otherwise should be allowed to do so.[149]

By the last third of March it was becoming clear that the four articles from the second part of the discussions were the main sticking points. John Frederick wrote to Philip of Hesse on 20 March that they had 'discussed and disputed all articles of our confession, up to these four: priestly marriage, communion in both kinds, the private mass, and monastic vows'.[150] Although they had not yet entered into a full discussion of these articles with

[146] TStWei, Reg. H. 106, fos 49–51 (good Latin copy), 31v–3v (German trans.); Reg. N. 736, fos 11–12v (mutilated Latin copy) [*DWA*, 58–65].

[147] TStWei, Reg. H. 106, fos 51–v (good Latin copy), 33v–4 (German trans.); Reg. N. 736, fos 12v–13 (mutilated Latin copy) [*DWA*, 64–5].

[148] TStWei, Reg. H. 106, fos 52–3 (good Latin copy), 34–5v (German trans.); Reg. N. 736, fos 13v–14v (mutilated Latin copy) [*DWA*, 66–9].

[149] TStWei, Reg. H. 106, fos 53–5 (good Latin copy), 35v–8v (German trans.); Reg. N. 736, fos 14v–17 (mutilated Latin copy) [*DWA*, 68–77].

[150] '[V]on allen artikeln e.l., unser, auch der andern confession bis auf die vier, der pfaffen ehe, die communion in baider gestalt, die bebstische mes und die clostergelubde betreffend, rede und disputation gehalten': Prüser, *England und die Schmalkaldener*, 295–6.

the English, the German theologians already suspected that they would be the cause of some difficulty. John Frederick had also been informed by Brück and Burchard that 'they should agree with our theologians on the other articles up to the aforementioned last four'.[151]

The ambassadors, in fact, did not have a commission to agree or disagree with any articles of religion. Rather, their brief was to find out where the likely problem areas with the king would lie, so preparing the ground for further discussions in England. Given their background, it might be supposed that the ambassadors would have agreed with all the articles discussed. But it was the king's views that mattered. The ambassadors must take care not to act in opposition to these at so early a stage in the development of Anglo-Schmalkaldic relations. To do so would be to run the risk of wrecking the progress which had already been made. Thus they did not commit themselves on the four articles from the second part of the discussions. They would give their provisional assent to the articles from the first part of the discussions, but steer clear of any endorsement of the others. Meanwhile the results thus far could be sent back to England for the king to consider. As Martin Luther wrote to John Frederick towards the end of March, 'since they are not sure how their king will take the articles, especially the last four, they have decided to take time in which to show the same to his majesty'.[152] Now the ambassadors' attention must shift to persuading the Schmalkaldeners to send a return embassy to England. This was what the king wanted. It was also what the English evangelicals wanted. In England, with the full weight of the evangelicals behind the negotiations, the remaining problems would surely be ironed out. As Brück and Burchard reported to John Frederick, 'the embassy has assured that there will be no difficulty with the king, if only the League despatches an embassy so that the king himself can negotiate and talk with the embassy and the divines'.[153] For the remainder of their stay in Germany the ambassadors would concentrate their efforts on achieving this.

Before moving on to look at the remaining events of 1536, it will be useful briefly to consider the subsequent career of the articles discussed at Wittenberg.[154] Historians have tended to argue that they were taken back to

---

151 '[W]eren sie mit unsern gelerten der andern artikel halben bis auf die berurten vier vorglichen': ibid. 297.

152 'Weil sie aber nicht wissen, wie dieselben yhr herr konig wird an nehmen, sonderlich die letzten vier, haben sie der halben einen hindergang genomen, solchs S.Ko.Mt. anzuzeigen': WABr vii. 383.

153 '[D]ie botschaft vortrostung gegeben, als ob bei k. w. nit wurde mangel sein, wo allain die botschaft von unser, der einungsvorwanten, wegen geschickt wurde und k. w. selbs mit der botschaft und dem gelerten hiraus handeln und reden wurde': Prüser, England und die Schmalkaldener, 297.

154 The articles are printed in Die Wittenberger Artikel von 1536, ed. G. Mentz, Leipzig 1905, and cited here as DWA. In their German translation they were entitled Artikel der cristlichen lahr, von welchen die legatten aus Engelland mit dem herrn doctor Martino gehandelt anno 1536

England by Foxe, where they 'were a main source of the royal Ten Articles, produced a few weeks later', and in the following year of the Bishops' Book too.[155] This view is supported by the presence in the Ten Articles and Bishops' Book of sentences and sometimes paragraphs which appear to be verbatim English translations of the Wittenberg articles. It might also be significant that it was the bishop of Hereford, the same Edward Foxe who had spent much of the preceding year in Germany, who actually introduced the Ten Articles to convocation on 11 July 1536. Nevertheless, a warning note should be sounded. There is a close similarity between the Wittenberg articles and previous Lutheran formularies of the faith, most notably the Confession of Augsburg and the *Loci communes*: there are no authorities or arguments in the Wittenberg articles which could not have found their way into the Ten Articles or Bishops' Book independently by way of those earlier formularies, which themselves were widely available in England long before the Anglo-Schmalkaldic discussions at Wittenberg. The Confession of Augsburg, for example, had become so well known by 1536 that during the Pilgrimage of Grace it was one of the documents which the rebels singled out for repudiation.[156] As for the *Loci communes*, Melanchthon dedicated that work to the king and sent copies to Henry and Cranmer in August 1535.[157] Foxe's instructions cited it as offering arguments which could be applied to the divorce[158] and the embassy took a copy to Germany as one of its source

('Articles of the Christian faith which the ambassadors from England discussed with Dr Martin Luther in the year 1536'). Although it is convenient to use Mentz's term, 'the Wittenberg articles', to refer to the results of the 1536 discussions, the impression of an Anglo-Schmalkaldic theological agreement should be avoided. Even the agreement given to the thirteen articles from the Confession was only provisional, and there was no endorsement of the four from the Apology. Though Mentz alludes to this in his brief introduction (pp. 1–16) he compounds the problem by listing the articles in the sequence used in the German translation of the articles prepared for John Frederick by Burchard. Burchard had silently inserted the four disputed articles among the thirteen which were found more acceptable; in following this Mentz heightens the false impression of homogeneity.

155 Scarisbrick, *Henry VIII*, 402. See also A. Kreider, *English chantries: the road to dissolution*, London 1979, 121–3; Prüser, *England und die Schmalkaldener*, 134 n. 1; Rupp, *Studies*, 109–14; P. Hughes, *The Reformation in England*, London 1963, i. 355; ii. 51–2; Tjernagel, *Henry VIII and the Lutherans*; J. A. Ridley, *Thomas Cranmer*, Oxford 1962, 113–14; C. W. Dugmore, *The mass and the English reformers*, London 1958, 106–8; Doernberg, *Henry VIII and Luther*, 110. For a more cautious assessment see, for example, Dickens, *Thomas Cromwell and the English Reformation*, 142, and *The English Reformation*, 244, and also R. A. W. Rex, who states in *Henry VIII and the English Reformation*, Basingstoke 1993, 146–7, that 'It is wrong to read into the [Ten] articles an attempt to compromise with Lutheranism or smuggle it in through the back door.' More recently, MacCulloch, *Cranmer*, 161–2, has tended towards the view that the Wittenberg articles may have had some influence on the Ten Articles and the Bishops' Book.
156 C. Cross, *Church and people, 1450–1660*, London 1976, 67.
157 *LP* ix. 223–5.
158 PRO, SP 1/96, fo. 19v [*LP* ix. 213.i].

books.[159] Furthermore, there is the example of the 'sixty-seven abuses', which the conservative bishops sought to have condemned by convocation before Foxe's return in June 1536. These were indeed what one early historian called 'Protestantism in ore', and they show clearly that there was no shortage of sources in England for heterodox opinion.[160] Any suggestion, therefore, that a single formulary, whether the Wittenberg articles or another, provided the basis for the settlements of 1536 and 1537 should be treated with caution. This is not to deny that the Wittenberg articles could have had some influence on discussions in convocation in 1536 and 1537. It is only to remember that in the absence of any material or formulation unique to the discussions at Wittenberg any correlation is impossible to measure. It seems more likely that the Wittenberg articles were kept in storage until a return embassy from the League came to England to discuss them: had they been offered to convocation some of their conciliatory aspects, such as the long discussion on the importance of good works with its distinctive division into five parts, would probably have appeared in the Ten Articles or the Bishops' Book.

In any case, perhaps the greater significance of the Wittenberg articles rests elsewhere. For the discussions at Wittenberg give an early and important insight into the specific nature of the king's theology in the mid-1530s and the impact that theology would have on developments during the remainder of the decade. It is reasonable to suppose that when, in the weeks prior to the departure of the embassy, Edward Foxe was briefed by Thomas Cranmer on how he should conduct the theological negotiations that awaited him in Germany, he was instructed on the state of the king's theological mind and how to express it faithfully among the Lutherans. The official English position presented at Wittenberg largely reflected, therefore, the views of the king of England, rather than the private views of the ambassadors and their friends, prior to the embassy's departure in September 1535. The discussions suggest, on the one hand, that Henry appears to have had an open mind on the doctrine contained in the Confession (including, one suspects, justification and confession, both of which would evade unequivocally conservative definition for the remainder of the reign). On the other hand, they indicate that he seems to have been very worried about the doctrine on the abuses set out in the Apology: Henry would need a lot of persuading before he could be brought to accept a Lutheran position on private masses, communion in both kinds, priestly marriage and monastic vows. Certainly, the matter was by no means decided. But a crucial area of theological conflict had been disclosed: in retrospect, the evidence of 1535–6 can be seen as revealing that in spite of the break with Rome Henry still retained particular yet profound suspicions

---

159 BL, MS Cott. Tit. B.i, fo. 458 [LP ix. 213.v]: a remembrance listing the source books to be taken included 'Melanctons boke de Locis communibus'.
160 Quoted in Hughes, Reformation in England, ii. 23. Rex, Henry VIII and the English Reformation, 146–7, also argues that the Ten Articles could have been written from a range of sources independently available in England.

of Lutheranism. These suspicions were so great that they would bedevil the next round of Anglo-Schmalkaldic discussions, in 1538, and contribute substantially to the conservative reaction in England the following year. While it may be conceded that the Wittenberg articles might have had some influence on the English religious formularies of 1536 and 1537, perhaps their greater historical significance rests in what they reveal of the king's specific misgivings about Lutheran doctrine in the autumn of 1535, and in the subsequent relationship of those misgivings to the Anglo-Schmalkaldic theological discussions of 1538, the Act of Six Articles of 1539 and the ultimate breakdown of relations between England and the League in 1540.

Outcomes, February–September 1536

While negotiations on the divorce and the doctrine of the faith were taking place in Wittenberg, Henry and his advisers reviewed the articles which had been presented to the English ambassadors at Schmalkalden on Christmas Day 1535, and which they had sent back to England for consideration shortly afterwards.

As soon as the articles arrived in England, Henry began to seek the advice of his counsellors. Though Cromwell was by this time Henry's principal adviser, Henry did not simply listen to the minister and his friends and ignore all others. Recognition of the importance of faction politics to the second half of Henry's reign does not imply that the king was a plaything of faction. Henry could indeed be influenced by the factions around him, but he was also able, and indeed adept, at manipulating and balancing the competing political groups and their individual members himself.[161] One of the emerging themes in Anglo-Schmalkaldic relations during the second half of the 1530s will be the way in which Henry often sought opinions from a wide range of counsellors, avoiding a situation in which his only source of counsel was men like Cromwell.

This occasion was no exception. On 3 February Henry signed at the head a letter to Stephen Gardiner and John Wallop in France, which informed them that

> ye shal understand that the bishop of herford hathe sithens his departure sent unto us sundry letters not only conteyning his good acceptation and welcomyng by the duke of Saxe, the lansgrave van Hesse and other the princes there but also their conformyties to all thinges whiche he had in chardge to require of them and of their lerned men, with whom they doo right wel agree.

---

[161] The same sort of point as this is made in Starkey, *Personalities and politics*, 137–9, and in Redworth, *Gardiner*, 129. Bernard, 'Making of religious policy', 321–49, is reluctant to accept that a powerful, personal monarchy could coexist with active faction politicking.

. . . we send unto youe herwith certain capita gathered of his letters and diverse other copies.[162]

The following day, Henry decided to use this letter to widen the advisory process. He told Cromwell that he did not want simply to inform the French ambassadors of the progress in Germany, so that they could use that knowledge in their dealings at Francis's court. He also wanted Gardiner to provide some input on the question of what sort of response should be made to the Germans. Accordingly Cromwell wrote to Gardiner the next day saying that

ye shal by this berer receyve the kinges highnes letters. . . . And with the same certain copies conteyning aswel my lorde of Herfordes procedinges in Germany as thaffections of the princes there towardes the kinges highnes, the frenche king, the bisshop of Rome, the Counsail and otherwise whiche as his maiestie thought convenient to communicate unto youe. . . . Soo his pleasure is ye shall in your next letters signifie what ye shall doo therin, and what your opinion is touching every parte of the same.[163]

While advice was being gathered, Henry wrote a brief letter to John Frederick, dated 6 February, in which he indicated that he would need some time for further consideration on the points raised at Schmalkalden. He did not offer any definite opinion on the proposals the Germans had made.[164]

In the meantime, Gardiner looked through the papers he had been sent and in mid-February wrote to Cromwell from Lyon. Under the heading 'The opinion of me, the Bishop of Winchester, concernyng the articles presented to the Kinges Highnes from the princes of Germany',[165] he dealt with a number of practical difficulties which he thought the proposals might create. He suggested that it would be demeaning for Henry to enter into an association with princes who, except for John Frederick, were of inferior quality.[166] He then went on to raise a point which would be the cause of great difficulties in the future between Henry and the League: noting that the Germans asked for a sum of money from a great prince for their defence, he observed that 'as for a reciproque, I see noon to the Kinges Highnes for ther parte'. He also referred to possible clashes of interest arising from the fact that they 'calle themself thEmperours subgettes', and that 'if they take hym [Charles] as I gather by ther other wrytinges they doo, thenne our matiers, by waye of leage, shalbe somoch the more perplexe[d] with them'.[167]

Well targeted though these criticisms were, Gardiner scored his most

---

162 BL, MS Add. 25114, fos 134v–5 (final copy in Wriothesley's hand) [LP x. 235].
163 BL, MS Add. 25114, fo. 137 [Merriman, Life and letters of Thomas Cromwell, ii. 3; LP x. 255]. This was in Wriothesley's hand and signed by Cromwell.
164 TStWei, Reg. H. 105, fo. 75.
165 Letters of Stephen Gardiner, ed. J. A. Muller, Cambridge 1933, 72. Muller prints the original draft, in Gardiner's hand, as opposed to the seventeenth-century copy used in LP x. 256.
166 Letters of Stephen Gardiner, 72–3.
167 Ibid. 74.

telling points elsewhere with his assertion that to enter into an alliance with the League on the basis of the proposals which Foxe had been given would simply mean to swap the yoke of Rome for that of Wittenberg. This argument was a powerful weapon for the conservatives; a foreign involvement which even implicitly questioned the king's supremacy and the independence of the English Church would be one which Henry would find very difficult to accept:

> if this article [the first article from the Christmas articles, demanding English acceptance of the Confession of Augsburg] be granted unto, thenne shal the Kinges Highnes be bounde to the Church of Germanye, and, without ther consent, maye not doo that the Worde of God shal permitte, oonles ther comen consent doth concurre therunto.[168]

Gardiner was careful not to disgree with the king on the virtue of theological consultations with the League, noting that 'to here ther ambassadours, to commen also with them, to entertayne them, and with them to discusse the very truth, wer very good',[169] but he stressed that the proposed thoroughgoing religious and political alliance would rob Henry and his Church of that independence for which the king had so recently fought:

> I wold rather advise the Kinges Highnes to geve them money wherwith to defende truth, thenne to entre any leage with such men, which, as I feare, cannot be fast bounde again, and also dwel soo far of . . . but upon the Worde of God, to make a newe knot, wherof the oon ende shalbe in Germany, shal declare rather a chaunge of a bonde of dependaunce thenne a rydaunce therof.[170]

Gardiner's advice on preserving the independence of the English Church struck a responsive chord, for Henry had little interest in accepting verbatim a foreign formulary of the faith. Consultation and compromise on the way to achieving a mutually acceptable religious code was one thing; slavish obedience to the dictates of Wittenberg quite another. When Henry came to draw up a reply to the League in early March, the influence of Gardiner's advice on religious independence from Wittenberg was clear. A draft noted that Henry, 'being a king rekened somwhat lerned (though unworthy) having also so many excellent well lerned men within his realme thinketh it [not] mete to accepte at any creatures hande the observing of his and his realmes faith'.[171] A later draft developed the theme: 'it shuld not be sure nor honourable for his maiesty bifore they shalbe with his grace agreed upon a certain concorde of doctrine to take such a province upon his hieghnes'.[172] On the other hand,

168 Ibid. 72.
169 Ibid. 74.
170 Ibid.
171 PRO, SP 1/99, fo. 166 (early draft in Wriothesley's hand) [LP ix. 1016.iii].
172 BL, MS Cott. Cleo. E.vi, vol. 2, fo. 307v [LP x. 457].

where Gardiner had been negative in all respects, Henry's reply did show a willingness to accept most of the remaining German proposals. Indeed, apart from the need for religious compromise, he only asked for two conditions to be met before he consented to the articles. First, in return for the 100,000 crowns Henry was to contribute to the defence of the League, he wanted a firm undertaking from the princes to supply a number of ships, cavalry and infantry in the event of England's being attacked. Second, Henry would join the League and accept the title of its defender only after an Anglo-Schmalkaldic conference had taken place with the king and his theologians in England on the matter of English acceptance of the Confession of Augsburg.[173]

The background and content of Henry's reply to the Germans not only help demonstrate the king's ability to leap and manipulate the factional divide, but go a long way towards undermining the theories of those historians who argue that Henry was only interested in contact with them during times when invasion threatened. The reason for this is quite simple: England was no longer threatened by invasion. By the time the king's reply was sent to Germany, in early March, Catherine of Aragon had been dead for two months. As Henry exulted on the news of her death, ' "God be praised that we are free from all suspicion of war!" '[174] Or, as Cromwell wrote to Gardiner and Wallop on 8 January 1536, Charles had 'none other cause or querele to the kinges highnes. . . . being the onelie matier of the unkyndenes betwixt them now abolisshed by the deth of the saide lady'.[175] Yet in spite of the receding threat of hostilities, the king did not retreat from alliance with the League. Instead, the Schmalkaldeners were presented with the same forthright assertion of the need for flexibility in the discussions on the faith as had appeared in Foxe's instructions. They were also given a detailed proposal for an Anglo-Schmalkaldic alliance. The reply to the League, then, offers further evidence that England's Schmalkaldic policy did not rise and fall strictly in accordance with England's attitude to the other powers of Europe. Though it was influenced by wider European developments, England's Schmalkaldic policy had imperatives, ambitions and factional implications which were peculiar to itself.[176]

---

[173] PRO, SP 1/99, fos 166–8 (earlier English draft in Wriothesley's hand) [LP ix. 1016.iii]; BL, MS Cott. Cleo. E.vi, vol. 2, fos 306–8 (later English draft) [LP x. 457]; HStMar, PA 443, fos 47–50 (Latin copy), 51–4 (Latin copy), 55–61 (German trans.); PA 2561, fos 75–8 (Latin copy) [CR iii. 45–50].

[174] As reported by Chapuys: LP x. 141.

[175] BL, MS Add. 25114, fo. 126v [Merriman, Life and letters of Thomas Cromwell, ii. 2; LP x. 54].

[176] Prüser, England und die Schmalkaldener, 64–71, possessed by the idea of 'the dilatory intentions of Henry VIII's policy' ('die dilatorischen Absichten der Politik Heinrichs VIII'), argues that after Catherine's death Henry decided to retain the Protestants as possible allies against the emperor, but, in the less critical circumstances, to distance himself somewhat: thus to avoid an alliance, but make it possible for him to call on them in times of need. In

*

The king's reply to the League's proposals, given to John Frederick on 12 March by Foxe and Heath, was the subject of intense consideration by the League over the following weeks. Since Henry had effectively posited a continuance of Anglo-Schmalkaldic relations on a theological conference in England, the dominant question was whether the League should send the major embassy which he desired. On 20 March John Frederick wrote to Philip of Hesse. Enclosing a copy of Henry's response, he suggested that it should be considered at a meeting at Nordhausen between Saxony, Hesse and Lüneburg, which had already been arranged for general discussions. This would allow the necessary agenda for the forthcoming Schmalkaldic diet at Frankfurt to be arranged so that a final League decision on the matter could be reached.[177] Philip agreed, writing to John Frederick on 26 March that he had received his letter on English affairs, and had directed his counsellors to discuss the matters at Nordhausen with those of the duke.[178]

Three days later, Philip wrote again to John Frederick. He noted that since the matter of England concerned not just Saxony and Hesse but the entire League, it would be advisable for the English embassy to be present at the diet at Frankfurt for a final discussion on any outstanding political and religious matters and to receive the League's final decision on the question of a Schmalkaldic embassy to England.[179] The English ambassadors, eager to secure an undertaking for the despatch of a Schmalkaldic embassy to England, were themselves very keen to be at Frankfurt. On 5 April John Frederick told Philip of this. Further, he noted that they had expressed dissatisfaction with the indefinite answers to Henry's reply they had thus far received and hoped that it would be possible to give them a final decision at Frankfurt. Though John Frederick had misgivings about the English attending, in view

explaining why Henry put a detailed and demanding response to the Germans in March 1536, he offers the ingenious solution that this was simply 'a good means to prolong the negotiations; it also had the advantage of deceiving the naive Protestant politicians as to the barely honest intention of the English diplomacy. For if the English king sought a great deal from them in long negotiations, then it could only appear to them that he was serious about an understanding' ('ein gutes Mittel, diese Verhandlungen in die Länge zu ziehen; dazu hatte es den Vorteil, die naiven protestantischen Politiker über die wenig ehrliche Absicht der englishchen Diplomatie hinwegzutäuschen. Denn wenn der englische König in langer Unterhandlung viel von ihnen verlangte, so konnte das von ihnen nur so gedeutet werden, dass ihm ernsthaft an einer Verständigung gelegen wäre').

177 TStWei, Reg. H. 105, fos 78–87 (draft); HStMar, PA 443, fos 62–8 (copy); PA 2561, fos 70–4 (final copy) [Prüser, England und die Schmalkaldener, 295–9].

178 HStMar, PA 2561, fo. 101 (draft); TStWei, Reg. H. 120/122, fo. 70 (final copy).

179 HStMar, PA 2561, fos 102–3 (draft); TStWei, Reg. H. 120/122, fos 71–3 (final copy). Much of the content of this letter corresponds with an opinion by Philip's chancellor, Johann Feige, dated 28 March: HStMar, PA 443, fos 71–4. See also Prüser, England und die Schmalkaldener, 72–3.

of the enthusiasm of the ambassadors and that of Philip himself he relented and suggested that the details be arranged, along with the wider preparations for the English discussions and other matters at the forthcoming diet, by his and Philip's delegates at Nordhausen.[180]

Philip's instructions to his delegates, dated 2 April,[181] were that they should support Henry's request for the League to send an embassy to England. In particular, the opportunity to send Schmalkaldic theologians to England and possibly persuade Henry to accept the Confession of Augsburg was a valuable one. Though he did not name names, Philip suggested that one theologian from Wittenberg and one from his own region could be sent. If Henry did not accept the Confession of Augsburg, the League could still seek an agreement with him on a common policy with regard to a general council and a non-religious defensive alliance. If some of the League's members were unwilling to enter it, then they need not do so. If a flexible attitude were adopted the king would not be completely rejected, 'but held in the hand, and the almighty God might with time grant further grace'.[182] John Frederick's instructions, however, were not nearly so flexible. They contained little which had not been covered in the proposals presented to the English at Schmalkalden during Christmas, and in fact corresponded so closely to those proposals that it seems likely that they were written directly from them. John Frederick stressed that Henry would have to accept and defend the Confession of Augsburg. If he did not do this then no further diplomatic contact should be contemplated.[183] Given the contrast in the Hessian and Saxon instructions it is not surprising that little headway was made at Nordhausen. When the delegates met they informed each other of their instructions, but found themselves unable to go any further; they were quite unable to reach a decision on a combined Saxon-Hessian approach to the League diet at Frankfurt as they had intended, and had to accept the impasse. They agreed that they would return to their masters for further consultations and in the light of these continue the negotiations with the rest of the League at Frankfurt.[184]

While these negotiations were going on, the theological discussions in Wittenberg were drawing to a close. Foxe requested a farewell audience with John Frederick. However, the duke had other matters to attend to, and so the

---

180 TStWei, Reg. H. 120/122, fos 74–7 (draft); HStMar, PA 2561, fos 110–11 (final copy).
181 HStMar, PA 443, fos 79–84 (draft); PA 2562, fos 15–17 (final copy).
182 '[S]ondern an der handt behalten und mocht also mit der zeit der almechtig Got weither gnade geben': HStMar, PA 443, fos 83v–4 (draft); PA 2562, fo. 17 (final copy). Ironically, Prüser, *England und die Schmalkaldener*, 69, accuses Henry of duplicity in exactly the terms Philip uses here, saying that although Catherine was dead, Henry wanted the Protestants 'als Druckmittel gegen den Kaiser *an der Hand behalten*' (my italics). Philip's comments here hardly accord with Prüser's view of him (p. 69) as one of the 'naiven protestantischen Politiker'.
183 The several drafts of these instructions are extremely fragmentary and haphazardly arranged: TStWei, Reg. H. 105, fos 114–29.
184 Ibid. fos 145–50 (Saxon account of the Nordhausen diet).

bishop had to be satisfied with a declaration on his behalf given on 3 April by Franz Burchard.[185] In this Burchard emphasised that Henry's response to the Schmalkaldic proposals of Christmas 1535 could only be considered and answered by the League as a whole. John Frederick's own opinion was that Henry would have to accept the Protestant confession before he could be admitted to the League. If Henry did this and joined the League, he would have most of the military aid he sought. If, on the other hand, he refused or clung to the conditions in his recent reply (he did not specify which), John Frederick thought an embassy would be useless. Still, the duke wished to emphasise that this was only his opinion. The matter would have to be discussed by the other League members before any final answer could be given.[186]

On 6 April Foxe received a brief parting letter from John Frederick, who thanked the bishop for his efforts, hoped for a successful conclusion to the negotiations and wished him well.[187] Foxe was also given some additional correspondence to pass on, notably a letter of 9 April to Cromwell from Martin Luther.[188] Luther began by excusing himself for not having replied sooner to the letter which he had earlier received from Cromwell, and returned the compliment which Cromwell had paid him in it.[189] He then went on to note that 'Dr Barnes rejoiced me wonderfully, as he told me of the earnestness and propensity of your lordship's goodwill in the cause of Christ, and in particular because of your authority in the entire kingdom and about the king, with which you can do much.'[190] This, it hardly needs to be said, is the sort of letter which Luther would only have written to someone whose religious position he considered to be close to his own. It is also a letter which for the first time identified Cromwell in German eyes as a leading English

---

185 G. Mentz, *Johann Friedrich der Grossmütige, 1503–1554*, Jena 1903–8, ii. 83.

186 TStWei, Reg. H. 105, fos 93–6 (German draft), 97–100 (German draft), 101–4 (Latin draft), 105–6 (fragment of Latin draft) [CR iii. 60–3; *LP* x. 771]. Chancellor Brück also wrote to John Fredrick on 4 April that in accordance with the duke's instructions he had explained to the English that the League would provide a final answer, and directed them to proceed to Frankfurt to receive it: TStWei, Reg. H. 105, fos 107–9.

187 Ibid. fos 110–11 (German draft), 112–13 (Latin draft).

188 There were two other letters. One, quite unremarkable, from John Frederick to Henry, dated 8 April, praised the ambassadors and hoped for a successful outcome to their efforts: ibid. fos 130–4 (Latin draft), 135–7 (German draft), 138–40 (good German draft), 141–2 (good Latin draft) [CR iii. 63–4; *LP* x. 770]. The other, from the Wittenberg divine Justas Jonas to Cromwell, urged that a religious agreement be closed between England and the League, from which, he believed, a political alliance would naturally flow: BL, MS Harl. 6989, fo. 57 [*LP* x. 665]. The date of this letter is 13 April, which suggests that it might have been passed on to Foxe after he had left Wittenberg.

189 The letter from Cromwell is not extant.

190 'Mirifice vero me laetificauit D. Barnes, cum mihi narraret T[uae] D[ominationis] tam seriam & propensam in causa Christi voluntatem, praesertim cum pro autoritate tua, qua in toto regno & apud Sereniss. Dominum regem plurimum vales, multum prodesse posses': BL, MS Harl. 6989, fo. 56 (final copy written and signed in Luther's hand) [*WABr* vii. 396; *LP* x. 644].

---

evangelical. At Nuremberg in May 1534 the talk had been of a nameless group promoting reform about the king; increasingly, from 1535–36, the Germans would identify Cromwell as the man whose words and deeds represented the best hope for the Gospel in England.

Foxe wrote again to John Frederick on 8 April, asking again for a farewell audience.[191] But John Frederick's reply of 10 April only repeated his formal farewell of 6 April and made no mention of a final audience.[192] The ambassadors therefore decided that they would not wait any longer, and on the very same day rode out of Wittenberg and headed west for Frankfurt, arriving there a fortnight later, on 25 April.[193]

The instructions which John Frederick gave his Frankfurt delegates, Georg von Anhalt and Franz Burchard, demonstrated a more positive attitude to relations with England than had been evident from the discussions with the Hessian delegates at Nordhausen, or indeed in Burchard's declaration to the English at Wittenberg. This may have been an attempt to take account of the recent Hessian views expressed at Nordhausen. But it was probably also the result of the influence of an opinion on Anglo-Schmalkaldic relations written by Gregor Brück for John Frederick on 15 April. Brück sent this opinion from Wittenberg. Included with it was a brief report on the recently concluded theological negotiations, and a German and Latin copy of the seventeen theological articles which the German theologians and English ambassadors had discussed.[194] Brück did not hesitate to acknowledge that an agreement on theology with Henry must precede the admission of England to the League, and that such an agreement should not be contrary to conscience. Nevertheless, there was the League's evangelising duty to consider. After all, the evidence of the recent theological discussions was promising and, most important, there was the advocacy of Foxe and the evangelicals: 'the bishop also said to me that if he had any doubt concerning the king, then one can be sure that he would not have entered so far into that agreement. Also, it is said that many honest bishops and others in England are heartily inclined to these matters, and promote the same well'.[195] Thus Brück recom-

---

191 TStWei, Reg. H. 105, fos 143–4 (final copy).

192 WABr vii. 402–3.

193 LP x. 730. The ambassadors evidently stopped on their way; though no evidence appears to indicate where they went, they did not complete the two- or three-day journey to Frankfurt for a further two weeks. The only evidence for where they went is a letter of 9 April from John Frederick to the duke of Cleves, asking permission for the embassy to travel through his lands: TStWei, Reg. H. 105, fos 151–2. If they did take this less direct route, there is no evidence to suggest why they did so.

194 Ibid. fos 155–64.

195 '[S]o sagt auch der bischof zu mir wan er daran zweifel hette, k. w. halben, so solt man es gewisslich dafur halten das er in berueter vergleichung so weith nit wolt gelassen haben. Darzu so sagt man, das auch viel erliche bischove und andere in Engellandt sein, die den sachen hertzlich geneigt seint und dieselben wol vorstellen': ibid. fos 158r–v.

mended that an embassy should be sent. Its personnel should include Melanchthon, Burchard and Georg von Anhalt. As to the final details of financing, instructing, personnel and so on, these could be agreed at Frankfurt.[196]

John Frederick took account of some of this in his instructions for his delegates to Frankfurt. The duke indicated that he was now in favour of an embassy to England, even if agreement on religion and an alliance had not yet been reached. On the question of personnel, he agreed with Brück that Melanchthon should accompany Burchard and Anhalt.[197] He had even shifted ground a little on the question of the possibility of an understanding with England if not all religious articles could be agreed. This is especially notable in view of the fact that Luther, in response to a request from John Frederick, had tendered the opposite advice in a letter of 20 April. Luther had said that

> I leave the question of whether there should be a league with the king if there is not an agreement on all articles to the lords about my most gracious lord because it is a temporal matter: nevertheless, it strikes me as dangerous to unite externally, when the hearts are not of one spirit.[198]

But on this occasion Luther's advice appears not to have been the dominant influence. For if John Frederick remained strongly in favour of an agreement based on religious conformity, the Frankfurt instructions show that he was now prepared at least to admit the possibility of a limited political understanding with the English even if not all religious questions were agreed.[199] Philip of Hesse's instructions for his delegates Sigmund von Boineburg, Johann Walter and Georg Nusspicker said little more than those for Nordhausen. Indeed, the key sentence simply referred to those instructions, and said that 'such is still our opinion to negotiate with the delegates of the League: we do not wish to change our mind thereto at this time'.[200] The only other extant instructions are those which were provided for the Strassburg

---

[196] Ibid. fos 158v–60v.

[197] Although a fragment of a draft noted that 'at this time we cannot know if Master Philip or another will be needed thereto' ('konnen wir auch noch zur zeit selbst nicht wissen, ob wir Magr. Phillipum oder einem andern darzu gebrauchen werden': TStWei, Reg. H. 114, fo. 29), the fact that at Frankfurt his name was proposed as a member of the embassy suggests that the final version of the instructions followed the majority of the drafts and recommended his inclusion.

[198] '[O]b aber das Verbündnis mit dem Könige anzunehmen sei, im Fall dass er nicht in allen Artikeln mit uns stimmen würde, lass ich die lieben Herrn nebst meinem gnädigsten Herrn bedenken, weil es ein weltlich Ding ist: doch dunkt michs fährlich sein, wo die Herzen nicht eines Sinnes sind, äusserlich sich vereinigen': WABr vii. 404. Luther sent this letter to Franz Burchard in response to a request for advice on the question from John Frederick relayed by the vice-chancellor.

[199] This is a summary of a haphazard variety of fragments of instructions; no final copy exists: TStWei, Reg. H. 114, fos 10–15, 17–23, 24–39.

[200] '[S]o ist solche noch unsere meinung mit den gesandten der Bundestand also

delegation. Although these emphasised the desirability of an agreement on religious matters, they were just as inflexible as those of the Saxons. They suggested that so long as an agreement on the substance and main articles of religion could be achieved, it should be acceptable if 'the king of England, because he has such a large kingdom, cannot conform precisely with us in all points and ceremonies'.[201]

On 24 April 1536 the Schmalkaldic League Diet of Frankfurt began. In a letter to Philip of 25 April, the Hessian delegates reported that the English had arrived the same day and had invited the Hessian delegation to their lodgings for a conference. The English ambassadors had informed them of the extent of the agreement on theology at Wittenberg, and, with this evidence of progress, had urged the prompt despatch of an embassy to England. They had also mentioned that it might be possible to include Scotland (which at this time was also receiving diplomatic approaches from England) in a future Anglo-Schmalkaldic alliance.[202] The English ambassadors had to wait a further week before they got an answer to these or any other questions, while the League discussed more pressing business. Although Philip told his delegates on 26 April that he supported the English desire to have a Schmalkaldic embassy sent as soon as possible,[203] the English remained in the background for the remainder of the month.

Discussions on England finally got underway on 2 May. But still there were problems. Not all the delegates had arrived at Frankfurt with the necessary powers to close on the English matter, largely because the duke of Saxony had neglected to tell those members in his section of the League what was to be discussed.[204] Probably embarrassed, and apparently unsure of what to tell the English, the delegates sent for Foxe on 2 May. They asked if he had anything to report. Foxe replied that what he had said before still applied, repeating specifically only the suggestion that consideration should also be given to admitting Scotland and others to the League.[205] On 3 May, after further discussions, the delegates prepared a response. This explained that some of the delegates had not come with the required powers. It would therefore be necessary for all the League members to return to their masters to consult; a final opinion on whether to send the sought-after embassy to England would be provided within a month. In the meantime, the king would be sent an apology for the delay from the League.[206] On being given this response on

zuhandeln: darzu wir dieser zeit nichts zu andern wissen': HStMar, PA 440, fo. 9v (final copy). Earlier drafts are at PA 439, fos 21v–2v (first draft), 35v–6 (second draft).
[201] '[D]er kunig von Engelland mit einem solchen weiten reich nit sogleich in alln puncten und ceremonien mit uns vergleichn kund': PC ii. 355.
[202] HStMar, PA 443, fo. 29v (draft); PA 439, fo. 44v (final copy).
[203] HStMar, PA 439, fo. 34v.
[204] See McEntegart, 'England and the League of Schmalkalden', 171–3.
[205] PC ii. 364.
[206] TStWei, H. 106, fos 56–9 (Latin copy), 60–3 (German copy), 64–5 (Latin copy), 66–8 (German copy), 69–71 (Latin copy); HStMar, PA 443, fos 85–8 (Latin copy) [PC ii. 364–5].

4 May Foxe immediately indicated that 'he was not not very satisfied'.[207] The next day he sent for some of the delegates. He gave them back their response with a reply of his own and told them in no uncertain terms of his displeasure at this further delay.[208] His indignation and refusal to accept the League's proposal achieved little, however: he would simply have to wait. In any case, his anger may have been mitigated by the fact that the delegates did at least continue to discuss the question of an embassy to England. The aim, as Philip's men reported on 4 May, was to 'discuss the instructions and articles for the same [that is, the proposed embassy to England], so that they can be given to the League delegates' to take back as proposals for their masters to decide upon.[209] Discussions were concluded on 10 May;[210] a document was produced, setting down the proposed embassy's instructions and personnel, and outlining the administrative arrangements for reaching a final decision on its despatch.[211]

Conditions for Henry's membership of the League followed closely the articles suggested in late 1535: Henry must indicate his acceptance of the Confession of Augsburg and his preparedness to defend it at a general council; he should work with the League in opposing a papal council of the Church; neither side should provide aid against the other; England should provide the League with 100,000 crowns in time of war; and the League should provide England with 500 cavalry and 2,000 infantry against any aggressor.[212] An additional condition was inserted to the effect that in matters unconnected with the faith, the alliance's provisions would not apply to the emperor, the king of the Romans or the empire.[213] It was also noted that the League would not be involved in the divorce suit.[214] The document went on to outline arrangements for the finances, provisions and personnel of an embassy to England. In keeping with John Frederick's instructions to his delegates, it was proposed that Philip Melanchthon should lead the team of theologians (assisted, it was suggested, by Martin Bucer and Jorg Drach) and that Georg von Anhalt should be in overall charge.[215] John Frederick's instructions to his delegates on the possibility of a political agreement if Henry would not accept the Confession of Augsburg were also adopted: in such a case neither Henry nor the League would go to a general council

207 '[D]er nit wol züfriden gesin': PC ii. 365.
208 PC ii. 366.
209 '[I]nstruction und artickell derselbigen reden, so man den gesanten der stende mit geben': HStMar, PA 439, fo. 68.
210 PC ii. 365–7.
211 For convenience, the following citations are from the printed version in SchmBa ii. 105–14. Manuscript versions have been consulted in HStMar, PA 445, fos 24–35 (draft), 39–49 (copy); TStWei, Reg. H. 106, fos 72–85 (copy).
212 SchmBa ii. 106–11.
213 Ibid. ii. 109.
214 Ibid. ii. 111.
215 Ibid. ii. 112.

without the other, and neither would provide an enemy with aid against the other.[216] Finally, the document noted that 'as far as the embassy [to England] is concerned, the delegates of the League should, as soon as they return home, actively encourage their lords and masters to write their thoughts within a month of the date of this letter to the duke of Saxony and the landgrave of Hesse'.[217] The next day, 11 May, the English delegation had a final meeting with the representatives of Saxony, Hesse and Strassburg. Details are difficult to make out, the Strassburg delegates' account noting only that a parting resolution was made with Foxe. The bishop was in all probability as satisfied as he could be in the circumstances with the provisional undertaking to send an embassy to England.[218]

The English delegation remained a while longer, awaiting confirmation that the embassy would be sent. However the time was fast approaching when Foxe must return to England, with or without a final answer. In mid-May, in an effort to speed things up, he decided to send Mont to John Frederick.[219] Just as he was about to do so, however, he heard of a meeting between John Frederick and Philip scheduled to take place in Naumberg from 29 May to 3 June, and decided to send him there instead. Mont left Frankfurt for Naumberg in the last week of May. He took with him separate letters, dated 27 May, to John Frederick and Philip, both written in German in his hand and signed by Foxe. That to John Frederick explained that Foxe could not stay in Germany much longer and requested a final answer.[220] The letter to Philip repeated that Foxe must go soon, and similarly asked that

> your grace and the duke write a letter to the king's majesty, indicating therein if it has been decided to send a legation from all those in the Schmalkaldic League to negotiate further with his majesty. And together with such a letter to send a copy urgently to the bishop at Frankfurt with an explanation of who will be in the embassy, when it will be sent and approximately how one might do all that is necessary to effect its despatch.[221]

---

[216] Ibid. ii. 107.

[217] '[S]ovil die schickung betrifft, das die gesandten der stende, so balde ein jder anheimisch kompt, bei iren hern und obern zum vleissigsten fordern wolle, ir bedencken dem churfursten czu Sachssen und lantgraven zu Hessen in monatsfrist den negsten nach dato dis briffs zuczuschreiben': ibid. ii. 111–12.

[218] PC ii. 368.

[219] Mont to Cromwell, LP x. 860. Mont names the person who sent him as 'reverendissimus'; the editor of LP wrongly suggests that Mont was referring to Cranmer.

[220] TStWei, Reg. H. 106, fos 86–7.

[221] 'E.f.g. sampt dem Choerfursten eyne schrifft zu Koeniglicher Maiesteet doen willen warinnen aengezceygt wert wie man beschlossen hab eyne legation zu senden von wegen aller die im Evangelien bünt verfast syn seyner maiesteet weyter zu handeln. Und das man soeliche schrifft sampt eyner copy dar ab zum foerderlichsten dem Bischoff gen Franckfort zustellen wold mit weyter erclerung waaszerley personen sollen in soelicher legation gescheen werde und by waas weeg alles des ungeferlich auff das man zur noettorfft bequeme bestellung auff alle soelche sachen verschaffen moeg': ibid. fo. 88.

Mont's suit had some effect: Philip and John Frederick wrote from Naumberg the requested joint letters to Henry and to Foxe. To the king they explained the problem of getting a final answer from some of the League members, and said that unfortunately an embassy would have to be delayed until the coming autumn.[222] To Foxe they were rather more frank:[223] they asked the bishop 'not to complain that we do not give your ambassador [Mont] any further answer, since your grace [Foxe] can well understand yourself that we must first take notice of our members' answers and final thoughts'.[224]

Foxe had done just about as much as he possibly could in Germany, and was unwilling to wait any longer. With this final letter from Philip and John Frederick in his possession, he prepared the embassy to return to England. It left Frankfurt in June, arriving back in London on 4 July 1536.[225]

As Foxe and his fellow ambassadors were making their way back to England, the League finally began to make co-ordinated and effective efforts to reach a final decision on the proposed embassy. Throughout the second half of May and June a series of meetings took place within the membership of the Schmalkaldic League. The outcome was generally not favourable. Although Saxony, Hesse and Strassburg favoured the despatch of an embassy, most of the smaller members were against it, largely because they feared it would anger Charles V.[226] John Frederick sent copies of the decisions from his region to the landgrave on 19 June.[227] Philip sent those from his region to the duke on 26 June.[228] Nevertheless, that a number of the League members were not in favour of the embassy need not in itself prevent Anglo-Schmalkaldic relations from making any further progress. As Philip had said in late May, on the prospect of a split decision, those League members who did agree could go ahead with their own.[229]

But before any such plan could make progress, events in England upset all calculations. For in late May, news began to arrive in Germany of the fall of

---

222 HStMar, PA 443, fos 91–2 (German copy), 93–4 (Latin copy); TStWei, Reg. H. 106, fos 93–4 (German copy), 95–6 (Latin copy).
223 HStMar, PA 443, fos 89–90 (German copy); TStWei, Reg. H. 106, fos 89–90 (German copy), 91–2 (Latin draft).
224 '[N]it beschwerung tragen das wir bei disen iren gesanten dissmals weither antwort nit geben mügen. Dan E.l. kan selbs wol achten das wir der andern unsern mitverwandten anthwort, und entlich gemuth, in dem zuvor auch wissen und vernemen mussen': HStMar, PA 443, fos 89v–90 (German copy); TStWei, Reg. H. 106, fos 89v–90 (German copy).
225 LP xi. 80; Prüser, England und die Schmalkaldener, 92.
226 For more detail on this point see McEntegart, 'England and the League of Schmalkalden', 179–83.
227 HStMar, PA 2566, fos 10 (final copy of letter to Philip), 13–36 (copies of decisions); TStWei, Reg. H. 120/122, fos 116–17 (draft); Reg. H. 115, fos 18–24 (final copies of decisions).
228 TStWei, Reg. H. 115, fos 28–9 (final copy), 30–46 (copies of decisions); HStMar, PA 455, fos 2–6, 12–16 (copies of decisions); PA 1809, fos 56–7; PA 2065, fo. 25 (final copy).
229 HStMar, PA 2563, fo. 41v.

the Boleyns. The first reports were lurid. On 2 June John Frederick sent Philip news from a source in Brandenburg, which reported that 'on account of whoring and knavishness' Henry 'has imprisoned his queen, her brother, a bishop, and three other great lords in the country'. Moreover, Mary had been brought back to London and restored to the succession.[230] Another report from Antwerp alleged that Henry had imprisoned Anne and twelve or fifteen men of her chamber.[231] A little later the same source reported that Anne had been executed on 19 May and that the following day Henry had taken on a new, and already pregnant, 'hausfraue'.[232] The duke of Lüneburg reported 'a general outcry in the sea [Hanse] cities', that Henry had imprisoned Anne and some of her friends, and that she was about to be 'sent to the stake'.[233]

The mention of burning, mistaken though it was, helps indicate the chief concerns of the Protestants.[234] Though they had always supported Henry's first marriage, the Protestants knew well that Boleyn and her circle were supporters of the new ideas. They therefore made the natural deduction that the fall of the Boleyns was simply part of a wider reaction in England against Protestantism. If an anti-Protestant reaction had set in, it would make little sense to send an embassy to England. An assessment of the situation in England was first required.[235] Thus, on 19 June, Philip wrote to the Strassburg council that because

the king of England has executed his second wife and taken another, the despatch [of an embassy] will be held up. The duke and we have considered advisable, and have decided – since the king has executed his second wife, who it is said was well inclined to the gospel – that before we send an embassy we take cause to send a man there, to ascertain whether the king is still of the same opinion and supports the gospel.[236]

---

230 '[U]mb huren und buben . . . sein konigin gefangen hatt und iren bruder, ain bischoff, und sonst noch drey gros herren im land': HStMar, PA 2565, fo. 182 (enclosed with John Frederick to Philip, fos 173–80).

231 'News' (Zeitungen) from Johan von Quickelberg in Antwerp to Philip, 24 May: HStMar, PA 437, fos 45–6.

232 'News' (Zeitungen) from Johan von Quickelberg in Antwerp to Philip, 29 May: ibid. fo. 47.

233 '[S]ee stetten ein gemein geschrei . . . zuverprennen zulassen': HStMar, PA 2566, fos 35 (copy sent by John Frederick to Philip, 19 June), 10 (final copy); TStWei, Reg. H. 120/122, fos 116–17 (draft).

234 Though burning was also the formal penalty for certain types of treason in England, in the light of the Boleyns' well-known religious inclinations the Germans would have considered it to be the punishment for heresy.

235 Even John Foxe, normally very quiet on foreign policy, mentioned how the Boleyn affair shocked the Germans and caused them to hesitate to send an embassy to England: Acts and monuments, v. 137.

236 '[D]er konig zu Engellandt das zweite weib hat lassen richten und itzt ein ander genomen, wird solichs die schikung etwas ufziehen; dan der churfurst und wir haben fur gut angesehen, dieweil der konig das zweite weib hat lassen richten, die dan dem evangelio, wie man sagt, gneigt gewesen und das hat gefurdert, das wir irst, ehe dan wir die potschaft

*

Similarly, on 26 June, when Philip sent John Frederick the decisions of the cities in his region on sending an embassy, he repeated that though it seemed to him that there was sufficient support, first a man should be sent with a letter to the king in order to assess his attitude to Protestantism.[237] On 7 July John Frederick wrote back that he would take a little time to consider the precise course of action.[238] In a lengthy letter of 13 July, he gave Philip his opinion.[239] He doubted that there could be found a messenger with sufficient contacts in England to gauge the state of religion accurately. The best course, he said, would be to establish contact with those around the king who were sympathetic to Protestantism. Thus, he suggested that Dr Aepinus in Hamburg, or perhaps Luther or Melanchthon, should seek to obtain information from Barnes, whom he understood to have 'a good deal to do with the king's affairs, and is very friendly with Cromwell, who is regarded as one of the highest counsellors in England'.[240] John Frederick also wanted to know if the recent events in England had altered Henry's views on a general council; the Protestants should make further contact dependent on his continued opposition to the general council. He believed, however, that on the subject of a common theological policy at a general council it would be difficult 'to stand as one man with the king and be committed concerning it, since, as has already been sufficiently noticed, he understands little of religion'.[241] He suggested that the matter 'be let lie until your grace or we get a response from the king or the bishop of Hereford' to the letter which Philip and he had written for Foxe to take to Henry at Naumberg in early June.[242] If such a response was not forthcoming then 'the matter should on this side also be let rest'.[243]

It was also proposed to write again to Henry. On 3 August John Frederick wrote to Philip that steps were in hand to send a letter from Luther and Melanchthon through Hamburg to Barnes, in order to ascertain how the situ-

---

abfertigen, ein ursach nemen und einen hineinschiken wollen, zu erkunden, ob der konig noch der meinung sei und dem evanglio anhange': HStMar, PA 455, fo. 11 [PC ii. 378].
237 TStWei, Reg. H. 115, fos 28–9.
238 HStMar, PA 2566, fo. 58.
239 TStWei, Reg. H. 107, fos 1–6 (draft); HStMar, PA 2566, fos 72–7 (final copy).
240 '[V]iel gelegenhait umb des konigs sachen und soll ser wol sein an dem Cromwelle, welche der furnembsten Regentten ainer in England geachtet wirdet': TStWei, Reg. H. 107, fo. 2 (draft); HStMar, PA 2566, fo. 73 (final copy).
241 '[M]it dem konigk fur ainen Mhan zu stehen und des vorppflicht zu sein dieweyl er wie genugsam vormarckt von der relligion wenig verstehett': TStWei, Reg. H. 107, fo. 2v (draft); HStMar, PA 2566, fo. 73v (final copy).
242 '[S]tillgestanden werdenn solt bis E.L. und uns von koniglicher w. oder dem Bischoff von Hereford, schrieffte zukhemen': TStWei, Reg. H. 107, fo. 4v (draft); HStMar, PA 2566, fos 75v–6 (final copy).
243 '[M]an die sache auff dieser seytte auch schlaffen lasse': TStWei, Reg. H. 107, fo. 5 (draft); HStMar, PA 2566, fo. 76 (final copy).

ation stood in England; a copy of a letter to Henry was also sent for Philip's approval.[244] What became of the letter to Barnes is not known, but on 27 September Philip did note that the letter to Henry had been sent.[245] This, dated 1 September, played for time. It disingenuously explained the delay of the promised embassy to England on the fact that not all the League members had replied to the proposals made at Frankfurt. Otherwise it said very little, only asking Henry to declare to the League once more his mind on the articles drawn up at Schmalkalden the previous Christmas.[246]

Henry made no reply. He was hardly likely to repeat the message which he had sent to the League in March; what he now wanted was for the League to make up its mind and send to him the embassy which Foxe had sought and been assured of during the previous year. Moreover, during the closing months of 1536 England was in the grip of a national emergency, the Pilgrimage of Grace. Until that was dealt with, neither the king nor his counsellors would have the time or inclination to chase after the slow, indecisive Germans. For now it would be up to the Germans to make the running in forwarding Anglo-Schmalkaldic diplomacy. Only when domestic order was restored in 1537 would the king and his men have the luxury of securely sitting back and giving further consideration to Anglo- Schmalkaldic relations.

---

[244] TStWei, Reg. H. 120/122, fos 222–7 (draft); HStMar, PA 2566, fos 83–6 (final copy).
[245] HStMar, PA 2566, fos 140–5 (draft). In early October John Frederick acknowledged this report with thanks: TStWei, Reg. H. 120/122, fos 236–45 (draft); HStMar, PA 2566, fos 167–74 (final copy). Philip acknowledged John Frederick's letter on 12 October: HStMar, PA 2566, fos 210–13 (draft); TStWei, Reg. H. 120/122, fos 348–54 (final copy).
[246] LP xi. 388.

3

The Schmalkaldic Embassy to England, 1537–1538

Diplomatic contact revived, September 1536–April 1538

One of the enduring myths about Anglo-Schmalkaldic relations is that between 1536 and 1538 England ceased to show any interest in the League: that during the Franco-imperial war of 1536–8 Henry did not feel under any threat from abroad and so decided to ignore the League until such time as the French king and the emperor ceased hostilities. The survival of this interpretation is testimony to the continuing influence of the Froudean mechanic: from April 1536 to the treaty of Nice in June 1538 Charles and Francis were at war in northern Italy; *ergo* Henry ignored the Schmalkaldeners. In this scheme of rule-book diplomacy it is not necessary even to look at the wider evidence; one simply knows that when France and the empire are at war Henry automatically distances himself from the Germans, keeping them just close enough should they be required again later on. R. B. Wernham, for example, writes that

> the fact of the matter was that Hery now felt reasonably secure. Francis and Charles were fighting each other again. Their mutual jealousy would surely not cease when the war ended. And now that Henry's particular causes of quarrel with the emperor had been removed by the death of both Catherine and Anne, he might hope to be able to play off Charles against Francis as well as Francis against Charles. Besides, there were always the Lutherans as an additional lever upon Charles's behaviour if one were needed.[1]

And so, 'by the summer [of 1537] Henry felt so secure that he allowed the talks with the German Lutherans to die away'.[2] Similarly, Prüser argues that 'as long as Charles V and Francis I were at war, Henry's diplomatic situation was excellent'.[3] This would only change when the 'long feared reconciliation between the emperor and the king of France actually took place. At the end of 1537 this danger first appeared'.[4] Now a Franco-imperial enterprise against England threatened.

---

[1] Wernham, *Before the armada*, 134.
[2] Ibid. 137.
[3] 'So lange Karl V. und Franz I. sich im Kriege befanden, war Heinrichs diplomatische Lage glänzend': Prüser, *England und die Schmalkaldener*, 117.
[4] '[L]ange befürchtete Aussöhnung zwischen dem Kaiser und dem König von Frankreich wirklich erfolgte. Gegen Ende 1537 zeigte sich diese Gefahr zuerst': ibid. 118.

That was the same situation as had been evident in 1535, as Henry had set out to seek an understanding with the Schmalkaldic League. And so naturally he followed the same path as he had then and set in train negotiations [with the League] before a full union between Charles V and Francis I had been achieved.[5]

These accounts of Anglo-Schmalkaldic relations from 1536 to 1538 are difficult to accept.[6] They reduce England's diplomacy with the League to a series of simplistic adjustments wholly dependent on the movements of the great powers of Europe. To argue against them is not to say that England's Schmalkaldic policy was formulated in isolation from the wider foreign policy scene. Rather, it is to suggest that it also had its own independent influences: that it was not simply a dependent part of an Anglo-Franco-imperial machine; and that the course of Anglo-Schmalkaldic relations from 1536 to 1538 can only be understood by examining its own particular sources and context.

Certainly, there was a brief break in Anglo-Schmalkaldic contact. But that break is not exclusively to be explained by the war in Italy. Rather, the explanation lies in the fact that in late 1536 and early 1537 Henry was waiting on the return embassy from Germany which he had been promised by John Frederick and Philip in their letter of 1 September 1536, and that during this time the resources of the crown were stretched to breaking point in dealing with the Pilgrimage of Grace. Moreover, the break was not even coincident with the Franco-imperial war of April 1536–June 1538. Edward Foxe continued to negotiate in Germany until the summer of 1536, long after the death of Catherine of Aragon had reduced the likelihood of an English war with the empire and two months after the opening of hostilities in Italy. And it was during the summer of 1537, while Francis and Charles were still at war, that contact between England and the League was restored.

The first steps towards a renewal of relations were taken by the Germans. The growing threat of a general council caused the League to renew the contacts it had broken off in the wake of the Boleyn affair. Papal pressure had steadily risen since the appearance of the papal nuncio, Pietro Vergerio, at the Diet of Schmalkalden at Christmas 1535. Though the League had coolly dismissed him with a refusal to consider anything other than a free council on German soil, during 1536 the papacy went ahead with plans to summon a general council. On 2 June 1536 the formal summons was issued. This hardly allayed the Protestants' fears that they would not receive an even-handed

---

5 'Das war dieselbe Lage, wie sie sich 1535 gezeigt hatte, als Heinrich sich anschickte, eine Verständigung mit dem Schmalkaldischen Bunde zu suchen. Es war natürlich, dass er denselben Weg ging wie damals und dass die Verhandlungen schon begannen, ehe es zur völligen Einigung zwischen Karl V. und Franz I. gekommen war': ibid.
6 Prüser and Wernham are but two exponents of a universally accepted orthodoxy. Others who concur with their views include Merriman, *Life and letters of Thomas Cromwell*, i. 228–41; Hughes, *Reformation in England*, i. 355–7; Elton, *England under the Tudors*, 154–5, and *Reform and Reformation*, 276–7; Doernberg, *Henry VIII and Luther*, 111–13; Jacobs, *Lutheran movement*, 127–30.

hearing (at one point the summons spoke of 'the plague of the Lutheran heresy'), and towards the end of 1536 a diet was summoned to Schmalkalden to discuss the threatening situation.[7] One of the results of the diet was that in early 1537 it was decided to send Henry an explanation of the League's position on a general council.

This tract was completed in March 1537.[8] Instead of sending it to Henry with the major embassy of which the king had been assured in 1536, the League decided to give the pamphlet to the city of Hamburg to pass on quietly through one of its trade contacts with England. The man selected for the task was an anonymous Hamburg sailor. He appears to have left for England sometime in July 1537. Upon arrival at Dover, he made enquiries as to how he might gain access to the court and was eventually brought to one John Whalley, an acquaintance or agent of the Cromwell family. Whalley agreed to help the German, and on 29 July wrote for him a letter of introduction to Richard Cromwell. He reported that the sailor

> hathe brought letters ffrom grate men of Jarmeny unto the kynges highnes and also unto my lord your uncle; that he may come to my lordes presence and that my lord be good lord unto hym for his expedicion. I perceyve he lovythe my lord well and bycause of his fidelitie and love towardes my lord I have caused one to conduct hym to the courte bycause he cane speke no ynglishe. And the while he followeth the courte I pray you be good master unto hym that he may have some lodgyng.[9]

The same day he also wrote a letter of introduction for the German to Thomas Cromwell himself, explaining his reasons for coming to England and that he had 'desyered me to have him conducted unto you'.[10]

The sailor was accordingly conducted to the court.[11] When he arrived there, however, he made a very poor impression. His status and bearing were low, and once he had presented the tract from the League he departed the court unannounced, without even bothering to wait for a reply. This not only annoyed Henry, who on so important a matter had at the least expected an honourable messenger rather than a grubby seaman from the League. It also infuriated Cromwell and his evangelical friends, who saw in the recent defeat of the rebellious Pilgrims the ideal opportunity to press ahead with their plan to use relations with the German Protestants to promote reform in England.

---

7 W. P. Fuchs, *Das Zeitalter der Reformation*, Munich 1973, 178.

8 The tract was written in about early March 1537 (for dating see *LP* xii/1, 564.i): BL, MS Cott. Vit. B.xxi, fos 215–16 (English trans.) [*LP* xii/1, 564.ii]. It was conveyed with a covering letter from the League to Henry dated 26 March: BL, MS Cott. Cleo. E.vi, fos 295–6 (sealed final copy), 318–19 (English trans. in Vaughan's hand) [*LP* xii/1, 745].

9 PRO, SP 1/123, fo. 130 [*LP* xii/2, 363].

10 PRO, SP 1/123, fo. 129 [*LP* xii/2, 362].

11 What follows in this paragraph is based on a report on the sailor's appearance at the court which will be reviewed in detail at pp. 82–4 below: TStWei, Reg. H. 137, no. 64, fos 156–7 (copy enclosed with Philip to John Frederick, n.d., fos 155 [text], 158 [fly-leaf]).

After the appearance of the bedraggled sailor at the court, the evangelicals decided to inform the League of this. They would send a secret message to Germany, complaining at the inadequacy of the League's efforts and exhorting it to send a respectable embassy to the king.

Finding the right person to convey such an unofficial – and therefore highly dangerous – message would usually have been difficult. The messenger would have to be a trustworthy evangelical. He would also have to be well known to influential men in Germany, travelling to Germany on some other purpose and not one of the evangelicals' servants. Fortunately for the reformers, providence delivered into their hands just such a person: Thomas Theabold. Theabold was a godson of the earl of Wiltshire, Anne Boleyn's father. He had been sent to Germany in 1535 for the twin purposes of study in Tübingen under Joachim Camerarius and touring the various centres of Protestant Europe. Recently he had been staying in Strassburg.[12] In the summer of 1537 he unexpectedly arrived back in England, conveying books to the king on behalf of some of the Strassburg group of reformers. This was opportune for the English evangelicals. On 22 July Cranmer wrote a letter of introduction for him to Cromwell, saying that

> the berer herof, Mr Tybbold, one that hath exercised his studie in Almayne theis ii or iii yeres past, brought from Capito and Monsterus both letters and bokes to the kinges highnes. And if his graces pleasure be to rewarde theym for thair paynes and good hartes whiche thei bere unto his said grace, this man that browght the said letters shall very conveniently do the king good service in that bihalf, ffor he is goyng thether warde now agayn and is a very honest man and both loved and trusted of the lernyd men in thos parties with whome if it please your lordship to commone, he can well enforme you of the state of that countrye.[13]

This then was just the man. A reliably evangelical itinerant student, well known to, and trusted by, the theologians of Protestant Germany, he was the perfect agency through which to transmit information to the leadership of the Schmalkaldic League.

And so the young student was taken under the wing of the English reformers. They took care that his books were quickly brought to the king's attention, seeing to it that they were presented to Henry by Cranmer personally. They also made sure that their authors were rewarded. Cranmer wrote to one of them, Wolfgang Capito, of how Cromwell, Foxe and he, during a meeting together, had arranged to ensure this:

[12] J. Fines, *A biographical register of early English Protestants and others opposed to the Roman Catholic Church*, Abingdon 1985, ii. T–6; Prüser, *England und die Schmalkaldener*, 45 n. 1; *LP* xii/1, 377. See also E. W. Ives, *Anne Boleyn*, London 1986, 306–7 (where Theabold's name is rendered as Tebold). Theabold was to be one of Cromwell's continental agents for the remainder of the decade.

[13] PRO, SP 1/123, fo. 67 [*LP* xii/2, 314].

when the bishop of Hereford and I were together in company with the Lord Cromwell, the keeper of the privy seal, who is one of the privy councillors, and who has done himself more than all others together in whatever has hitherto been effected respecting the reformation of religion and of the clergy; we united in requesting him to put his majesty again in mind of you, which he has done, and a hundred crowns are assigned to you as a present, which he has ordered the bearer of this letter to take with him.[14]

And just as the evangelicals smoothed the way for Theabold, so they enlisted his services for their own purposes: conveying to Germany their annoyance at the League's recent negligence in sending a hapless sailor as ambassador to the king of England, and asking the League to make a greater effort in its relations with England so as to assist with the progress of the Reformation. When Theabold returned to Germany he made directly for Strassburg, where he delivered some letters and conveyed by word of mouth certain secret intimations.

The most interesting of the letters was from Thomas Cranmer to Strassburg's leading theologian, Martin Bucer.[15] Although it is not extant, Bucer's reply of 23 October survives, and shows clearly that Cranmer had both outlined the course of recent political developments in England and expressed the disappointment of the evangelicals with the recent efforts of the League in England. Responding to the information he had received 'by these letters, and by the conversation of Thomas', Bucer noted his optimistic outlook,

> for inasmuch as the Lord has united with you (not as Theseuses, but as Barnabases) the Latimers, the Foxes, and other endued with so much courage, so much activity, and, in fine, with so much zeal; what else can be inferred from this, but that he favours your purpose and undertaking, and that he will enable you to produce abundant fruit unto Christ throughout the whole kingdom?[16]

He went on to acknowledge the evangelicals' criticisms, lamenting

> that senselessness and all but treason of ours, who in a place and time so convenient and desirable have not aided you by the slightest exertions . . . how it shames and grieves both our senators here, and us ministers of the word, that besides all those betrayals (let me call it by the right name) of the kingdom of Christ among you [ie. the Pilgrimage of Grace], the letter of our Schmalkaldic

14 *Original letters relative to the English Reformation*, ed. H. Robinson, Cambridge 1846, 15 [*LP* xii/2, 315].
15 The only other known letter was an innocuous piece from Edward Foxe to Martin Bucer, which thanked Bucer for the dedication of the *Enarationes*, enclosed a copy of the recently published Bishops' Book and told him that in understanding the state of England 'he will find the bearer a youth of learning': *LP* xii/2, 410. As this last comment suggests, Foxe would convey the detail of his feelings on Anglo-Schmalkaldic relations by word-of-mouth.
16 *Original letters*, 520–1 [*LP* xii/2, 869].

council was sent in so disgraceful a manner! For what could be more disgraceful, or more shameful, what could be done so unworthy of us, as thus to send the letter of a council so eminent, as it seems to me, on a matter of such importance, to so illustrious a king, and one too who had before so honoured us beyond all expectation even of those who had hoped the best, and offered us of his own accord in a more than royal embassy those things which, if we really desired to advance the kingdom of Christ, it would have behoved us to obtain at the expense of all we have?[17]

But this was not all. For Theabold had not simply been charged with passing on letters which provided intelligence on developments in England and conveyed the dissatisfaction of the evangelicals with the League; he had also been directed to ask on the evangelicals' behalf that an embassy be sent again to England to capitalise on the opportunity which the previous one had missed. This message was to be passed on orally. Its content is revealed by a report which the Strassburgers subsequently decided to write on the letters and the oral message. This, compiled by a member of the town council, probably Jakob Sturm,[18] for the purpose of informing the leadership of the Schmalkaldic League, was sent to Philip of Hesse about late October. Philip in turn had a copy forwarded immediately to John Frederick.[19]

The report began by using the information which had been brought by Theabold to provide a survey of the revived progress of the Reformation in England:

today a man from England was here, who brought to our preacher a letter, in which was written that as a result of the recent uproar in England [ie. the Pilgrimage of Grace], the evangelical bishops very much have the king's ear, and that from day to day there is good hope of furthering the cause of the gospel in England.[20]

Moreover, because the rebels wanted

the Roman Church restored again in its glory and dignity, included in their ranks many papistical monks and priests, and named them captains and leaders of this holy pilgrimage (as the rabble called it) . . . the outcome has been

---

17 Original letters, 521 [LP xii/2, 869].
18 Philip of Hesse would shortly afterwards write to Sturm on the subject of Anglo-Schmalkaldic relations: PC ii. 464.
19 Unsigned copy forwarded to John Frederick: TStWei, Reg. H. 137, no. 64, fos 156–7 (copy enclosed with Philip to John Frederick, n.d., fos 155 [text], 158 [fly-leaf]). The original sent to Philip is not extant.
20 'Diser tag einer uss enngellandt hie gewesen der geschrifften an unser prediger bracht darinne geschrieben wirtt das die vergangen uffrur in Engellandt ursach geben, das die Evangelischen bischove vill gehor bey ko. Mat. haben und gute hoffnung seye die sach des Evangeli soll sich vonn tag zu tage inn Engellandt meheren': TStWei, Reg. H. 137, no. 64, fo. 156 (copy enclosed with Philip to John Frederick, n.d., fo. 155).

that those whose spiritual inclination is to the papacy have equally less of the king's trust and ear.[21]

But the League had failed to take advantage of this promising situation. Now came the evangelicals' oral message:

in relation to this, however, the Englishman has also told me how all the kind-hearted have complained bitterly that the embassy from my gracious lord the duke of Saxony, your grace and the other League members has not gone ahead and been sent to England, where it might promote the gospel.[22]

In driving this point home, Edward Foxe, the English evangelical most widely known and respected in Protestant Germany at this time, was the reformers' mouthpiece:

in particular he said that the bishop of Hereford, whom you know from his embassy, had commanded him to tell me that the king received a letter concerning the council from the duke of Saxony and your grace, which was brought by a sailor from Hamburg, that was so out of date that the sailor appears to have spent a good amount of time on the way, and that he had left before he could be given an answer. The king was particularly annoyed that in such an important matter the letter was not brought by a special and honourable ambassador, especially since he previously has sent a major embassy on this very question.[23]

In the light of this, Foxe recommended strongly that the League send an embassy to England, or at least write Henry a letter of apology and explanation. He was sure that in the current circumstances this would find a good response from the king. His name must not be mentioned, however, for this

---

[21] '[D]i Romische kirche wider in ir Ehr und würde restituirtt haben, sich vill Babstlicher münchen und pfaffen zu inen geschlagen und sich zu dieser heyligen bilgerfart, dann also nannten sie iren hauffen, fur hauptleut und furer dargegeben . . . dann gefolgt das di so des glaubens halb noch Babstisch seindt desto weniger glauben und gehor bei dem konig haben': TStWei, Reg. H. 137, no. 64, fo. 156 (copy enclosed with Philip to John Frederick, n.d., fo. 155).
[22] '[D]aneben aber hatt mir der obgemelter Engellander auch gesagt, wie alle gutherzigen eine grosse beschwerde emphangen das di bottschafft von meinen gesch. hn. dem Churfursten zu Sachsen und E.F.G. und andere Evangelischen nit fur sich gangen und in Engellandt geschickt worden dann sey furdenus dem Evangelio gegeben haben': TStWei, Reg. H. 137, no. 64, fos 156r–v (copy enclosed with Philip to John Frederick, n.d., fo. 155).
[23] '[S]onderlich sagt er das ime der Bischoff von herefordt so yhr in Bottschafft wyss herauss gewesen bevolhen mir zu sagen das dem künig ein brieve von dem Churf. zu Sachssen und E.F.G. das Concilium betreffen durch ein schiffman von hamburg zu khommen der sey nun am datum etwas alt gewesen also das er ein gute zeitt uff dem wege und ehe er uberantwurt verhalten worden sei. Dorab der konig einer sonder beschwerdt emphangen das in einer solchen wichtigen sach im die brieve nit durch einen eigenn und ehrlichen botten zugeschickt worden, besonderlich weil er hievor ein so statlich botschafft eben in dieser sachen hierauss geschickt hette': TStWei, Reg. H. 137, no. 64, fo. 156v (copy enclosed with Philip to John Frederick, n.d., fo. 155).

was a private initiative on the part of the evangelicals: Foxe's involvement must be kept secret, the report noted in closing, 'so that he does not come into any danger with his lord the king'.[24]

Theabold's messages arrived at exactly the right time, as, in the second half of 1537, increasingly favourable indications on the religious orientation of England began to find their way to Germany from other sources. In August Melanchthon was able to express his pleasure at the news that Robert Barnes was no longer under the threat of persecution he had earlier apparently faced,[25] while Martin Bucer commented to Cranmer in October that he was pleased with religious progress in England and that 'the agreement of our Churches is making fair progress'.[26] Moreover, the death of the religiously conventional Jane Seymour in October removed what had been perceived in Germany as a possible obstacle to continued Anglo-Schmalkaldic relations.[27] Even the message brought by the sailor from Germany on the general council which had so annoyed Henry, evoked a response from the king which had a positive effect on the Protestants. The report on Theabold's appearance at Strassburg related that because Henry was so angered by the ignorant manner in which the message was presented he had responded, not by replying to the Protestants, but simply by publishing his own tract against the general council, without any reference to the Germans.[28] This action, however, intended as a counter-insult, did not have the desired effect. Far from it; Henry's pungent attack on Rome's efforts to summon a general council profoundly impressed the Protestants. The pamphlet appeared in Wittenberg in a Latin version and was immediately printed and widely distributed. Such was its popularity that it reappeared shortly after in three German translations; two editions, one from Augsburg, the other from Strassburg, were printed and quickly sold out.[29] The Hessian chancellor Johann Feige wrote to Philip on 7 October that 'the king of England and his men have written and published in print a strong attack on Pope Paul III and his letter summoning a council. In this he despises and condemns the papacy no less than Dr Martin or any other ever has'.[30] Melanchthon too wrote in early October that he was

---

[24] '[D]omitt ime khein gefar bey seiner herren dem konig dorauss entstande': TStWei, Reg. H. 137, no. 64, fo. 157 (copy enclosed with Philip to John Frederick, n.d., fo. 155).
[25] CR iii. 395–6 [LP xii/2, 433].
[26] LP xii/2, 969.
[27] For example, Luther's suspicions as to Jane's religious inclinations: LP xi. 475.
[28] TStWei, Reg. H. 137, no. 64, fo. 156v (copy enclosed with Philip to John Frederick, n.d., fo. 155). The tract was entitled A protestation in the name of the king, and the whole council and clergy of England, why they refuse to come to the pope's council at his call.
[29] Prüser, England und die Schmalkaldener, 119.
[30] 'Es hat der konig von Engellandt und seine stend des reichs in Engellandt ein heftigk stusschreiben widder Bapst Paulu der dritte und sein uberschreiben pro roguit concilii in drugk aussern lassen darin er des bapst thumb nicht mynder verachtet und verwirfft dan doctor Martino oder kein andere ye gethan haben': HStMar, PA 469, fos 172v–3.

'surprised at the freedom of his [Henry's] writing, for he inveighs with the utmost bitterness against the pope'.[31]

Thus circumstances favoured a positive German response to the urgings of the English evangelicals. When Philip sent the report on Theabold's visit to John Frederick in October, he suggested that they should send an embassy to England immediately – and if not an embassy then at the least a letter. In a postscript, Philip emphasised the need to keep Foxe's involvement a secret, so as to hide from the king the extent of behind-the-scenes agitation in favour of Anglo-Schmalkaldic relations, 'for your grace knows that in these matters the king is not to be joked with'.[32] On 15 November John Frederick replied that it would be unwise for the two of them to send an embassy to Henry on their own account, without first consulting the other League members. Henry wanted an agreement with the whole League and to open negotiations without all the members' consent, only to find that they were not willing to carry them through could be counterproductive. Moreover they would have to meet all the costs of the embassy themselves and deal with any problems that resulted from it on their own. Better, he proposed, would be to adopt the alternative suggestion and send a letter to Henry. Accordingly, he had enclosed a letter to Henry, dated 14 November, for Philip to read. If the landgrave found it satisfactory, he might countersign and counterseal it for despatch to England forthwith. In the meantime they could meet with the other League members and seek to get them to agree to an embassy to England.[33] In a letter of 20 November, Philip agreed to John Frederick's proposal and sent back the letter to Henry, having added his signature and seal.[34] This, dated 14 November and signed by both John Frederick and Philip to Henry, and a very similar letter signed by John Frederick alone of the same date, were despatched to England. The princes began by lavishing praise on Henry's recent written attack on a papal council. They went on to apologise for the inappropriate manner in which they had last written to him, explaining that they had understood at the time that the pope was about to summon a general council very soon and so had exercised the greatest haste, entrusting the despatch to the 'senate of Hamburg, which city has almost daily commerce with England; and in so doing did not mean to displease him'. After commenting favourably on his religious opinions, the princes proposed opening a round of discussions to plan what to do should a council be summoned. They also requested that Henry pass on his religious views so that they could debate them at their next diet.[35]

---

31 *LP* xii/2, 844–5.

32 'Dann E.L. wissen das mit demselben konig in disen sachen nit zuschertzen ist': TStWei, Reg. H. 137, no. 64, fo. 158.

33 Ibid. fos 159–61 (draft); HStMar, PA 2569, fos 115–16 (final copy) [Prüser, *England und die Schmalkaldener*, 302–4].

34 HStMar, PA 2569, fo. 98 (draft); TStWei, Reg. H. 146, no. 70, fo. 6 (final copy).

35 Letter from John Frederick and Philip: HStMar, PA 2569, fos 117–20 (German copy);

The letters to Henry were well timed. Cromwell, Cranmer and their evangelical friends were more firmly entrenched as the king's most influential
counsellors than they had been at the time of Theabold's visit, advocating
from a position of strength closer relations with the League of Schmalkalden.
Indeed, even before John Frederick and Philip wrote to Henry, the evangelicals had been able to persuade the king to consider despatching an ambassador to Germany, as a letter of early October from William Fitzwilliam to
Cromwell shows:

> this afternoone the kinges hignes riding to Hanworth shewed me by the weye
> that he had forgotten to commone with you in oon thing, which is that in the
> Instructions to bee gyven to hym that shall goo into Jermanye his maiestie
> thinkes it good that there bee an article put to knowe what the states there
> will doo for his grace in caase themperor, the ffrenche king and the Bisshop of
> Rome doo joyne and conclude upon a generall Counsaill and doo at the same
> anything which shuld bee contrary to the lawes of god, his purpose and
> theirs.[36]

This, incidentally, speaking as it does of an afterthought concerning France,
the empire and Rome, supports the view that it is wrong to connect
Anglo-Schmalkaldic relations too closely with the actions of Francis, Charles
and the pope. For clearly Cromwell and Henry had in the initial discussion
mentioned by Fitzwilliam analysed relations with the League without any
accompanying in-depth analysis of the activities of Henry's main European
rivals. On the other hand, of course, Fitzwilliam's letter also shows that it
would be equally wrong to deny that the other powers of Europe had any relevance to Anglo-Schmalkaldic relations. Certainly, it is likely that as the
houses of Habsburg and Valois tentatively opened peace talks towards the
end of 1537, Henry's interest rose in the idea of developing an alternative
alliance in Germany in case both Charles and Francis turned against him.
Moreover, with the possibility of a general council looming ever larger by the
end of 1537, it is likely that Henry became increasingly aware that the
Schmalkaldic League was the only ally with which to work to prevent the
papacy from turning a general council to its advantage. Once again, then, it is

---

121–2 (Latin copy) [CR iii. 448–50 n.; LP xii/2, 1088]. Letter from John Frederick: CR iii.
448–51 [LP xii/2, 1089]. The citation is from LP xii/2, 1088. As if to acknowledge the role
Strassburg had played in mediating the intimations from the evangelicals and thereby
reopening relations with England, Philip also sent a copy of this letter to Jakob Sturm, probably the author of the report which had related Theabold's arrival and the messages he had
brought. The course of action the League leaders had taken was well appreciated in
Strassburg: Sturm wrote back on 12 December to say that 'I have received and read your
grace's letter and the copy of the letter sent to the king of England, and the apology
contained therein pleases me well' ('E.f.g. schreiben sampt uberschickter copei an den konig
von Engelland hab ich empfangen, verlesen und mir die entschuldigung wol gefallen lassen':
PC ii. 464).
36 PRO, SP 1/125, fo. 107 [LP xii/2, 814].

not that these wider European developments had no influence on Henry's relations with the League, but only that they were not the exclusive or even principal determinants of his actions.

The Saxon ambassador who arrived in England with the letters from John Frederick and Philip appears to have had his charge declared by Cromwell late in the year.[37] After some discussion he was given a letter dated 2 January 1538 from Henry to John Frederick and Philip to take back to Germany, which expressed pleasure at the Germans' attitude to a general council and agreed with their suggestion that Anglo-Schmalkaldic negotiations be continued.[38] Henry undertook to send an embassy to Germany for this purpose forthwith and requested that a return embassy from the League be sent to England, among whose number should be learned men 'with sufficient power or authority' to conclude an alliance without delay.[39] Finally, Henry noted that he found the Germans' apology for the way in which the previous message to England had been conveyed 'friendly and satisfying'.[40]

Cromwell's involvement in all this was manifest. He was with the king at Greenwich on New Year's Day when the matter was probably at the final stage of discussion[41] and, in his remembrances, he reminded himself 'to depeche the duke of Saxons messanger'.[42] Moreover he seems to have been in charge of arranging the despatch of the embassy to the League, announced in Henry's letter of 2 January.[43] Cromwell's servant Christopher Mont was once again chosen to represent the king. His letters of introduction to John Frederick and Philip, signed by Henry on 25 February, simply stated that Henry wanted Mont to discuss with the princes his religious views and the action he and the princes should take in the event of a general council. They also requested the earliest possible despatch to England of the Schmalkaldic League embassy which had been promised in 1536.[44]

The instructions, drafted by Wriothesley, were more expansive.[45] Clearly,

---

37 BL, MS Cott. Tit. B.i, fo. 444 [*LP* xii/2, 1151. ii]: 'to declare the newes of Germanye' (this item was cancelled, as if Cromwell had already seen to it).

38 HStMar, PA 1800, fos 3–6 (German trans.; Latin original is not extant).

39 '[M]it genugsamen gewald oder Auctoritet': ibid.

40 '[F]reuntlich und wolzufriedenn': ibid.

41 *LP* xiii/1, 24. This is the well-known letter from John Hussee to Lord Lisle on the presentation of New Year's gifts to Henry at Greenwich. It suggests that Cromwell was one of the few with the king at this time, and was therefore dominating the flow of advice even more than usual. Hussee noted that 'there was but a small court'.

42 BL, MS Cott. Tit. B.i, fo. 444 [*LP* xii/2, 1151.ii].

43 Cromwell's involvement is suggested by, among other things, his remembrances about this time: BL, MS Cott. Tit. B.i., fo. 439v [*LP* xii/2, 1151.iii].

44 Letter for Philip: HStMar, PA 1800, fo. 11 (final copy); BL, MS Cott. Vit. B.xxi, fos 170–2 (draft) [*LP* xiii/1, 353]. Letter for John Frederick: BL, MS Cott. Vit. B.xxi, fo. 173 (good draft) [*LP* xiii/1, 352].

45 PRO, SP 1/129, fos 140–55 [*LP* xiii/1, 367]. A close German paraphrase of these instructions is in TStWei, Reg. H. 165, no. 78.i, fos 1–10.

Henry was still interested in joining or forming an alliance with the League. Mont was directed to ask for details of the League, in particular

> howe many princes and states be ioyned with them, and whether the king of Denmark be oon of the confederates, and howe and after what sort they be bound oon to thother, whether for defence in cause of religion onely or for mutuel assistence in cace of invasyon for that or anny other matier, and howe farre their ayde do extend.[46]

The general council also remained a central concern. Mont was instructed at some length to tell the League that Henry was pleased that 'It apperethe that right prudently and wiselye they doo forsee the purpose and intent of the Bisshopp of Rome in the setting furthe of his pretended counsail.'[47] However, Henry could not 'a litle marvail' at recent rumours that the Germans might be relenting in their attitude to the pope's authority to summon a council.[48] If by some chance they had so given 'unto him therein a greater preemynence thenne he can by anny colour almost clayme',[49] Henry urged them to reconsider, and ensure 'that hereafter they gyve unto him again no suche libertie nor colour to clayme that thing which in dede he hath not'.[50] Finally, the instructions also suggest that Henry's interest in theological consultations with the League remained as strong in 1538 as it had been in 1536. The princes were to be told of how

> his grace hath travaylled and howe moche he laborethe dayllye by sundry most discreate and prudent meanes to bring his people to the true knowleage of god and his woorde and . . . what conformytie he hathe brought all his subiectes unto by his wisdom and temperannt ministring his medycynes lyke a good and most perfyct physicyan as his grace might perceyve the Stomakes of the patientes hable to bere and susteyne them.[51]

Henry wanted the League to send to him 'suche men of wisdom lernyng and gravitie to that province as may soo indifferently waye all matiers with at their cumyng hether'.[52] In particular, Henry wanted the Germans to 'appoynt Philipp Melancton to be coming in that legacion specially for that his hieghnes hathe conceyved a very good opinion of his vertue, lernying, temperaunce and gravitie, and wold gladly conferre with him at his cumyng in sundry of the pointes of Religion'.[53]

These were very positive instructions and likely to be favourably received

---

46 PRO, SP 1/129, fos 147v–8 [LP xiii/1, 367].
47 PRO, SP 1/129, fo. 145 [LP xiii/1, 367].
48 PRO, SP 1/129, fo. 146 [LP xiii/1, 367].
49 PRO, SP 1/129, fos 146r–v [LP xiii/1, 367].
50 PRO, SP 1/129, fo. 146v [LP xiii/1, 367].
51 PRO, SP 1/129, fos 144r–v [LP xiii/1, 367].
52 PRO, SP 1/129, fos 143r–v [LP xiii/1, 367].
53 PRO, SP 1/129, fo. 150 [LP xiii/1, 367].

by the Schmalkaldeners. But Cromwell and his evangelical friends had worked much too carefully over the last few months on promoting Anglo-Schmalkaldic relations to leave anything to chance. This time the League must not be allowed to renege on the major embassy to England as it had done in 1536. Thomas Cromwell decided to take steps to ensure this. He decided to contact the Schmalkaldic leadership personally. On 20 January 1538, still a month before Mont's letters of credence were signed by Henry, Cromwell put his own signature to a private letter to Philip of Hesse.[54] He assured Philip that

> I have conceived a firm hope and trust that it will come to pass that such friendship as exists most harmoniously at this time between the king's majesty, the illustrious lord and duke of Saxony and your excellency, will be mutually most useful. And I will not neglect any occasion, nor such offices as I possess, with which to strengthen and establish such friendship daily with a strong bond.[55]

Cromwell was revealing quite a lot here. Yet there was still more he wanted to say. This, however, was evidently too secret to be put down on paper, and would be conveyed by his servant. Cromwell told Philip that Mont would shortly be sent to Germany, not only to negotiate on behalf of the king, but also to pass on certain secret intimations: 'I have directed that something be explained to your excellency in my name, to which I heartily request you give certain credence, and not burden yourself but to judge me most studiously.'[56]

What then was it that Mont was to pass on? The 'official' evidence reveals little. Mont left England in late February 1538, and arrived in Germany in time to attend a Schmalkaldic League diet at Braunschweig, arranged for late March. In April he was given a reply from the League to take back to Henry. The League claimed that it had never said that the pope had a right to call a council as Henry had suggested. They should like to explain further the purpose of their League, as Henry had requested they do, but it would be difficult to instruct Mont on the matter, and to put it in writing would be dangerous. They had therefore decided to send a small interim legation to England to explain it to the king and discuss doctrine, so that when the requested major embassy was sent its work would be simplified. The major embassy would, if the general council were deferred, soon be sent to England;

---

[54] HStMar, PA 1800, fo. 7 (Latin final copy, signed in Cromwell's hand at the foot: 'Obsequendi studiossis, Thomas Crumwell'). A contemporary German translation is at fo. 9.

[55] '[S]pem certam fiduciamque concepi, futurum aliquando ut haec amicitia quae inter suam Regiam Maiestatem ac Illustriusimum Dominum Saxoniae Ducem atque vestram Excellentiam iam est coniunctissima sit aliquando utrique maxime utilis nullamque ego omittam occasionem nullumque officii genus elabi sinam quo tenacioni in dies nexu firmetur stabiliaturque': HStMar, PA 1800, fo. 7.

[56] '[M]eo quoque nomine eidem vestrae Excellentiae exoneda communisi cui impense rogo ut certam fidem habere meque sui studiosissimum existimare non gravetur': ibid.

however, it was noted that if the general council proceeded the League would have to keep its chief divines in Germany.[57]

But what of Cromwell's secret intimations? This evidence reveals nothing. Rather, it is necessary to turn to a private letter from Christopher Mont to Philip of Hesse of 27 April, which the English agent paused to write and give to a messenger he had happened to meet near Grave in the province of Brabant, as he made his way back to England.[58] Mont began by noting that 'I would have been glad to have had a discussion with your grace at Braunschweig concerning my gracious lord the king of England.'[59] But, he explained,

> I could not comfortably do this because your grace had various business which occupied you at the diet. Also, the departure [from the diet] took place so quickly that I could not follow your grace, for I received my answer at eight [o'clock in the morning] on that same day on which your grace rode for Cassel at four [o'clock in the morning]. Thus, I have not let this messenger go by, but have given him this letter to your grace.[60]

So Mont had not been able to have the private conversation with Philip which Cromwell had directed. That then was the reason for this letter. The information to which Cromwell had referred in his message of 20 January would not be delivered by word of mouth after all. Instead it would be conveyed in Mont's letter.[61] Mont continued:

---

57 PRO, SP 1/130, fos 226–35 [*LP* xiii/1, 648]. Various Latin fragments of drafts and copies of this survive in TStWei, Reg. H. 165, no. 78.i, fos 11–26.

58 HStMar, PA 1800, fos 19–20 [Prüser, *England und die Schmalkaldener*, 304–6]. Mont's orthography exhibits certain English influences; his occasional anglicisms such as 'and' instead of 'und', 'has' instead of 'hat', 'newlich' instead of 'neulich' etc. have been retained.

59 '[I]ch het gans gern mit euer furstilichen gnaden mich bereedt zo Brunswick, meines gnedigen hern, des konings von Englant halben': HStMar, PA 1800, fo. 19 [Prüser, *England und die Schmalkaldener*, 304].

60 '[H]ab ichs nit bequeemlich mogen doen ursach mangerlei geschft halben, mit welchen eure gnad auf dem tag beladen geweest ist. Auch ist der abzweg so gans geschwind gescheen, das ich euren gnaden nit hab moegen folgen. Den ich hab meine antwort um 8 entfange[n] des dags, welchen eure gnad um 4 nach Cassel geritte[n] ist. So hab ich disen boten nicht moege[n] lasse[n] geen sunder [ihm diesen] brief aen e.f.g. [gegeben]': HStMar, PA 1800, fo. 19 [Prüser, *England und die Schmalkaldener*, 304–5].

61 Cromwell is not mentioned by name in this letter. But that is not suprising given that he had instructed Mont to pass information to Philip orally, most probably to ensure it could not be traced (and Foxe, after all, had told Theabold specifically to keep his name out of the frame only a few months earlier; with Cromwell's higher profile an even greater caution was probably judged necessary). What follows should be regarded as the information which Mont would have conveyed to Philip had he been able to meet him, but with Cromwell's name excised for security reasons. Incidentally, it should not be thought that in this letter Mont was revealing information 'as of himself' on Henry VIII's behalf; there is no suggestion in his detailed instructions that he should do this.

Gracious lord, I want to beg your grace, both for the honour of God and the promotion of his holy word, that your grace will seriously endeavour to send a number of your grace's councillors and those of the duke of Saxony to the king, in accordance with the answer given to me at Braunschweig, which discussed and promised this. For I hope with some certitude that this despatch should be the way and preparation for a great and powerful act for God and the world; I trust that through your ambassadors the king and the whole kingdom of England will be won and conquered for God, the Almighty.[62]

Like Theabold the previous year, Mont had been directed to emphasise the favourable conditions which existed in England for a Schmalkaldic embassy:

the king's majesty, with the leading lords in the entire kingdom, and also the commonality, are very well inclined to the matter and have through God's grace made a good beginning with the holy gospel. Thus if you only keep God's glory before your eyes, you will not let this opportunity slip to bring a whole kingdom to the holy gospel and to conduct them further into a recognition of God's word, in which they have already made good progress. For the pope, the root and foundation of all superstition and lies, has by God's grace been proscribed and banished from the kingdom. And there is also available the scripture of the old and new testaments in the English language, along with good preachers, from which it is also to be hoped that there will be a welcome recognition of God's word.[63]

Mont had also been briefed by Cromwell to point to Henry's status and the significance of the efforts he had made in the past with regard to the League:

if one will now cast an eye over the course and affairs of the world, then such a king – whom the emperor, the French king and indeed the whole world courts – is not to be spurned by you. Moreover, he has first approached you with a

---

62 'Genediger her, ich will e. f. g. gans flissig gebeten haben, beide um der eer gottes wollen and sines heligen worts promotion, das eure furstliche gnad mit ernst sich beerbeten woll, das ia etliche eurer gnaden reed samt des choerfursten von Saxen mit dem fürderlichsten aen koenigliche maiastaat gesent werde[n], glich als in der antwort, mir zo Brunswick geben, begriffen und versprochen ist. Dan ich verhoff mich gewislich, das dise sendung sal ein weeg and bereitung sin eines groessen and gewaltigen wercks kegen got and der weelt. Den ich verhoff, das ir durch eure gesanten sollet den koenig and das gans reich von Englant got, dem almechtigen, gewinnen and erobern': HStMar, PA 1800, fos 19r–v [Prüser, *England und die Schmalkaldener*, 305].

63 '[K]oenigliche maiest. mit den foernemesten hern in ganzen reich, darzo die gemein, ist der sach gans woel zogetaen and hat durch gottes gnad einen goeten fortgang in dem heligen evangelio getaen. So ir allein gottes eer foer augen habt, so ist Euch soeliche occasion nicht zo verseumen, woorbi ir ein gans koenigrich zo dem heligen evangelio brengen moeget und ferner in die erkantnis des worts gottes zo leiten, waarinne sie den nu eine schoene baen gemacht habe[n]. Den der babst sein wurzel and fundament aller sup[er]stition and loegen ist aus dem reich bi der gnad gottes verbant and proscribirt. So hat man die schrift des alte[n] and neuen testaments in der englischen zunge and darzo gute predige[r], daraus den zo hoffen ist ein wolkomne erkantnis des worts gottes': HStMar, PA 1800, fo. 19v [Prüser, *England und die Schmalkaldener*, 305].

costly and magnificent embassy – that led by the bishop of Hereford, which was with your grace in Germany in 1536 – and therefore honesty demands that a further despatch be made to the king.[64]

He had even been instructed to play the German card, pointing out that

I am the king's servant, but I certainly have not forgotten my fatherland. I therefore might note, that were great utility and progress not to result from this – both for the promotion of the almighty God and his holy word, and against the world's quick infidels and offenders – I sincerely would not advise in the matter as I have done.[65]

And in closing Mont told Philip that since

I have seen come to light before my eyes great and certain signs that the matter will progress well, I cannot refrain but advise with all diligence that your grace will ensure that your ambassadors are despatched most expeditiously to the king's majesty; for I trust that the result of all this will be in accordance with God's honour and glory.[66]

The evidence of 1537 and early 1538 suggests that, as a result of domestic developments, England's relations with the League had entered a new stage: the twin crises of the period, the Boleyn affair and the Pilgrimage of Grace, had sharpened and defined English faction politics.[67] Whereas from about 1533 to 1536 religiously-based faction politics was in the process of emerging – as goals, loyalties and groupings slowly crystallised – the events of 1536–7 brought factional affiliations and tensions out into the open. When Theabold told the Strassburgers that as a result of the Pilgrimage the 'evangelical

---

64 'So man nu das aug auf der weelt leuf and hendel richten will, so ist ein sodaener koening, um welchen der keiser, der franssoes, ia die ganze weelt boolet, euch nit zo verschmehe[n]. So ir irst euch mit einer koestlichen prachtliche[n] legation ersoecht has, als mit dem bischof von Herfort, welcher den anno 36 bi eurer furstlichen gnaden in Teuschslant geweest ist, darum soll ia redlicheit erfordern, witer aen den koenich zo senden': HStMar, PA 1800, fos 19v–20 [Prüser, *England und die Schmalkaldener*, 305].
65 '[I]ch bin des konigs diener, ia doch bin ich meines vatterland nach nit vergessen. So ich deet vermirken, das nit ein goetes nuts und foertgang hieraus erfolge[n] sol, beide, zo dem almechtige[n] got und sines heligen worts furtgang and kegen der weelt geschwinden infel and aenstoes, so wolt ich warlich so neulich nicht zo der sach raten': HStMar, PA 1800, fo. 20 [Prüser, *England und die Schmalkaldener*, 305–6].
66 'Nachdem ich aber groesse and gewisse zeichen foer auge[n] and am tag sehe, das die sach einen guten fortgang haben wirt, kan ichs nit unterlasse[n], sunder mit alle[m] fleis raten, das eure furst: gnad daraen woll sin, das eure gesenten mit dem furderlichste[n] an koenigliche ma: gesent werde[n]; den ich verhoff, al ding sal erfolgen nach gottes eer and glory': HStMar, PA 1800, fo. 20 [Prüser, *England und die Schmalkaldener*, 306].
67 It has been suggested that these two episodes were connected; that in the wake of Cromwell's alleged double-crossing and defeat of the Aragonese in the Boleyn affair, the Pilgrimage of Grace, planned by those same Aragonese, went off without the support at the top necessary for its success: Elton, *Reform and Reformation*, 260–70. Though the evidence for the connection is circumstantial, the argument is broadly plausible.

bishops very much have the king's ear', while those whose 'spiritual inclination is to the papacy have equally less', he was effectively reporting a hardening of the lines of factional division. This was especially the case where
those who inclined towards the Gospel were concerned. The fall of the
Boleyns had left Cromwell, closely allied with Cranmer, as the principal focus
of power among the reformers. Those who might previously have seen themselves more in alliance with the Boleyns (men like Latimer and perhaps also
Foxe) now gravitated quickly and unequivocally towards this group. This
process was only hastened by the events of the Pilgrimage. By the time
Cranmer wrote of recent developments in England to Bucer in mid-1537 the
consolidation of the reformers into a single group was becoming increasingly
clear. As Bucer observed in response to Cranmer's letter, 'the Lord has *united*
[my italics] with you . . . the Latimers, the Foxes and other endued . . . with so
much zeal; what else can be inferred from this, but that he favours *your*
purpose and undertaking [my italics]'. The italicised words say it all: unity in a
common purpose and undertaking. The unity was a faction; the common
purpose and undertaking was to work for the advancement of the Gospel.
The evidence that has been accumulating since 1533 – Cromwell's consistent
involvement in Schmal- kaldic affairs, the Nuremberg diet of May 1534, the
fraternal tone of Cromwell's correspondence with Barnes and Luther in
1535–6, the messages conveyed to Germany by Theabold and Mont in
1537–8 – has established an unmistakeable pattern of behaviour. Henceforth
it is reasonable to stop speaking of the evangelicals in hypothetical, general
terms, and to begin referring specifically to an evangelical faction as an
evidentially discernible political grouping: an alliance of elite politicians
under the leadership of Cromwell and Cranmer, whose principal 'purpose and
undertaking' – whose very reason for existence – is to strive for the ascendancy of Protestantism in England.

It should again be emphasised that this argument rests on the assumption
of a powerful and knowledgeable king. As in 1533–36, the only reason the
evangelicals in 1538 wanted an embassy from the League to discuss theology
with the king was that Henry had shown an interest in such discussions. The
evangelicals were following the lead set by the king on Anglo-Schmalkaldic
relations; without his pre-existing interest there would have been no
Schmalkaldic diplomacy. The divergence between the king and the faction
was not on the question of whether there should be diplomacy with the
League but why: aside from the diplomatic benefits, the king saw the League
as no more nor less than a consultative source to help him achieve a codification of the English faith; the evangelicals, however, saw Anglo-Schmalkaldic
relations as a Trojan horse for introducing into England a full programme of
reform along continental lines. Now, in the wake of the conservative debacle
that was the Pilgrimage of Grace, the evangelical faction had every reason to
think that, as Theabold reported, there was 'good hope of furthering the
gospel in England'. It appeared that England was on the verge of giving
herself completely to the Reformation. The evangelicals apparently needed

only a push from abroad; for an embassy from the League to be 'sent to England, where it might promote the gospel'. Whether the League would fulfil the role which the evangelicals had envisaged remained to be seen.

Preliminary discussions, April–June 1538

Important though Mont's letter to Philip is for the insight it offers into the motives and actions of the evangelical faction, his efforts at persuasion came too late to have any influence on events. Though his pleas for the despatch to England of an embassy were principally concerned with the major legation which had been promised at Braunschweig, the decision to send a minor exploratory embassy first had already been taken. Even as Mont wrote to Philip of Hesse, discussions on the matter were underway between John Frederick and Philip. On 24 April three days before the letter was sent, John Frederick wrote to Philip that the embassy to England would leave from Hamburg shortly. Philip should send whomever he had appointed to it to Hamburg on 12 May. He also asked that Philip add his signature to the letter of credence and return it to Saxony so that it could be finished.[68] Philip, however, was not about to give John Frederick such exclusive control over the embassy. In a letter of 29 April he informed the duke that he had not decided whom he would send to England and because of this would not be able to sign the letter. Instead, he suggested that John Frederick's ambassadors bring their own letters and his would do the same. He added that he would not be able to send his ambassador to Hamburg until 19 May.[69] On 6 May John Frederick wrote to Philip, agreeing with the changed arrangements, and urging that any further delays be avoided.[70]

Philip eventually decided to appoint as his ambassador Georg von Boineburg, a Hessian nobleman and experienced diplomat. For his part, John Frederick settled on Franz Burchard, Friedrich Mykonius and Bernhard von Mila. Burchard, John Frederick's vice-chancellor, was an outstanding Latinist and a well-travelled diplomat. Mykonius, the little known superintendant of Gotha,[71] was the embassy's chief theologian, and had been sent in place of the much sought-after Melanchthon.[72] Mila, a knight with some business ex-

---

68 HStMar, PA 2572, fos 56–8 [Prüser, *England und die Schmalkaldener*, 306–7].
69 HStMar, PA 2572, fos 59–60 [Prüser, *England und die Schmalkaldener*, 308–9].
70 TStWei, Reg. H. 198, no. 91, fos 45–8. John Frederick had written to the Hamburg council the day before, asking it to alter accordingly the arrangements for the transport of the ambassadors to England: Reg. H. 165, no. 78.i, fos 104–6.
71 Mykonius' only biographer, P. Scherffig, *Friedrich Mecum von Lichtenfels*, Leipzig 1909, reviews Mykonius' activities in England at pp. 115–19.
72 Melanchthon wrote a letter of recommendation for the embassy, which praised the ambassadors and explained his own absence, saying that it was necessary for him to remain

perience in England, would play no great part in proceedings. He returned to Germany after only three weeks.

While the personnel was being selected, instructions were drawn up. These principally directed the ambassadors to explain that the League was unable at this time to send the major delegation which Henry had requested through Christopher Mont because of the possibility of a general council and the need to keep the League's foremost theologians at home. The ambassadors were to outline the reasons for which the League had been formed and explain its defensive character. They should also inform Henry that the king of Denmark had joined it. However, the main purpose of the embassy was to ascertain the religious differences between England and the League, so as to prepare the ground for the major follow-up embassy to negotiate Henry's inclusion in the League. The ambassadors were to ask Henry to declare his own views and explain just what it was that he found lacking in the Confession of Augsburg.[73]

Supplementary instructions, which John Frederick issued to his ambassadors, developed all these points.[74] Because theology dominated discussions in England in 1538, they are of particular interest where they touch on religious matters. The ambassadors were instructed to 'stop on your way at Wittenberg to consult with Dr Martin, Philip and the other divines, and also take copies of the agreement which was made with the king's ambassadors two years previously'.[75] With an eye to the theological differences on the abuses which had been revealed in the second part of the 1536 disputations at Wittenberg, John Frederick directed his ambassadors to consult on

> the four points which remain unresolved, and which must almost be considered the pillars and very foundations of the pope and his adherents: the permitting of communion in both kinds, the abrogating of the private mass . . . [the article] concerning monastic vows, and the fourth article concerning the marriage of the priesthood, or celibacy.[76]

---

behind and help in matters touching the Reformation in Germany: Prüser, *England und die Schmalkaldener*, 124.

73 PRO, SP 1/130, fos 236–9 [*LP* xiii/1, 649.i]; BL, MS Cott. Cleo. E.vi, vol. 2, fo. 303 [*LP* xiii/1, 649.ii]. There are various drafts at TStWei, Reg. H. 165, no. 78.i, fos 27–75, 110–21.

74 TStWei, Reg. H. 165, no. 78.i, fos 79–92 (copy), 93–103 (copy) [Mentz, *Johann Friedrich*, iii. 376–83].

75 '[W]an sie iren wegk uf Wittenbergk zu nemen, bei doctori Marthino, philippo und den andern bericht, auch copei nhemen der vergleichung, die mit des konigs botschafft doselbst vor zweien jharen bescheen': Mentz, *Johann Friedrich*, iii. 381.

76 '[D]er vier punct, welche doch vhast die seulen und die furnemliche unterhaltung des babstes und seines standes geacht mussen werden, unverglichen plieben sein, nemlich der zulassung der communion in beider gestalt, domit doch fallen mussen die privatische messe . . . die clostergelubde belangende. Und zum vierten den artikel priesterehe oder celibat anlangende': ibid. iii. 381–2.

Ominously, the duke pointed out that 'if the king persists in these articles, which are almost the most important points in the struggle with the pope and papacy, then there will remain a great shortfall in the agreement between his majesty and us'.[77]

During the first half of May the embassy's personnel and papers were finalised.[78] About the middle of the month the Hessian and Saxon ambassadors made their separate ways to the meeting point at Hamburg. Boineburg met the three Saxons at Hamburg on 19 May, and after some preliminary disputations between Mykonius and Boineburg, the men made ready to depart for England.[79] They sailed from Hamburg on 20 May and arrived in England seven days later after a stormy crossing.[80]

The embassy's first few days in England were taken up with administrative matters.[81] Upon their arrival, the ambassadors took the first shelter they could get and sent ahead one of their 'servants, to lord Cromwell, the highest counsellor in England, who is most favourably inclined and affectionate towards the affairs of the Christian religion and the German nation'.[82] The servant was instructed to deliver the embassy's introductory papers and to ask that the ambassadors be granted more comfortable and permanent lodgings. Cromwell responded swiftly. He saw to it that the next day the ambassadors were visited in their temporary accommodation and were assured that better rooms would be found for them as soon as possible. The following day he made good his promise, arranging for them to be collected by Sir 'Christoff Moriz' and taken away to be installed in more suitable lodgings,[83] apparently in the City of London.[84] Of the standard of accommodation, Cranmer would later write to Cromwell that the Germans

---

[77] 'Wo der kunig nun uf den punkten verharrete als vhast die wichtigsten punct des streits mit dem babst und babstum, so were auch noch ain grosser mangel an der vergleichung zwuschen seiner koniglichen wirden und uns': ibid. iii. 382.

[78] Letters of credence were also written up around this time. They were substantially the same as the main instructions: BL, MS Cott. Cleo. E.vi, vol. 2, fos 284–94 [LP xiii/1, 650].

[79] Mykonius to Gregor Brück, Hamburg, 19 May 1538, in 'Epistolae reformatorum', ed. N. Linde, Zeitschrift für Kirchengeschichte v (1877), 164–5.

[80] Report on the crossing in the opening of letter from Burchard and Mila to John Frederick, 1 June, HStMar, PA 2574, fos 45–7 (copy enclosed with John Frederick to Philip, 2 July, fo. 29) [Prüser, England und die Schmalkaldener, 309–12].

[81] Much of what follows in this section, from the arrival of the ambassadors until their first audience with Henry on 2 June, relies on Franz Burchard's account. Unfortunately, this does not provide any detail on the embassy's activities outside this period: TStWei, Reg. H. 165, no. 78.i, fos 171–83.

[82] '[D]iener an dem hern Crumellum als obersten regenten in Englandt, und dem die sachen der Christlichen religion, und auch der deutschen nation, zum hochsten gewogen und zugethan': ibid. fo. 172 (Burchard's account).

[83] Cromwell had probably delegated Morice to the ambassadors because of his previous experience with Germans on military matters. DNB mentions Morice's missions to Germany seeking the services of military men there.

[84] At one point (TStWei, Reg. H. 165, no. 78.i, fo. 175v) Burchard speaks of sailing back to

ar very evill lodged where thei be. ffor beside the multitude of Ratts daily and nyghtly runnyng in thair Chambers, whiche is no smale disquietnes, the kechyn standeth directly agaynste thair parlar, where thei daily dine and suppe, and by reason therof the house savereth so yll that it offendith all men that come into it.[85]

Interestingly, the German evidence makes no such mention of dissatisfaction with the new lodgings; indeed, Franz Burchard would note with evident approval the interior fittings and the supplies that had been made available to them.[86] Perhaps the archbishop and his circle were more demanding about such things – whatever the case, these quarters would remain the ambassadors' place of residence for the next four months.

The day after they moved into their new lodgings, the ambassadors got down to business. Their first step was to take a barge up the Thames to Westminster for a preliminary meeting 'in the king's house' with Cromwell.[87] They gave him a letter from John Frederick,[88] and discussed their instructions. Cromwell informed the Germans that Henry had said that they could have an audience with him on the coming Sunday, and wished to know 'whether the ambassadors desired a public audience, or would prefer to be heard by the king in private'.[89] The ambassadors replied that they thought it would be best to see the king with his 'most privy councillors',[90] but that they would be happy to conform to the king's wishes. They were later informed that Henry agreed with their suggestion of a meeting with the king and his council.[91]

The next day, Saturday 1 June, Burchard sailed alone up the river to Westminster once more. Unlike the formal introductory meeting of the previous day, his purpose this time was to enter into private discussions with the two leading evangelicals, Cromwell and Cranmer. He stopped first at Westminster to talk with Cromwell. 'Do not doubt', said the minister to the German,

> that such a despatch as this should lead to the promotion and propagation of God's word and otherwise to great Christian unity and excellence between the

London after a meeting at Westminster. Also, all the ambassadors' letters from England would be dated from London (as opposed, say, to Westminster or Greenwich, locations to which the ambassadors would at various times refer with a specificity which suggests that they recognised the City of London as a distinct area).

85 BL, MS Cott. Cleo. E.v, fo. 225 [Burnet, *History of the Reformation*, vi. 165; *LP* xiii/2, 164].

86 Burchard's account (TStWei, Reg. H. 165, no. 78.i, fo. 173) made no complaint about the new lodgings, but did mention approvingly that they contained some tables and provisions.

87 '[I]n die ko. Mt. häus': ibid. (Burchard).

88 John Frederick's letter to Cromwell, ibid. fo. 109. It is a colourless letter, introducing the ambassadors and stating in general terms the aims contained in their instructions.

89 '[O]b die gesanten eine offentliche audienz begerthen oder ob sie leber in geheim von ko. mt. wolten gehort wurden': ibid. fo. 173 (Burchard).

90 '[V]ertrautsten rethe': ibid. fo. 173v.

91 Ibid.

king's majesty and the whole kingdom of England and those of our League. For the king's majesty is agreed with almost all the articles of the Christian religion of the League; only in one or two articles does the king's majesty still have reservations, but with time he should also be moved on these.[92]

Cromwell also assured Burchard that nothing in the kingdom would be hidden from the ambassadors and that if they needed anything the king would grant them it.[93] Burchard then crossed the river to meet Cranmer at Lambeth and pass on letters to the archbishop from John Frederick. Cranmer, like Cromwell, 'showed that this despatch pleased him most highly and that it should not be doubted that it should serve Christian unity and the promotion and dissemination of the godly truth and gospel'.[94] Cranmer had also 'given a wide ranging report on how religious matters in the kingdom stand; how far they have come and where they are still wanting', and had provided an optimistic assessment of the likelihood of continued reform.[95]

Greatly encouraged by the day's events, Burchard returned to his lodgings, took up pen and paper and wrote an enthusiastic letter to John Frederick, reporting what he had heard from Cromwell and Cranmer. The king, he wrote,

is very well inclined to the gospel and God's word; after all, he has let the League's Confession and Apology be put into English and published in print throughout the kingdom, and the same should happen with the Bible and New Testament. Everyone has great hope that shortly the ungodly abuses and ceremonies will be done away with, once the people are better advised by Christian preachers.[96]

---

[92] 'Zweifle auch nicht solche schickung solte zu forderung und ausbreitung des gotliche worts und sunste zu vilen guthen christlichen einickeit und feinheit schafft zwischen ko. mt. und dem ganzen reich zu Englant und unseren gnedigste und gnediger hern sampt iren zugewanthen gedeien, dan die ko. mt. were fast in allen artickeln der Christlichen religion, mit der confession des churfursten zu Sachssen etc. und s. ch. f. g. zugewanten einig, allein einen oder zweien artickel hatte sein ko. Mt. noch bedencken halten aber es solten mit der zeit die ko. Mt. darinnen auch zubewegen sein': ibid. fo. 174.
[93] Ibid. fos 174r–v.
[94] '[A]ngezaigt das er dieser schickung zum hochsten erfreuet sei auch ungezweifelt es soll solches zu christliche einickeit und forderung und ausbreitung der gotliche warheit und Evangelii dinstlich sein': ibid. fo. 175v.
[95] '[F]erner allerlei bericht gethan wie es mit der religion sachen in konigreich Englandt gelegen wie weit man komen und woran noch der mangel sei': ibid. fo. 176.
[96] '[Z]u dem evangelio und gotlichen wort vor ire person ganz geneigt. Dan es haben ire konig. mat. euer cur- und f.gn. und der andern christlichen stend getane und offentliche in druck ausgegangene confession und apologia in engelische sprache vordolmetschen und offentlich alhier in irem konigreiche in druck ausgehen lassen, desgleichen auch mit der biblia und neuem testament gescheen sein soll. Und stehet jederman in trostlicher und guter hofnung, es sollen kurzlich die ungotliche misbreuche und ceremonien, wan die leute durch die cristliche prediger bas berichtet, auch abgetan werden': HStMar, PA 2574, fos 43r–v (copy enclosed with John Frederick to Philip, n.d., fo. 29) [Prüser, *England und die Schmalkaldener*, 310].

He then went on to speak of the men from whom he had learnt this. 'Herren Crumellus', he continued, is

> very well inclined towards matters concerned with promoting the gospel, and he has pursued the same with great diligence up to now. He has also told us that the king would unite completely with the Christian faith of your grace and the other League members. His majesty only has reservations about the article [i.e. from the Wittenberg articles] concerning the marriage of the priesthood, but he hopes that there will not be any further problems. The same goes for the Archbishop of Canterbury, who was very obliging with regard to your grace's letter, and who was confident that everywhere in the kingdom a satisfactory end will be reached in matters concerning religion. And they, both Cromwell as the highest counsellor in all England after the king and the archbishop of Canterbury, appeared to be delighted at our arrival and were of the highest hope that the embassy should meet with success.[97]

The next day this optimistic outlook was put to the test as the ambassadors arrived for their first audience with Henry:

> in the king's house behind Westminster [ie. Whitehall], in the presence of his majesty's foremost councillors, such as the archbishop of Canterbury, the duke of Norfolk, the duke of Suffolk, the lord chancellor, lord Cromwell and some others.[98]

The ambassadors introduced themselves to Henry in the customary fashion and were in turn embraced by the king. As they stepped back, Henry nodded to indicate that they might begin. Burchard then began his address, which was heard not only by the king, but also by the five or six councillors who stood beside him. After this he handed over the letters of credence. With the same five or six councillors Henry retreated to a bay window to examine and discuss the papers. After a while, he returned to his former position and commanded the ambassadors to approach him until they were standing right

---

97 '[D]ie sachen des evangelii zu furdern ganz genaigt, dasselbige auch bisher mit allem vleis getan. Er hat uns auch angezaigt, das konigliche mait. mit euer chur und furstlichen gnaden und der andern ainungsvorwandten bekannte cristliche ler durchaus ainig sein wurden. Sein konig. mait. hette allain in dem artikel, der priester ehe belangende, noch etwas bedenken, daran es doch seins vorhoffens nach kain mangel haben wurde. Desgleichen auch der erzbischof zu Candelberg sich ganz gutwillig auf euer churf. gnaden schreiben erboten, gibt auch guten trost, das die sach alhie im konigreich sich allenthalben mit der religion recht schicken werden. Und seint baide, obgemelter Crumellus als oberster regent nach konig. mait alhier zu Engeland und itztgenanter erzbischof zu Candelberg unser zukunft zum hochsten erfauet gewesen, der genzlichen hofnung, es sol zu allem guten geraichen': HStMar, PA 2574, fo. 43v (copy enclosed with John Frederick to Philip, n.d., fo. 29) [Prüser, *England und die Schmalkaldener*, 311].
98 '[S]einer mt. haus hinder Westminster in beisein seine mt. treffliche rethe als des ertzbischoff von Candelbery, hertzoge von nortfoc, hertzoge von sutfoc, des Reichs cantzler, des hern Crumellii und etliche anderen': TStWei, Reg. H. 165, no. 78.i, fo. 176v (Burchard's account).

beside him. He then directed them to declare their instructions in full detail. This went on for the best part of an hour, as the ambassadors went through their instructions with the king in Latin, negotiating almost from word to word.[99]

When they had finished, the ambassadors stepped back and Henry retreated again to the bay window to talk for quite some time with the same councillors. Eventually they returned and Thomas Cranmer came forward to declare Henry's mind. He said that the king was glad at the ambassadors' arrival, in particular because they came with the intention of promoting the true religion, something which he valued very highly and was trying to promote in his own kingdom. Because the ambassadors' instructions were long and touched on many important matters, Henry wanted them to be put in writing and presented to him. He would then consider them and in due course provide an answer. The ambassadors' first response was to pause to confer among themselves. They then replied that they would put their instructions into writing as Henry wished, adding that they were glad to hear of Henry's religious inclinations and that they trusted he would continue to extirpate the abuses and errors of Rome.[100]

Henry now spoke up himself. He observed that he did indeed value Christian matters highly, and suggested that since they were of such great importance, Philip Melanchthon surely should have been sent to discuss theology with him, 'for his majesty doubts not that in such Christian affairs his presence should be most useful and beneficial'.[101] To this the ambassadors replied that if, as they doubted not, Henry was willing to accept the League's religious principles and defend them at a council, Melanchthon would be sent with the next embassy. Now came an exchange which exemplified the major difference between the attitudes of Henry and the League to theological negotiations. Henry answered that he would happily accept the German confession,

> but his majesty noted that some articles of the confession require explanation and discussion, and that some are widely contended, concerning which he would gladly talk with Master Philip. And each side must concede to the other, so that one may well achieve complete unity for the promotion of the holy truth and all Christendom.[102]

99 Ibid. fos 176v–8.
100 Ibid. fos 178–80v.
101 '[D]en seine mt. zweifelt nicht seine gegenwertickeit solte in solchen christlichen sachen vil nutzes und gutes schaffen': ibid. fo. 181.
102 'Es achtet aber seine Mt. darvor das etzliche artickel gemelte confession noch ercklerung und beraths bedurfften zu dem das in etzliche auch weit gesthritten darvon seine Mt sich gern mit M. Philippo unterreden wolte. Und muss ein teil den andern teils weichen do mit man zu volkomen einickkeit zu forderung der gotliche warhait und ganzer Christenhait zu guthe komen mochte': ibid. fo. 181v.

The League, of course, had little inclination to offer Henry any compromise beyond that in the Confession of Augsburg: the ambassadors informed the supreme head that the Confession of Augsburg was grounded in Scripture, and that the League would not consider any alteration to it.

Though this statement provided a clear hint that the League would not consider the sort of compromise formula which Henry envisaged, the ambassadors avoided any immediate impasse. They hastily added the assurance that, knowing Henry's reputation as they did, the minor problems he had detected would surely raise few difficulties. Moreover, they continued, one of the reasons for their visit was to establish just where these slight problem areas might lie. In order to do this and explain the Confession of Augsburg more fully, they offered to place at Henry's disposal their theologian, Friedrich Mykonius. Henry, now 'with a happy expression',[103] declared himself satisfied. It was agreed that Mykonius should come to him at the first opportunity for a private discussion of Protestant theology. Henry then brought the audience to an end, embraced the ambassadors again, bid them farewell and dismissed them to their lodgings.[104]

Mykonius returned the following week, on 10 June, to discuss the Confession of Augsburg with Henry. Details of what they talked about do not appear, but Henry was impressed by Mykonius' erudition and during discussions suggested that the Germans might like to enter into a round of doctrinal negotiations with his own theologians. The ambassadors were at first reluctant to involve themselves in such a major and potentially lengthy disputation, but pressed by the evangelicals they eventually agreed. 'For', wrote Burchard and Mila to John Frederick,

> lord Cromwell explained to me, the vice-chancellor, that it would not require any drawn-out disputation, since the king, thank God, is agreed and united with almost all the articles in the Confession and Apology, and it should not be doubted that such a discussion with the king's theologians and scholars will have good consequences.[105]

Thus reassured, in mid-June the Germans prepared to join a group of English theologians for discussions at Lambeth. By now they were very optimistic as to the prospects for the Gospel in England. As Mykonius wrote just before the theological discussions began,

---

[103] '[M]it froliches gemuet': ibid. fo. 183.

[104] Ibid. fos 181–3.

[105] '[D]iweil sich gemelter herr Crumellus gegen mir, dem vicecanzler, erclert, das es keiner weitleuftigen disputation bedurfen wurde, dan die konigl. mait were got lob fur ire person numer fast in allen artikeln mit der confession und apologia verglichen und einig, und solten nit zweiveln, es wurde solich gesprech mit kon. mait. theologen und gelerten zu allem guten gereichen': HStMar, PA 2574, fo. 103v (copy enclosed with John Frederick to Philip, 2 July, fos 83–4) [Prüser, England und die Schmalkaldener, 317].

I find, that by great godly grace there is very good hope that the Almighty will spread his holy word to every corner of the entire English kingdom. Then for one thing, the king has ordained by proclamation throughout the whole kingdom that all priests and ministers should preach and teach the holy gospel to all people, pure, loud and clear. And now preaching takes place every Sunday, which previously was a rare thing in England. Four ministers, of whom Dr Robert Barnes is one, have been named, who have a public commission to instruct the people wherever in the kingdom they consider it necessary. There are also some bishops, such as he of Canterbury, he of Worcester (named Latimer), and other fine learned men, who teach pure and true, and they are permitted faithfully to instruct that human works as a means of grace, consecrated salt, water, extreme unction and indulgences, confirmation, saints and so on are certainly the devil's deceptions, which lead man away from Christ. God is to be thanked that the people are willing and favourably inclined towards evangelical doctrine, as the preachers have reported and I myself have noticed. There is still a lack of well taught and diligent preachers, since the realm is very big and the workers few; nevertheless, given that this country has many learned people, we are of the hope that God will achieve good counsel in this kingdom.[106]

The ambassadors' experiences and optimistic comments during their first two weeks in England reflect the fact that they had arrived in London at the peak of the Henrician Reformation. By the early summer of 1538, the conservative cause was in disarray, its leading lights scattered or on the run. Henry was encouraging the pillaging of shrines and had lent his support to the attack on superstitions. The incorrigible bishop of London, John Stokesley, seemed finally to have been run down by Cromwell; indicted for praemunire, the worse fate of Friar Forest, Catherine of Aragon's erstwhile confessor, who in May had been tried and executed as a heretic for holding Romish opinions,

---

[106] 'Und befinde, das aus grosser gotlicher gnad sehr gute hoffnung ist, der almechtig werd seinem hailigen worte allen raum und platz im ganzen engelischen reich geben. Dann erstlich ist gereidtan durch koe. mt. durch offentliche mandat durchs ganze reich geboten, das alle pfarrer und predicanten das heilige evangelion rain, lauter und clar an allem menschenstand und zusatz predigen und lehren sollen, und wird nun alle sontag gepredigt, das zuvor ein seltzam ding in Engeland gewesen ist. Es seint auch vier predicanten verordent under welichen doctor Anthonius Garves einer, die da offentliche bevel haben, an welichem ort im reich sie sehen, das es notig, das volk zu underrichten. Es seint auch etliche bischof, als der von Kandelberg, der von Ungarn, Latimerus genant, item andere feine gelerte menner, die rain und treulich lehren, und ist inen frei und zugelassen, das sie treulich underrichten mugen, das die menschenwerk als walfart, geweihet salz, wasser, olung und aplas, firmelung heiltum und dergleichen mit des teufels betrug, dadurch man von Christo gefurt wurde, gewislichen sei. Es ist auch gotlob, wie mich die predicanten berichten und ich selbst vermerk, das volk zu der lehr geneigt und willig. Es feilet aber noch an treuen gelehrten und fleissigen predigern; dan dies land ist sehr gross und der arbeiter wenig; doch hoffen wir, weil das Land viel gelehrter leute hat, es werde got hier auch rat schaffen': HStMar, PA 2574, fos 86–v (copy enclosed with John Frederick to Philip, 2 July, fos 83–4) [Prüser, *England und die Schmalkaldener*, 314–15].

might well await him.[107] Elsewhere, the two most doughty and politically respectable defenders of orthodoxy were exiled from the centre of power, Stephen Gardiner as ambassador in France and Cuthbert Tunstall as president of the council of the north. These then appeared to be propitious times for the English reformers. If the Schmalkaldic embassy was not the sought-after major delegation led by Philip Melanchthon, it was the next best thing; a successful conclusion to it would lay the foundations for the doctrinal reformation of the English Church.[108]

However, the appearance of imminent evangelical victory was deceptive. For, although the twin crises of 1536–7 had been the springboard for evangelical ascendancy in the short term, in the long term they had damaged the cause of reform. As a result of the Boleyn affair Cromwell's grip on the council had been weakened. The execution of Anne's brother Rochford had removed his principal noble supporter there, the man best placed to offset the anti-Cromwellian feelings of conservative noblemen like the duke of Norfolk. Certainly, he still had Foxe, Cranmer and Audley, but Foxe had died a couple of weeks before the arrival of the German ambassadors in May 1538, Cranmer was of limited value as a political operator and Audley too was politically weak. At court, Cromwell's faction was rather more secure, but even there the lack of a close alliance with the queen, of the kind he had enjoyed with Anne, most probably weakened him too. Finally, the long-term situation of the evangelicals in the Church had been shaken by the Pilgrimage of Grace. Although Cromwell had worked to pack it with fellow evangelicals – for example, Foxe, Latimer, Shaxton and Hilsey each received their bishoprics during 1535 through the patronage of the Boleyn–Cromwell network[109] – the Pilgrimage of Grace had sown the first seeds of doubt as to the wisdom of continued reform. The Bishops' Book of 1537, diluting as it did the crypto-Protestantism of the Ten Articles of the previous year, was the first sign that the Pilgrims had achieved some success in slowing down the pace of reform.

And just as there were long-term domestic problems for the cause of reform, so it gradually became evident that the Schmalkaldic visit would not go quite so easily or favourably as the evangelicals had initially expected. An early sign of this is the appointments which were made to the theological committee to discuss doctrine with the Germans. It soon became clear that some of England's most conservative theologians would be included, most remarkably, the bishop of London, John Stokesley, who shortly after the arrival of the ambassadors was pardoned of his praemunire charges.[110] His

---

107 For Cromwell's longstanding campaign against Stokesley see Brigden, *London and the Reformation*, 232–8, 282–5.
108 This picture of the evangelicals on the verge of victory in the early summer of 1538 is supported ibid. 285: 'Hopes that the conservative nobles and Bishops might thwart the plans of the heretics now faded. In 1538 the gospellers were firmly in power, and might realise their old ambition to bring the Gospel into England.'
109 Elton, *Reform and Reformation*, 230.
110 Brigden, *London and the Reformation*, 282–5.

presence would be supplemented by that of another conservative, the bishop of Chichester, Richard Sampson.[111] The question of who decided which theologians would discuss doctrine with the Germans is an interesting one. The best explanation is probably to be found in the German evidence, which suggests that it was Henry who decided upon the composition of the committee.[112] It would seem that Henry decided to balance the strong Protestant presence with the appointment of two bishops of reliably orthodox views. None of this, it should be noted, is to say that Henry wanted the German Protestants completely outnumbered, for Thomas Cranmer and Robert Barnes would also be directed to join the theological committee. Rather, it is to suggest that Henry wanted there to be a genuine discussion of the German views: the ambassadors would not simply preach to the converted. Such a balancing of men from different factions was a well-established feature of the king's political management. It has already been seen, for example, that early in 1536 Henry sought the views of Stephen Gardiner in France on the proposals made by the Schmalkaldic League over Christmas 1535. And there is the revealing testimony of Thomas Cranmer, who in 1537 wrote to one of the reformers whose books had been brought to the king by Theabold that summer of how Henry usually took advice on such matters:

> The king, who is a most acute and vigilant observer, is wont to hand over books of this kind that have been presented to him, and especially which he has not the patience to read himself, to one of his lords in waiting for perusal, from whom he may afterwards learn their contents. He then takes them back, and presently gives them to be examined by some one else of an entirely opposite way of thinking to the former party. When he has thus made himself master of their opinions, and sufficiently ascertained both what they commend and what they find fault with, he at length openly declares his own judgement respecting the same points.[113]

In 1538 Henry would employ a similar technique. He would set in train doctrinal discussions which would involve both sides of the religious divide. He would listen to the deliberations which emerged from those discussions. He would make himself master of the opinions which were given. And then, finally, he would apply the results to his own Church.

The shadowy role of Cromwell in the 1538 discussions is something of a surprise. Cromwell's commitment to the success of Anglo-Schmalkaldic relations should by now be clear. The consistency of his words and deeds since 1533 point to this, and his comments to the newly arrived 1538 ambassadors provide further evidence of his interest in bringing England and the League together. But for one whose commitment was so strong, Cromwell would remain curiously ineffective and uninvolved in the vital doctrinal negotia-

---

[111] Sampson was also the king's confessor and dean of the chapel royal.
[112] See Mykonius' letter to John Frederick: Prüser, *England und die Schmalkaldener*, 315.
[113] *Original letters*, 15 [LP xii/2, 315].

tions of 1538. In the hundreds of folios which the discussions would produce there would not be so much as a scratch from a pen wielded by Cromwell. Diarmaid MacCulloch has suggested that Cromwell's less than active involvement might be explained by his immersion in the factional machinations which would finally surface in August as the Exeter conspiracy.[114] Cromwell may also have been taken up during the summer with preparations for the issuing of the second Injunctions, which would appear in September. Yet although these matters and others must have distracted him, perhaps his complete absence from the theological discussions with the Germans can also be explained by something else, by a problem that became increasingly evident to him during the later 1530s: Cromwell was a layman – and not a scholarly layman of the universities or inns of court, like a St German, the sort of figure contemporaries would refer to as 'learned'. Cromwell's status as a lay and, in formal terms, relatively uneducated man precluded his playing a direct part in discussions on the faith.[115] His involvement could not go beyond the administrative and political. He could, for example, take charge of setting up discussions between the Germans and English theologians at Lambeth,[116] or he could arrange for Richard Moryson, a reformer from his following, to take the German ambassadors 'forth to the pleasur of huntyng'.[117] He could order a reluctant Richard Sampson to have the ambassadors to dinner,[118] or he could deal with complaints from Cranmer that the Germans were poorly lodged.[119] He could even direct Moryson to inform the arch conservative Stokesley of 'in what expectacion the kinges hyghenes is' for talks with the ambassadors at Lambeth,[120] or he could write to Sampson charging him with propounding Romish opinions in discussions with the Germans.[121] But such activities as these represented the limits of Cromwell's powers: what he could not do was exert direct control over the course and substance of the theological discussions.

None of this, of course, is to deny that Cromwell's influence over religious affairs in general was very considerable. After all, as vicegerent he chaired convocation, and in such religiously relevant activities as the dissolution of the monasteries or issuing the 1536 and 1538 Injunctions or determining

---

114 MacCulloch, *Cranmer*, 215–16.
115 MacCulloch is sceptical about this argument: ibid. 216 n. 150.
116 PRO, SP 1/133, fo. 28 [*LP* xiii/1, 1176].
117 PRO, SP 1/133, fo. 253v [*LP* xiii/1, 1297]. The Germans could not be persuaded to go hunting.
118 PRO, SP 1/133, fo. 250 [*LP* xiii/1, 1295]. Even though the bishop of Chichester reported that he had 'neyther ale, no bere, no wyne, nor any other thing erthely that shuld be in a howse'.
119 BL, MS Cott. Cleo. E.v, fo. 225 [Burnet, *History of the Reformation*, vi. 165; *LP* xiii/2, 164].
120 PRO, SP 1/133, fo. 251v [*LP* xiii/1, 1296].
121 BL, MS Cott. Cleo. E.v, fos 306–7 [*LP* xiii/2, 278]. Cromwell reassured the frightened Sampson a few days later: PRO, SP 1/136, fos 146–7 [*LP* xiii/2, 339].

episcopal appointments he had played a central role.[122] These, however, were areas of applied, or practical, theology; it was in areas of pure, or doctrinal, theology that Cromwell's competence and authority were limited. The best the minister could do to influence the formulation of doctrine was to orchestrate and seek to exploit the views of competent people of similar opinions. The 1537 discussions surrounding the formulation of the doctrine in the Bishops' Book are instructive in this respect. When Cromwell wanted Protestant doctrine to be considered in convocation's discussions on the content of the Bishops' Book he did not seek to put forward reformist propositions himself, but brought along the Scottish reformer, Alexander Alesius, to speak on his behalf. And when the conservative bishops protested against the radical views being proposed by Cromwell's guest it was not Cromwell but Edward Foxe who came to the Scotsman's defence – Cromwell remained silent throughout the exchange.[123] In the gathering of the critical input to the Bishops' Book itself, Cromwell was similarly unable to participate directly. Though he made corrections to the preface and commencement of one draft,[124] and to the instructions for the use of another,[125] in neither case did he offer any comments on the doctrine which made up the substance of the book. Once again, the best he could do to influence consideration of the doctrine in the Bishops' Book was to advance the views of others, as two of his remembrances demonstrate: 'to shewe Seynt Jermayns opynyon upon the busshopes boke',[126] and 'Remembrances to be remembryd to the kynges highnes . . . item, the determynacyon of Mr Day,[127] Heth,[128] Thyrlby,[129] and Skyppe,[130] upon the x comandementtes, justyffycacyon and purgatorye'.[131]

Cromwell was therefore dependent on a strong theological ally in the discussions with the Germans. He and the evangelical cause had lost a formidable adherent with the death of the widely respected Edward Foxe in May. By the summer of 1538, Cromwell was left with just one major and widely

122 For Cromwell as vicegerent see S. E. Lehmberg, 'Supremacy and vicegerency: a re-examination', *EHR* lxxxi (1966), 225–35, and F. D. Logan, 'Thomas Cromwell and the vicegerency in spirituals: a re-visitation', *EHR* ciii (1988), 658–67. For Cromwell's packing of the episcopate see Elton, *Reform and Reformation*, 230.

123 *LP* xii/1, 790.

124 PRO, SP 6/2, fos 158–70 [*LP* xii/2, 401.vi].

125 PRO, SP 6/2, fos 102–4 [*LP* xii/2, 618].

126 BL, MS Cott. Tit. B.i, fo. 444 [*LP* xii/2, 1151.ii].

127 At this time George Day was Provost of King's College, Cambridge; subsequently he was to be bishop of Chichester. Although he was well known later in life as a religious conservative, he would later admit that during the early years of the Reformation he had gone along with the new trends; during this period he probably occupied the middle ground between those favouring and those resisting continued reform: *DNB*.

128 Heath was, of course, sympathetic to the new ideas during the 1530s.

129 Thirlby, also a conservative in later years, was not averse to the Reformation in the 1530s: *DNB*.

130 *DNB* categorises Skip as an evangelical.

131 PRO, SP 1/126, fo. 193–v [*LP* xii/2, 1122.ii].

acceptable theological friend: Thomas Cranmer. Cranmer's friendship was not an insignificant string for Cromwell to have to his bow. He was the foremost cleric in England, and his ability to get around the king was already well known. Yet Cranmer's episcopal pre-eminence, while providing obvious advantages, also demanded a certain discretion and impartiality. Although he would be appointed chairman in the forthcoming discussions with the Germans, Cranmer knew well that any blatantly sectarian opinions or activities would compromise his position dangerously. When, for example, the possibility was later raised that the obstructive Stokesley could be removed from the discussions, Richard Moryson would inform Cromwell that 'my lord of Canterbury wold in no wyse it were so, albeit he saith they myght do moch better if he were away. Men would talke, or at the lest thinke evyl, if he shold be taken from their assemble.'[132]

Thus, although on the eve of the Anglo-Schmalkaldic discussions the stage seemed set for a triumphant conclusion for the evangelicals, the issue was far from settled. Evangelical ascendancy in the wake of the Boleyn affair and Pilgrimage of Grace concealed long-term weaknesses; Henry wanted a genuinely critical examination of the Germans' doctrinal principles; Cromwell's influence on the theological discussions was limited; and Cranmer had to preserve an impression of impartial chairmanship. Certainly, the evangelicals seemed to have the advantage. But the upholders of orthodoxy still had a great deal to play for.

The Anglo-Schmalkaldic theological discussions which began in mid-June 1538 can be divided into three phases. The first, on the doctrine in the Confession, began at Lambeth on 14 June under Cranmer's chairmanship and continued until around the end of July. The second, which dealt with the doctrine in the Apology, began with a letter of 5 August from the German ambassadors to Henry, which the king, assisted by one of his theologians, examined, researched and answered in a reply which the Germans appear to have been given shortly before their return to Germany. The third was concerned with the matters which had been raised in the German letter to Henry of 5 August: it began on 19 August, with a debate arranged by Cromwell and Cranmer between the Germans and a group of conservative bishops.

---

[132] PRO, SP 1/133, fo. 251v [*LP* xiii/1, 1296].

First phase: the committee and the Confession, June–July 1538

The first phase of the discussions was arranged quickly. During his discussion with Mykonius on 10 June, Henry indicated that he wanted to see a discussion of doctrine take place between the Germans and a group of English divines.[133] Mykonius wrote to John Frederick that

> the king's majesty has directed that the Archbishop of Canterbury, the Bishop of London (who is an evil old papist and sophist), the Bishop of Chichester, Archdeacon Heath and three other doctors should negotiate with us and, if God lends his grace, seek to achieve a resolution with our confession.[134]

When Mykonius wrote his history of the Reformation a few years later, he gave a brief account of the 1538 discussions, and included a full list of the English participants. Apart from the four mentioned in his letter to John Frederick – Cranmer, Stokesley, Sampson and Heath – he also named Nicholas Wilson,[135] George Day[136] and Robert Barnes.[137] Thus Henry ensured that all shades of opinion, from German Lutheran to rabidly anti-Protestant, were represented. And to achieve a still finer balance, he even adjusted the composition of the German and English committees a little further so as strengthen the German side, 'the king', according to the chronicler Wriothesley, 'admittinge Doctor Barnes to be of their partie'.[138] With the parties so balanced, Henry bid the men join in a conference, 'which sate every week two or three tymes'.[139] The discussions began on 14 June.[140]

The doctrine contained in the Confession was that which had caused the least problems and had been provisionally accepted in the first part of the theological discussions at Wittenberg in 1536. The content and course of the discussions in England are revealed by both English and German sources. In England, there are the numerous drafts produced by the duscussions. In

---

[133] In their letter of 10 June Mila and Burchard told John Frederick that Henry had that day requested such a disputation: HStMar, PA 2574, fos 45–7 (copy enclosed with John Frederick to Philip, 2 July, fos 83–4) [Prüser, *England und die Schmalkaldener*, 312–13].

[134] 'Es hat auch konig. mt. verordent, das der erzbischof von Kandelberg, der bischof von Lunda, welicher ein alter poser papist und sophist ist, der bischof von Cicestrien, der archidiaconus Nicolaus Heito und sonst noch drei gelerte doctores sich mit uns in gesprech und handlung begeben mussen, ob got gnad verleihen wolt, das sie sich mit unser confession vergleichen mochten': Prüser, *England und die Schmalkaldener*, 315.

[135] The king's chaplain, and a conservative sufficiently dangerous for Cromwell to send him, together with Sampson, to the Tower in the early summer of 1540: his appointment lends further weight to the view that Henry wanted a strong conservative presence at the discussions.

[136] For George Day see n. 127 above.

[137] Mykonius, *Historia reformationis*, 57–8.

[138] Wriothesley, *Chronicle of England*, 81–2.

[139] Ibid. 82.

[140] This date is suggested by the contents of Cranmer's letter to Cromwell of 13 June: PRO, SP 1/133, fo. 28 [*LP* xiii/1, 1176].

Germany, there is the Latin final version of the articles discussed[141] and a translation of this into German.[142] The Latin version contains critical marginal annotations in the hand of Martin Luther, while the German version (probably provided for John Frederick) has marginalia by the ambassadors themselves, showing where they were unable to agree with the English.

The many drafts provide a first indication of the level of disagreement which each issue raised.[143] The most intensely debated article, on penance, generated eight drafts, and from one draft to the next demonstrated substantial differences of opinion. On the other hand, most of the remaining articles generated fewer drafts, and these were relatively uniform in content, suggesting that they aroused comparatively little debate. The article on orders[144] produced only one draft; those on images,[145] the veneration of saints,[146] civil affairs[147] and the last judgement[148] produced only two each; those on original sin,[149] the Creed,[150] the dual nature of Christ[151] and the ministry of the Church,[152] three; those on baptism,[153] ecclesiastical rites,[154] the real presence[155] and the use of the sacraments,[156] four.

---

141 TStWei, Reg. H. 165, no. 78.ii, fos 35–54.

142 Ibid. fos 55–85.

143 In the following paragraphs those articles which corresponded closely to the text of the Wittenberg articles, analysed in chapter 2, will not be examined in detail.

144 PRO, SP 1/134, fos 63–78 [*Miscellaneous writings and letters of Thomas Cranmer*, ed. J. E. Cox, Cambridge 1846, 484–9; *LP* xiii/1, 1307.xix].

145 *Miscellaneous writings of Cranmer*, 484 [*LP* xiii/1, 1307.xvii, xviii; only *LP* xiii/1, 1307.xviii, is extant, interspersed with the article on saints in PRO, SP 1/134, fos 54–62].

146 *Miscellaneous writings of Cranmer*, 484 [*LP* xiii/1, 1307.xvii, xviii; only *LP* xiii/1, 1307.xviii, is extant, mixed in with the article on images in PRO, SP 1/134, fos 54–62].

147 PRO, SP 1/134, fos 15–19 [*Miscellaneous writings of Cranmer*, 478–80; *LP* xiii/1, 1307.i], 35–3 [*LP* xiii/1, 1307.xiv].

148 PRO, SP 1/134, fos 19 [*Miscellaneous writings of Cranmer*, 480; *LP* xiii/1, 1307.i], 39–40 [*LP* xiii/1, 1307.xv].

149 PRO, SP 1/134, fos 2 [*Miscellaneous writings of Cranmer*, 472–3; *LP* xiii/1, 1307.i], 21 [*LP* xiii/1, 1307.ii]; BL, MS Royal 7.c.xvi, fo. 193 [*LP* x. 585].

150 PRO, SP 1/134, fos 2 [*Miscellaneous writings of Cranmer*, 472; *LP* xiii/1, 1307.i], 21 [*LP* xiii/1, 1307.ii]; BL, MS Royal, 7.c.xvi, fo. 193 [*LP* x. 585].

151 PRO, SP 1/134, fos 2v–3 [*Miscellaneous writings of Cranmer*, 473; *LP* xiii/1, 1307.i], 21v [*LP* xiii/1, 1307.ii]; BL, MS Royal, 7.c.xvi, fo. 193v [*LP* x. 585].

152 PRO, SP 1/134, fos 12v–13 [*Miscellaneous writings of Cranmer*, 477; *LP* xiii/1, 1307.i], 25 [*LP* xiii/1, 1307.ii]; BL, MS Royal, 7.c.xvi, fo. 197v [*LP* x. 585].

153 PRO, SP 1/134, fos 6–7 [*Miscellaneous writings of Cranmer*, 474–5; *LP* xiii/1, 1307.i], 22v–3 [*LP* xiii/1, 1307.ii]; BL, MS Royal, 7.c.xvi, fos 194v–5 [*LP* x. 585]; BL, MS Cott. Cleo. E.v., fos 5v–6 [Strype, *Ecclesiastical memorials*, i/2, 444–5; *LP* xiii/1, 1307.iii].

154 PRO, SP 1/134, fos 13–14 [*Miscellaneous writings of Cranmer*, 477–8; *LP* xiii/1, 1307.i], 25v–6 [*LP* xiii/1, 1307.ii]; BL, MS Royal 7.c.xvi, fos 197v–8v [*LP* x. 585]; PRO, SP 1/134, fos 33–4 [*LP* xiii/1, 1307.xiii].

155 PRO, SP 1/134, fos 7 [*Miscellaneous writings of Cranmer*, 475; *LP* xiii/1, 1307.i], 23 [*LP* xiii/1, 1307.ii]; BL, MS Royal 7.c.xvi, fo. 195 [*LP* x. 585]; BL, MS Cott. Cleo. E.v., fo. 5v [Strype, *Ecclesiastical memorials*, i/2, 444; *LP* xiii/1, 1307.iii].

156 PRO, SP 1/134, fos 11v–12v [*Miscellaneous writings of Cranmer*, 477; *LP* xiii/1, 1307.i],

Naturally, before proceeding from one article to the next there would have been close examination and cross-examination of the principles involved; it would be wrong to assume that a small number of uncorrected drafts automatically indicates that little discussion or revision of the article in question took place. Indeed, the German evidence shows that the articles on the veneration of saints and ecclesiastical rites each contained a paragraph which the ambassadors found questionable.[157] Moreover, an article on free will does not even appear in draft form, yet the German evidence shows that it was discussed, that its generally faithful reproduction of Lutheran doctrine was modified in two places by the German ambassadors,[158] and that Martin Luther objected to material in the Latin final copy which he examined.[159] Nevertheless, these are the exceptions: there remains a general correlation between the number and content of the drafts and the level of disagreement which each article raised, and this correlation suggests that the foregoing articles took up less time than the remaining ones, on the Church, justification and penance.

Discussions on the Church were probably less an occasion for disagreement than for caution.[160] This was because Henry took up one of the five drafts and corrected it. To the definition of the Church, which stated that it is that congregation 'of all men who have been baptised in Christ and who have neither openly renounced Christ nor have been excommunicated', he added 'justly or have been impenitent'.[161] A little further on he added an assertion that 'this is our catholic and apostolic Church, with which neither the bishop of Rome nor any other prelate or bishop has anything to do except in his own diocese'.[162] These additions were not likely to offend any Lutheran, and most of the subsequent drafts incorporated them silently in their text. The German

25 [*LP* xiii/1, 1307.ii]; BL, MS Royal 7.c.xvi, fo. 197 [*LP* x. 585]; BL, MS Cott. Cleo. E.v, fo. 130 [Strype, *Ecclesiastical memorials*, i/2, 449–50; *LP* xiii/1, 1307.xii].

157 TStWei, Reg. H. 165, no. 78.ii, fos 65 (ecclesiastical rites: the ambassadors objected to an assertion that ceremonies must also be obeyed by the command of God, who says we must do as commanded by the temporal authorities), 82v–3 (veneration of saints: the ambassadors disliked the suggestion that saints have a function as mediators of God's word).

158 Ibid. fos 76, 78.

159 Ibid. fos 43v, 44.

160 PRO, SP 1/134, fos 4–6 [*Miscellaneous writings of Cranmer*, 473–4; *LP* xiii/1, 1307.i], 22 [*LP* xiii/1, 1307.ii]; BL, MS Royal 7.c.xvi, fo. 194 [*LP* x. 585]; BL, MS Cott. Cleo. E.v, fo. 4 [*Miscellaneous writings of Cranmer*, 474; Strype, *Ecclesiastical memorials*, i/2, 442–3; *LP* xiii/1, 1307.iii]; PRO, SP 1/134, fos 27–8 [*Miscellaneous writings of Cranmer*, 474; *LP* xiii/1, 1307.vii].

161 '[O]mnium hominum qui baptizati sunt in Christo, et non palam abnegarint Christum, nec sunt excommunicati'. Henry inserted 'juste' before 'excommunicati', and added 'aut obstinati' after it: BL, MS Cott. Cleo. E.v, fo. 4 [*LP* xiii/1, 1307.i; *Miscellaneous writings of Cranmer*, 474; Strype, *Ecclesiastical memorials*, i/2, 442–3].

162 'Ista est ecclesia nostra catholica et apostolica, cum qua nec pontifex romanus, nec quivis aliquis praelatus aut pontifex, habet quicquid agere praeterquam in suas dioceses': ibid.

evidence confirms the impression of general agreement: neither Martin Luther nor the ambassadors made any comment on this article.[163]

The article on justification, however, gave rise to some impassioned discussion.[164] Mykonius wrote to John Frederick of a great debate in which, nevertheless, the Lutherans had been victorious: this article of the faith, he said, 'has been dragged through fire, and were it not made of gold, it would surely have melted. But God lent it his support; and all their arguments ran like the lead from silver, and thence became ashes.'[165] There are seven drafts of this article, which suggests a fair amount of discussion and revision, but they are all very much of a Lutheran character, bearing a substantial similarity to the corresponding item in the Wittenberg articles. And though Martin Luther did add a clarification to a sentence dealing with the relationship between justification and good works, neither he nor the German ambassadors registered any actual disagreement;[166] it would appear that Mykonius' confidence that the Lutheran doctrine had won the day was, as it were, justified.

The remaining article, and the only one for which there is clear English and German evidence of both substantial disagreement and a failure on the part of the German theologians to achieve a manifestly Lutheran formulation, is that which in most of its eight drafts was entitled 'de poenitentia'.[167] This item was a curious admixture of the Lutheran doctrine of grace and Roman doctrine on the sacrament of penance. The first half rehearsed the doctrine of grace in similar terms to the corresponding sections of the Wittenberg articles; all the drafts were uniform in their adherence to the Lutheran explanation of how man achieves salvation.

However, acceptance of Lutheran doctrine changed after the discussion of the doctrine of grace. Incongruously, there followed a lengthy discussion of

---

163 TStWei, Reg. H. 165, no. 78.ii, fos 36v–7 (Latin version annotated by Luther), 60v–2 (German trans. annotated by ambassadors).
164 PRO, SP 1/134, fos 3–4 [*Miscellaneous writings of Cranmer*, 473; *LP* xiii/1, 1307.i], 21v–2 [*LP* xiii/1, 1307.ii]; BL, MS Royal 7.c.xvi, fos 193v–4 [*LP* x. 585]; BL, MS Cott. Cleo. E.v, fos 4v–5 [Strype, *Ecclesiastical memorials*, i/2, 443–4; *LP* xiii/1, 1307.iii], 102 [*LP* xiii/1, 1307.v], 7 [*LP* xiii/1, 1307.vi]; PRO, SP 6/6, fos 114–15 [*LP* xiii/1, 1307.iv].
165 '[D]urchs feuer gezogen, das, wo er nicht gulden gewest, hat er zerschmelzen mussen. Aber got hat in auch erhalten, dass alle ire argumenta haben mussen wie das blei von silber ablaufen und zu aschen werden': Prüser, *England und die Schmalkaldener*, 315.
166 TStWei, Reg. H. 165, no. 78.ii, fos 36–v (Latin version annotated by Luther), 58v–9v (German trans. annotated by ambassadors).
167 PRO, SP 1/134, fos 7–11v [*Miscellaneous writings of Cranmer*, 475–7; *LP* xiii/1, 1307.i], 23–5 [*LP* xiii/1, 1307.ii]; BL, MS Royal 7.c.xvi, fos 195–7 [*LP* x. 585]; BL, MS Cott. Cleo. E.v, fos 123–5 [*LP* xiii/1, 1307.xi], 126 [Strype, *Ecclesiastical memorials*, i/2, 445–6; *LP* xiii/1, 1307.ix.1], 127 [*LP* xiii/1, 1307.ix.2], 128–9 [Strype, *Ecclesiastical memorials*, i/2, 446–9; *LP* xiii/1, 1307.x]; PRO, SP 1/134, fos 29–32 [*LP* xiii/1, 1307.viii; *Miscellaneous writings of Cranmer*, 475–7, indicates Cranmer's corrections].

confession which clearly contradicted the marginal importance attributed to it by the German Protestants. The most hostile of the drafts was probably the work of one of the two conservative bishops present, Stokesley or Sampson.[168] It insisted that confession should 'not only be retained in the Church, but also its use is necessary'.[169] Whereas the Apology asserted that confession is of human authority, this draft claimed that it was of divine origin and that, moreover, the ministry has the power to absolve the sinner from sin: 'he who truly condemns confession, condemns the keys of the Church, which bequeath an ordination of God. For He gives this power to his ministry, so that when they remit sins they are remitted.'[170] Overt hostility to the German Protestant position culminated in the statement that 'it is, therefore, impious to do as the Apology of the Germans professes and remove this absolution from the Church'.[171]

Though so explicit a rejection of Protestant doctrine was not repeated in subsequent drafts, an essentially orthodox position was retained. In all the remaining drafts it was maintained that in confession 'the priest has the power of absolving the person who confesses from all sins, including those which are usually called special cases'.[172] The assertion of the divine ordination of confession was also retained, though in a slightly different form: it was claimed that 'if there are some who condemn or reject confession, they are certainly neglecting and showing contempt for that which was instituted in God's word'.[173]

These forthright statements of orthodoxy did not pass unopposed. There is one draft which Cranmer went over, in which he clearly attempted to move the article towards a formulation which would be more in keeping with Protestant doctrine.[174] Where it was stated that confession is 'highly neces-

---

[168] BL, MS Cott. Cleo. E.v, fo. 127 [LP xiii/1, 1307.ix.2].

[169] 'Haec absolutio non modo retinenda est in ecclesia sed etiam eius usus necessarius est': BL, MS Cott. Cleo. E.v, fo. 127v [LP xiii/1, 1307.ix.2].

[170] 'Qui vero eam contemnit ecclesiae claves, qua dei ordinationem tradunt, contemnit. Hanc enim potestate suis ministris dedit ut que remiserint peccata, remissa sint': ibid.

[171] 'Est ergo impius hanc absolutionem tollere, ab ecclesia, ut germanorum apologia fatetur': ibid.

[172] PRO, SP 1/134, fos 7–11v [Miscellaneous writings of Cranmer, 475–7; LP xiii/1, 1307.i], 23–5 [LP xiii/1, 1307.ii]; BL, MS Royal 7.c.xvi, fos 195–7 [LP x. 585]; BL, MS Cott. Cleo. E.v, fos 123–5 [LP xiii/1, 1307.xi], 126 [Strype, Ecclesiastical memorials, i/1, 445–6; LP xiii/1, 1307.ix.1], 128–9 [Strype, Ecclesiastical memorials, i/2, 446–9; LP xiii/1, 1307.x]; PRO, SP 1/134, fos 29–32 [LP xiii/1, 1307.viii; Miscellaneous writings of Cranmer, 475–7, which indicates Cranmer's corrections]. The citation is from Miscellaneous writings of Cranmer, 476: 'sacerdos potestatem habet absolvendi confitentem ab omnibus peccatis, etiam illis qui soliti sunt vocari casus reservati'.

[173] 'Quod si qui sunt qui eam vel damnant, vel rejiciunt, hi profecto se et in verbo Dei institutionem . . . negligere et contemnere ostendunt': ibid. The citation is from the Miscellaneous writings of Cranmer, 477.

[174] PRO, SP 1/134, fos 29–32 [LP xiii/1, 1307.viii; Miscellaneous writings of Cranmer, 475–6].

sary', Cranmer suggested 'most advantageous'.[175] Where it was asserted that the ignorant cannot be advised and instructed anywhere 'more correctly or better than in confession', Cranmer proposed 'advantageously' in the place of 'correctly'. He then added the qualification, 'so long as they can find a learned and pious confessor'.[176] Where confession was described as 'useful and necessary', Cranmer suggested 'useful and advantageous'; a few sentences later he proposed an identical substitution.[177] Finally, in the margin, near to the place at which it was asserted that confession had been instituted in God's word, Cranmer observed that although confession might be retained in the Church, 'it is not a precept in scripture'.[178]

Cranmer was not alone in opposing sections of this article. In the German translation, the ambassadors indicated that they too had found much of it objectionable. Where it was claimed that confession has the virtue of encouraging a man to submit himself to another as if to God, the ambassadors inserted a bracket and wrote 'we did not agree with all this that is indicated by the line, since it comprehends a thing which in no writing is commanded by God'.[179] Where the scriptural authority of confession was maintained, the ambassadors were at one with Cranmer in claiming that confession might be kept in the Church, 'although it is not in the holy scriptures or instituted by Christ'. They went on to note that 'though the archbishop also wrote the same in his book, this remained unresolved, and was not entirely agreed'.[180] Where it was suggested that it is dangerous to refrain from confession, the ambassadors instead proposed that abstaining was merely ill-advised. Once more they added that although Cranmer 'also wrote the same in his book, with the others it again remained unagreed'.[181]

Very few of the suggestions made by Cranmer and the Germans figured in other drafts or in the final version, and those which did reappear were relatively innocuous; none of the substitutions of 'advantageous' for 'necessary'

---

175 '[S]umme necessariam'. Cranmer suggested 'commodissimam': PRO, SP 1/134, fo. 30 [LP xiii/1, 1307.viii; Miscellaneous writings of Cranmer, 476].
176 '[R]ectius'. Cranmer suggested 'commodius', and added, 'modo confessorem doctum et pium nacti fuerint': PRO, SP 1/134, fo. 30v [LP xiii/1, 1307.viii; Miscellaneous writings of Cranmer, 476].
177 '[U]tilis et necessaria'. Cranmer's alternative reading would have been 'utilis et commoda': PRO, SP 1/134, fo. 31 [LP xiii/1, 1307.viii; Miscellaneous writings of Cranmer, 476]. Cranmer proposed a similar alteration at fo. 31v.
178 '[N]on sit praecepta in scripturis sacris': PRO, SP 1/134, fo. 31v [LP xiii/1, 1307.viii; Miscellaneous writings of Cranmer, 477].
179 'Dises alles so seither es mit der linien bezeichnet haben wir nicht ainnen wollen. Den es uns zuvil deckt ein dingk das godt ihn keine schrifft gepoten': TStWei, Reg. H. 165, no. 78.ii, fo. 74.
180 '[W]iewol sie yhn gotliche schrifft nicht gepoten noch von Christo eyngesetzt . . . wiewol der Erzpischoff solchs yhn seyn puch auch geschrieben. Ists doch hangend blieben und nicht gentzlich vereyneget': ibid. fo. 74v.
181 '[S]olches yhn seyn puch auch geschrieben. So ist es gegen den anderen auch unverglichen hangend bleiben': ibid. fo. 75.

were retained, nor was the blunt denial of confession's scriptural authority repeated. The impression that a conclusion unsatisfactory from the reformed point of view was reached is reinforced by Martin Luther's comments on this article. He used more ink on this article than on any of the others. Where Cranmer had changed 'highly necessary' to 'most advantageous', Luther, with characteristic directness, simply drew a line through the former; further on he made a similar deletion to deny again the necessity of confession.[182] Finally, in the section which claimed that confession has the virtue of encouraging a man to submit himself to another as if to God, Luther scratched the entire argument out and in the margin wrote, 'not a whit'.[183]

Thus from the first phase of the discussions confession emerged as the most hotly disputed article, and the only one on which the Germans and their English supporters were defeated. Indeed, this may be why, when the Germans wrote to Henry in August, they singled it out for specific mention in their preamble as one of the foremost abuses in the Church.[184]

---

182 Ibid. fos 38, 40.
183 '[N]ihil': ibid. fo. 40.
184 Burnet, *History of the Reformation*, iv. 369. The isolation of confession as the principal point of dispute is the most significant result of the first phase of the discussions. In the nineteenth century H. Jenkyns found a draft from these discussions, entitled the 'Thirteen Articles', mistakenly thought it to be a theological agreement between the English and the Germans and speculated that it had been used as a source in drawing up the Edwardian Forty-two Articles and the Elizabethan Thirty-nine Articles: *The remains of Thomas Cranmer*, Oxford 1833, i, pp. xxiii–iv. His interpretation has been adopted by, among others, *DWA*, 15–16; Prüser, *England und die Schmalkaldener*, 134 n. 1; Rupp, *Studies*, 112, 117–18; Doernberg, *Henry VIII and Luther*, 114; Tjernagel, *Henry VIII and the Lutherans*, 184–9; *Documents of the English Reformation*, ed. G. Bray, Cambridge 1994, 184 (a collection which provides the first English translation of the points discussed in the first phase of the discussions). As with the Wittenberg articles, I think that any such evolutionary interpretation of the significance of these discussions for subsequent English formularies is best avoided; those Lutheran aspects of Jenkyns's Thirteen Articles which 'reappeared' in 1553 and 1562 were, like those of the Wittenberg articles which 'reappeared' in 1536 and 1537, more likely to have come from the great German confessional statements of the early 1530s than from the Anglo-Schmalkaldic theological discussions of 1536 and 1538. It should be emphasised that there was nothing unique to those Anglo-Schmalkaldic discussions which was transmitted to any English formulary of the faith; moreover the enumeration of thirteen articles is misleading. The final copy of the 1538 articles in the Weimar archives shows that in fact seventeen articles were discussed, and that these did not have the character of an agreement (there is not a single document with a signature upon it), but of a summary of the discussions, which would provide a basis from which the subsequent embassy from the League would hammer out a final agreement on the faith.

Second phase: the king, the bishop and the Apology, July–September 1538

The second phase of the discussions was concerned with an examination of the doctrine contained in the Apology, otherwise known as the abuses. Henry's doubts about Lutheran doctrine on the abuses had been signalled at Wittenberg in 1536, when Edward Foxe's delegation refused to accept the formulation of articles offered to them on private masses, communion in one kind only, priestly marriage and monastic vows. John Frederick had specifically instructed his ambassadors to attempt to reach a settlement with the king on those questions which had caused difficulty in the second part of the 1536 discussions. If Henry could not be brought to an agreement on these points, then the ambassadors should at least discuss them with him in preparation for the major embassy which would follow to conclude an alliance between the League and England.[185]

As the first phase of the discussions entered its closing stages, however, obstacles to opening a similarly thoroughgoing second round of talks on the abuses began to emerge. It was a question of time. The first phase had taken much longer than Cromwell had led the ambassadors to expect; as the embassy entered its third month in England the Germans' thoughts began gradually to shift away from the importance of the task facing them and increasingly towards the prospect of a return home. Burchard wrote to John Frederick on 27 July that although the ambassadors had been delayed by the theological discussions, they hoped to be able to return to Germany in three weeks, on the next available sailing to Hamburg. He spoke optimistically of the course of the talks, reported the continuing attack on shrines, and predicted that an agreement between England and the League would be forthcoming.[186]

Burchard made no mention of how the ambassadors expected to discuss the abuses before that next sailing. Nevertheless, it would seem that as the first phase of the discussions dragged slowly towards a conclusion the ambassadors took steps to avoid similarly protracted talks on the abuses. They decided to sidestep further oral discourse altogether. Instead, they would execute their commission by writing a letter to Henry on the abuses, recommending that he and his theologians discuss the views contained therein. This letter, completed on 5 August,[187] was sent with a covering note to

---

185 Mentz, *Johann Friedrich*, iii. 376–83.
186 HStMar, PA 2575, fos 131–2 (copy sent enclosed with John Frederick to Philip, 30 Aug., fo. 130). In relation to the shrines, he noted that Henry had agreed 'to remove the greatest shrine in England, called Maria Parathalassia [i.e. Our Lady of Walsingham], of which Erasmus of Rotterdam has also written' ('konig. Mait. die groste walfahrt in Engellandt Maria Paratalassia genant davon auch Erassmus Roterdamus geschrieben abschaffen': fo. 131v).
187 TStWei, Reg. H. 165, no. 78 i, fos 122–3 (early draft of opening section), 124–60 (draft); BL, MS Cott. Cleo. E.v. fos 186–221 (final version) [Burnet, *History of the Reforma-*

Cromwell, asking him to promote it with the king so that they could leave in two weeks time.[188]

Henry's response was greatly influenced by the circumstances of his court at the time. The court was away from London on the summer progress, which this year was much more peripatetic than usual. The French ambassador noted in mid-June that Henry had decided to spend the summer inspecting his southern ports,[189] and, in addition, he appears to have spent time variously hunting and visiting shrines earmarked for disposal; between 13 July and 24 September he stayed at at least thirty different places. Such constant movement was very disruptive to government. Even though the more normal, leisurely progresses, changing location every week or so, were themselves fairly disturbing, three or four days would usually be sufficient to re-establish the political and administrative lines of communication to the capital. During the summer of 1538, however, links with London were severed completely and Henry and his court became even more isolated than was usual during the progress time.

The significance of this for the German letter of 5 August is simple: there was only one theological counsellor available to the king to give advice on how to respond to the Germans, and that man was none other than the conservative bishop of Durham, Cuthbert Tunstall. Three weeks before the progress had set off, Tunstall had been ordered to discharge himself from the presidency of the council of the north and come to court on what appears to have been a temporary secondment.[190] When, however, the letter on the abuses arrived at court, Henry decided to extend his temporary posting, so that Tunstall could function as his adviser in drawing up a reply. Hence the king wrote to the council of the north to appoint a new president, explaining that

> for certain purposes of greate importance wherin we thought convenient to use the counsail of the right Reverand father in god our right trusty and right welbiloved counsailor the bisshop of Duresme, we did lately call the same unto us, being sithens his arryval mynded to contynue his demore here about our personne.[191]

And use Tunstall in replying to the Germans he most certainly did. As one of Tunstall's chaplains would relate the following year, 'the servanntes that went

---

tion, iv. 352–72; LP xiii/2, 37]. In the following analysis the German letter on the abuses will be cited according to the page references in Burnet, *History of the Reformation*.

188 LP xiii/2, 38.

189 LP xiii/1, 1405.

190 On 27 June Tunstall wrote to Cromwell, saying that he was coming to join the king forthwith as directed: PRO, SP 1/133, fos 211–12 [StP v. 128–9; LP xiii/1, 1267].

191 PRO, SP 1/133, fo. 213 [StP v. 129; LP xiii/1, 1268].

last yere but this with my lord told me that the kynges majestie dyd call upon my lorde many tymes and talke with hym on the way'.[192]

This was a great opportunity for the upholders of orthodoxy. Since 1535 Henry had shown himself to be suspicious of Lutheran doctrine on the abuses. Now he had to pass judgement on that doctrine, not in the context of the two-sided colloquy that he had sought, but in an isolated court where his sole theological counsel was a conservative bishop. Certainly, the king should not be seen as the passive or manipulated party. The evidence suggests that it was Henry who chose Tunstall as his adviser: he could just as easily have selected a theologian of reformed views – or indeed one from the more conservative wing of the episcopate. As with the first phase of the discussions, Henry appears to have wanted a genuinely moderate examination of Lutheran doctrine. Still, the isolation of the court was not good for the evangelicals: over the next few weeks there would be no possibility of introducing into the deliberations alternative voices that might mollify the king's pre-existing concerns about the abuses. Moreover the man whom Henry had chosen to help him with the reply to the Germans had distinctive characteristics. Tunstall was no crude fanatic who, like some of the conservative bishops, might present an easy target for harassment. Bright and subtle, a highly educated humanist, he knew Lutheranism inside out, from his personal atten-dance at the celebrated confrontation between Luther and Charles V at Worms in 1521 to his efforts in identifying and restricting Lutheran influ-ences in England during the 1520s.[193] Now he had six weeks before the court returned to London, alone with the theological mind of the king. It was not long, but it was to be enough. For as the court made its way around southern England during August and September, Henry and Tunstall closeted them-selves away in deep theological deliberations; and as the results of their labours inched into the light of day, it became increasingly clear that Tunstall had used their time together to very good effect.[194]

---

[192] PRO, SP 1/155, fo. 199 [LP xiv/2, 750 iii].

[193] C. Sturge says nothing on the role Tunstall played as the king's theological adviser during the summer progress of 1538, although he provides some useful material on Tunstall's earlier career: *Cuthbert Tunstall*, London 1938, 213–14.

[194] Though the progress was unusually itinerant, it should not be thought that the court was a small one. Indeed, a report by Chapuys and Mendoza (*LP* xiii/2, 232), who attended an audience with the king about Arundel on 21 August, suggests the reverse. They noted that Tunstall, Cromwell, Derby, Dorset, Wiltshire, Wallop and Carew were in attendance. Apart from Tunstall and Cromwell, court theologian and minister respectively, Derby and Dorset were non-office holding nobles, Wiltshire and Wallop were councillors, and Carew was a councillor and a member of the privy chamber. The main point about the court at this time, however, is not its size but the fact that its highly itinerant nature made it an even more isolated political world than usual, and thus Tunstall was able to dominate the flow of theo-logical advice to the king. Had the court been less peripatetic, or nearer London, Cromwell might have been able to bring alternative influences, such as Cranmer or Latimer, to bear upon the king; with the court cut off from the wider political world, however, he had little choice but to stand back and let Tunstall do what he would.

The Germans' letter was based on essays on three of the abuses. Missing was a discussion of monastic vows. Why the ambassadors did not follow John Frederick's specific instructions and discuss them too is not stated in the evidence, but a plausible explanation can be offered. It is simply likely that the ambassadors had seen during the two months they had spent in England that the dissolution of the English monasteries was so advanced that any discussion on monastic vows could only be superfluous; that its inclusion in the letter to Henry would be an unnecessary complication.[195]

Henry's reply to the Germans was likewise based on three essays, though on the question of priestly marriage he expanded the scope considerably so as to deal also with the importance of keeping vows made to God, a subject which the Germans had avoided by excluding monastic vows. The methodology employed in composing the reply shows how seriously Henry took the questions raised by the Germans. He had Tunstall prepare a summary of the original letter;[196] he had pertinent scriptural and patristic sources adduced and commentaries on them drawn up which he examined and commented upon;[197] on at least one occasion he made notes in preparation for drafting;[198] and, assisted by Tunstall, he corrected many of the drafts personally.[199] The resulting document was no indiscriminate side swipe at Lutheranism, but was the result of deliberate and careful royal consideration.[200]

The first head which the Germans discussed was communion in both kinds. They developed their argument along two broad lines. The first dealt with scriptural authority for giving communion thus, while the second discussed the historical and contemporary examples of Churches which followed this practice.[201]

There was a wide-ranging preliminary analysis of the question by Henry and Tunstall. The extant opinions probably represent only a fraction of the papers produced during the initial consultation stage, and of these a number were modified or even dropped altogether in the drafting process. For example, an anecdote from Eusebius' history of the Church, concerning a sick man who was only able to receive the eucharist in one kind, was not repeated verbatim in any of the drafts, but it bore a strong conceptual similarity to an

195 A similar point is made by Prüser, *England und die Schmalkaldener*, 135.
196 BL, MS Cott. Cleo. E.v, fos 222–4 [*LP* xiii/2, 37.ii]. This was 'reabridged' in an anonymous hand at BL, MS Cott. Cleo. E.v, fo. 266 [*LP* xiii/2, 37.iii].
197 PRO, SP 1/135, fos 157–77 [*LP* xiii/2, 166.i–iii]; BL, MS Cott. Cleo. E.v, fos 167–70 [*LP* xiii/1, 1307.xx], 174–7 [*LP* xiii/1, 1307.xxii]; PRO, SP 1/134, fos 41–5 [*LP* xiii/1, 1307.xvi; *Miscellaneous writings of Cranmer*, 480–2].
198 BL, MS Cott. Cleo. E.v, fo. 133 [no *LP* ref.; Strype, *Ecclesiastical memorials*, i/2, 392].
199 PRO, SP 1/135, fos 151–6 [*LP* xiii/2, 165.iii], 178–91 [*LP* xiii/2, 166.iv]; BL, MS Cott. Cleo. E.v, fos 151–60 [no *LP* ref.], 144–50 [*LP* xiii/2, 165.ii]; CCCC, MS 109, fos 7–57 [no *LP* ref.].
200 BL, MS Cott. Cleo. E.v, fos 228–38 [Burnet, *History of the Reformation*, iv. 373–91]. Unless otherwise noted, this letter will be cited according to the Burnet page references for the remainder of this section.
201 Burnet, *History of the Reformation*, iv. 354–5.

argument which would later emerge: that the German demand that all Christians must receive both kinds of the sacrament was unfair to those who are physically unable to do so.[202] Similarly, a citation from Ambrose, which related the story of his brother Satyrus, who communicated by wrapping a napkin with bread in it around his neck, may have provided the basis for the later claim that it is permissible to communicate spiritually, without actually consuming the bread or the wine.[203]

Other papers were more directly related to the early drafting process. One piece, lavishly studded with 'note well' from Henry's pen, discussed Old Testament examples of Jewish equivalents for communicating with bread alone,[204] while another discussed – in a paper largely concerned with the private mass – the experience of the biblical travellers to Emmaeus, whom Luke described as having been given bread only by Christ.[205] These two themes were incorporated into a larger paper, which added a discussion of the main biblical commentary on the Last Supper (1 Corinthians x, xi) and a citation from Acts which described a fellowship of believers whose religious activities included the breaking of bread alone.[206]

In what appears to have been the first draft, the examples from the Old Testament were dropped and the discussion of Corinthians heavily modified, but the commentary on Luke was followed closely and the citation from Acts was repeated verbatim. This draft was written in an anonymous clerical hand and was corrected by Tunstall.[207] Its structure was not duplicated in the second draft, but its main arguments and authorities were reordered, repeated and developed. Henry took a liberal helping of ink to the second draft, crossing out and rewriting much of the introductory section, and correcting and adding to the following folios. Tunstall worked with him on this draft, providing additional corrections and criticism.[208] A third draft incorporated these corrections and additions, and was the subject of further revision and development at the hands of both men.[209] These were then incorporated into an expanded fourth draft,[210] which in turn was repeated verbatim in the relevant section of the reply to the Germans.[211]

The finished product began by refuting the German claim that Scripture

---

202 PRO, SP 1/135, fo. 158 [LP xiii/2, 166.i]. The authority was Eusebius' *Ecclesiastica historia* vi.44 (not ch. 34, as the opinion has it).
203 PRO, SP 1/135, fo. 158v [LP xiii/2, 166.i]. The authority was Ambrose's *De obitu Satyri fratris*.
204 PRO, SP 1/135, fo. 167v [LP xiii/2, 166.i].
205 PRO, SP 1/135, fo. 168v [LP xiii/2, 166.i]. The discussion was based on Luke xxiv.13–35.
206 PRO, SP 1/135, fos 176–7 [LP xiii/2, 166.iii]. The citation was from Acts ii.42–7.
207 BL, MS Cott. Cleo. E.v, fos 151–60 [no LP ref.].
208 PRO, SP 1/135, fos 151–6 [LP xiii/2, 165.iii].
209 CCCC, MS 109, fos 3–21 [no LP ref.].
210 BL, MS Cott. Cleo. E.v, fos 144–50 [LP xiii/2, 165.ii].
211 BL, MS Cott. Cleo. E.v, fos 228v–31v [LP xiii/2, 165.i].

gave no authority for providing communion in one kind, citing Luke and Acts. Henry then sought exegetically to prove both that at mass the elements could be dispensed separately, and that in spite of this separation either the bread or the wine alone would still contain the complete body and blood of Christ. To demonstrate separation, two verses from 1 Corinthians were analysed. On the one hand, it was noted that at the last supper Christ 'took bread, and when he had given thanks he broke it and said, "this is my body, which is for you; do this in remembrance of me" '.[212] On the other hand, when giving the wine Christ said, ' "do this, whenever you drink, in remembrance of me" ';[213] the additional words 'whenever you drink', it was argued, indicated both that the wine could be taken separately from the bread, and that an element of choice over its use had been ordained by Christ.[214] To demonstrate that following consecration the bread or the wine alone still contains Christ's entire body and blood, the verbal hair-splitting was taken a step further. The following passage, from the same chapter of Corinthians, was cited as evidence: 'whoever eats the bread or drinks the cup of the Lord in an unworthy manner will be guilty of sinning against the body and blood of the Lord'. This passage, it was argued, proved the totality of Christ's presence in either the bread or the wine alone because the conjunction which linked the unconsecrated elements was disjunctive, whereas that which linked them following consecration was copulative; if one could, say, unworthily eat the bread alone and still be guilty of both Christ's body and his blood, then it followed that one could eat it worthily and rejoice in both parts of the Lord.[215]

Having thus discussed the scriptural basis for communion in only one kind, Henry moved on to consider the German claim that the scriptural injunction that all should drink from the chalice must be taken literally; that offering the sacrament in both kinds was not a matter indifferent, but a divine ordination which could not be altered.[216] Henry set out to defend the Christian's freedom to choose whether he take communion in one or both kinds. He corrected the second draft himself so that it stated that while communicating in both kinds was not contrary to God's word, neither was communicating in one.[217] In the third draft he personally developed this further, writing in his own hand an inventive and even enlightened note which proposed that there were in fact four permissible ways of communicating.[218]

---

212 1 Cor. xi.23–4.
213 1 Cor. xi.25 (my italics).
214 Burnet, *History of the Reformation*, iv. 375–6. This distinction was sharpened through Tunstall's insertion in the third draft: CCCC, MS 109, fo. 9v [no LP ref.].
215 1 Cor. xi.27 (my italics); Burnet, *History of the Reformation*, iv. 376–7.
216 Burnet, *History of the Reformation*, iv. 354.
217 PRO, SP 1/135, fos 152–6 [LP xiii/2, 165.iii]. Henry inserted the words '[non] verbo dei adversetur'.
218 CCCC, MS 109, fo. 13. This note was the work of Henry alone; Tunstall made but a few additions when Henry presented it to him for discussion and checking. The note forced the

The first was communicating in both kinds: a layman might take this if his piety was judged sufficient, his mental state competent and his motives not disruptive of the Church. The second and third were bread or wine only; if impediments of nature or tradition barred the person from taking both kinds, then one kind should suffice. The fourth posited a spiritual form of communicating for those who for physical reasons could not keep the sacrament in their stomach; they should at least be shown the sacrament, so that the memory of Christ's sacrifice could be communicated spiritually.[219] Turning on the Germans, Henry asked why those who championed Christian liberty as they did would not allow men the freedom to choose how the sacrament be communicated. His defence of Christian liberty and the sufficiency of one kind was crowned by an attack on the injustice of the German position for people who, for climatic reasons, have restricted access to wine, such as those who inhabit the northern regions, or Africa and the tropics: are these people, he asked, 'not able under one kind to partake of the full body of Christ?' Tunstall scribbled onto the end of the second draft his judgement of this proposition: 'that would be reprehensible'.[220]

Finally, Henry dealt briefly with the patristic and contemporary practices which the Germans had cited in defence of taking the eucharist in both kinds. He acknowledged that the custom had been followed in the patristic age, but asserted that it had been abandoned and Christ's legacy of Christian freedom adopted so that the Church began to administer the sacrament in one kind only. As to the Germans' argument, that the practice of the orthodox Greek Church should be followed as a laudable contemporary example, Henry dismissed it with the observation that although the Greeks had long been free from the Roman tyranny, they had been even longer under that of the Turks, and their Church had in consequence a limited degree of Christian liberty.[221]

The longest of the essays the Germans sent Henry was that on the private mass. This rambling and ill-structured piece, punctuated with overdone populist attacks on the papacy, contained the same three essential points as the corresponding unagreed article of 1536: first, that the mass had been

---

introduction of a new folio of text to elaborate the four-way distinction he had insisted upon (fo. 17). Henry further checked this new folio and made a number of corrections to it. His note and the new folio were directly inserted into the text of the fourth draft in an anonymous clerical hand and thence were put into the final copy.

[219] Henry may have developed this interesting fourth alternative from a reading or discussion with Tunstall of Ambrose's *De obitu Satyri fratris* (cf. n. 203), which described an instance of communicating when the eucharist was not consumed: PRO, SP 1/135, fo. 158v [*LP* xiii/2, 166.i]. The principle is also briefly mentioned in a note at fos 172–4 [*LP* xiii/2, 166.ii].

[220] '[S]ub una non integrum Christum capere possent?': Burnet, *History of the Reformation*, iv. 379. Tunstall's addition ('[I]d quod absit') to SP 1/135, fo. 155, figured in the third and fourth drafts, and in the final copy.

[221] Burnet, *History of the Reformation*, iv. 379–80.

corrupted by the Roman views that mere acceptance of the sacrament *ex opere operato* confers grace and that one can apply in this way for the remission of the sins of others; second, that the mass does not involve offering a sacrifice to God; third, that the mass should be corporate and celebrated on appointed days.[222]

All the extant papers on this issue followed lines appropriate to the king's conservative views. A number did not get much further than the initial drafting stage. These included an Augustinian commentary on the difference between Old Testament sacrifice of animals and the concept of the sacrificial mass in the New Testament,[223] a number of writings by Augustine amd Jerome on Melchizedek and the eucharistic sacrifice,[224] and a piece by Chrysostom on the mystery of the mass.[225] Though these papers figured initially in the drafting process,[226] they were excluded subsequently. The most notable of the exclusions was a draft paper entitled 'In the mass prayers are made on behalf of the living and the dead'. This very orthodox piece carried Henry's marginal observation, 'note: on behalf of the dead'.[227] Yet in spite of his approbation and the fact that the paper was developed in the first draft and approved by Henry again, it did not appear thereafter.[228] There are a number of possible reasons for this. It may be that Henry realised that its inclusion would constitute so uncompromising a rejection of one of the most important Lutheran tenets that any chance of finding common ground with the League would be lost. Alternatively, it may have been noted that arguing in favour of prayers for the dead would would not sit well with the wholesale destruction of intercessory institutions in the dissolution of the monasteries. Or, it might have been pointed out to Henry that pronouncing in favour of prayers for the dead would rest uneasily with the assertion that they were of doubtful scriptural authority in the sections on purgatory in the Ten Articles and Bishops' Book.

The first extant draft, featuring a number of corrections and additions in Henry's hand, included all these questions.[229] For no obvious reason they all failed to appear in the second extant draft, even though a number of other passages and authorities from the first draft were repeated. The second draft appears to have been produced fairly late in the composition process. There are no major corrections and the text is almost exactly the same as the final

---

222   Ibid. iv. 355–65.
223   PRO, SP 1/135, fo. 159 [*LP* xiii/2, 166.i].
224   PRO, SP 1/135, fo. 160 [*LP* xiii/2, 166.i].
225   PRO, SP 1/135, fos 160v–1 [*LP* xiii/2, 166.i].
226   PRO, SP 1/135, fos 178–91 [*LP* xiii/2, 166.iv].
227   This was entitled: 'In missa pro omnibus oratur tum vivis tum defunctis'. Henry's marginal comment reads 'Nota pro defunctis [sic]': PRO, SP 1/135, fo. 161 [*LP* xiii/2, 166.i].
228   PRO, SP 1/135, fos 189–90 [*LP* xiii/2, 166.iv].
229   PRO, SP 1/135, fos 178–91 [*LP* xiii/2, 166.iv].

version.[230] It was probably from the second draft that the relevant section of the reply given to the Germans was directly copied.[231]

Though Henry ultimately chose to ignore the argument against prayers for the dead which the Germans had set down in their letter, the response he put in its place must have been infuriating for them none the less. The opinion was based on a paper[232] which, in conjunction with the relative section in the first draft,[233] was largely repeated verbatim in the second draft and final copy.[234] It was uncomplicated: Henry simply asserted that all masses, whether public or private, must necessarily contain those very things which the Germans villified, and that to argue for abolishing one would be to imply the same for the other. Assuming the private mass was carried out properly, Henry wanted the Germans to explain what it was that diffentiated it from the public mass. After all, 'at the beginning of every private mass is a general confession by the public of all sins; pardon is asked of God and absolution is imparted by the priest in accordance with God's word, just as in the public mass'.[235]

Henry then moved on to express his amazement at the Germans' aversion to the idea that when taking communion the recipient is actually offering a sacrifice to God. He dropped the arguments which had been adduced from the Old Testament (which he had approved) and sidestepped the standard Roman explanation of this doctrine (that the priest is offering, in Christ's name, Christ as a sacrifice to the father). Perhaps building on a related work by Chrysostom which he had approved at several points,[236] Henry used an argument which in the first draft he marked approvingly and which was for the most part repeated verbatim in the second draft and the final copy.[237] It proceeded on the basis of an idea which seems less a triumph of ingenuity – as the Catholic historian Philip Hughes appeared to regard it[238] – than a suspiciously syllogistic Henricianism: namely, that in the sacrament is the body and blood of Christ; Christ was sacrificed for our sins; ergo in the sacrament is the sacrifice of which the church Fathers speak. Why then, asked Henry, should the Germans dispute this? It was, surely, only for this reason that the

---

230 CCCC, MS 109, fos 27–39 [no *LP* ref.].
231 BL, MS Cott. Cleo. E.v, fos 231v–4v [*LP* xiii/2, 165.i].
232 PRO, SP 1/135, fo. 168 [*LP* xiii/2, 166.i].
233 PRO, SP 1/135, fos 187–8 [*LP* xiii/2, 166.iv].
234 For the second draft see CCCC, MS 109, fos 27–39 [no *LP* ref.]; for the final version see Burnet, *History of the Reformation*, iv. 380–1.
235 '[I]n exordio omnis missae privatae publica sit peccatorum omnium generalis confessio; venia postulatur a Deo, absolutio impartitur a sacerdote secundum Dei verbum, quemadmodum in missa publica': Burnet, *History of the Reformation*, iv. 380–1 (quotation at p. 381). It is verbatim in the draft: PRO, SP 1/135, fos 187r–v [*LP* xiii/2, 166.iv].
236 PRO, SP 1/135, fo. 162 [*LP* xiii/2, 166.i].
237 PRO, SP 1/135, fos 181v–2 [*LP* xiii/2, 166.iv]. For the second draft see CCCC, MS 109, fos 27–39 [no *LP* reference]; for the final version see Burnet, *History of the Reformation*, iv. 383.
238 Hughes, *Reformation in England*, i. 358–60.

ancient writers such as Basil, Chrysostom, Jerome and Augustine had called the mass a sacrifice; 'since there is Christ our sacrifice in the sacrament'.[239]

Much of the second draft and the final copy was occupied with the third point which the Germans had advocated: that the mass should be celebrated publicly, at regular times every week (rather, it would seem, than privately several times daily) and in the vernacular.[240] The latter issue was ignored completely, but the first two certainly concerned a king whose fondness for repeated daily masses was well known. The Germans had cited the current practices of the orthodox Church, but once again Henry was dismissive of eastern practices, retorting that in Greece, 'where you assert there is one public mass every Sunday, very rarely does anybody communicate in the sacrament, as we have learned from worthy confidants, who themselves attended the worship of the Greeks'.[241]

On the question of how often the mass should be celebrated Henry suspected that the Germans had selected the rules to suit themselves. Here again the question of a Christian's liberty of choice was raised. If the Germans should be allowed to choose to have less frequent masses, why should not others be free to celebrate more frequently?

Indeed you cite Epiphanius, who asserted that in Asia the mass is celebrated three times every week, and that this custom was introduced by the apostles. But now in Greece the people go to worship only every Sunday; if it is thus possible to change there from the tradition introduced by the apostles, so that the people congregate more rarely than the apostles arranged, why is it not also possible to change so that the people meet more often, whereby the memory of Christ's death will more frequently be celebrated?[242]

The third issue which the Germans raised in their letter to Henry concerned priestly marriage.[243] The only evidence which affords clues as to the composition of the English reply are a series of patristic authorities which Henry

---

239 '[Q]uod ibi sit Christus sacrificium nostrum in sacramento': Burnet, *History of the Reformation*, iv. 383. It is verbatim in the draft: PRO, SP 1/135, fo. 182 [*LP* xiii/2, 166.iv].
240 For the second draft see CCCC, MS 109, fos 27–39 [no *LP* reference]; for the final version see Burnet, *History of the Reformation*, iv. 356–9.
241 '[U]bi singulis Dominicis diebus fit missa publica uti asseritis, raro admodum communicat in esu sacramenti quisquam e populo, uti a fide dignis accepimus, qui ipsi Graecorum sacris interfuerunt': Burnet, *History of the Reformation*, iv. 381 (German citation of Greek practice at iv. 357–8).
242 'Quod vero Epiphanium citatis qui singulis septimanis ter celebratam synaxim in Asia asserit, eumque morem ab apostolis inductum, cum jam tantum in Graecia singulis Dominicis fiat populi conventus ad sacra, si mutari mos potuit ab apostolis inductus, ut rarius quam statuerunt apostoli populus congregaretur, cur non etiam mutari potuit ut saepius conveniret, quando per hoc celebrior fit mortis Christi memoria': Burnet, *History of the Reformation*, iv. 381. MacCulloch points out that this reference to the Orthodox Church probably originated in Tunstall's interest in the Greek Church: *Cranmer*, 220.
243 Burnet, *History of the Reformation*, iv. 365–9.

examined and approved,[244] and a note in Henry's handwriting, apparently drawn up in preparation for drafting, containing scriptural citations.[245] Almost all this pre-drafting material figures in the only extant draft, which also features a number of corrections in Tunstall's hand.[246] The text and corrections of the draft are substantially the same as the final version, and it is probable that it was the draft from which the final version of the reply to the Germans was drawn.[247] Two concerns were addressed in the pre-draft notes and in the draft and final copy, the main issue of priestly marriage and the subsidiary one of keeping vows made to God.

Most of the patristic sources dealt with priestly marriage. Writings from Chrysostom, Theophilactus, and Jerome on Matthew xix were marked approvingly by Henry,[248] and though they were not repeated in the final copy, they must have formed the backbone of the sources consulted for the discussion of Matthew in the reply sent to the Germans. A citation from Origen, though approved by Henry, appears to have been dropped in the drafting process.[249] Henry's own holograph note contained scriptural citations from 1 and 2 Timothy and 1 Corinthians, all of which were either developed or repeated verbatim in the final copy. He also included a brief description of the priesthood, and mentioned that Chrysostom, Athanasius and Jerome agreed that marriage was a purely secular affair.[250]

In the draft and the final copy Henry dealt directly with the German assertion that Scripture does not forbid priests from marrying. Leaning on the patristic sources which had been prepared on Matthew xix, he cited the evidence of the three eunuchs, the third of whom Christ described as having assumed that state for the kingdom of heaven.[251] It was argued that those who, like the third eunuch, can assume the celibate office of priest are invited to do so by the words 'he who is able to receive it, let him receive it'.[252] By these words Christ invites only those who are suitable for the celibate life; those who consider the invitation must examine themselves carefully, for though Christ gives them a choice about whether to enter the priesthood, he

---

244 PRO, SP 1/135, fos 163–5 [LP xiii/2, 166.i].
245 BL, MS Cott. Cleo. E.v, fo. 133 [LP xiv/1, 1068.i; Strype, *Ecclesiastical memorials*, i/2, 392]. Scarisbrick, *Henry VIII*, 418, and *LP* associate this with the parliamentary discussions on the Act of Six Articles. The correlation between its arguments and authorities and those in the reply to the Germans, however, show that is was written for the reply to the Germans in August and September 1538 during the summer progress.
246 CCCC, MS 109, fos 41–55v [no *LP* ref.].
247 BL, MS Cott. Cleo. E.v, fos 234v–8 [LP xiii/2, 165.i].
248 PRO, SP 1/135, fos 163–4 [LP xiii/2, 166.i].
249 PRO, SP 1/135, fo. 165 [LP xiii/2, 166.i].
250 BL, MS Cott. Cleo. E.v, fo. 133 [LP viv/1, 1068.i; Strype, *Ecclesiastical memorials*, i/2, 392].
251 Matt. xix.12.
252 Ibid.

gives them no choice about revoking its conditions once they have entered.[253]

The patristic and historical sources cited by the Germans in support of priestly marriage were refuted point for point by Henry. Priests had become celibate after the examples of Paul and Timothy, he claimed, and, contrary to the German argument concerning the early councils, those of Nicaea and Chalcedon had endorsed the practice.[254]

Henry ignored the German contention that prohibiting priests from marrying will only inflame their lust.[255] Instead, he suggested that just as the sacerdotal vocation makes such demands that a priest would be unable to be a proper husband, so does marriage distract the priest from his profoundly important office. In his preliminary notes Henry had quoted a passage from 2 Timothy, and this was one of a number of scriptural authorities which were cited along with exegetical commentaries from Augustine, Jerome and Cyprian in support of the view that the priesthood required so much of a man that it could not possibly be combined with the duties of married life.[256]

The subsidiary element in the article on priestly marriage was that of keeping vows made to God. The title of one patristic source (Ambrose) examined and approved by Henry summed the question up: 'After vows of celibacy one is not allowed to marry.'[257] Henry's interest in this question was confirmed by a note he made on vows in his pre-drafting paper: 'A description of a vow: it is a vow of something good; with deliberation, a promise made to God.'[258]

In the draft and final version this concern emerged in a passage which argued that vows of continency, once made to God, must not be broken. Evidence was cited from 1 Timothy, showing that widows who broke their vows to God were damned.[259] Of the half dozen scriptural authorities which were trotted out to show that 'God's word itself openly opposes everywhere the breaking of vows',[260] that from Numbers was typical: 'When a man makes a vow to the Lord or takes an oath to bind himself by a pledge, he must not

---

253 Burnet, History of the Reformation, iv. 384–5. The draft discussion based on Matt. xix is in PRO, SP 1/135, fos 163–4 [LP xiii/2, 166.i].

254 For the German evidence see Burnet, History of the Reformation, iv. 366–7. Henry's response is at pp. 386–7.

255 Ibid. iv. 368.

256 Ibid. iv. 388–9. In his preliminary notes, Henry cited 2 Tim. iii.4, which was repeated in the final version: BL, MS Cott. Cleo. E.v, fo. 133 [LP xiv/1, 1068.i; Strype, Ecclesiastical memorials, i/2, 392; repeated in Burnet, History of the Reformation, iv. 388].

257 'Post votum celibatus non licet nubere': PRO, SP 1/135, fo. 165 [LP xiii/2, 166.i].

258 'Descriptio voti. Est autem votum alicujus boni, cum deliberatione, Deo facta promissio': BL, MS Cott. Cleo. E.v, fo. 133 [LP xiv/1, 1068.i; Strype, Ecclesiastical memorials, i/2, 392].

259 1 Tim. v.11–12; Burnet, History of the Reformation, iv. 386.

260 'Verbum ipsum Dei palam adversatur ubique ne rumpantur vota': Burnet, History of the Reformation, iv. 386.

break his word but must do everything he said.'[261] Augustine and Jerome provided the patristic ammunition: Augustine's commentary on Psalm lxxv was cited in support of the view that 'a vow once made must be served',[262] while Jerome was quoted as saying 'a virgin who is sworn to God will be damned if he marries'.[263] It should be pointed out that in the reply to the Germans no explicit statement was made to the effect that vows of celibacy made to God must be kept. But in preparing this aspect of the essay on priestly marriage Henry had clearly been brought to the point at which effecting that mental leap would be but a sensible and logical development.

Third phase: the embassy departs, August–October 1538

The brief third phase of the Anglo-Schmalkaldic discussions began while Henry and Tunstall were still in the country on the summer progress, labouring over their systematic rejection of Lutheran doctrine on the abuses. It took place largely at the instigation of Cromwell and Cranmer. On 18 August Cranmer replied to a letter from Cromwell which the minister had sent him three days earlier.[264] Cranmer said that in accordance with Cromwell's letter he had asked the Germans to wait until the king returned to London before they set off back to Germany. He had told them that 'thair tarying should grow unto some good successe concernyng the poyntes of thair commission, whiche I moche put theym in hope of on your bihalf'.[265] It would appear that Cromwell had begun to get an idea of the way in which the deliberations of Henry and Tunstall were moving, and wanted the Germans to remain in England so as to keep alive the possibility of achieving something with face-to-face discussions when the court arrived back in London. However, the Germans were reluctant to remain in England any longer.

As Boineburg wrote to Germany on 22 August, he had told Cranmer that he was not sure whether they had powers 'to wait so long on these matters, especially in view of the fact that your graces intend to send another embassy next spring, which will have powers to discuss everything, and to conclude'.[266] But Cranmer, he said, had been persistent, asking the ambassadors 'to stay on another month, and for us to negotiate with the gathered bishops and other learned men on the abuses, such as the mass, the sacrament

---

261 Num. xxx.2; Burnet, *History of the Reformation*, iv. 386.
262 '[V]otum semel emissum servandum esse': Burnet, *History of the Reformation*, iv. 386.
263 '[V]irgo quae se Deo dicavit, si nubat, damnationem habet': ibid. iv. 386.
264 Cromwell's letter is not extant, but he was with the king at Arundel at this time: *LP* xiii/2, 151. Its date is given in Cranmer's reply.
265 PRO, SP 1/135, fo. 116 [*StP* i. 580; *LP* xiii/2, 126].
266 '[D]ise dinge so ferr abzuwarten, in sonderlicher ansehung, das ew. c. u. f. g. ein andere botschaft auf den kunftigen lenzen zu schicken bedacht, wilche allenthalben zu handeln, auch zu schliessen bevelch haben wurden': Prüser, *England und die Schmalkaldener*, 321.

in both kinds, priestly marriage and monastic vows'.[267] He had also told them that the king had impounded the ship in which they wished to go home (so that by remaining, presumably, they would not lose their passage), and that if they stayed they would be very likely to gain the answer they wanted from Henry. This last point was especially persuasive: Cranmer wanted 'us also for this purpose, so that we would get a good satisfactory answer from the king'.[268]

A letter of 23 August from Burchard to John Frederick provides additional detail on the pressure which the evangelical faction was putting on the ambassadors. Cranmer had asked the Germans 'to consider the many thousands of souls in England' who might be saved by their remaining an extra month.[269] In a desperate gamble, Cromwell, who appears to have commuted between the progress and London at this time, went so far as to tell the Germans that not only was Henry largely in agreement with most aspects of the Confession of Augsburg, but that as a result of his consideration of the particular questions from the Apology which the ambassadors had raised with him he was about to accept reformed doctrine on the abuses – indeed, he already had accepted that doctrine to some extent:

> lord Cromwell assured us most highly and showed us that the king is agreed throughout with the substance of the confession. The exceptions are the mass and priestly marriage, but on those points too he is in daily disputation and it is very much to be hoped that he will allow himself to be led by the holy writ. Then the king is agreed with us on the article which concerns both kinds of the holy sacrament of the body and blood of our lord Christ, and the same goes for that which concerns monks' vows. It is only that during this time we have some patience.[270]

And so the Germans relented, and agreed to stay another week: because 'the archbishop and lord Cromwell showed us the importance attached to such a postponement, we agreed to wait the designated time for the promotion of

---

[267] '[N]och einen monat alhie zu verharren und uns mit den verordenten bishofen und andern gelerten von wegen der misbreuch, als nemlich der messe, von dem sacrament beiderlei gestalt, von der priester ehe und der geistlichen geluebd, auch zu unterreden': ibid.
[268] '[U]ns auch diese gewisse verwenung tun, das mir [this must be a misprint or misreading for "wir"] alsdan von ko. mat. ein gute richtige antwort bekommen': ibid.
[269] '[V]iel Tausent Shelen in Engeland betrachten': HStMar, PA 2575, fo. 249v (copy enclosed with John Frederick to Philip, 21 Sept., fo. 245).
[270] '[U]ns der herr Crumel zum hochsten vortrostet und angezaigt das die konig. mait. durch aus mit der Confession inn der Substanz aynigk, ausgeschlossen die mas und priester ehe, darvon doch sein konig. Mait. auch teglich disputiert und sey genzlich zuverhoffen sein konig. Mait. werde sich hierinnenn auch durch die gotliche schriefft weyssen lassen. Dan den Artickel baiderley gestalt des hochwerdigen sacrament des leybs und bluts unsern herren Christ belangend sey sein konig. Mait. mit uns ainigk, des gleichi der Munchen gelubde halbenn. Allain das wir die Zeit uber gedult trugen': ibid. fos 250v–1 (copy enclosed with John Frederick to Philip, 21 Sept., fo. 245).

God's word and to please the king'.[271] The Germans' insistence that the discussions be recorded in their 'book', as had been the other articles, suited Cromwell and Cranmer perfectly. However, while the two evangelicals found the Germans persuadable, the conservative bishops were much less malleable: they refused point blank to pre-empt the king's judgement on the abuses by committing anything to writing. Although they entered into oral discourse with the Germans on 19 August, Cranmer could not get them to put anything down on paper. 'I have syns', wrote the archbishop to Cromwell,

> effectiously moved the bisshops therto, but thei have made me this answer, that thei knowe that the kinges grace hath taken upon hymself to answer the said Oratours in that bihalf and therof a boke is alredie devised by the kinges maiestie. And therfore thei will not medell with the abuses, leste thei should write therin contrarye to that the king shall write.[272]

The bishops instead suggested that the four 'Roman' sacraments be discussed, but Cranmer saw this for the distraction it was, suggesting 'that the bisshops seke only an occasion to breke the concorde'.[273] Thus he asked Cromwell to get Henry's command to have the discussions recorded, since 'nothing shalbe don unles the kinges graces special comandemente be unto us therin directed. ffor they manifestly see that thei cannot defende the abuses, and yet thei wold in no wise grannte unto theym'.[274]

But no command came from Henry, and the discussions soon began to deteriorate, producing only a few inconclusive papers from the Protestant side in favour of communion in both kinds[275] and against private masses.[276] As the talks bogged down in late August the Germans became increasingly distracted. Burchard and Boineburg squabbled over Reformation trivia, the Saxon betting one English parrot and 120 new florins against the Hessian's 112 florins (some of which were old, overweight pieces) that Martin Luther had been formally awarded his doctorate when he posted the ninety-five theses.[277] Mykonius, who at the outset of the third phase of the discussions

---

[271] '[D]er Erzbischoff auch der her Crummel uns angezaigt was treflich an solchen vorharren gelegen haben wir bewilligt zufurderung des Gotlichen Worts und konig. Mait. zugefallen die bestimbte zeit abzuwarten': ibid. fo. 250 (copy enclosed with John Frederick to Philip, 21 Sept., fo. 245).

[272] BL, MS Cott. Cleo. E.v, fo. 225 [Burnet, *History of the Reformation*, vi. 165; LP xiii/2, 164].

[273] Ibid.

[274] Ibid.

[275] BL, MS Cott. Cleo. E.v, fos 167–70 [LP xiii/1, 1307.xx], an anonymous article which followed Lutheran doctrine very closely; BL, MS Cott. Cleo. E.v, fos 174–7 [LP xiii/1, 1307.xxii], a paper which lists some of the principal scriptural and patristic sources supporting communion in both kinds.

[276] PRO, SP 1/134, fos 41–5 [LP xiii/1, 1307.xvi; *Miscellaneous writings of Cranmer*, 480–2]. This is a paper on the private mass which resembled the corresponding article in the Wittenberg articles, and featured a number of corrections in Cranmer's hand.

[277] Mykonius ran the book and signed the betting docket. Later, in Germany, he attached a

had been confident of success,[278] began to behave badly, writing to Cromwell on 7 September that he was too sick to carry on and that he desperately needed to be allowed back to Germany, with or without the others.[279] By the middle of the month the discussions had petered away to nothing.

It is likely that the conservative bishops were reluctant to record the discussions in writing because they did not wish to miss the opportunity to fall in behind Henry should he come down against the Germans on the abuses. If they were to subscribe to some Lutheran interpretation of the abuses, as Cranmer seems to have thought any written formula would certainly be, they would find this very difficult. Until the Germans left England, and in the absence of a specific command from the king, mere conversations were all that they would involve themselves in. For now a waiting game was required. Only when Henry returned to London and his current views on German theology were better known would the time for action come.

The king arrived back at the end of September and the Germans were granted a farewell audience. There are no records to indicate what was discussed. The ambassadors were given letters dated 1 October from Henry to Philip and John Frederick which praised the ambassadors' erudition, expressed satisfaction at the progress that had been made, and asked that Philip Melanchthon be sent with the promised follow-up embassy to continue the discussions and to conclude an agreement.[280] The ambassadors appear to have departed for Germany shortly afterwards and to have arrived back home towards the end of the month.[281]

---

copy of Luther's doctorate to the docket in order to settle the matter: P. Scherffig, *Friedrich Mekum von Lichtenfels*, Leipzig 1909, 118–19.

[278] Mykonius to John Frederick, 23 Aug. 1538, in *Der Briefwechsel des Friedrich Mykonius (1524–1546)*, ed. H.-U. Delius, Tübingen 1960, 50–1.

[279] Ibid. 51–2.

[280] Henry to John Frederick, TStWei, Reg. H. 165, no. 78.i, fos 165 (final version), 166 (copy), 167–8 (German trans.), 169–70 (German trans.) [*LP* xiii/2, 497]. Henry to Philip, HStMar, PA 1800, fos 58 (final version), 59 (German trans.).

[281] Hussee reported on 27 September that the Germans had left that day (*LP* xiii/2, 434), but letters from Henry to John Frederick and Philip (n. 280 above), signed 'prope Londinium', suggest that their farewell audience with the king was on 1 October.

4

Conservative Resistance and Reaction, 1538–1539

Initial signs of reaction, August–November 1538

The German letter of 5 August 1538 was an error of judgement. In it Henry was given certain specific issues to consider; not a wide body of doctrine, but a sort of theological multiple choice: a limited range of distinct questions admitting of only acceptance or rejection. It concentrated his mind. Moreover here was no random selection of doctrine, but explosive questions about which the king had had misgivings since the earliest theological discussions with the Schmalkaldic League. Not only did the Germans force Henry to pass judgement on the most specific range of Lutheran doctrinal questions he had considered since the writing of *Assertio*; they also did this at a time when his answer would be produced in the context of an isolated royal progress during which his only source of theological counsel was the conservative Tunstall. This combination boded ill for the cause of reform. Ever since the mid-1530s, Henry had demonstrated a consistent interest in using consultations with the League to help settle the faith of his own Church. Now that these consultations had begun and he had been cast into the middle of the ensuing debate – not in his usual supervisory position, but as a 'hands on' contestant – his interest in applying the results of Anglo-Schmalkaldic discussions to the process of English theological codification was given even greater momentum.

Henry meant what he said when he closed the response to the Germans which he and Tunstall had composed with the assurance that 'concerning these articles which we have discussed, we will as soon as possible consider them with our theologians, and only then establish that which we judge to advance the glory of Christ and the propriety of his covenanted Church'.[1] As if to emphasise this intention, in his farewell letter to the Germans, Henry reiterated that 'as the matter of our negotiations concerns the glory of Christ, and the discipline of religion, it requires mature deliberation'.[2]

Accordingly, upon his return to London from the summer progress, Henry set in train theological discussions on the five main points of contention

---

[1] 'De articulis vero quos jam disseruimus maturius cum theologis nostris quamprimum vacabit agemus, atque ea demum statuemus quae ad Christi gloriam ecclesiaeque sponsae ejus decorem conducere existimabimus': Burnet, *History of the Reformation*, iv. 391.
[2] *LP* xiii/2, 497.

which had surfaced during the discussions of 1538. These now became five of the crucial issues over which the forces of reform and orthodoxy fought: from the first phase of the discussions, auricular confession, and from the second, communion in both kinds, private masses, the necessity of keeping vows made to God and clerical marriage.

It is about this time that it is possible to discern the first emergence of an actual faction of conservatives, as opposed to the disparate and incoherent grouping of conservative elements which had previously been evident. The continuing rehabilitation of Stokesley was an early indication of the developing strength and cohesion of the conservative forces. Still more significant was Tunstall's new lease of life. Upon his return from the summer progress to London he found himself installed on the council, occupying the seat vacated at Foxe's death.[3] Moreover, his performance during the summer had clearly raised him in the king's esteem as a special adviser: on 27 November 1538 he would write to Cromwell from Hampton Court that he was personally assisting the king in penning instructions for ambassadors to the Low Countries.[4] Also significant was the return of Stephen Gardiner from France. On 28 September Gardiner took his first steps on English soil in three years, and although he lived in some danger for his first thirty-six hours back in England and was kept from the court and council in the following months, it would not be long before he too was working with the other leading conservatives against the evangelical cause.[5] For the conservatives, the events of the summer constituted a long-awaited opportunity to drag themselves back into favour. As news of Henry's uncompromising rejection of the German letter on the abuses inevitably leaked out, their stubborn refusal during the third phase of the 1538 discussions to accept Cranmer's instruction to join with the Germans in setting down a statement on the abuses, before Henry's judgement was known, was vindicated. Now that Henry had shown his hand, the conservatives had the opportunity to support his orthodoxy fully and push for an appropriate religious settlement.

For the evangelicals, on the other hand, the Schmalkaldic embassy had gone badly wrong. Not only had it not been a major embassy led by Philip

---

[3] On 28 September 1538 Husee reported to Lisle that the council had met. Among those present were Tunstall, Cromwell, Audley, Cranmer 'and others' (Norfolk and Suffolk were at the court): *LP* xiii/2, 446. At *LP* xiv/1, 1048.xviii, there is a record of Tunstall's signature on a bill for dinners in 'the council Chamber'. It is tempting to conjecture that Tunstall was originally recalled from the council of the north to replace Foxe. However, Henry's letter to that body, requesting the appointment of a new president, indicates that Tunstall's recall to London was initially only temporary; his role as king's theological adviser during the 1538 progress probably led to his promotion to Foxe's seat on the council.

[4] *LP* xiii/2, 916.

[5] Redworth, *Gardiner*, 86–7. MacCulloch, *Cranmer*, 198, also makes the point that it is probably more than coincidence that during the three years that Gardiner was in France the evangelical cause prospered, while from the time of his return religious policy began to turn in a conservative direction.

Melanchthon, but it had proved to be anything but a stepping stone to further doctrinal reform. After the first couple of months it had become steadily more and more unhelpful, sending Henry the disastrous letter of 5 August, staying on longer only after intensive pleas by Cromwell and Cranmer, and even then opting out of the third phase of the discussions after only a few weeks. The result had been to put the evangelicals very much on the defensive.

As the Schmalkaldic ambassadors made their way home, to the five contentious issues which they had raised and which had subsequently become the subject of theological discussion was added the question of the real presence. Denial of the real presence was the characteristic doctrinal tenet of two continental heresies which began to manifest themselves in England during the later 1530s: anabaptism and sacramentarianism. The existence of anabaptism in England was only revealed to the authorities at all because of a tip-off from the Schmalkaldic League. In August 1538, the League had come across documents indicating that there was an incipient anabaptist movement in England. After a brief consultation it was decided that Henry should be warned of this and advised on how to deal with it. A letter was first drafted in Saxony on 1 September, and, after some further revisions in Hesse, a final version was despatched to England on 25 September.[6] It appears to have arrived at court within four or five days. Thomas Cromwell took immediate action. His reformist friend Richard Moryson provided a full English translation of the Latin,[7] and on 1 October Cromwell signed a royal commission which appointed Cranmer, Stokesley, Sampson, Skip, Thirlby, Heath, Gwent, Barnes and Crome, 'or any three or four of them, to search for and re-examine anabaptists, receive back into the Church such as renounce their error, hand over those who persist in it to the secular arm for punishment, and destroy all books of that detestable sect'.[8]

Just as the evangelicals were in the van of efforts to destroy the anabaptist heresy in these months, so they were also involved in restricting the growth of sacramentarianism. This may be demonstrated by looking at the case of the sacramentary, John Lambert, which appears first to have come to light in October; that is to say, in the weeks following Cromwell's appointment of the commission to seek out and destroy anabaptism. About this time John Taylor, a reformist preacher who would be deprived of the bishopric of Lincoln in

---

6   For Saxon–Hessian correspondence concerning the discovery of intelligence, the decision to send letter to Henry and its composition and despatch see TStWei, Reg. H. 191, no. 88, fos 44–5; Reg. H. 207, no. 94, fos 32, 69–72, 81–99, 106, 125–31; HStMar, PA 2575, fo. 114. The English translation by Richard Moryson of the final version of the letter, 25 Sept., is at PRO, SP 1/137, fos 19–28 [LP xiii/2, 427; StP viii. 47–50]. LP xiii/2, 264 is an abstract based on a version in CR, which was copied from a draft of 1 Sept. in TStWei, Reg. H. 207, no. 94, fos 92–4.
7   PRO, SP 1/137, fos 19–28 [LP xiii/2, 427; StP viii. 47–50].
8   LP xiii/2, 498.

Mary's reign,[9] gave a sermon at St Peter's Church in London. At the end of the service Lambert, who had been in the congregation, approached Taylor and proceeded to contest the affirmation of the real presence which had been made in the sermon. Taylor reported the matter to Robert Barnes, who advised that it be referred to Thomas Cranmer.[10] The archbishop immediately brought the case to the attention of Thomas Cromwell, who in turn lost no time in ordering that Lambert be imprisoned.[11] Once in detention, Lambert made his difficult situation even worse by writing a long and forthright letter to Henry, explaining why Christ could only be figuratively present in the sacrament.[12] At this point Henry seems to have decided to make an example of him. On 16 November the sacramentary was brought to face trial at Westminster, in a public hearing which the king, assisted by his bishops, personally conducted. After five hours of one-sided bullying the trial ended with the sorry but unrepentant Lambert led away to suffer the consequences.

The involvement of leading members of the evangelical faction in the measures against anabaptism and Lambert raises some interesting questions. In particular, it provides an opportunity to consider the specific nature of their religious beliefs. It has been suggested that Cromwell and Cranmer might have been sympathetic to deniers of the real presence, for it is said that they protected, and even promoted, sacramentarian activities at Calais in the later 1530s. Admittedly, Cromwell and Cranmer do appear to have underestimated the extent of religious radicalism there; perhaps Cromwell's difficult relationship with Lord Lisle caused him to disregard some of the deputy's entreaties to suppress religious radicalism at Calais, judging them less as a call for action against sacramentaries than a veiled attempt to get authority to act against evangelicals generally in the Pale. Be that as it may, it would be incautious to take literally the accusations of sacramentarianism levelled by the ideological foes of Cromwell and Cranmer. Even if the taint of sympathy with sacramentarian heresy would cause recurrent problems for Cromwell in particular during 1539 and 1540, it is unlikely that either he or Cranmer were sacramentaries. The only evidence against them is that provided by their enemies; it can be adequately refuted by the evidence of the leading roles they played in apprehending and destroying the sacramentary Lambert and in their willingness to take action against sacramentaries in Calais when they were sure that such actually were active.[13]

---

9   DNB.

10 Foxe, *Acts and monuments*, v. 227–8.

11 Lambert referred to his imprisonment at Cromwell's direction in his holograph letter to him: PRO, SP 1/139, fos 129–30 [*LP* xiii/2, 849.ii].

12 Lambert referred to this in the same holograph letter: ibid. Foxe, *Acts and monuments*, v. 236–50, says that Lambert wrote the letter while 'he was in the archbishop's ward at Lambeth, which was a little before his disputation with the king', and prints it *in extenso*.

13 The argument for Cromwell's partiality towards the Calais sacramentaries was originally expounded in *The Lisle letters*, ed. M. St Clare Byrne, London 1981, v, passim. An alternative view is provided in P. J. Ward, 'Thomas Cromwell and Calais, 1530–40', unpubl. BA

Yet if Cromwell and Cranmer were not sacramentaries, what sort of Protestants were they? This has long proved to be a vexatious question, especially where Cromwell is concerned. Certainly, no one any longer believes Merriman's anachronistic portrayal of him as a secular-minded, proto-modern statesman. But there has been little to replace those views other than a steadily growing acknowledgement that Cromwell supported some sort of evangelical reform.[14] John Guy, in the most recent general history of the period, declines to give the minister's Protestant beliefs any specific categorisation, since Cromwell 'did not deny the real presence in the Eucharist or teach the doctrine of justification by faith alone'.[15] That is true – Cromwell explicitly affirmed or denied little where theology was concerned, and he was not qualified to teach any doctrine. But such caution as this is probably unwarranted; it should be possible to use Cromwell's acts and deeds to come to a firmer conclusion on his religious convictions. This study has noted such pertinent clues to his religious beliefs as his correspondence with Martin Luther, his friendship with England's foremost Lutheran, Robert Barnes, the assessment of him by the Lutheran ambassadors of 1538 and his role in the actions against the anabaptists and Lambert. More generally, it has high-

---

diss. Armidale, NSW 1988, and 'The politics of religion: Thomas Cromwell and the Reformation in Calais, 1534–40', *Journal of Religious History* xvii (1992), 152–71. Though I do not agree with Ward's broader conclusions on Cromwell's religious convictions, I believe he demonstrates effectively that the most Cromwell was guilty of in dealing with the Calais sacramentaries was indecision. The only slight doubt about the Lambert evidence is that cast by Foxe's assertion that 'it is reported of many that Cromwell desired him [i.e. Lambert] of forgiveness' on the day of his burning: *Acts and monuments*, v. 236. Purely on the face of it, this suggestion that the minister would have associated himself in such a way with a condemned heretic – and especially one he had helped bring to book – is highly unlikely. Moreover, the story comes from oral sources ('it is reported of many'), and while Foxe was remarkably reliable with documentary evidence, his handling of oral evidence was often incautious and liable to distortion. Foxe, of course, had great difficulty in explaining the actions of his evangelical heroes in the Lambert affair. In seeking to mitigate their central roles in the burning of the sacramentary, he resorted (v. 234) to the imagined machinations of 'wily Winchester': 'through the pestiferous and crafty counsel of this one bishop of Winchester, Satan (who oftentimes doth raise up one brother to the destruction of another) did here perform the condemnation of this Lambert by no other ministers than gospellers themselves, Taylor, Barnes, Cranmer and Cromwell'. In his interpretation of the Lambert affair, Foxe was imposing his mid sixteenth-century understanding of correct reformed views on the real presence on those of the 1530s: during the 1530s there was in fact no contradiction at all in being an evangelical and opposing denial of the real presence. The Lutherans opposed it, and in recent years its only proponents had been the revolutionary anabaptists of Münster and the still obscure reformers of upper Germany and Switzerland who were uncertainly following in Zwingli's footsteps.

14 This has mainly been on the back of the view of Cromwell presented in Dickens, *Thomas Cromwell and the English Reformation*. An excellent presentation of Cromwell and his evangelical connections is to be found in S. Brigden, 'Thomas Cromwell and the "brethren" ', in Cross, Loades and Scarisbrick, *Law and government*, 31–49. A dissenting voice is Bernard, 'Making of religious policy', 341–5.

15 Guy, *Tudor England*, 178.

lighted his long-standing and unusual interest in the Lutherans of the Schmalkaldic League. Consideration may also be given to other religiously relevant aspects of his career, such as his sponsorship of Richard Tavener's English translation of the Lutheran Confession of Augsburg or the significance of his double portrait on the title page of the Great Bible of 1539.[16] This evidence, taken with further material which will be presented as this study progresses, provides sufficient indications as to the colour of Cromwell's reformist beliefs: though he carried no membership card nor made any formal declaration of the faith, Cromwell's actions suggest that the form of Protestantism to which he inclined was Lutheranism.[17]

The same may be said of Cranmer during the 1530s. Quite apart from the archbishop's actions, he did put thoughts down on paper which reveal his faith. His close adherence to the position of the Lutheran negotiators in 1538 has already been noted, but perhaps the best evidence is a letter he wrote to Cromwell in August 1538 concerning one of the men causing trouble at Calais:

> As concerning Adam Damplip of Calice, he utterly denieth that he ever taught or said that the very body or blood of Christ was not really present in the sacrament of the altar, and confesseth the same to be there really; but he saith that the controversy . . . . was because he confuted the opinion of transubstantiation, and therein I think he taught but the truth.[18]

These words are unambiguous: a man who affirms the real presence but denies transubstantiation is professing consubstantiation. This is a distinctively Lutheran doctrine. Cranmer's approving pronouncement on it suggests that his Protestant beliefs in the first decade of the English Reformation were also of a Lutheran hue.[19]

---

16 Ibid. 179. For the title page of the Great Bible see MacCulloch, *Cranmer*, 238–40.

17 For cautious support for this interpretation see Dickens, *English Reformation*, 247 (['Cromwell's] leanings toward Lutheranism should be taken quite seriously'); for cautious scepticism see G. R. Elton, *Reform and renewal: Thomas Cromwell and the common weal*, Cambridge 1973, 35 ([Cromwell's] 'Lutheran leanings do not look entirely convincing'). Elton did, however, later give greater credence to Cromwell's Lutheran inclinations in 'Thomas Cromwell redivivus', in his *Studies in Tudor and Stuart politics and government*, Cambridge 1974–83, iii. 377–8. See also B. W. Beckingsale, *Thomas Cromwell: Tudor minister*, London 1978, 77 ([Cromwell's] 'Lutheran leanings never amounted to a total acceptance of Lutheranism'). In 1530 Cromwell is said to have cursed the advent of Martin Luther, though in a comment made to Cardinal Wolsey: Elton, *Reform and Reformation*, 171.

18 *Miscellaneous writings of Cranmer*, 375.

19 This is the view of most historians who have commented on Cranmer's theology, from Foxe, *Acts and monuments*, v. 500–1 (Cranmer at the time of his interview with Damplip was 'but a Lutheran'), to P. N. Brooks, *Thomas Cranmer's doctrine of the eucharist: an essay in historical development*, London 1965, 7–37 (which also provides a survey of the historiography on this question). More recently Diarmaid MacCulloch has taken the same view: *Reign of Henry VIII*, 170, and *Cranmer*, 179–82. Some, for example Dugmore, *The mass and the English reformers*, 182, have suggested that at this time Cranmer might have been

It might be suggested that there were three broad religious categories in England at this time: the Anglo-Catholics (those who accepted Catholic doctrine in all respects but the supremacy);[20] the evangelical Protestants (those who inclined to a Lutheran form of Protestantism); and the radical Protestants (those who denied the real presence – effectively sacramentaries or anabaptists). The conservative faction was drawn from the first category and the evangelical faction from the second. The latter category, however, the radical Protestants, had no representation or support at the upper level of government. Theirs was a lower level movement, often filled out by foreigners and especially prevalent at Calais.[21] Radical Protestants were not, therefore, centrally involved in faction politics.[22]

This, then, was the fundamental difference between the doctrinal issue of the real presence which emerged during the second half of 1538 and the five questions which the 1538 Schmalkaldic embassy had raised. Whereas the five were issues of contention mainly at the factional level, the real presence was a controversial issue at the popular, grass-roots level. At the upper level of the regime, opposition to denial of the real presence was an 'all party' issue, on which the competing evangelical and conservative factions saw eye to eye. Its proscription, therefore, would not be something which could properly be counted as part of a conservative reaction, nor would it be something which could cause difficulties with the Schmalkaldeners, since they too upheld the real presence.[23]

Just six weeks after Henry's return to London from the summer progress, the first official pronouncement was made on the six major doctrinal questions which had come to dominate theological debate. On 16 November two signals were sent on the current state of this debate. The first of these was the trial of John Lambert. As a signal it was intended purely for the benefit of the wider populace; it was not relevant to English faction politics or to Anglo-Schmalkaldic relations.[24] The other signal, however, concerned both

---

rejecting both transubstantiation and consubstantiation as the means by which the real presence is effected in favour of the scholastic doctrine of impanation. This is improbable: in view of the archbishop's close interest in Lutheranism at this time, consubstantiation is much more likely to have been the eucharistic doctrine to which he was attracted (the argument on this in Brooks, *Cranmer's doctrine of the eucharist*, 7–37, is compelling).

[20] For a three-way subdivision of this conservative group see MacCulloch 'Henry VIII and the reform of the Church', 168–9.

[21] Ibid. 171–2.

[22] However, just as the conservatives could be falsely accused of loyalty to the papacy, so the evangelicals would at times be open to accusations of involvement with radical Protestants, particularly sacramentaries.

[23] A letter from John Frederick to Philip of 10 January 1539 noted intelligence from Hamburg on the process against Lambert, described the public trial and said that Lambert had been condemned as a heretic for holding false opinions on the sacrament of the altar: HStMar, PA 2578, fos 48v–9.

[24] Dickens, *English Reformation*, 238–40, describes the proceedings against Lambert, and at p. 239 suggests that a public spectacle was made of him because of Henry's diplomatic needs:

the fortunes of the evangelical faction and England's relations with the League. Through the medium of a royal proclamation, not only were the 'all party' concerns of sacramentarianism and anabaptism dealt with, but also the first traces of a new doctrinal direction which can properly be described as conservative indicated.[25] What was initially intended was a short-term response to the combination of information on anabaptism which had recently arrived from Germany and the continuing sacramentarian activities at Calais. But it would seem that in the course of the drafting of a proclamation to deal with these heresies against the sacrament of the altar, the conservatives persuaded Henry to extend it as a catch-all for other current theological concerns. In particular, it was to provide an interim indication on the current progress of the 'mature deliberations' on the questions raised by the recent Schmalkaldic embassy which Henry had set in train upon his return to London. The only extant draft of the proclamation probably dates from the second half of October. The final manuscript versions (which do not survive) were probably produced during the first two weeks of November; they were signed and the great seal applied on the day of Lambert's trial.[26]

The bulk of the proclamation represented little gain or loss for either of the leading factions,[27] for it was concerned with exiling anabaptists and sacramentaries, forbidding discussion of the eucharist and regulating the importation and printing of those books in English which were giving rise to the new popular heresies. These were all questions on which evangelicals and conservatives were in broad agreement. One new matter temporarily joined the six major doctrinal questions at issue and made an appearance in the proclamation. It was concerned with the keeping of ceremonies not already abolished. This article has sometimes been cited as an early example of the

he was disappointed with the Lutherans and wanted to placate the Catholic powers. Although there is no conclusive evidence for or against the influence of diplomacy on the Lambert trial, it is more likely that Henry wanted a show trial to warn his own people against joining heresies against the sacrament of the altar rather than as part of some European propaganda exercise.

25 The proclamation is printed in P. L. Hughes and J. F. Larkin (eds), *Tudor royal proclamations*, New Haven 1964–9, i. 270–6. The only extant draft is in BL, MS Cott. Cleo. E.v. fos 356–83 [*LP* xiii/2, 848.ii]. G. R. Elton, *Policy and police: the enforcement of the Reformation in the age of Thomas Cromwell*, Cambridge 1972, 255–8, examines the proclamation, and concludes (p. 27) that 'how such disparate pieces ever came to be joined together is a mystery'. Light will be shed on its genesis and implications in the remainder of this section.

26 For the procedures involved in producing a royal proclamation see the introduction to Hughes and Larkin, *Tudor royal proclamations*, and also P. A. Neville, 'Richard Pynson, king's printer (1506–1529): printing and propaganda in early Tudor England', unpubl. PhD diss. London 1990, 66–9.

27 This argues against Elton, *Policy and police*, 257: 'the main part of the proclamation represents a victory for the conservative faction, but the reformers managed to add a second part which, though harmless on the surface, would remind people that things had not changed right round again'. In what follows it will be suggested that only one article in the proclamation posed a serious problem for the evangelicals.

gathering strength of conservative reaction.[28] But its significance should not be overestimated. Though it probably did represent a minor victory for the upholders of orthodoxy, it only commanded observance of those ceremonies not already abolished (that is to say, it did not reintroduce any previously banned), and it did so in a way which implicitly recognised a fundamental Protestant tenet on ceremonial matters: the realm, it stated, should 'use the same [ceremonies] without superstition, and esteem them for good and laudable ceremonies, tokens, and signs to put us in remembrance of things of higher perfection, and none otherwise, and not to repose any trust of salvation in them'.[29] The only aspect of this article offensive to reformed opinion was that it made observance of existing ceremonies compulsory rather than optional. And even this little triumph for orthodoxy was reduced by a further couple of points which did not appear in the draft but which were later added by the evangelicals and appeared in the final version. One of these enjoined the realm to avoid any superstitious practices, while the other removed Thomas Becket from the calendar.[30]

There was, in fact, only one article in the proclamation which represented a genuine and unambiguous setback for the evangelicals. This was directly related to Henry's work with Tunstall during the summer and the subsequent theological discussions ordered by him. It sprang from the theologically least complicated of the issues which Henry and Tunstall had worked out: priestly marriage and the necessity of keeping vows. The relative simplicity of these questions, allied to the king's very strong personal feelings on them, probably explains why they alone of the issues raised by the Schmalkaldeners were, at the vigorous prompting of the conservatives, chosen to figure at such an early stage in the discussion process as part of the proclamation.

As the work on the proclamation entered the drafting stage, in about late October, Henry joined the deliberations himself. He examined the drafts and applied a number of corrections to one of them which demonstrate the influence on his thinking of the summer collaboration with Tunstall. Where the draft noted that 'Finally his majestie understanding that a fewe nombre of this his realme being prestes aswell religious as other have taken wifs and maryed themselfs contrary to',[31] Henry superscribed in his own hand a passage citing the same authorities he had used in his pre-drafting holograph note during the summer and which had figured in the final version of the reply he and Tunstall had composed: 'the holsumme monissions off saint palle ad thimotheum ad titum and ad corintheos bothe first and seconde and contrary alsoo to the oppinions off meny off the olde faders and expositers off

---

28 For example in Elton, Policy and police, 256–7; Brigden, London and the Reformation, 295–6.
29 Hughes and Larkin, Tudor royal proclamations, i. 274.
30 Ibid. i. 274–6.
31 BL, MS Cott. Cleo. E.v, fo. 382 [LP xiii/2, 848.ii].

scripture'.[32] At this point Henry then caused a new clause dealing with vows to appear, adding 'not estimyng also', before returning to the text, 'the avowe and promyse of chastitie which they made at the receyving of their holye ordres'.[33] Thus the summer's more generalised concern with keeping vows made to God now emerged, with Henry's help, in the proclamation as a distinct and more narrow concern with keeping vows of chastity made to God. The emerging distinction between clerical marriage and vows of chastity as separate issues may seem pernickity and even redundant, but the groundwork for it had been laid in the summer, and in the months ahead it would be even more fully worked out.[34]

The setback which the proclamation's one unambiguously orthodox pronouncement caused the reformers was bad enough, but the problem did not end there. For the other issues of doctrinal contention which had emerged during the summer discussions with the Schmalkaldic embassy were also threatening to be the subject of a conservative settlement at this time. The fact that they did not appear in the proclamation may probably be explained by their greater complexity and therefore the need for lengthier discussion, and the fact that the king's mind was not yet as firmly settled on them as it was on priestly marriage and vows of chastity. Nevertheless, they were being discussed and the orthodox position was winning through. A letter to Henry from Germany in early 1539, for example, would refer to the ongoing debate and that the conservative position was prevailing, noting that 'we understand there, that our articles of the mass, of the use of the whole sacrament of the Lord's supper, and of celibacy, be still called into question'.[35]

And so, within six weeks of Henry's return to London and the departure of the Schmalkaldic embassy to Germany, the advantage had shifted from the promoters of reform to the upholders of orthodoxy. Henry's views on the issues he had examined with Tunstall during the summer were now common knowledge. There was also the sign of a swing towards orthodoxy evident in the 16 November proclamation. Thus the stage was set for the conservatives to push home their advantage and agitate for the earliest possible settlement of all five of those contentious questions which the Schmalkaldeners had brought to the fore of English faction politics.

---

[32] Ibid.

[33] Ibid.

[34] A further confirmation of the influence of the summer disputations on this article is to be seen in the penalty, deprivation, which was prescribed for priests who had married. This was precisely what Henry had recommended to the German princes in his reply to the 5 August German letter on the abuses.

[35] This was a letter from John Frederick and Philip to Henry: Strype, *Ecclesiastical memorials*, i/2, 400 [*LP* xiv/1, 698]; TStWei, Reg. H. 260, no. 111, vol. 1, fos 6–12 (Latin draft); BL, MS Cott. Cleo. E.vi, vol. 2, fos 297–302 (Latin final copy).

Evangelical responses, November 1538–April 1539

Although Henry had comprehensively rejected Lutheran doctrine on the abuses during the summer and had pronounced on clerical marriage and vows of chastity in November, it should not be thought that a thoroughgoing orthodox settlement of these issues was inevitable by the close of 1538. Henry's mind was certainly moving in a conservative direction on these matters, but he was still interested in further consultations with the League: the farewell letters which he had given to the ambassadors to take back to John Frederick and Philip had emphasised that he wished to continue discussions with a major theological delegation from the League.[36] Thus the ultimate fate of the doctrine which the Schmalkaldeners had thrust to the front line of English theological debate rested in some part with the Germans themselves. The issues remained open. If the League would send Melanchthon and the promised delegation to England for a further disputation, a mutually acceptable accommodation on the outstanding points might yet be found.

This, then, was one line for the evangelicals to pursue as 1538 drew to a close. They would urge that the League be contacted by an English embassy to ask for the despatch of a major delegation from Germany to England so as to continue the theological discussions and seek to conclude an Anglo-Schmalkaldic alliance. Towards the end of the year the evangelicals began advocating such a plan. In so doing, Cromwell and the evangelicals had the advantage of being able to point to the threatening international situation, as the pope finally issued the long threatened bull of excommunication against Henry in December 1538,[37] and Charles and Francis began to show signs of forming an alliance to enforce the papal decree. Though the proposed embassy should not be seen as an operation of the Froudean mechanic, it is likely that the mounting threat of invasion in late 1538 allowed people like Cromwell to attach greater urgency to the need to continue the efforts to establish an Anglo-Schmalkaldic alliance.

This was not the only strategy which Cromwell had now decided to pursue to bring England and the League together, however. For in mid-1538 he had also begun cultivating an alternative approach, a marriage alliance which he probably decided to unveil towards the end of that year as the conservatives began to seize the advantage in religious matters. Such an alliance would operate as a fail-safe device to bring England and the League together if the

---

[36] Letter to John Frederick: TStWei, Reg. H. 165, no. 78 i, fos 165 (final version), 166 (copy), 167–8 (German trans.), 169–70 (German trans.) [*LP* xiii/2, 497]; letter to Philip: HStMar, PA 1800, fos 58 (Latin final version) [Prüser, *England und die Schmalkaldener*, 322–3], 59 (German trans.). It is therefore wrong to suggest that the 1538 Anglo-Schmalkaldic discussions were broken off in acrimony, as have some historians, for example Ridley, *Cranmer*, 162; G. Redworth, 'A study in the formulation of policy: the genesis and evolution of the Act of Six Articles', *Journal of Ecclesiastical History* xxxvii (1986), 50.
[37] *LP* xiii/2, 1087.

Anglo-Schmalkaldic discussions ran into further difficulties. It would be effected through marrying into Germany either Henry or princess Mary, both of whom remained unmarried at this time in spite of wide-ranging efforts to find them suitable partners.[38] The first definite evidence of this plan appeared on 23 August 1538.[39] In a letter to John Frederick, Franz Burchard reported that 'lord Cromwell, who is most favourably inclined to the German nation, wants most dearly that the king should wed himself with the German princes'.[40] Cromwell subsequently engaged in a private correspondence with John Frederick on this question,[41] and as the situation for the evangelicals worsened during November he probably first floated the idea of a German marriage with the king.[42] The choice of marital partner was Cleves, a suggestion which had the added weight of offering a strategically useful ally for Henry, positioned between the emperor's German and Burgundian possessions. Henry considered the proposal, and after some no doubt vigorous persuasion from Cromwell decided to go along with it.

Cromwell then set about arranging for an embassy to Germany. Christopher Mont would once more be at its head. Appointed as his assistant was one Thomas Paynell, a man who appears to have been an associate of Barnes at Louvain and Cambridge and who had been in contact with Cromwell during 1538 concerning the suppression of monasteries at Boston.[43] The ambassadors were given two sets of instructions, the principal one signed by Henry, the other by Cromwell.

---

38 For efforts to find Henry a bride after the death of Jane Seymour see Scarisbrick, *Henry VIII*, 355–61; A. Müller, 'Die Beziehungen Heinrichs VIII. zu Anna von Cleve', unpubl. DPhil. diss. Tübingen 1907, 1–16; Warnicke, *Marrying of Anne of Cleves*, 38–62.

39 There is an earlier report of talk about an Anglo-German marital alliance in a letter of 17 June 1538 from the imperial ambassadors to Charles (*LP* xiii/1, 1198). But the 1538 Schmalkaldic ambassadors had brought no such proposals and made no report of such discussions at this early stage of the embassy. The imperial ambassadors' confusion is confirmed by their false assertion that Mewtas and Holbein had been sent to Germany to obtain portraits of the people in question (Holbein and Mewtas were, in fact, in France in mid-1538: Scarisbrick, *Henry VIII*, 356, 359). They were either referrring to other marital negotiations going on at this time or perhaps had heard some early mutterings by Cromwell and his men about a possible Anglo-German marital alliance.

40 '[H]err Crumellus, welcher zum hochsten der Teutschen Nation genaigt ist, wolte am liebsten das sich seine Mait. mit den Teutschen fursten befreien det': HStMar, PA 2575, fo. 251v (copy of a letter from Burchard to John Frederick, enclosed with John Frederick to Philip, 21 Sept. 1538, fo. 245).

41 See Cromell's instructions for Mont, speaking of John Frederick, 'as he hath written by his letters to his lordshipp': BL, MS Cott. Vit.B. xxi, fo. 174 [*LP* xiv/1, 103.ii].

42 See *LP* xiii/2, 923, a letter from Henry to Wyatt of 28 November 1538, in which the king directed his ambassador to the emperor to mention the possibility of an Anglo-Cleves marriage, and to judge Charles's reaction. At *LP* xiii/2, 1162, 30 December 1538, the French ambassador in London mentioned discussions on 'the Cleves marriage'.

43 *DNB*. There was a contemporary with the same name who was well known as a translator of books. Though the *DNB* suggests that it was he who accompanied Mont to Germany, the associations with Barnes and Cromwell and the religious views of the other Paynell make this unlikely.

Henry's instructions directed Mont to begin by seeking out John Frederick, using Burchard to learn of the 'ocurranntes' there and to gain access to the duke. Once in his presence, he was to thank him and the landgrave for the recent letters which had been sent to England 'concerning the detestable secte of the Anabaptists', and advise that the problem had already been dealt with.[44] He was then to say that Henry

> merveyleth much that sythens his orators went awaye from hens with suche convenyent wedder as by all likelywode they shuld have ben spedely and within fewe dayes at home as it is reaported they were arryved his hieghnes hath hard from the saide duke no maner of thing, howe they have ben accepted at their retourne nor any other annswere of his mynde uppon such matiers as were commoned of here with his said orators nor what he doothe intende theruppon.[45]

To this Mont should add that Henry was also concerned about rumours that the Germans were about to conform to the emperor's demands, and ask for further information on this matter.[46] In closing, Mont was to come to one of the two central reasons for his despatch: he should 'solicite the sending of the notable legation hether to his Majestie that was spoken of at the said dukes orators last beyng here'.[47]

The king's instructions also dealt with the other main reason for Mont's despatch: 'for sundry other causes', Mont was to investigate 'what disposition and inclinacion both dukes of Cleve, father and sonne, with their familie be of towardes the furtherance and mayntenannce of the truthe'.[48] If the duke and family 'be of the olde popishe fashon and the same to be observed yet in their contreis', Mont should find out whether they would be likely to 'altere thair myndes easely and to ioyne with the other princes in the leage and with them to be bounde to furthar, mayntayn and defende the truthe of the gospell and withstande the abuses of the Church of Rome'.[49]

Cromwell's supplementary instructions concerned themselves exclusively with the Cleves marriage. They also went further than the king's on the matter. Where Henry's instructions had directed the ambassador simply to gather information on Cleves, Cromwell's ordered Mont actually to pursue the marital alliance. He directed that

> the said [Christopher] Mount shall at his being ther take occasion to com-mon[e and con]ferre with ffranciscus Burgartus the said dukes vicecha[ncellor] and late his orator here in Englande. And on the biha[lf of] the said lorde Crumwell with hartye and affectuous co[men]dations by mouth besides his

---

44 PRO, SP 1/142, fo. 105 (final version, signed at its head by the king) [*LP* xiv/1, 103.i].
45 PRO, SP 1/142, fo. 105v [*LP* xiv/1, 103.i].
46 PRO, SP 1/142, fos 105v–6 [*LP* xiv/1, 103.i].
47 PRO, SP 1/142, fo. 106v [*LP* xiv/1, 103.i].
48 PRO, SP 1/142, fo. 106 [*LP* xiv/1, 103.i].
49 PRO, SP 1/142, fo. 106v [*LP* xiv/1, 103.i].

lordshippes letters to the said [Bur]gartus diverted, shall declare unto him that wheras [at] a conference bitwen his lordshipp and the said Burgartus [at] suche tyme as he was here orator concerning an alliaunce of maryage to be contracted bitwen the yonge duke of Clev[es] and his daughter the lady Marye . . . That the lorde Crumwell muche tendering the kinges alliaunce in Germany, If he could fynde any occasion wolbe gladd to employe himself ernestly to induce and persuade the kinges hieghnes his soverain lorde rather to Ioyn with them, then otherwise, specyally for the duke of Saxonyes sake, who is allyed ther, and to mak[e] a crosse maryage bitwen the yong duke of Cleves and my lady Mary as is aforesaide And of the kinges hieghnes with the said older daughter of Cleves.[50]

There should be no doubt as to the partisan nature of this marital proposal. Cleves was not attractive as a marital partner because it occupied the religious middle ground between Rome and Wittenberg, or simply for its strategic value.[51] The evidence of Henry's instructions shows clearly that Cromwell had been counselling a Protestant marriage: the central concern of Henry's instructions was for Mont to investigate not only whether Cleves was disinclined to Rome but also whether it would be prepared to join the Schmalkaldic League. Why then had Cromwell not pushed for a direct marital alliance with an actual member of the Schmalkaldic League? The answer to this is simple. Outside of England, Henry could marry no lower than a duchess, and the League possessed no suitable candidates at this time. Cleves was the next best thing: the only available duchy with strong Schmalkaldic connections (the sister of the duke of Cleves was John Frederick's wife) and eligible duchesses.

From the outset, the Cleves marriage was a factional gambit, designed to back up and complement efforts to bring a major theological embassy to England to discuss and conclude an alliance. That is why Cromwell saw fit to give Mont supplementary instructions directing action where Henry had only ordered observation. It is also why Cromwell used such an enthusiastic and involved tone in his instructions: why he asked for pictures of the candidates to be sent to 'thentent his lordshipp might the better persuade his Majestie therby';[52] why he enjoined great haste 'before [con]clusion shuld be made with another';[53] why he assured that 'some good successe shuld succede therof

---

50 BL, MS Cott. Vit. B.xxi, fos 174–v (final version, signed at its foot by Cromwell) [LP xiv/1, 103.ii].

51 For the argument that the Cleves match was less an evangelical ploy on Cromwell's part than an element in the king's search for a middle way see Bernard, 'Making of religious policy', 344. Warnicke, Marrying of Anne of Cleves, 71–2, also stresses the king's interest in the religious position of the duke of Cleves as part of a broader argument (pp. 72–4, 94–6, 176) that the Cleves match was primarily a diplomatic event, intended if anything to communicate the king's orthodoxy rather than to lead to a closer association with the Schmalkaldic League.

52 BL, MS Cott. Vit. B.xxi, fos 174v–5 [LP xiv/1, 103.ii].

53 BL, MS Cott. Vit. B.xxi, fo. 175 [LP xiv/1, 103.ii].

in the effect of [an] alliance',[54] and that 'having the lorde privie seale moche desirous therof, they ought to hope well'.[55]

Mont and Paynell set off on 20 or 21 January 1539. Bad weather kept them at Dover for three days, but once at Calais they made their way east quickly and arrived at Antwerp on 27 January.[56] From Antwerp they appear to have travelled directly to the duke of Saxony. Mont was admitted to an audience with John Frederick sometime during the first half of February, when he was assured that the duke would support the matters on which he had been despatched. John Frederick added, however, that he could not take any action until he had met with the other League members at a diet scheduled to convene at Frankfurt on 12 February. After the audience Mont and Paynell appear to have decided that they themselves should also attend the diet. There they could confer with the rest of the League and receive a final answer to their suit. They probably left Saxony for Frankfurt in the second week of the month, arriving there on about 15 February.[57]

A Schmalkaldic diet had been summoned principally for the purpose of talks with an imperial delegation led by the archbishop of Lund on the new low point which had been reached in imperial-Schmalkaldic relations. Once again the Germans faced threats from Charles, and rumours were current that Francis was about to join a Catholic coalition against them. Indeed, it had begun to appear that Henry might be the only ally upon whom the Protestants could count. As early as November 1538 John Frederick had commented optimistically to Philip on the return of the Schmalkaldic embassy from England that 'the king of England, as we understand, is well inclined in matters of religion and, with God's grace, before too long will be completely united with us'.[58] Now he made notes in his own hand in preparation for the diet, suggesting that in the current situation it made sense to continue negotiating with Henry, since 'he will not abandon us in an emergency'.[59] Accordingly, at Frankfurt, the duke of Saxony's delegates initially declared their master to be in favour of establishing an alliance between the League and England, and did not even emphasise the necessity

---

54 Ibid.

55 Ibid.

56 PRO, SP 1/142, fos 171–2 [StP viii. 135–7; LP xiv/1, 157].

57 This account of the movements of Mont and Paynell between Antwerp on 27 January and Frankfurt on 15 February is based on a letter from them to Cromwell dated from Frankfurt on 5 March. This is not extant but is summarised by Cromwell in a letter to Henry of 18 March: StP i. 604–6 (the abstract in LP xiv/1, 552 is a little unreliable). The date of arrival in Frankfurt is based on the presentation date at the city endorsed on Henry's letter to Philip of Hesse: HStMar, PA 1800, fo. 60. For a brief sketch of the English ambassadors' negotiations in Frankfurt see P. Singer, 'Beziehungen des schmalkaldischen Bundes zu England im Jahre 1539', unpubl. DPhil. diss. Greifswald 1901, 7–32.

58 '[D]ie K.W. zu Engellandt, als wir vermerken, zu den sachen der religion geneigt und, ob got wil, in kurz mit uns genzlich einig sein wirdet': Mentz, Johann Friedrich, ii. 160–1.

59 '[E]r würde uns in vhal der nodt nit verlassen': ibid. iii. 426.

145

of first achieving a religious agreement. The landgrave's delegates expressed a similar view.[60]

Thus the English ambassadors seem initially to have made reasonably good progress. Letters of 18 and 19 February from Mont and Paynell to Cromwell were sufficiently encouraging on the marital question for Cromwell to be able to advise them in a letter of 10 March that Henry had decided to send Edward Carne, Nicholas Wotton and Richard Birde to Cleves to investigate further the possibility of an Anglo-Cleves marriage, 'and specially concernyng the mariage of his highnes, leaving thother [marriage of Mary] to be conferred of and upon overture or requisicion to be made on thair behalf'.[61] On the question of a major embassy from the League, his letter also seemed reasonably optimistic, though the ambassadors were reminded to urge that the embassy be despatched to England to conclude an alliance as soon as possible.[62]

However, just as Anglo-Schmalkaldic relations appeared to be on the verge of making some substantial progress and helping to recover the ground lost in England since the previous summer, there was a setback. For during late February and March the negotiations between the League and the archbishop of Lund began to produce results which offered a genuine hope of an imperial-Schmalkaldic peace. Before long a truce would be agreed, the Frankfurt Interim, under which there would be a cessation of imperial-Schmalkaldic-papal hostilities until a religious colloquy could be convened at a mutually agreed German location (this would eventually take place in 1541, at the Diet of Regensburg). The Frankfurt Interim proved from the outset to be a constraint on the League's English diplomacy. It soon became clear that the League had a diminishing interest in keeping to the promises to send a major embassy to Henry which had been made in writing at Braunschweig in April 1538 and personally to the king during the summer on a number of occasions.

Mont did his best to secure an embassy led by Melanchthon, but in increasingly difficult circumstances. The Strassburg delegate to the diet, Jakob Sturm, wrote on 3 March that he 'still desires that a considerable embassy will be sent to England and that it will be permitted that Philip

---

60 Prüser, *England und die Schmalkaldener*, 155–6.
61 BL, MS Cott. Vit. B.xxi, fo. 145v [Merriman, *Life and letters of Thomas Cromwell*, ii. 187; *LP* xiv/1, 490] (Cromwell's letter of 10 March to Mont and Paynell referring to letters from them of 18 and 19 February which are not extant).
62 BL, MS Cott. Vit. B.xxi, fos 145–7 [Merriman, *Life and letters of Thomas Cromwell*, ii. 186–90; *LP* xiv/1, 490]. Around this time the despatch of Robert Barnes to the Lutheran king of Denmark to seek an alliance was also arranged. Though this mission was focused on Denmark as a power in itself, rather than as a member of the Schmalkaldic League, and although it was of lesser importance (Cromwell did not mention it in any of his letters to Henry) and would soon fade into the background, it should be noted as an indication of the favour with which the development of relations with the Protestants of northern Europe was being regarded at this time. The details of Barnes's mission, including Hessian and Saxon advice, sought by the king of Denmark, are dealt with in Prüser, *England und die Schmalkaldener*, 183–91.

Melanchthon rides with it'.[63] But his efforts were to no avail. On 18 March Cromwell had to inform Henry that although the marital negotiations were proceeding well, with reports of the elder duchess's appearance very promising and a portrait of her being arranged, 'Christophor doth diligently Instante and sue for the sending of an honorable ambassiate, but he hath yet no answer.'[64]

As Schmalkaldic reluctance to provide an appropriate response grew Henry began to lose patience. Cromwell wrote to the ambassadors on 22 March, telling them that Henry marvelled at the lack of response from Philip and John Frederick to his desire for an alliance. He directed them to approach them once more to warn against any accommodation with the emperor and papacy, and to investigate the matter of an alliance for the defence of the Gospel,

> requiring and pressing them therfore that [without a]ny further protract or delayes they woll send [unto the k]inges highnes thair resolute mynd and Intencion [a]nd to shewe themselfes no les gratefull and thankfull to take and accept his good will and zele towardes them then it hath proceded of his highnes to have sent you thither. And so plainly to shewe his graces mynd unto them Inducing them to give you som resolute answer without further protract, by all suche reasons as your discation (seing the circumstantes therof) may better gether and allege for your purpose, and for inducing them to send ernestly som person or persons Instructed to conclude with his maiestye, orelles to give you full advertisment of thair purposes and procedinges.[65]

Cromwell went on to speak at length of the common ground shared by England and the League, noting that there would be nothing so disheartening or worrying to the 'papistes, ner more to the encoragement of the Evangelicall company, then to see all the professours of the same ioyned and united togeder in an indossoluble knott'.[66] But in closing he emphasised that these offers of friendship could not remain open indefinitely, without any response from the League. If the Germans continued to show no interest, 'ye shall no further presse them for the maters of allyaunces but take your iorney hither thorugh the duke of Cleves domynions, And there to mete with the Kinges oratours ther, Dr Owton and Mr Berde'.[67] If the League were set on abandoning England, then Cromwell would still pursue his policy of estab-

63 '[B]egert noch, das man ein ansehenlich botschaft in Engelland schicken wolt und Philippum Melanchton inen zugeben, das er mitritte': PC ii. 562.
64 BL, MS Cott. Vit. B.xxi, fo. 96v [StP i. 605; Merriman, Life and letters of Thomas Cromwell, ii. 201; LP xiv/1, 552].
65 BL, MS Cott. Vit. B.xxi, fo. 160v [Merriman, Life and letters of Thomas Cromwell, ii. 204; LP xiv/1, 580].
66 BL, MS Cott. Vit. B.xxi, fo. 162v [Merriman, Life and letters of Thomas Cromwell, ii. 206; LP xiv/1, 580].
67 BL, MS Cott. Vit. B.xxi, fo. 163 [Merriman, Life and letters of Thomas Cromwell, ii. 206; LP xiv/1, 580].

lishing a common alliance with Protestant Germany through a marriage with Cleves.

Upon receiving Cromwell's letter, Mont and Paynell redoubled their efforts. Mont made clear to his German friends the setbacks which the cause of the Gospel had suffered in England and the need for German help. Jakob Sturm reported that Henry 'has issued an open mandate in England in which priests and monks are forbidden to marry. And still he allows the private mass with all its accretions to remain.'[68] John Frederick and Philip were also told of the reversals which had followed the king's return from the summer progress, and were persuaded to write to Henry of their distress that the issues of the private mass, communion in both kinds and celibacy were still being called into question.[69] Melanchthon wrote to Henry on 26 March,[70] 1 April[71] and 10 April.[72] He also wrote supportive letters to Cranmer on 30 March,[73] to Cromwell about the same time[74] and to Nicholas Heath on 1 April.[75] Melanchthon's letter of 1 April paid particular attention to the royal proclamation of which Mont had evidently advised him. He lamented the articles on clerical marriage and on the enforced observance of ceremonies and provided arguments to show why each should be rescinded.[76] In his letter to Cranmer, Melanchthon was rather more frank, complaining bitterly at the articles on marriage and ceremonies in the proclamation. Nevertheless, he did acknowledge reports he had heard which had 'not only extolled Cranmer's piety but explained the dangerous conflicts in which he is engaged and the constancy and moderation which he maintains'. He also recognised the efforts which the evangelical faction had made to lessen the impact of the proclamation's directives on ceremonies by means of the final two articles which had been appended to it, saying that 'I do not accuse you, Cromwell or Latimer, who I think have sought to soften the edict by the addition of a clause promising public correction of abuses.'[77]

Yet if these letters were helpful, what was really wanted was the promised major embassy, including, if possible, Henry's favourite Lutheran, Philip Melanchthon. In spite of the difficulties, Mont plugged away valiantly on this point. And, finally, his efforts met with a measure of success. Although in the light of the progress being made with Charles the Germans declared them-

---

68 '[H]at ein offen mandat in Engelland verkunden lossen, dorin er den pfaffen und munchen die ehe verbeutet. so lost er noch die privatmessen mit allen iren anhengen pleiben': PC ii. 562.
69 Strype, *Ecclesiastical memorials*, i/2, 400 [LP xiv/1, 698].
70 BL, MS Cott. Cleo. E.v, fos 251–3 [LP xiv/1, 613].
71 BL, MS Cott. Cleo. E.v, fos 256–63 [LP xiv/1, 666].
72 LP xiv/1, 737. This letter was sent with the May 1539 embassy to England.
73 LP xiv/1, 631 [CR iii. 676–9].
74 A letter from Melanchthon to Cromwell is mentioned and partly quoted in summary and verbatim in the minister's letter to Henry of 24 April: LP xiv/1, 844.
75 CR iii. 679–81 [LP xiv/1, 667].
76 BL, MS Cott. Cleo. E.v, fos 256–63 [LP xiv/1, 666].
77 LP xiv/1, 631 [CR iii. 676–9].

selves unwilling to send a major embassy to England,[78] in early April they did at least agree to open negotiations on the English matter.[79] After a few days of discussions a decision was reached: though the League remained firm that a major embassy would not be sent to England, it did consent to despatch a minor mission to enter into discussions with Henry.[80] On 8 April it was ready to leave.[81]

The Act of Six Articles, April–June 1539

While Mont and Paynell were working away in Germany, theological discussions continued in England. These were still dominated by the six major issues: the real presence, communion in both kinds, private masses, clerical marriage, vows of chastity and auricular confession. The only other important question at this time was ceremonies, but by the early months of 1539 this had been satisfactorily settled and had ceased to be an issue of dispute. A royal proclamation of February 1539 reinforced the November directive on the observance of ceremonies, but again included the reformist *caveat* that

> neither holy bread nor holy water, candles, bows, nor ashes hallowed, or creeping and kissing the cross be the workers or works of our salvation . . . . as the word doth no good to him that abuseth it, nor unworthily receiveth it, so is not the ceremony fruitful to him that would superstitiously abuse it.[82]

Though a gushing observer would later wax lyrical in an oft-cited letter to Lord Lisle at Henry's creeping to the cross on Good Friday and his regular use of ceremonies at this time, it should be remembered that the correspondent failed to realise (or at least to mention) that the November and February proclamations meant that Henry was doing these things in a way which Protestants would find adiaphoristically acceptable.[83] Certainly, a group of London Protestants appear to have been satisfied with the proclamation when they wrote on 8 March to a continental reformer that

> ceremonies are still tolerated, but explanations of them are added; so that now the holy water, as it is called, is for no other purpose than to refresh our minds

---

[78] Strassburg, which favoured rejecting the imperial negotiations and joining with England, was the exception: PC iii. 577–9, 580, 581.
[79] Jakob Sturm reported that negotiations had begun on 3 April: PC ii. 588.
[80] Sturm reported this to Strassburg on 8 April: PC ii. 594.
[81] Prüser, *England und die Schmalkaldener*, 169.
[82] Hughes and Larkin, *Tudor royal proclamations*, i. 279.
[83] *LP* xiv/1, 967. Some historians have also ignored this important qualification: Brigden, *London and the Reformation*, 302; Starkey, *Personalities and politics*, 153; Scarisbrick, *Henry VIII*, 422.

with the remembrance of the sprinkling of the blood of Christ. . . . These things are retained for the sake of preventing any disturbances.[84]

Thus the issue of ceremonies was something that all the main religious persuasions could live with. Discussions on the other matters, however, continued unabated. Because the real presence was disputed only at the popular level, those about the king soon agreed that it should be put forward for immediate settlement. Since neither the king's evangelical nor his conservative advisers felt threatened by the issue, it was commonly agreed to adopt the most authoritative attitude possible. Sometime near the end of winter, it was proposed to settle the question by means of a legislative instrument in parliament (which had recently been scheduled to convene in the forthcoming summer). The factional innocuousness of the proposal to deal with doctrine by statute is demonstrated by the fact that the suggestion for parliamentary action first emanated from one of the evangelical faction. As Stephen Gardiner would write in the next reign: 'And I shall never forget that the Lord Audelay, late Chauncelor, told me . . . that when our late soveraigne lord devised with hym how to resist the detestable heresie against the Sacrament of thAltar, he advised the King's Majestie to make an acte of parliament of yt.'[85] Thus was born a piece of legislation to abolish diversity in opinion; it began life as a one-article device, in which only the popular, factionally irrelevant issue of the real presence would be dealt with. This is why it was Thomas Audley, since the death of Edward Foxe the third ranking evangelical, who first proposed the legislation. And it is why Cromwell would have had no qualms about noting in his remembrances in early March that there would be a 'devise in the parliament for the unitie in religion';[86] an act to outlaw diversity of opinion on the real presence was perfectly acceptable to him and the evangelical faction.

The other five issues, however, had as yet not been considered for final settlement. They remained very much alive, contested heavily by the evangelicals and conservatives, clearly some way from the sort of general agreement which had been reached on the real presence. On 8 March a letter to a continental reformer mentioned that 'nothing has as yet been settled respecting the marriage of the clergy, although some persons have very freely preached before the king on the subject'.[87] Alluding to another point of dispute from 1538, it was also noted that 'the mass is not asserted to be a sacrifice for the living and the dead, but only a representation of Christ's

---

84 *Original letters*, 624 [LP xiv/1, 466].
85 Gardiner to the privy council, 30 Aug. 1547, in Muller, *Gardiner's letters*, 369. Gardiner said that Audley had told him this during Easter 1543. The example was cited as part of a thesis arguing that acts made by parliament could only be undone by the same.
86 PRO, E 36/143, fo. 67 [LP xiv/1, 655]. For the dating of this remembrance see Elton, *Studies*, i. 205.
87 *Original letters*, 624 [LP xiv/1, 466].

passion',[88] a comment which if rather optimistic does reflect the fact that the private mass too was a subject under discussion at this time. Nevertheless, for the moment no immediate settlement of these issues was envisaged; not only were they still being worked out at the upper level of government, but they were issues which Henry wished first to be debated with the major theological delegation from the Schmalkaldic League.

The embassy which the League sent to England from Frankfurt in April 1539 was not the major delegation the evangelicals had hoped for and Henry expected. Nevertheless, it could still do a lot of good both for the fortunes of the English Reformation and for Anglo-Schmalkaldic relations. If Henry could be offered attractive terms of alliance and promised a future theological disputation with Melanchthon and other learned men, he might well put on hold any final settlement of the five issues which had come to prominence during the summer of 1538. Although Henry had shown himself to be unfavourable to Lutheran doctrine on the abuses as early as 1535, he had also shown since the mid-1530s a consistent interest in theological consultations with Philip Melanchthon. The fact that he had renewed this request in his letters to John Frederick and Philip of 1 October 1538 and through Mont and Paynell very recently shows that he remained interested in a thoroughgoing consultation with the League on disputed points of doctrine with a view to reaching an agreement.

The League, however, failed to appreciate any of this. Not only were the ambassadors sent to England in April led by two laymen, Franz Burchard and the Hessian nobleman and diplomat Ludwig von Baumbach, but their instructions also contained very one-sided political demands. To make things even worse they conveyed a letter from the League to Henry which dismissed completely the king's interest in continuing the theological discussions between England and the League which had been going on since 1536. There were two sets of instructions. The supplementary instructions were the more reasonable. They were chiefly concerned with explaining to Henry the implications of the Frankfurt Interim for Anglo-Schmalkaldic relations. In particular, it was pointed out that although clause seven of the agreement made with Charles stated that the League could not admit any further members, this did not mean that England and the League could have nothing to do with each other. The ambassadors were to tell the king that although the Frankfurt Interim did not allow the League to admit Henry as a member, 'the words "to admit to your League" do not go so far as to prevent the League members from making a supplementary agreement with the king, particularly in the event that we or the king are attacked or injured on account of the papacy and religion'.[89] The ambassadors' main instructions were not

---

88 Ibid.
89 '[E]rstegken sich di wort "in ire bundtnus zu nemen", nicht so weit, das die stand daneben mit I.Kön.W. nicht ainen nebenverstandt machen mochten, sonderlich uf den fal, da I.Kön.W. dergedacht des babsts und religion halben vergewaltigt oder beschwert werden

especially enticing from an English point of view. They dealt with the possible forms which an alliance with England might take. They directed the ambassadors to propose that Henry should contribute 15,000 crowns a year for the next eight years, with an additional 30,000 crowns to be contributed in the event of war. In return for this, the Protestants offered nothing to Henry – nothing, that is, unless one counts helping him recruit mercenaries in Germany at his own cost (or, at the very most, with the costs of mustering and getting the soldiers as far as the sea paid for by the Germans).[90]

The introductory letter which the ambassadors brought to Henry from the League was similarly unhelpful. Most significantly, it contained a unilateral declaration that the Anglo-Schmalkaldic theological discussions were at a close:

> concerning an embassy, in which the king's majesty desireth that some excellently learned men might be sent to him for a further disputation; it cannot now be resolved, for such causes especially as we have partly signified to the king and partly understood by the very circumstances of the times. And let the king take this in good part. We judge the opinion of our men is sufficiently known to the serene king, and the learned in England, as well by our confession as by those disputations which the ambassadors of the most serene king [had] three years ago, and lately the English bishops had with our men, sent thither.[91]

These papers, reflecting the moderating influence which the Frankfurt Interim had had on the League's diplomacy, offered Henry nothing in political terms and refused him any possibility of the major theological discussions he had so long sought. They were at best unlikely to gain a positive response from the king; in the event they would produce results which would be disastrous both for the purposes of the evangelical faction and for the general development of Anglo-Schmalkaldic relations.

On 8 April 1539, the German ambassadors left Frankfurt. They met Mont and Paynell in Cleves, and travelled with them to England, arriving in London on 23 April, five days before the opening of parliament.[92] From the outset, things began to go wrong. First, Cromwell contracted a serious illness just as the ambassadors arrived. On 19 April he wrote to Henry that 'I fynde upon me some grutge of an ague', making it impossible to give 'my due and promised attendaunce upon your highnes'.[93] The ague soon developed into a

solte und hinwidderumb': TStWei, Reg. H. 260, no. 111, vol. 1, fo. 29 [Mentz, *Johann Friedrich*, iii. 433].

[90] TStWei, Reg. H. 260, no. 111, vol. 1, fos 31–41.

[91] The letter was actually from the League's two leaders, John Frederick and Philip: Strype, *Ecclesiastical memorials*, i/2, 399–400 [*LP* xiv/1, 698]; TStWei, Reg. H. 260, no. 111, vol. 1, fos 6–12 (Latin draft); BL, MS Cott. Cleo. E.vi, vol. 2, fos 297–302 (Latin final copy).

[92] Prüser, *England und die Schmalkaldener*, 169.

[93] BL, MS Cott. Tit. B.i, fo. 271 [Merriman, *Life and letters of Thomas Cromwell*, ii. 214; StP i. 610; *LP* xiv/1, 806].

tertian fever, which confined Cromwell to house until 10 May.[94] This sickness came at the worst time possible for Cromwell. Later in the year he would confide to a visiting German embassy that the conservative dominance of the events of this time had only been achieved 'by some bishops during his illness',[95] a remark which suggests that had he been in full health he might have been able to forestall the workings of his enemies. As it was, his conservative opponents would now have the court to themselves for the next three weeks. In that short time Cromwell's rivals would use his absence from political life to devastating effect.

For the moment Cromwell did what he could from his sickbed at St James's. On 24 April he wrote to Henry of the arrival of Burchard and Baumbach.[96] Given that most of Cromwell's communications with Henry were oral, this letter provides a fascinating insight into Cromwell's approach when giving the king counsel. To begin with he noted that John Frederick and Philip 'do contynue styll in their loving and frendely observacion towardes your maiestie, very Joyouse of your graces allyance and confederacion'.[97] He went on to use the Germans to voice reservations about the factionally relevant points which had been raised in the November proclamation, saying that the

> Landgrave hath found that part of your graces proclamacions somwhat strange wherin it is spoken de coniugio sacerdotum, sayeng that thesame was agenst the true doctrine of the votes which they professed, and herupon also Melanchthon hath writen unto me that he hath seen that proclamacion wherin certain evill doctrines be forbeden [ie. the popular heresies against the sacrament of the altar: sacramentarianism and anabaptism], and also certain true doctrine whiche they professe in Alemayn concernyng de votis et coniugio, but that he hopeth forasmoch as in the said proclamacions your highnes promisseth to abolishe abuses that your grace shal consydere thesame more exactely and at the last mitigate thesame.[98]

Thus Cromwell artfully advanced objections to two distinct points in the November proclamation, those added, with the help of Henry's insertions, to the article on clerical marriage: vows of chastity on the one hand, and priestly

---

94 S. E. Lehmberg, *The later parliaments of Henry VIII, 1536–1547*, Cambridge 1977, 55–7. The date is that of Cromwell's first appearance in parliament; he missed the opening on 28 April, and Lehmberg suggests that the date of his first attendance should be taken as the date of his recovery, since he would have appeared as soon as his health allowed.

95 '[D]urch etzliche bischoff dohin bracht in seiner schwocheit': TStWei, Reg. H. 260, no. 111, vol. 2, fo. 31v (the account, from September 1539, of Burchard and Dolzig which will be examined in greater detail in chapter 5).

96 BL, MS Cott. Cleo. E.v, fo. 185 [Merriman, *Life and letters of Thomas Cromwell*, ii. 219–22; *LP* xiv/1, 844].

97 BL, MS Cott. Cleo. E.v, fo. 185 [Merriman, *Life and letters of Thomas Cromwell*, ii. 220; *LP* xiv/1, 844].

98 Ibid.

marriage on the other. This was a typical example of the evangelicals' use of the League as an instrument of faction. There was more to follow. In suggesting that Henry might reconsider his position on vows, Cromwell mentioned a comment to the Germans by Mont, who had said that

> he might well affirme that your highnes is not to scrupulouse in the matier de votis and that sundry nonnes and religiouse women have ben discharged oute of their houses with honest pensions during their lyves and not forbeden but suffred to marye.[99]

Turning to priestly marriage, Cromwell used Mont's observations obliquely to suggest the possibility of an eventual revision of the official line on Henry's pet theological subject:

> as for prestes he thinketh the cause of the prohibicion was bicause they must preach the worde of god and that it is thought that the common people as yet weake in the knowlege of the worde and of other thinges myght therby conceyve an opinion of concupiscence in them, and by reason thereof contempne their preachinges and the worde of god. But what your grace wold do after ward whan the people shall wexe stronger and hable to eate solide meate, he answered he could not diffine nor Juge.[100]

Apart from using the Germans to make doctrinal points, Cromwell also employed them to attack those conservative bishops who were agitating in favour of a conservative settlement on the abuses. Henry's favourite German was again the mouthpiece:

> Melanchton further writeth unto me his opinion of your graces bishops by thies wordes, ['at this time many excuse the abuses with cunningly thought interpretations, or mitigate them, so that by artifice they support them. . . . I see this pernicious sophisticate of the Church acting like high priests among you. Indeed care must be taken, so that the truth is not again overwhelmed by this sophisticate . . . ['] This is theffect of Melanchthons lettere to me.[101]

Finally, Cromwell did what he could to persuade Henry to consider agreeing to an alliance with the League:

> the leage evangelike is allways stedfast and constantly sett to byde in their opinion yea and rather to dye then relente. . . . I am assured thise oratours

---

99 Ibid.
100 Ibid.
101 BL, MS Cott. Cleo. E.v, fo. 185v [Merriman, *Life and letters of Thomas Cromwell*, ii. 221; *LP* xiv/1, 844]. The citation from Melanchthon was rendered in its original Latin: 'Multi ubique hoc tempore astute cogitatis Interpretationibus excusant abusus aut leniunt, ut arte stabiliant eos . . . hanc sophisticam perniciosam ecclesie video Imitari Mitratos apud vos. Sed cavendum est ne hac sophistica rursus obruatur veritas.'

cummyng shalbe very formidable to the bishop of Rome and to other of his adherentes also. ffor doubtles, If your majestie shal happen to joyne with them the papistes in my Jugement shalbe half indesperate.[102]

But Cromwell's efforts were badly handicapped by his inability to see the king. The court was far away at Richmond and Cromwell was sick. Though he could write to the king, his rivals could speak to him; as he and they knew, face-to-face contact was always the more effective in seeking to win Henry over to a particular viewpoint or course of action. It was perhaps at this stage that the enemies of Cromwell began to press around the king and seek to turn the arrival of the small legation from the League to their own advantage. Serious efforts now began to be made by the conservatives to persuade the king to settle in parliament, as adjuncts to the planned legislation on the real presence, the five issues of dispute which had been raised by the Schmalkaldic embassy of 1538. They could point to the renewed failure of the Germans to send a major theological delegation. They could argue that the small embassy which had arrived amounted to a rejection of Henry's interest in continued theological discussions. They could therefore persuasively advise that Henry should now press ahead with a doctrinal settlement of the five remaining unresolved theological issues without seeking further input from the Germans.

Henry probably gave careful consideration to such advice, but perhaps refrained from any final decision. Parliament would certainly pass an act abolishing popular diversity in opinion on the real presence, but whether it would also abolish factional diversity in opinion on the five issues from the summer of 1538 would remain for now an open question. First he and his council would meet and examine the German embassy and its instructions. Then a decision would be made. They would all have to gather at Westminster on 28 April for the opening of parliament. The day following could be set aside for an audience with the Germans. Thus, on 29 April, Henry and his councillors met the Germans for a preliminary audience. Though Cromwell was too ill too attend the opening of parliament, he made the special effort necessary to be present at the meeting with the Germans. Before it could get very far, however, his health failed him and he declared himself unable to continue. The audience was therefore concluded: Henry asked the ambassadors to have patience and told them that the discussions would be resumed as soon as Cromwell's health allowed.[103] It may have been at this meeting that the League's letter of 4 April, making clear that the Germans were disinclined to discuss theology further with Henry, was handed over. As the king and his conservative councillors, in the absence of the sick Cromwell, later examined the letter Henry began to take more seriously the advice being offered him. It

---

[102] Ibid.
[103] Merriman, *Life and letters of Thomas Cromwell*, i. 272–3.

was clear that the Germans were not going to provide him with the theological consultations he had so long desired; now he should go ahead with a settlement of the five outstanding theological issues. But perhaps he still deferred a final decision. At least he would wait until Cromwell was well enough to see through a full meeting with the Germans which would allow for a complete examination of their instructions and a final assessment as to the fate of the abuses.

Three days later, on 2 May, Cromwell was sufficiently fit and 'the ambassadors were directed to lord Cromwell's house [presumably because he was still too ill to venture out] in London', to resume talks with the king's 'councillors; namely, both dukes Norfolk and Suffolk, the chancellor of the kingdom of England [ie. Audley], the High Admiral [ie. Southampton], lord Cromwell, and the bishop of Durham, who is called Tunstall'.[104] Discussions were not held up by Cromwell's illness this time, and it was possible to examine all aspects of the ambassadors' instructions. At the conclusion of the discussions, the councillors, most probably in the absence of the housebound Cromwell, left 'to inform the king's majesty of all the matters which had been treated'.[105]

Perhaps it was at this meeting that the one-sided political demands of the Germans and their unwillingness to enter into any form of theological discourse or accommodation with Henry were finally confirmed. When Henry later received an account of the ambassadors' demands from his councillors he decided to accept the advice of those dominating the advisory process in the absence of Cromwell. Now he directed that the five outstanding theological issues from the previous summer should be included in the parliamentary settlement of 1539.[106]

---

[104] '[S]indt die gesanten in hern Crummello hausz zu London erfordert. . . . rethe alsz nemmelich die bayde herczogen Norfoick vnd Soyffoick desz richz engelant cantzeller der oberste ammerall her Crumellus vnd der bisschoff von Derm Tunstallius genant': ibid. i. 273.

[105] '[D]er ding allenthalben koniglicher mayestät zu berichten auff sich gennommen': ibid. i. 274.

[106] There is very little direct evidence for what finally made Henry decide to enact the religious legislation of the 1539 parliament or precisely when he made his decision; the account given here, like all previous work on the act, must be speculative. Nevertheless, the general view that the League's diplomatic hesitancy provided Henry's conservative advisers with a golden opportunity to push for a conservative settlement will be supported in chapter 5 by the detailed citation of a German letter which conveyed secret complaints from the evangelical faction on the Schmalkaldeners' diplomatic negligence and the role it had played in the making of the 1539 religious legislation. Redworth, 'Study in the formulation of policy', 51–3 (his views are also taken on board by Brigden, London and the Reformation, 303–4, and MacCulloch, Cranmer, 247–8), suggests that the final trigger for the act was the revelation to Henry, during Cromwell's illness, of sacramentarian heresies at Calais. Though the reconstruction offered in this study has stressed the influence of Anglo-Schmalkaldic relations on the king's decision to settle the five outstanding theological issues, it might be that the difficulties at Calais which burst upon the court in early May – even if they were only concerned with the heresy against the sacrament of the altar – gave heightened urgency to Henry's move towards a settlement of religion by statute. That notwithstanding, it remains difficult

In their report, the German ambassadors noted that after the meeting of 2 May, 'the matter took a delay of some days because the aforementioned king's councillors daily had to be in the parliament'.[107] While the Germans waited, Henry got on with his religious settlement. On 5 May Thomas Audley announced to the House of Lords that in order to extinguish diversity in opinion, the Lords should select a committee to examine certain issues. Although these were not specified and no record of the subsequent discussions exists, their probable content is revealed by the actions of the duke of Norfolk on 16 May. Norfolk announced to the Lords that the theological committees had been unable to resolve the issues put to them, and therefore the king wanted the House to provide resolutions on six questions: the real presence; communion in both kinds; vows of chastity; private masses; priestly marriage; auricular confession.

This boded ill for the reformers. The conservatives had managed to 'factionalise' even the previously innocuous question of the real presence, having it introduced to the Lords in an explicitly Roman form that asked not simply whether Christ was present in the sacrament, but whether his presence was effected specifically by the agency of transubstantiation.[108] The questions on vows of chastity, priestly marriage, private masses and confession were also provocatively put, framed so as to ask not whether acceptance of them was merely necessary or advisable, but whether they were enjoined 'by God's law'.[109]

Meanwhile – indeed the very same day that Norfolk announced the six questions to the Lords – Henry directed his councillors back to the German ambassadors for a meeting at St James's Palace. Though Cromwell had now been well for a week, he was unable to help the embassy. The councillors had been sent with specific instructions from the king, and these not even a healthy Cromwell could bend. Henry wanted the ambassadors to be notified of his dissatisfaction with the League's diplomacy, and in particular the one-sided nature of their instructions. His irritation was derived partly from information which had been received suggesting that under the Frankfurt Interim the League could not admit new members. The ambassadors, however, were able to explain satisfactorily that the League could still arrange a supplementary agreement with Henry.[110] The other problem which surfaced

---

to see how Calais could have contributed to the substance of the final five 'factional' articles.

[107] '[H]aben sich die dinge etliche tage vorczugen ausz ursach desz koniglicher mayestät rethte obgemelt teglich insz parlament haben sin mossen': Merriman, *Life and letters of Thomas Cromwell*, i. 274 (ambassadors' account).

[108] 'An Eucharistia verum sit Corpus Dominicum, absque Transubstatione': *Journals of the House of Lords*, i. 109.

[109] '[D]e Jure divino': ibid.

[110] Ambassadors' report in Merriman, *Life and letters of Thomas Cromwell*, i. 274. This explanation was given in accordance with their supplementary instructions, discussed at p. 151 above. Merriman, unaware that the ambassadors had instructions to explain that the

on 16 May, however, proved much more difficult to resolve: this was the question of reciprocal military aid. The ambassadors were told that Henry could only consider an alliance if obligations and duties were the same for each side. The ambassadors, however, were unwilling to shift from their instructions. They informed the councillors that in an alliance with the League Henry must be prepared to provide substantial military aid for the Germans while receiving very little for himself.[111]

After this meeting the councillors went back to discuss these questions with Henry. The king, doubtless now even more convinced of the political and religious intransigence of the Germans, directed them to return to the ambassadors to reject the Schmalkaldic offers. On 18 May the councillors and the ambassadors met again at St James's Palace. They told the Germans that Henry would only conclude an agreement with them if their powers were extended so that he could be offered a military package equivalent to that which they sought from him. The councillors said that Henry considered the ambassadors' instructions 'very narrow and restricted', and suggested that they write back to Germany for expanded powers.[112] But the Germans remained unyielding. They refused to shift from their instructions, and even audaciously sought to convince the councillors that the unequal military conditions would in fact be of equal benefit to Henry.[113]

Not surprisingly, such arguments as these were to no avail. The ambassadors were now left to themselves for the following eight days. In the meantime, the battle over the six theological questions continued. During the period from 19 May to the temporary prorogation of parliament on 23 May the main debates took place in the Lords, as Cranmer publicly opposed the conservatives and Henry appeared in the chamber on 19 and 21 May to lend weight to the movement towards a conservative settlement.[114] During the prorogation from 23 to 30 May, the six questions were discussed by convocation and the process of forming them into a coherent piece of legislation was begun. As the legislation entered its closing stages in the last week of May, Henry emerged to exert a decisive influence on its final shape. His close in-

---

Frankfurt Interim would not prevent the Germans from concluding an alliance with Henry, wrongly assumes that his anger at clause seven of the agreement made with the emperor precipitated the collapse of the negotiations.
111 Ambassadors to John Frederick, 16 May, TStWei, Reg. H. 260, no. 111, vol. 1, fos 54–5 (cypher), 56–7 (decypher).
112 '[S]ere enge vnd restringirt': Merriman, Life and letters of Thomas Cromwell, i. 275.
113 Ambassadors' report, ibid. i. 274–5. The ambassadors argued that the proposed alliance would in fact be of equivalent benefit to Henry because not only would the king be able to muster foot and horse soldiers in Germany, but the continued existence of the League would in itself be an advantage to England, since it could only be a hindrance to the pope and his adherents. Thus, they were sure that such a reputed and rich king as Henry would not mind contributing a sum of money for the defence of Christian affairs.
114 The most recent narrative account of this period is in Redworth, 'Study in the formulation of policy', 58–9. See also Lehmberg, Later parliaments, 65–8; Ridley, Cranmer, 178–84.

volvement in the drafting process at this time is especially clearly seen in the evidence of the one extant bill, which features corrections in his own hand throughout. It was during this stage that the influence of the 1538 theological deliberations on Henry's thinking and the shape of the legislation became most plainly apparent.

There was, of course, one issue which was not relevant to the Anglo-Schmalkaldic discussions of 1538: the real presence. Indeed on this, the first item in the bill, Cranmer and the evangelical bishops were able to persuade Henry that the conservative advance should be moderated. The bill dropped the factionally relevant word 'transubstantiation' which Norfolk had introduced on 16 May and simply dealt with the real presence in its broader sense, asking 'Whither in the most blessed sacrament of the aulter remaineth after the consecration the substance of breade and wyne or noo'.[115] This question was answered in the negative: only the substance of Christ remained in the sacrament after consecration. This response, though it failed to include the substance of the bread and wine with Christ's body and blood in the eucharist, as Lutheran teaching demanded, avoided an explicit endorsement of transubstantiation and hence could be acceptable to all parties.

The remaining articles were quite different, however. The second article, on communion in both kinds, bore unmistakeable traces of the parallel pronouncement Henry had made in his reply to the Germans the previous year. As Edward Foxe had made clear as early as 1536, Henry was decidedly wary of the Lutheran view that communion must be dispensed in both kinds, and that this was not a matter indifferent but required by the law of God. In his reply to the German letter on the abuses in 1538, Henry had not said that communion in both kinds was wrong – indeed, under certain conditions he had approved the practice – but had argued that it was not the only way of communicating. In the draft bill Henry ensured that this line of reasoning was followed precisely. Even in the preamble, where it was asked whether it 'be necessary that all men' should communicate in both kinds, Henry inserted the qualification 'by godes law', so as to focus the question of dispute on whether God actually required communication in both kinds or whether there was an element of choice.[116] In the answer to this question, Henry confirmed the continuing influence of the 1538 reply to the Germans. Where the opening stated that 'communion in bothe kyndes is not necessary'; Henry added 'ad salutem by the lawe of god':[117] in case anyone had missed the point, Henry wanted it spelt out, as it had been in his letter to the Germans, that taking communion in one kind only would not endanger one's chances of salvation. Henry then went on to add an elaboration which borrowed directly from the reasoning of 1538 that one could communicate with bread or wine only, because each on its own contained the entire body and blood of Christ.

---

[115] BL, MS Cott. Cleo. E.v, fo. 327v.
[116] Ibid.
[117] Ibid. fo. 330.

The labyrinthine verbal analysis of 1 Corinthians which had figured in 1538 was not repeated, but its reasoning was followed closely in Henry's holograph addition, which stated 'and that it is to be belevyd and not dowted off but that in the flesse under forme of brede is the very bludde and in the blude under forme off wyne is the very flesse as well appart as thowght they wer bothe togyder'.[118]

The third article in the bill concerned priestly marriage. This had been earmarked as a point of major disagreement between Henry and the Schmalkaldeners when Cromwell informed the newly arrived German ambassadors in 1538 that Henry had misgivings about that article from the 1536 Wittenberg discussions. The uncompromising line which Henry took in his 1538 reply to the Germans was then echoed in the November proclamation. Once again, in the summer of 1539, Henry's corrections to the draft bill strongly suggest that he was leaning on the reasoning he had employed with Tunstall the previous year. The principal argument against clerical marriage in 1538 had been that priests cannot have a divided allegiance to a wife and to God. Henry applied this argument to the question in the preamble, adding after the words 'whither priests', the clause, 'that is to sey, men dedicate to god'; and inserting after the words 'ordre of presthode', the qualification, 'by whyche they dedicate themselfe to cryst first'.[119] The bill then went on to pronounce on clerical marriage with a remarkable severity, declaring that priests may not marry by the law of God.[120] No pope would ever claim that priests were forbidden to marry by divine law (it was considered a matter of ecclesiastical discipline); the formulation of this article was one of the two most extreme in the bill.

The fourth article concerned the necessity of keeping vows of chastity and widowhood. This appeared as a result of the arguments on the necessity of keeping vows made to God which were considered in drawing up Henry's reply on clerical marriage in 1538; it had subsequently appeared, thanks to Henry's holograph insertions, as a distinct aspect of the November proclamation's article on priestly marriage. At the draft bill stage in 1539, Henry again made a number of corrections to the article which reflect the influence of his deliberations with Tunstall in 1538. Although the bill spoke only of the divine necessity of keeping vows of chastity, Henry inserted into the question in the preamble and the article itself the words, 'made to god advysedly', so as to highlight, as he and Tunstall had done in 1538, the importance of a vow

---

118 Ibid.
119 Ibid. fo. 327v.
120 It might also be noted that the reply to the Germans in 1538 had suggested that priests should follow an unmarried life because they entered under such orders willingly. Although the addition 'wyllyngly takyng on them', which Henry proposed to put before, 'the ordre of the presthode', was deleted, it does at least show again that Henry was maintaining the theological line on this question that he and Tunstall had worked out during the previous summer: ibid.

made to God.[121] Henry also personally expanded the scope of this article so as to include vows of 'wyduhode';[122] the necessity of keeping vows of widowhood had also been directly anticipated in Henry's reply to the Germans in 1538, with the citation of evidence from 1 Timothy demonstrating that widows who broke their vows to God would suffer damnation.[123] Thus emerged the other extreme article in the bill, which stated that vows of chastity or widowhood made to God must be observed by the law of God.

The fifth article in the bill dealt with the private mass, one of the main obstacles to persuading Henry to accept reformed doctrine. The Germans had sought to achieve a resolution of the matter with Foxe's embassy in 1536 and had failed; they were no more successful with Henry in 1538. Nevertheless, in 1539, this article was not an unmitigated triumph for the conservatives. The question announced by Norfolk on 16 May had been whether private masses were necessary 'by divine law'.[124] By the time the question appeared at the draft bill stage, however, this had been changed to 'stande with the law of god'; a small but definite retreat from Catholic orthodoxy.[125] When it came to the article itself, Henry crossed out entirely the version in the draft bill and substituted in his own hand a formula which also avoided saying that private masses were necessary by divine law and instead stressed their efficacy in a manner which again strongly recalls his deliberations with Tunstall in 1538: 'it is mett and necessary that private masses be continuyd and admyttyd in thys our englice Churche and congregation as wherby good and chrysten peaple (orderyng themselfe accordyngly) do resayve bothe godly and goodly consolations and benyfites and it is agreable allso to godes law'.[126]

The sixth article was concerned with the necessity of confession. This was the issue which had come to prominence during the first phase of the 1538 Anglo-Schmalkaldic discussions, when the conservatives had managed to prevail with an orthodox pronouncement on auricular confession. Nevertheless, in this as in all the articles under discussion in the summer of 1539, the support of the king was essential to success, and on confession Henry was somewhat ambivalent. Though Norfolk's questions on 16 May asked whether confession was necessary 'by divine law',[127] this soon came under attack from the evangelical side. As, in the last week of May, the conservatives sought to push in convocation for an endorsement of the divine authority of confession they found the king unwilling to accept the unequivocally orthodox statement which the Lutheran ambassadors had conceded the year before. Though the 'expedient and necessary' formula which Cranmer and the

---

121 Ibid. fos 328, 330.
122 Ibid. fos 328 (spelt 'widuhode'), 330.
123 1 Tim. v.11–12; Burnet, *History of the Reformation*, iv. 386.
124 '[D]e Jure divino': *Journals of the House of Lords*, i. 109.
125 BL, MS Cott. Cleo. E.v, fo. 328. Henry personally changed the original formulation of the question, from 'agreable to the lawe of god', to the formulation cited.
126 Ibid. fo. 330.
127 '[D]e Jure divino': *Journals of the House of Lords*, i. 109.

German ambassadors had quibbled over in 1538 was included, Henry supported the reformed view in omitting the claim that confession was a practice instituted by God. And when Tunstall, perhaps overestimating the degree of influence he had attained in the king's theological counsels, persisted in trying to convince Henry that he was misguided, he received a strong royal ticking-off for his troubles.[128] Thus the formulation which Henry examined and accepted at the draft bill stage represented a partial victory for the reformers: it stated that it was expedient and necessary to retain confession in the Church, but said nothing of divine ordination.

As deliberations over the final shape of the religious legislation entered their closing stages, Henry granted the Schmalkaldic ambassadors a last audience on 26 May. He told them that he was well inclined towards the idea of an alliance with the League, but that the suggested conditions of mutual aid were unfair. What he desired was 'an honourable, honest and mutually useful understanding'.[129] But since the ambassadors had no further powers than those which they had revealed thus far, he was left with no choice other than to dismiss them. Perhaps on the prompting of one of the evangelical faction, the ambassadors at this point saw fit to question Henry's actions in 'letting some articles of religion be negotiated in the parliament', asking the king that he be guided only by the truth in those matters.[130] This was difficult ground for two lay representatives of an alliance which had in the previous month refused to send theologians to Henry for doctrinal discussions, and in the ensuing conversation 'the king entered into a hefty disputation with the ambassadors on priestly marriage', before finally dismissing them, bullied, beaten and no doubt rather frightened.[131]

The course of this final audience epitomised the decline in Anglo-Schmalkaldic relations since the summer of 1538. Cromwell made a last desperate proposal designed to salvage something and keep the negotiations alive, suggesting an arrangement whereby a sum of money would be contributed by all parties and be available to whichever were attacked first. But even this was not discussed by the ambassadors, who claimed that they were barred from any further negotiation by their lack of appropriate powers.[132] The failure of the embassy was complete. On 31 May the Germans left England with three short letters.[133] Two of these were identical letters to John Frederick and Philip from Henry, in which he complained that the ambassadors

---

128 BL, MS Cott. Cleo. E.v, fos 131–2 (one of the longest extant letters in the king's hand).
129 '[E]yn rumelich erlich und baidersicz trostlich vorstentnisse': Merriman, *Life and letters of Thomas Cromwell*, i. 276.
130 '[E]tczliche artikel der religion im parlament handeln lassen': ibid.
131 '[D]ie konigliche mayestät in eyne hefftige disputacion desz artikelsz die priesterehe belangend': ibid.
132 Ambassadors' report, ibid. i. 276–7.
133 Scarisbrick, *Henry VIII*, 367 n. 2, mistakenly asserts that the ambassadors 'lingered in England until the end of the summer'. He seems to confuse here the Schmalkaldic embassy of the early summer with the Saxon ambassadors of the late summer who accompanied the Cleves delegation to England (see chapter 5).

had insufficient powers and that the proposals on non-reciprocal military assistance were unacceptable.[134] The other was from Cromwell to John Frederick, in which he regretted the outcome of the embassy, but assured him that he was doing all he and his offices would allow to advance the Gospel and establish an alliance between Henry and the princes of Germany. In closing he said that he had had conversations with the ambassadors which he hoped the duke would consider well, and that he would make further efforts to return the friendship which Henry bore for him.[135]

On 10 June 1539, the Act of Six Articles became law. Its format and substance were virtually identical to the corrected version of the bill which Henry had examined in the last week of May.[136] The argument which this study has presented for the emergence of the act is a novel one. Heretofore, historians have generally seen it as a monolithic piece of legislation, containing six articles of roughly similar provenance and equal importance.[137] It has been explained principally as a response to domestic and foreign demands. J. J. Scarisbrick, for example, has suggested that it is

difficult to explain fully, but certainly it was partly prompted by two motives: to assuage a largely conservative nation at a moment when it was supremely necessary to avoid all domestic unrest; to take the sting out of the foreign crusade against a heretical king then being mooted. The act was probably above all else a panic-measure, therefore, a sudden display of orthodoxy to disarm enemies at home and abroad.[138]

J. A. Williamson has also asserted that the legislation was passed so as 'to soften foreign discontent and please the great non-Protestant majority of his own people',[139] and a similar view has been put forward by J. A. Muller.[140] Others have tended to stress the effect of either domestic or foreign exigencies, rather than both together. The interest of the king in dealing with a restless population has been emphasised by Susan Brigden,[141] while David Loades has also noted that the legislation 'was not a surrender to continental pres-

---

134 HStMar, PA 1800, fo. 66 (final version of letter to Philip); TStWei, Reg. H. 260, no. 111, vol. 1, fos 63 (final version of letter to John Frederick), 64–6 (German trans.).
135 TStWei, Reg. H. 260, no. 111, vol. 1, fo. 67.
136 G. R. Elton, *The Tudor constitution: documents and commentary*, Cambridge 1960, 391.
137 Some historians (for example, Wernham, *Before the armada*, 145–6; Redworth, 'Study in the formulation of policy', 46; Jenkyns, *Remains of Thomas Cranmer*, i, pp. xxiv–xxv; J. H. Blunt, *The Reformation of the Church of England*, London 1878, 472–3) have noted the coincidence between the points of controversy in 1538 and some or all of the latter five articles of the Act of Six Articles. On the basis of this they have suggested a connection. None, however, has examined the 1538 discussions in any detail or dealt with the events between the summer of 1538 and the summer of 1539 in order to demonstrate its nature or development.
138 Scarisbrick, *Henry VIII*, 365.
139 Williamson, *Tudor age*, 162.
140 J. A. Muller, *Stephen Gardner and the Tudor reaction*, London 1926, 79–80.
141 Brigden, *London and the Reformation*, 299–306.

sures so much as an attempt to allay the anxieties of conservative Henricians and strengthen the "national front" against the pope'.[142] The influence of foreign threats on the calculations which led to the Act of Six Articles has been stressed by a wide group of historians from R. B. Merriman – Henry demanded the act simply 'to facilitate a reconciliation with Charles and Francis; for such a statement would remove the main pretext of the emperor and French king for an attack on him, namely that they were undertaking a crusade to suppress heresy'[143] – to Glyn Redworth, who in his article on the origins of the act argued that

> the background to a conservative settlement of religion was inextricably bound up with the king's own perception of diplomatic problems and of the proposed means to their resolution. . . . As the epitome of Catholic orthodoxy,[144] the conservative Six Articles fitted in with Henry's decision to express solidarity with the Catholic powers of Europe.[145]

These interpretations are difficult to accept. To take the domestic question first: though the first article of the act was undoubtedly designed to suppress the popular heresies against the sacrament of the altar which had emerged with the Lambert affair and continued to bubble in Calais, the other five articles were not concerned with issues which had caused unrest among the English people. These were issues of major contention at the upper governmental, or factional, level only. The only diversity in opinion which the latter five articles were intended to abolish was that which existed among the small group of people around the king. Thus, the domestic argument only works where the first article of the statute is concerned. The bulk of the act should not be characterised principally as an effort to calm the domestic population. Had domestic concerns been the primary concern, it would only have added to the first article on the real presence similarly contentious questions of popular piety, such as images, ceremonies, the observance of saints' days and so on.

It is similarly difficult to grant any credence to the argument that the act was simply a response to foreign Catholic pressure. In the first place, it goes against the central tenet of the early English Reformation: that the king, and not some foreign authority, was the supreme arbiter in English religious affairs. It is hard to accept that some four years after expelling the pope for

---

[142] D. M. Loades, *Politics and the nation, 1450–1660: obedience, resistance and public order*, London 1979, 190.

[143] Merriman, *Life and letters of Thomas Cromwell*, i. 254.

[144] The suggestion that the Act of Six Articles was the 'epitome of Catholic orthodoxy' is debateable. See Scarisbrick, *Henry VIII*, 409–10, 419; Kreider, *English chantries*, 147.

[145] Redworth, 'Study in the formulation of policy', 49. This selection of authors is necessarily brief. Others who adhere to the view that the act was largely a response to foreign pressure include J. D. Mackie, *The earlier Tudors, 1485–1558*, Oxford 1952, 403; Smith, *Prelates and politics*, 209–12; Sturge, *Tunstal*, 214; Ridley, *Cranmer*, 177; Gairdner, *Lollardy and the Reformation*, ii. 204–5; Tjernagel, *Henry VIII and the Lutherans*, 194–5.

interfering in English religious affairs, Henry would have admitted his two European rivals to the process of English theological definition by consenting to an act primarily designed to satisfy their religious views. Moreover, the argument which explains the Act of Six Articles as a reaction to the threat of a Franco-imperial offensive relies on a selective reading of the evidence. It will by now be clear that this study is suspicious of historiographical theories which are based on deterministic observations as to the effects of the perceived alignments of the great powers on domestic policy at any one time. But those who wish to pursue such theories should at least be consistent. They are not being so when they apply their theories to the Act of Six Articles. They fail to explain why it was that on at least three other occasions during the late 1530s, when a Franco-imperial alliance threatened, Henry exhibited, not slavish theological good conduct, but the desire for a close association with the heretics of the Schmalkaldic League. They ignore the fact that at the very time that Charles and Francis stopped fighting with each other in Italy in late 1537 Henry was in the process of reopening relations with the Schmalkaldic League; that during the highly publicised and threatening Franco-imperial truce agreed at Nice in mid-1538 and the subsequent meeting between Francis and Charles at Aigues-Mortes the king was openly involving himself in theological discussions with the League; and that during the Franco-imperial invasion scare of the winter of 1539–40, less than six months after the passing of the Act of Six Articles, Henry was involving himself more closely than ever before with the German Protestants. They ignore this evidence of Henry's close association with the League during times when he faced threats from Charles and Francis, and yet ask the reader to believe that as a result of one Franco-imperial invasion scare in early 1539 Henry turned away from Protestantism and the German Protestants.[146]

Finally, it should be mentioned that even had Henry wanted to send a signal of his orthodoxy either to his people or to Francis and Charles, it is doubtful that he would have sent such a convoluted and confusing one as the Act of Six Articles. Few of the standard interpretations pause to consider why the particular six questions which appeared in the act were chosen for debate

---

[146] The only evidence which can be produced in support of the view that Henry passed the act in order to satisfy foreign opinion is a comment by the French ambassador Marillac in a letter to Montmorency of 13 July 1539. He suggested that Henry had mentioned to him that the legislation had been passed in order to prove that what the pope said about him was untrue: *LP* xiv/1, 1261; Scarisbrick, *Henry VIII*, 365; Gairdner, *Lollardy and the Reformation*, ii. 204–5. The king's comment was in all likelihood no more than a momentary piece of opportunism; a claim not made previously and never again. When discussing the act in letters of 9 June Marillac made no mention of it (*LP* xiv/1, 1091–2), and letters detailing meetings with the king on 20 June (*LP* xiv/1, 1136–7), and again on 5 July (*LP* xiv/1, 1207–8), also show that when the king had the chance, soon after the passing of the act, to explain why it had been promulgated he did not claim that he saw it as a proof of his orthodoxy to the outside world. If Henry had seen the act principally as a demonstration of his orthodoxy to the rest of Europe, it is unlikely that he would have mentioned it only once. Marillac's letter probably records an unconsidered, off-the-cuff, remark.

in the first place. This is a crucial omission, for it avoids dealing with the possibility that Henry sponsored the act because he was genuinely concerned with the issues upon which it focused. It avoids the fact that there are numerous simpler and more emphatic ways in which the king could have made a public demonstration of his orthodoxy. Why not restore Thomas Becket to the calendar? Or if recognition of Becket might implicitly cast doubt on the king's supremacy, why not a relatively innocuous figure like Our Lady of Walsingham? It was the attack on shrines, after all, which had so enraged the papacy and its adherents in 1538. And why not actually say in the act that it had been conceived as a demonstration to the world of Henry's Catholic orthodoxy in all matters but the supremacy? The reason the act did nothing like this is that it was not a simple statement of orthodoxy. The Act of Six Articles was in fact a complex and eclectic piece of legislation; and it is that very complexity and eclecticism which point to origins that are more genuine and go deeper than a short-term desire to satisfy the English people or foreign potentates.

This study has proposed a new explanation for the origins and emergence of the Act of Six Articles. It has argued that the conservative essence of the act emerged as a result of England's negotiations with the Schmalkaldic League. It has suggested that the act began life as a one-article piece of legislation (proposed by the evangelical Thomas Audley), designed only to proscribe the popular heresies against the sacrament of the altar. However, because of the status and instructions of the minor Schmalkaldic embassy which arrived in England in late April, Henry was persuaded that the Germans had no further interest in theological negotiation. This led him to put forward for parliamentary settlement the five controversial issues which had surfaced during the Anglo-Schmalkaldic discussions of the summer of 1538. These were entered as the latter five articles of the act. Unlike the first article, settlement of each of these represented some degree of conservative reaction. Without this crucial development in Anglo-Schmalkaldic relations, therefore, not only would the legislation have had only a single article, but it would also have been difficult to speak of the act and the 1539 parliament as milestones in the conservative reaction of the second half of Henry's reign.

The popular title, the 'Act of Six Articles', gives a false impression of homogeneity; a title more appropriate to its evolution would be the 'Act of One plus Five Articles'. This would reflect not only the differences in background of the various articles, but also the correspondingly distinct measures for enforcement: the most severe and inflexible penalties were attached to the first article, while a series of graduated penalties were established for the remaining five. Moreover, the German reaction to the act bears out this interpretation: when the League came to complain about the act it fulminated at length about the latter five articles, but on the first had very little to say.

5

Evangelical Triumph and Disaster, 1539–1540

Evangelical pleas for help from the League, June–September 1539

In the wake of the passing of the Act of Six Articles the evangelicals decided to approach the Schmalkaldeners again. Once the dust thrown up by the act had settled the evangelical faction decided to send to the League a message, rather like that sent in 1537 through Thomas Theabold. The details of who conveyed this message, how its despatch was arranged and so on, were, not surprisingly, shrouded in secrecy. What, however, is clear is that sometime in late August a man fleeing England on account of the Act of Six Articles was given a message by the evangelicals to pass on to the Schmalkaldic League. This man appears to have sailed from England to Hamburg sometime in early September. From the north German seaport he then made his way south, to deliver the message at the town of Strassburg.[1]

On 17 September 1539 the Strassburg council wrote to Philip of Hesse. The letter referred to the Act of Six Articles and explained that some men had recently arrived in Strassburg from England, escaping persecution under the legislation. One of these men had brought certain information, in which it was shown that the only way in which the conservative advance could be halted was by the despatch of an embassy from the League to England. The town council supported this request, saying that by sending such an embassy the opportunity for bringing the Gospel into England might be restored, which 'through the League's previous dilatory negotiations . . . has been squandered'.[2]

The intimations conveyed to Strassburg were outlined in much greater detail by Martin Bucer, in 1539 as in 1537 the 'primary target' for this secret message. In a long letter of 16 September to Philip of Hesse, Bucer reviewed and discussed the information which he had received.[3] Beginning with an outline of the content of the Act of Six Articles, the fate of those who had suffered under it and the character of those conservatives who had advised

---

[1] This reconstruction is based on evidence which will be reviewed in the following paragraphs.
[2] '[D]urch die verzüglich handlung gemainer ständ hievor . . . versaumt worden ist': PC ii. 630.
[3] BwP i. 99–105 (transcribed from the original at Marburg) [CR iii. 775–82; LP xiv/2, 186]. It should be noted that CR is a transcript of the Hessian copy sent to Saxony and is not always reliable, and that LP is an abstract of CR. Bucer's letter is about 3,000 words long. In the following paragraphs reference is to BwP.

Henry towards acceptance of the act,[4] he then moved on to deal with the central thrust of the information from England: that the conservatives had only been successful in persuading the king to enact the legislation because of the bad diplomatic behaviour of the League. The king, he explained, had noticed 'that we negotiated with him so slowly and, as he took it, regarded him but little. And so it came to pass that he considered that he had little reason to value our help.'[5] As a result of this the conservatives now stood

> in special fame and trust, whereas the evangelicals ['die Unseren'] at this time are somewhat askew and in very little repute. This has mainly been caused by the fact that those pious men had much assured the king of our princes and allies and yet have still not been able to gain anything from us that would be well regarded by the king. Moreover, the fact that Master Philip has been denied him so often, that embassies [ie. the oft sought after and promised major legations] too have not been sent, and that all negotiations with him have been set to our advantage and have offered him nothing which he might appreciate; these things he has taken to be a great contempt of his person.[6]

And so, the evangelicals felt, the League had paved the way for the conservative triumph that was the Act of Six Articles:

> we – we, that is, who will recognise the truth – cannot completely absolve ourselves of guilt for this downfall and misery in England, given that such a great opportunity to raise up the empire of Christ in this kingdom was not more enthusiastically grasped and given that Master Philip, whom the king so dearly wanted to hear . . . was not sent on such a great mission; for on this, as one understood from the embassy [this appears to be a reference to the messenger conveying these intimations to Strassburg], the king principally depended.[7]

---

4 *BwP* i. 99–101. Personal blame was mainly attributed to Stephen Gardiner, probably to shield Henry's interest in the act.
5 '[D]ass wir so langsam mit ihm gehandelt und seinen [so] so wenig, wie ers ufnimmt, geachtet, auch dahin bracht ist, dass ers dafur haltet, er habe sich unser hilf wenig zu getrösten': ibid. i. 100.
6 '[I]n besonderem Ansehen and Glauben sind, die Unseren aber dieser Zeit etwas verschlagen und in gar geringem Ansehen: welches daher zum meisten komet, dass dieselbigen frommen Männer den König unser Fürsten und Ständen viel vertröstet und aber ihm an uns das noch nit haben erlangen mögen, das bei ihm etwarfur geachtet wurde. Dann das man ihm M. Philippum so oft abgeschlagen, auch sunst nicht Botschaften zugesandt und dann alle Handlung mit ihm uf unser Vortheil gesparet, auch nichs ihm anbotten, das bei ihm scheinbar wäre, dies hat er zu schwerer Verachtung sein ufgenomen': ibid.
7 '[W]ir, so wir die Wahrheit bekennen wollen, uns der Schuld an diesem Fall und Jammer in Engelland nit gar rein machen konden, demnach man so einen grossen Anlass, das Reich Christi in diesem Königreich ufzubringen, nit herzlicher ufgenommen und M. Philipum, den der Konig doch so gern gehört hätte . . . zu solchem grossen Werk gesandt hat, nämlich da man doch von der gesandten Botschaft vernomen, waran der König vurnämlich hange': ibid. i. 102.

What, then, did the evangelical faction want the League to do to make up for the damage it had caused? The answer was predictable. The same thing the evangelicals had sought from the League since 1534:

> now the pious, dear people, who have preached Christ with the greatest risk and diligence, know no counsel better (through which they will be able to remain still in the liberty of Christ's Church), than that we gravely undertake right now to despatch Master Philip along with other zealous people to the king. For there are two things which have brought them into this difficulty. One is that the king thinks that we have held him in contempt and demonstrated with our own affairs that we are uncertain and risky – that is to say, that no one could rely on our help. The second is that he was persuaded to accept the aforementioned articles [ie. the Act of Six Articles] by pretty periphrasis and crafty sophistry. Thus the pious people have hope that if our princes and allies were to despatch a considerable embassy to England and with true devotion look after the religion and the pious Christians there, it would yet be of great benefit to them.[8]

Melanchthon in particular would make a great difference:

> Master Philip would well and truly eliminate the sophistical clutches and illusory arguments with which the aforementioned articles were dressed up and by which the king was persuaded. He would also secure the truth with well fixed reasons against all sophistry. For they all hold that though the king is as he will, if it were shown that the previously made decision [ie. the Act of Six Articles] did not stand with God's word, he would not stick with it. And although the previous embassy [of Burchard and Mykonius] lacked nothing in themselves, still Master Philip (given that the king has so diligently sought his presence) is held by the king in greater repute in such matters.[9]

---

[8] 'Nun wissen aber die frommen theuren Leut, so Christum mit höchster Gefahr und Arbeit in Engelland geprediget haben, keinen anderen Rath mehr, dadurch sie bei etwas Freiheit des Reichs Christi nunmer bleiben konden, dann so wir uns ihrer mit Ernst doch jetzund annehmen und nochmals M. Philippum mit anderen eiferigen Leuten zum Konig sandten. Dann weil sie zwei Ding in diese Noth bracht haben, das ein, dass der Konig meinet, wir haben ihn zu viel verachtet und beweisen uns auch in unsern eignen Sachen, dass unser Ding ongewiss und gefahrlich seie, also dass sich unser Hilf Niemand viel getrösten möge, das ander, dass man ihm die vorerzäleten Puncten mit schoner Verblühmung und geschwinder Sophisterei ufgeredt hat, so hätten die frommen Leut Hofnung, wa unser Fursten und Stände nochmals ein taugliche Botschaft in Engelland schickten und sich der Religion des Orts und der fromen Christen mit wahren Treuen annehmen, es wurde ihnen noch zu grossen Statten erschiessen': ibid. i. 102–3.
[9] '[W]urde M. Philippus die sophistischen Griffe und die Scheinargument, damit man die oftgemeldten Articul ufgemutzet und dem Konig eingeredt hat, wohl und stattlich uflösen und die Wahrheit mit recht ansichtigen Gründen wider alle Sophisterei befestigen. Dann sie es alle dafur halten, der Konig sie, wie er wölle: wann es dannoch gewiesen wurde, dass vorgemachter Beschluss mit dem Gotteswort gar nicht bestohn möchte, er wurde nochmals nit darauf beharren. Und ob wohl die vorige Botschaft, so viel an ihnen, in dem nichs versaumet hat, jedoch so hätte M. Philippus bei dem Konig, weil er sein so fleissig begehret, mehr Ansehens in solchen Sachen': ibid. i. 103.

All this, Bucer argued, was the League's Christian duty. By way of demonstrating this he pointed to the example of Christ:

> in order to help us, our lord Jesus took on our form, gave himself from heaven unto our squalor, and suffered a cruel death. He forsook the ninety-nine lambs in order to seek the one hundredth.[10] He has also endowed us greatly, and demands from us that we faithfully help others, since he has given us greater powers for the performance thereof: and he will repay us one hundredfold in this life and with eternal salvation in the next. His message is: go into the wide world and preach the gospel to all creatures.[11]

In closing, Bucer summed up the appeal from the evangelicals, saying that they wanted

> that an embassy, including Master Philip, be despatched to the king to seek that which God will grant and abet. It is no slight thing, to win and preserve such a kingdom; one should therefore make a great effort. For the pious people stand in good hope, that this work would not be in vain and that Master Philip will accomplish much with the king.[12]

This information – the role the League had played in the passing of the Act of Six Articles, the king's deep respect for, and wish to discuss theology with, Melanchthon and so on – could only have come by way of a briefing from the evangelical faction: that is to say, from that elite group of evangelicals within the circle about the king. However, the evidence of Bucer's letter thus far does not allow any more specific identification; the only references made to the English source are to anonymous 'pious men' and 'dear people'. Nevertheless, there is a postscript to the letter which helps solve the problem, for in it Bucer provided information which suggests that only two men could have been responsible for briefing and despatching the messenger to Strasburg:

> our previous embassy, the vice-chancellor [Burchard] and Mykonius, are pious and learned men, but the belief that they were the measure of those practised sophists which England has is, I fear, mistaken. Moreover, they proceeded

---

10 This is a reference to the parable of the lost sheep in Matt. xviii.10–14.
11 'Unser Herre Jesus hat sich unser anders angenommen, hat sich, uns zu helfen, vom Himel in unser Elend begeben und den bitteren Tod erlitten, hat die neunundneunzig Schäflin verlassen und das hundertist gesuchet, hat uns auch hoch begabet, und forderet von uns, dass auch wir anderen soviel getreulicher helfen, soviel er uns hiezu mehr Vermögen verliehen hat: das wille er uns hie hundertfältig und dort mit ewiger Seligkeit vergelten. Es heisst: geht in die ganze Welt und predigen das Evangeli allen Creaturen': *BwP* i. 103.
12 '[D]ass ein Botschaft zum Konig geschickt, und M. Philips mit, die doch versuchten, was Gott noch geben und helfen wollte. Es ist je kein geringes, ein solich Konigreich gewinnen und erhalten, darumb man ja billich viel und grosses versuchen solle. So haben die frommen Leut dennoch noch gute Hoffnung, es sollte diese Arbeit nit vergeben sein und M. Philippus werde bei dem Konig viel ausrichten': ibid. i. 104.

most illadvisedly,[13] when, *in spite of the fervent requests and applications of the pious men in England* [my italics], they hurried back home before the disputations had been concluded.[14]

In 1538 there were just two men who had done all they could to persuade the Germans to stay on longer: Cromwell and Cranmer.[15] This passage, then, provides strong circumstantial evidence that it was Cromwell and Cranmer who, as with Theabold in 1537, were responsible for the despatch of this secret messenger to Germany.[16]

Unlike 1537, however, the evangelical faction was not likely this time to strike a responsive chord with the League. Though the Strassburg circle supported the evangelicals' suit, the rest of the League was unlikely to be impressed by Bucer's arguments. The reason for this, of course, was the Act of Six Articles. The Schmalkaldic ambassadors who had returned to Germany from England in June 1539 had said little about the act. Their report only mentioned the parliamentary debates in passing and devoted most of its attention to the impasse which had been reached with Henry on the question of mutual military assistance. Upon the ambassadors' return, John Frederick was generally optimistic, speaking only of the difficulties associated with the reciprocation problem and remaining hopeful that a religious and political agreement with Henry would eventually be reached. In particular, he told Philip of Hesse on 21 June, he held out hope for support from the leader of the evangelical faction: 'because Cromwell is so favourably inclined in matters of religion, he will with God's help not neglect to maintain these matters about the king'.[17]

Before long, however, the first reports of the substance and enforcement of the new legislation began to appear in Germany. On 29 June Philip wrote to John Frederick of rumours that Henry had suppressed some articles of the League's religion, mentioning by name clerical marriage and the mass. He suggested that if this was so, 'then we do not know if there is much to nego-

---

13 CR iii. 781, has mistakenly transcribed this passage and the previous sentence, which is the reason for the nonsensical translation at *LP* xiv/2, 186.

14 '[U]nser vorige botschafft, der vicecantzler und Myconius, sind fromme und gelerte menner, aber das sie gegen denen erubten sophisten, so Engelandt hat, gemessen sien, besorge ich es habe noch fel. Doch wie dem, so haben daran am alleronrathlichsten gefaren, das sie uber so fleissig bitten und anhalten der frommen christlichen menner in Engeland heim geeilet haben, ee dann uff die gehalten disputationen etwas beschlossen ware': *BwP* i. 104.

15 See the final section of chapter 3.

16 This passage also supports the view that the 1538 German ambassadors had behaved counterproductively in seeking to shorten the 1538 discussions with their letter to Henry of 5 August, agreeing only with great reluctance to the pleas of Cromwell and Cranmer to stay on a little longer and then opting out of the third phase of the discussions as soon as possible.

17 '[W]eil der Crumellus sowol an den Sachen der Religion ist, der werde durch Gotliche Vorleyhung nitt undterlassen, bey dem konige die Sachen zuundterhalten': HStMar, PA 2581, fo. 85.

tiate with him'.[18] The vague first reports were soon followed by detailed accounts of the act and oppression under it. By 30 July, Philip was responding to a piece of intelligence which had alleged a bloody implementation of the act with the characteristically passionate assessment, 'if the king is doing that, then in our view he is certainly the most evil man whom we have ever known or heard of'.[19] By the time Philip wrote these words, news of the act was known throughout Germany and virtually the entire League had abandoned any thought of doing further business with Henry.

The difficulty of the task faced by Bucer and the Strassburgers in persuading the League to act was emphasised by the response to the unexpected appearance of Christopher Mont in Germany in early September. It appears that at about the same time as the undercover message was being prepared and sent to Strassburg, Cromwell also persuaded Henry that it would be useful to send Christopher Mont to John Frederick and Philip to assure them of his friendship and explain that the Act of Six Articles did not change this.[20] The English sources are silent on the details of Mont's visit to Saxony and Hesse. However, identical letters in Mont's own hand to John Frederick and Philip and his letter of credence, dated 15 August at Donington and signed by the king, do explain the purpose of his mission.[21]

The letters in Mont's own hand give no hint of any factional advocacy. It appears that Mont's mission was an official one, counselled by Cromwell to keep open the formal lines of communication between Henry and the Schmalkaldic leadership rather than to push his faction's policy as the secret messenger to Strassburg was doing. Mont's letters emphasised that the recent League embassy to England had failed because the ambassadors had insufficient powers and instructions to reach a satisfactory agreement. On the question of religion, Mont's letters declared that

> although his majesty and the entire theological fraternity – moved by mature counsel, considerable reasons and eternal truths – do not agree with your doc-

---

[18] '[S]o wissen wir nit wol was viel mit im zuhandeln sein solt': ibid. fo. 117v.
[19] 'Tut aber der kuning ain solchs so wirdet er gewislich unsers ermessens der bosest mensch sein, von dem wir ie gehort oder erkant haben': Prüser, *England und die Schmalkaldener*, 190. The intelligence on which this comment is based is not extant.
[20] It is tempting to suspect that it was Mont who conveyed these messages to Strassburg, but this seems unlikely, for when Bucer heard of his arrival in Germany his comments to Philip of Hesse and to Cranmer suggest surprise and curiosity about his mission: *BwP* i. 105–13; *Original letters*, 526–30. Moreover, had Mont gone first to Strassburg, his next stop would surely have been Hesse (given that it was on the way to Saxony); in fact he went to Saxony first.
[21] HStMar, PA 1800, fos 85–8 (letter to Philip in Mont's own hand) [Prüser, *England und die Schmalkaldener*, 327–9]; PA 2582, fos 88–9 (copy of letter from Mont to John Frederick, enclosed with John Frederick to Philip, 20 Sept., fos 86–7); TStWei, Reg. H. 260, no. 111, vol. 2, fos 18–19 (letter in Mont's hand to John Frederick), 20–2 (copy of letter from Mont to Philip, enclosed in Philip to John Frederick, 24 Sept., fo. 17); letter of credence from Henry to John Frederick: TStWei, Reg. H. 260, no. 111, vol. 1, fo. 105.

trine on priestly celibacy, vows, the private mass and so on, nevertheless his majesty wants resolutely to hold and defend your determinations and decrees against his and your common enemy, the bishop of Rome, his unholy superstitions and his self aggrandised power.[22]

In conclusion the letters stated that Henry still wished to receive a properly instructed embassy in order to conclude an Anglo-Schmalkaldic agreement, and that even if such an agreement was not concluded he wished to assure the Germans of his friendship.

The response of the duke of Saxony, dated 16 September, was hostile. He blamed Henry entirely for the collapse of the negotiations in the middle of the year. Had the League known that Henry wanted mutual aid, he said, they would not have sent the embassy to England. He claimed that the League had always made it clear that if Henry wanted an alliance of mutual aid an agreement on religion would have to be concluded first: a purely secular alliance based on mutual aid was an impossibility. He argued that the question of the embassy's insufficient powers had simply been a pretext for Henry to dismiss the ambassadors. Turning to the Act of Six Articles, John Frederick said that it constituted the gravest obstacle to Anglo-Schmalkaldic relations. As against English suggestions that it did not deal with the most important aspects of doctrine, he said that maintenance of the act would threaten the most vital areas of evangelical doctrine, particularly the repudiation of private masses. He also accused the king of disingenuousness: he claimed that Henry must have known of the imminent religious settlement when he sent Mont to Frankfurt in January and certainly when the ambassadors arrived in England. Yet he had continued to play the Protestants along in negotiations, knowing that a religious settlement which would offend the Schmalkaldeners was in the offing.[23]

Philip's reply, of 24 September, was a little more compromising. He did, certainly, maintain that the instructions which the May 1539 ambassadors had taken to England had been sufficient, express his disappointment at the recent religious developments in England and, like John Frederick, emphasise that the current English position on celibacy, vows and the private mass struck at the heart of Protestant doctrine. On the other hand, he hoped that Henry might be persuaded onto the right track, noted his pleasure at Henry's

---

[22] '[W]iewoel ire ma. und der gans geistlich stant, aus reifen raat, trefflichen ursachen and standhaftigen fundamenten beweegt und verursacht, stimt nit gar zo mit ewrer leer de celibatu sacerdotum, de votis et privatis missis etc., nichtsdeweniger will ire ma. ire determinationes und decreta kegen seiner ma. und e.f.g. gemeinem fiant, dem bishof von Rom, seine misgleubige superstitiones und selbst angenomen gewalt steedfastiglich erhalten und defendirn': Prüser, *England und die Schmalkaldener*, 328–9.

[23] TStWei, Reg. H. 260, no. 111, vol. 1, fos 146–51 (German draft), 152–8 (good German draft), 159–65 (Latin copy) [Mentz, *Johann Friedrich*, iii. 437–40]; HStMar, PA 2582, fos 90–5 (copy enclosed in John Frederick to Philip, 20 Sept., fos 86–7).

continued attitude to the papacy and undertook to discuss the English question at a diet with the other League members.[24]

But even in Philip's letter there was little to suggest that the Schmalkaldic leadership, convinced as it was of the correctness of its conduct, would be prepared to adopt the sort of policy towards England which might assist the course of the English Reformation. Mont returned to England empty-handed, an English approach to the League once more rejected by the Germans.

It now remained to be seen if Bucer's specific entreaties, conveyed on behalf of the evangelical faction, would succeed where Mont's official and more general embassy had failed. Philip wrote back to Bucer on 30 September. Apart from answering the points made in Bucer's letter of 16 September, he enclosed a copy of his and the duke's answers to Mont and defended the stance which he and John Frederick had taken. He began by asserting that he too had long thought that Melanchthon should be sent to England, but that John Frederick had always stood in the way. Now, however, he thought that it would be too dangerous for Melanchthon to go to England, and doubted that his presence there would be beneficial. He felt sure that John Frederick would be of a similar view. Still, he said he would send Bucer's long letter to John Frederick, and attempt at least to get Melanchthon to write to Henry.[25] Accordingly, he wrote to John Frederick on the very same day, enclosing a copy of Bucer's letter and asking Melanchthon to write an 'expostulation' to Henry.[26]

Bucer wrote back to Philip on 14 October. He acknowledged Henry's fundamental responsibility for the turn against Protestantism, but argued that the circumstances warranted extending a friendly hand towards England, since 'God has placed so many thousands of pious people under his rule and such a beginning of gospel has been made there.'[27] He congratulated Philip on the reasonableness of his reply to Mont, and added that John Frederick should have replied in a similar vein.[28] Finally, he acknowledged that a letter from Melanchthon to Henry might be productive, but stressed that a personal visit would be more likely to achieve success, both because it would allow the sophists to be confronted face-to-face and because 'these monarchs consider the sending of an embassy to be a special honour'.[29]

Bucer, however, ran into implacable opposition when his letter of 16 September arrived in Saxony. On 7 October John Frederick wrote to his

---

[24] HStMar, PA 1800, fos 89–92 (copy) [Prüser, *England und die Schmalkaldener*, 329–31]; TStWei, Reg. H. 260, no. 111, vol. 2, fos 24–6 (copy enclosed in Philip to John Frederick, 24 Sept., fo. 17).

[25] *BwP* i. 105–6. The letter from Melanchthon to Henry was written and sent on 1 November 1539: *BwP* i. 106 n. 2.

[26] HStMar, PA 2582, fo. 149 (draft); TStWei, Reg. H. 282, no. 118, fo. 185 (final version).

[27] 'Gott im so fil tausent frommer leut underworffen hat und ein solicher anfang des Evangeli des orts ist': *BwP* i. 107.

[28] Ibid. i. 107–8.

[29] '[B]otschafft schicken achten dise monarchen fur ein besondere eer': ibid. i. 108.

chancellor, Gregor Brück, on the arguments put forward by Bucer.[30] He rejected completely the suggestion that 'the guilt should be ours for the king of England's enacting his unchristian articles against our doctrine'.[31] John Frederick insisted that the sole responsibility for the Act of Six Articles must rest with Henry, adding in the margin in his own hand that

> it is obvious that the king has never been serious about the gospel and has only done what he has done in order to drive the pope and his overlordship out of England, to set himself in that same place and to enrich himself with the treasures and income of the Church.[32]

He dismissed Bucer's suggestion that Melanchthon be sent to England, but added darkly that since 'Bucer believes that such a despatch and what would result from it would be a Christian, useful and good work, we would agree with it and be satisfied, if he along with others should be sent to England.'[33]

On 11 October a reply was sent to Philip, echoing these views. Though John Frederick recognised that Bucer meant well, noting that 'he has written his letter in response to some intimations from England',[34] he refused to accept the Strassburger's views. He refuted Bucer's charge that the Protestants had not previously been sufficiently forthcoming or willing to compromise with Henry, and reviewed the course of the previous negotiations in 1536, 1538 and 1539 to demonstrate this. He considered the recent developments in the English Church, argued that a revocation of the Act of Six Articles seemed extremely unlikely and asserted that Henry alone was to blame for the failure of the Anglo-Schmalkaldic negotiations. As for sending a theological delegation to England, he thought the proposal worthy of consideration, but insisted that Melanchthon could not go because of the possible threat to his life; once again he added the dark suggestion that Bucer would be an ideal alternative.[35]

30 TStWei, Reg. H. 260, no. 111, vol. 1, fos 210–12v [Mentz, *Johann Friedrich*, iii. 440–2].
31 '[D]ie schuldt unser sein, das der kg. zu Engellandt seine unchristliche artikel wider unser warhaftige lere zu halten solt verordent haben': TStWei, Reg. H. 260, no. 111, vol. 1, fo. 210v [Mentz, *Johann Friedrich*, iii. 441].
32 '[I]st wol zu fernemen, das dem konik des ewangeliums halben nie ernst und ist im allein darumb zu tuen gewesst, das er den bast mit seiner uberkeit aus Engellant gebracht und sich selbest an sein stat gesetzt und das er sich mit dem reichtumb der kirchen scheze und einkommen hat pfeisten mugen': TStWei, Reg. H. 260, no. 111, vol. 1, fo. 211 [Mentz, *Johann Friedrich*, iii. 441].
33 'Nachdeme aber Bucerus meint, wie ein christlich, nutzlich und guet werk solche schickung sein und was damit ausgericht werden solt, so lassen wir wol gescheen und seind zufriden, das er neben andern in Engellandt geschickt werde': TStWei, Reg. H. 260, no. 111, vol. 1, fo. 211–v [Mentz, *Johann Friedrich*, iii. 441].
34 '[S]ein schreiben getan hat uf etzlicher anzaigung aus Engeland': HStMar, PA 2582, fo. 211v [Prüser, *England und die Schmalkaldener*, 334].
35 HStMar, PA 2582, fos 208–13 [Prüser, *England und die Schmalkaldener*, 331–6].

The next day John Frederick wrote to his theologians in Wittenberg, asking them to provide an opinion on Bucer's letter.[36] A week and a half later, both Brück (answering the duke's letter of 7 October) and the theologians replied. Brück acknowledged Bucer's scholarly credentials, but said that he doubted that 'even had he, Philip, and others been sent to England, that they would have changed the king's mind and withheld him from his godless determination'.[37] Turning to the English complaints conveyed by Bucer on the conduct of the 1538 embassy, he accepted the general view that it had been badly handled. However, whereas Bucer had suggested that the ambassadors had broken off negotiations too early, he argued that they should not have entered into them at all. Instead, they should have stuck to their instructions to prepare the way for a major embassy led by Melanchthon. Nevertheless, he admitted that if his recent re-reading of the ambassadors' relation showed that they had given nothing away in the 'Lundenischen Disputation', they had certainly done less with their time than others might have done. He also noted that Bucer was right in suggesting that the embassy 'had certainly been lacking in the authority' which someone like Melanchthon had, and that such things were important to godless potentates.[38] Yet if Brück accepted some of Bucer's arguments, in closing he rejected the principal proposal to send a major embassy to England: Henry was so godless that 'even if the most considerable embassy were now despatched to England, with regard to the king it would only be flogging a dead horse, and would achieve nothing'.[39]

Brück's advice that the pleas of the English evangelicals should be rejected was echoed by the Wittenberg theologians Luther, Jonas, Bugenhagen and Melanchthon. They too wrote a joint letter to John Frederick on 23 October.[40] They acknowledged Bucer's good intentions, suggesting that he had been induced in good faith to write by fugitives who had come from England through Hamburg. Nevertheless, they refused to contemplate further relations with a king who acted against his conscience and 'damns the doctrine more severely than the pope, who has not yet asserted that priestly

---

[36] WABr viii. 562–6.

[37] 'Wenn gleich er, Philippus und andere in England wären geschickt worden, dass sie des Königes Vorhaben würden geändert und von seiner gottlosen Determination ihn abgehalten haben': CR iii. 795 [LP xiv/2, 378].

[38] '[H]at es doch an der Auctorität gemangelt': ibid.

[39] '[W]enn gleich die stattlichste Botschaft nunmehr hinein in Engelland verordent werd, so sey es doch des Königes halben ein lauter leer Stroh gedroschen, und nichts ausgerichtet': CR iii. 796 [LP xiv/2, 378].

[40] WABr viii. 572–7 [CR iii. 796–800; LP xiv/2, 379]. On the same day Luther wrote separately, saying that Bucer had written to him in the same terms as to Philip of Hesse. He had replied that there was no hope for further diplomacy with the king: WABr viii. 577–8 (for Luther's letter to Bucer of 14 October and another of the same date to Bucer or the Strassburg theologians in general see WABr viii. 568–72).

marriage is against God's law'.[41] They had little time for Bucer's argument that it was the Protestants' Christian duty ' "to go into the world and preach etc.": we do that with writings; also to leave our present calling is not required of us'.[42] As for the plea to send Melanchthon to the king, the theologians alleged that Henry had recently received writings from Melanchthon with great displeasure, and suggested that his theological arguments were so sophistical that it made little sense to negotiate further with him personally. The best course would be to send an 'expostulation' as Philip of Hesse had suggested. In closing, they noted that they would complete such a tract as soon as possible.

Thus, the secret efforts of the evangelical faction to engage the assistance of the Schmalkaldeners largely fell on deaf ears. On 16 October Bucer wrote despairingly to Philip that given the Saxon hostility to England evinced in the answer given to Mont,[43] perhaps the landgrave alone would write to Henry. In a long and rambling letter Bucer tried every form of persuasion possible, particularly stressing the Christian's missionary duty, to encourage Philip to do something to help the Reformation in England.[44] However, there is a strong hint of desperation in the letter, suggesting that Bucer sensed that the chances of restoring Anglo-Schmalkaldic relations by this means were slim and slipping away.

Discussions on the Cleves match, September–October 1539

Anglo-Schmalkaldic relations would most probably have collapsed by the late summer of 1539, had Cromwell's efforts only been directed through the secret messenger to Strassburg and Mont's official embassy. Throughout 1539, however, he had kept open and continued to develop that other line of contact: the marriage negotiations with Cleves. Where other efforts since the summer of 1538 had failed to draw the Germans into assisting the evangelical faction in its efforts to reform the Church, this one had proceeded with increasing success. Even as the information from England conveyed by Bucer and the messages brought by Mont were being rejected by the League, the Schmalkaldeners were being slowly but surely drawn back towards England by Cromwell's increasingly successful prosecution of the match between Henry and Anne, the elder duchess of Cleves.[45]

---

[41] '[V]erdammet dise lahr herter denn der Bapst, der noch nie gesagt, das Priester ehe wider Gottlich gesetz sey': WABr viii. 573 [CR iii. 797; LP xiv/2, 379].

[42] ' "Gehet In alle welt, prediget etc." das thun wir mit schrifften; weiter gegenwertigen beruff zu verlassen, ist uns nicht beuolhen': WABr viii. 575 [CR iii. 799; LP xiv/2, 379].

[43] As has already been noted, Philip had sent to Bucer copies of his and John Frederick's replies to Mont along with his letter of 30 September: BwP i. 105–6.

[44] Ibid. i. 109–13.

[45] For monograph surveys of the background to, and development of, the Cleves marriage up to the late summer of 1539 see Müller, 'Beziehungen Heinrichs zu Anna von Cleve',

The growing success of the marriage plans was in fact but one aspect of Cromwell's broad rehabilitation in the wake of the 1539 parliament. On the domestic front things had also improved for him. As the year entered the progress time his position had appeared precarious.[46] Apart from the general decline of the evangelicals in the king's favour which the secret messenger to Strassburg had described, there had been specific plots. A renascent group of conservatives comprising Sir William Kingston and the half brothers Fitzwilliam and Browne had begun to formulate a plan to overthrow Cromwell. They had turned to Cuthbert Tunstall to lead a campaign to supplant him as the king's minister, but had found that that shrewd old survivor did not covet the position, observing by way of explanation to his suitors that 'treacherous is the place of primacy about kings'.[47] As they looked about for an alternative leader, the plot stalled. Now Cromwell fought back. Taking no chances with the cautious Tunstall, he had apparently secured the exclusion of the bishop from the council. Then he had moved against those others who might lead a conservative challenge to his position, attacking and managing also to exclude Stephen Gardiner, Richard Sampson and John Clerk.[48] By August all anti-Cromwellian intrigues had been driven underground, and Cromwell had resumed his dominance of the king's affairs. With his opponents in disarray and the success of his sponsorship of the Cleves marriage becoming clearer by the day, Cromwell's return to the king's favour was complete.

By the summer of 1539 Cromwell's efforts to bring England and Cleves together by way of a marriage alliance had begun to bear fruit. In July William Petre and Hans Holbein were despatched to Cleves, respectively to negotiate terms of marriage and to paint the duchesses.[49] The vital stage in the negotiations came soon after in August 1539, when Holbein's portraits of Anne and

---

16–35; W. Bouterwek, 'Anna von Cleve: Gemahlin Heinrichs VIII, Königs von England', *Zeitschrift des Bergischen Geschichtsvereins* iv (1867), 337–70; Warnicke, *Marrying of Anne of Cleves*, 63–93. Diarmaid MacCulloch produces remarkable evidence to suggest that Archbishop Cranmer, perhaps mindful of the linguistic difficulties he had encountered with his own wife, counselled Cromwell not to pursue a German match for Henry but one with a suitable English bride, perhaps even the teenage Catherine Howard: *Cranmer*, 257–8.

46 The following is based on the interrogatories in *LP* xiv/2, 750.

47 'Lubricus est primus locus apud reges': *LP* xiv/2, 750, 278.

48 The relevance of at least Gardiner's exclusion to Cromwell's Protestant foreign policy is suggested by the following: 'the bp. of Winchester was put out of the Privy council because my lord Privy Seal was displeased with him for objecting to Dr Barnes, a man defamed of heresy, being ambassador. But touching the bp. of Chichester he did not rehearse or know any cause why he was put out of the Privy council': *LP* xiv/2, 750, 279. The exclusion of Tunstall and Clerk from the council at this time is suggested by the testimony of Marillac (*LP* xv. 486), who spoke the following year of Henry's intention to restore them to the council. Though the Frenchman made no mention of when they were excluded, this period when Cromwell fought back from the effects of the Act of Six Articles is probably the most likely.

49 *LP* xiv/1, 489, 920, 1193.

Amelia were completed and sent back to England. After a brief consideration Henry decided upon Anne as his fourth wife.[50]

Now Cromwell and the evangelicals had an excellent opportunity to draw John Frederick and the League into an evangelical alliance. For even if the Schmalkaldeners despised Henry, they could not avoid him if he married into one of the principal German noble families, and especially one so closely related to the duke of Saxony. An Anglo-Cleves marriage would make an alliance with the German Protestants a virtual certainty, whether the Protestants liked it or not. And this is in fact what happened. Not unnaturally, as the marital plans began to take shape Duke William of Cleves decided to seek the advice and help of his relative John Frederick, who had had so much experience in dealing with the English king, and who would be included in the inheritance provisions of any marriage involving Cleves. On 5 August John Frederick wrote to Philip.[51] He discussed the progress of Anglo-Cleves contacts and mentioned a recent request from Cleves for help: 'our uncle and brother-in-law the duke of Cleves wrote to us a few days ago that we should send some councillors to his grace who, with regard to the marriage, should travel to England with some of his grace's councillors'.[52] He took a very dim view of the marriage proposals, suggesting that 'our brother-in-law and his dear wife, mother, and sister will have little joy or favour with it'.[53] He told Philip that he was sending Hans von Dolzig and Franz Burchard to discuss the Anglo-Cleves marital plans with him in Cassel, and then to go on to Cleves to confer with the duke of Cleves. 'In view of the king's inconstancy', however, he remained unwilling at this stage to allow them to go to England.[54]

By the end of August, however, his attitude was beginning to change. On 31 August John Frederick wrote again to Philip on the Anglo-Cleves marriage plans.[55] He reported that Dolzig had returned from Cleves with a letter from Duke William, in which he said that the plans were well advanced and that John Frederick should send ambassadors to accompany a Cleves delegation to England. After some consideration, John Frederick had decided to relent a little:

we have approved after all that our same councillors [ie. Burchard and Dolzig] go to England, for the sole reason that they may support our brother-in-law's

50 *LP* xiv/2, 117.
51 HStMar, PA 2581, fos 244–9.
52 'Unser ohem und schwager der herzog von Julich vorwenigen tagen geschrieben etzliche unsere Rethe seiner lieb zuschicken welche furder mit etzlichen seinen Lieb Rethen in Engeland solchs hyrads halben Rayssen soltenn': ibid. fo. 249.
53 '[U]nser schwager und seine lieb frau, mutter und schwester werden darzu nit grossen lust oder naygung haben': ibid. fo. 249v.
54 '[W]eil des konigs unbestand dermassen': ibid. fo. 249.
55 HStMar, PA 2582, fos 27–31.

councillors and act as the maiden's good counsel. However, they should not make any special advertisement to the king on our behalf.[56]

John Frederick was now being dragged along by the momentum of events. On 12 September he responded to a letter from Philip on the possible advantages of an Anglo-Cleves marriage.[57] He admitted that although he still had misgivings about the proposed marriage, it was unrealistic to try to ignore what was going on: 'we do not like the idea of the marriage, and should like it if the same were to be reversed. But since it has come so far that it cannot go back, as our uncle and brother-in-law has explained, then we must let it proceed'.[58] Thus, he repeated his earlier decision to allow his ambassadors to go to England with the Cleves delegation. He emphasised again, however, that they must not enter into any special discourse with Henry.

Burchard and Dolzig left Germany in the second week of September. They arrived in England on 18 September, a few hours after the Cleves delega-tion.[59] On the orders of Thomas Cromwell, they were met by a number of 'distinguished people', who saw to it that they were put up in comfortable lodgings.[60]

On 20 September the Saxon ambassadors were conducted to Cromwell for preliminary talks. The first subject of discussion was the Act of Six Articles. Cromwell sought to allay the League's concerns, explaining that 'the thing was introduced by some bishops during his illness [i.e. Cromwell's tertian fever of 18 April – 10 May]. . . . However, up to now no execution has taken place, and he believes very strongly that because it has not at this time that the execution of the act will not proceed.'[61] Why did Cromwell feel so confi-dent about this? Partly it was because he had been able to turn the king against the conservatives. Henry, Cromwell asserted, 'is not inclined with great grace to those who caused the legislation. Their heads are hanging and

---

[56] 'So haben wir doch gewilligt das dieselbigen unsere Rethe mit in Engelland allain unsers schwagers Rethen beystendig und zu des freuleins bestenn Retig zu sein mitziehen. Sie sollen aber kain sonderliche werbung an den konig von unsern wegen thun': ibid. fo. 30v.

[57] Draft of Philip's letter to John Frederick of 5 Sept. 1539, ibid. fo. 50; signed final version of John Frederick's reply of 12 Sept., ibid. fos 63–4.

[58] '[W]ir denselben hairat nun ungern sehen, machten auch wol leiden dass derselb hairat gantz zuruckh ganngen were. Aber weil es nun so weit kommen dass man nit zuruckh kan wie unser oheim und schwager zuerkennen gegeben so mussen wir es auch geschehen lassen': ibid. fo. 63v.

[59] Most of the following is based on the Saxon ambassadors' account in TStWei, Reg. H. 260, no. 111, vol. 2, fos 31–9. For the date of arrival see fo. 31v.

[60] '[A]nsehentliche personen': Burchard and Dolzig to John Frederick, 20 Sept. 1539, TStWei, Reg. H. 260, no. 111, vol. 1, fo. 171 (final version); HStMar, PA 2582, fo. 239 (copy enclosed in John Frederick to Philip, 22 Oct., fos 230–4).

[61] '[W]ere die ding durch etzliche bischoff dohin bracht in seiner schwocheit. . . .]doch aber es bisherkeine execution erfolget Ehr achtet es auch genzlich darfur do es die Zeit nicht aussgangen es wurde nun nicht mehr geschen': TStWei, Reg. H. 260, no. 111, vol. 2, fo. 31v (account of Burchard and Dolzig).

they are subdued, as we ourselves would see.'[62] Partly it was because Cromwell had re-established his control over the central decision-making apparatus: 'there are several of the same', Cromwell had related, 'who since then have been excluded and segregated from the privy council'.[63] And partly it was because fate had intervened to decrease the conservative majority in the Church: 'also' the ambassadors had been told, 'the bishop of London has died'.[64] Cromwell urged the Germans to see the act in its true light as the result of a factional contest: it was, he had explained, 'contrived by the opponents of the gospel because they wanted to extirpate the lord of Canterbury, the chancellor [Audley] and lord Cromwell'.[65] Cromwell told them that he had pointed this out to Henry, and that the king had been sympathetic to his suit, assuring the minister that he need only bring a little patience to bear on the matter.[66]

Having explained the reasons for the act, and diplomatically refrained from demonstrating how the League had contributed to its genesis, Cromwell moved onto the Cleves marriage. He emphasised that it would bring England back onto the evangelical path, assuring the ambassadors that 'we should have no doubt that if the marriage proceeds, which he hopes to effect, all matters will be despatched favourably'.[67] He also stressed its factional advantages. It would, he assured, serve to bring England and the League together. He

> mentioned that the opponents of the gospel are very frightened at our arrival and would prefer that the king only enter into negotiations with Cleves. But the king wants very much to have the friendship of our gracious lord the duke; and so it [i.e. the marriage] will with God's grace achieve all that is beneficial.[68]

All this was very encouraging to the Germans. That evening they wrote back

---

[62] 'D]enjennigen nicht mit grosse gnad genaigt, dieses mandats ursacher gewesen. Sie hingen auch itzunder die kopff, und were klein lauth, wie wir selbst sehen und vormercken wurden': ibid. fos 31v–2.

[63] '[E]s were etzliche der selbige sindt der Zeit auss dem geheimsten rath aussgeschlossen und abgesundert': ibid.

[64] '[Z]u dem das der bischoff von Lunden in des mit todt abgangen': ibid. Stokesley died on 8 September.

[65] '[V]on den widersacher des Evangelii die ding doher gespilet das sie D. Cant., Cancell. und D. Crum. wolten ausheben': ibid.

[66] Ibid.

[67] '[W]ir solten keine zweifel haben do der heirath ein vortgang, wie ehr hoffet erreichet, wurden sich all sachen zum besten schicken': ibid.

[68] '[V]ormelden das die widersacher des Evangelii unsere ankunpfft hoch erschrecket und wolten lieber do es je nicht anders sein mocht das sein die ko. mat. mit den Julichschen allein in handlung sich einlasse, aber die ko. Mat. were zum hochsten begerig mit u. gn. hern dem churfursten freuntschafft zuhaben. Und es wurde ob goth wol zu allen guthen gereichen': ibid. fo. 33.

to John Frederick to inform him of what they had been told.[69] Cromwell, they said, had

> showed himself to be delighted at our arrival, and the same goes for all the good hearted, who are well inclined to the pure teaching of the gospel. And they stand in hope that the Almighty will despatch and turn all things here to his holy exaltation. For although the parliamentary decree [i.e. the Act of Six Articles] has gone out, no commission has been assembled and therefore its execution has been withheld. Moreover, there is hope that during the next parliament, which is to be summoned in the coming October, a change will take place.[70]

The ambassadors passed on the good news that 'one of the greatest enemies of the gospel . . . namely the bishop of London, died a few days ago', and repeated that the impression they had been given was that the chances of spreading the Gospel to England appeared to remain very good.[71]

In the days that followed the news only got better. On 23 September the Saxons accompanied the Cleves delegation to Windsor for an audience with the king. It went very well. Henry declared himself satisfied with the proposals in principle and directed that the marital negotiations should begin forthwith.[72] On 25 September the German ambassadors and the council therefore began their work on examining and negotiating treaties, dowries, blood-lines and so on.

On 27 September, in a break from their labours, the Germans were taken to join Henry hunting.[73] On the way Burchard had another long and detailed discussion with Cromwell. The minister emphasised once again the importance of a successful conclusion to the marital negotiations if the Act of Six Articles were to be fully reversed and the opponents of the Gospel prevented from returning to the king's favour. He explained that since the negotiations had now gone so far, if the Schmalkaldeners were to back out the conservatives would have a golden opportunity to poison the king's mind against the

---

69 TStWei, Reg. H. 260, no. 111, vol. 1, fos 171–3 (final version); HStMar, PA 2582, fos 239–40 (copy enclosed in John Frederick to Philip, 22 Oct., fos 230–4).

70 '[E]r unser ankunfft zum hochsten erfreuet gewesen desgleichen auch alle guetherzige die der reynen lere des Evangelii zugethan und gewogen. Und stehen in gantzer hoffnung der Almechtige gott werde all ding in Engelland zu seinen gotlich lob schicken und wenden. Dan ob wol des perlaments decrett ausgegangen so seind doch noch zur zeit kaine Comissarii verordent und wirdt also mit der Execution innegehalten und man stehet in hoffnung das uf das negst perlament welchs den kunftigen monat Octobris wiederumb vorgenhomen werden soll, enderung ervolgen werde': TStWei, Reg. H. 260, no. 111, vol. 1, fo. 171v (final version); HStMar, PA 2582, fos 239v–40 (copy enclosed in John Frederick to Philip, 22 Oct., fos 230–4).

71 '[D]er grosten veindt eyner des Evangelii. . . . nemlich der bischoff von Lunden, vor wenig tagen verstorben': TStWei, Reg. H. 260, no. 111, vol. 1, fo. 172 (final version); HStMar, PA 2582, fo. 240 (copy enclosed in John Frederick to Philip, 22 Oct., fos 230–4).

72 Account of Burchard and Dolzig: TStWei, Reg. H. 260, no. 111, vol. 2, fos 33v–4.

73 Ibid. fo. 34v.

evangelicals. He said that so long as the Germans were co-operative,'we should not have the slightest doubt that with God's grace the matter will work out well in all respects, for he knows that the king is favourably inclined to it. And such an opinion was also voiced by the archbishop of Canterbury'.[74]

And indeed, matters continued to progress well. They hunted and ate with Henry, who during dinner assured them that he was very interested in the idea of including the League in an Anglo-Cleves alliance.[75] The next day the ambassadors again dined at Henry's table and were treated with good humour and friendliness. On 30 September after two further days of negotiations with the council, the ambassadors were invited to join Henry once more. Before going to table, Burchard was pulled aside by Henry for a short discussion. Their conversation is notable for the fact that Henry told Burchard that he 'desires nothing more than that Master Philip should come to his majesty, for his majesty wants very much that a concord will be made in religion'.[76] Henry's continued interest in theological negotiations was further emphasised after dinner, when he discussed again with Burchard his desire for a religious agreement with the League. This time he also stressed the need for a conciliatory approach to such discussions. His comments on this question emphasise just how unacceptable he found the League's previous insistences that there must be complete agreement with all aspects of their doctrine. 'One should not be so unrelenting', the king told Burchard, 'that one is prepared to give way on nothing, for it might be that certain articles have gone too far, and these might without injury be conceded.'[77]

This conversation shows that Cromwell and the evangelicals had not been clutching at straws or misrepresenting the situation in England when they sent a secret messenger to Strassburg to ask for Melanchthon to be sent to England. Cromwell was, and always had been, pursuing a perfectly sensible policy in promoting relations with the Schmalkaldic League. Though he and his friends had agitated to promote Anglo-Schmalkaldic contact – at times independently of the king – they were basing their efforts on the knowledge that Henry himself, notwithstanding the Act of Six Articles, had his own strong interest in the German Protestants. Henry retained in the autumn of 1539 – as he had since the mid-1530s – an interest in theological consultations with Melanchthon and a major embassy from the League. By bringing the Cleves marriage forward as a means of contact between England and the

---

74 '[W]ir solten ganz nicht zweifeln, die ding wurden ob goth wol sich allenthalben noch recht schicken, dan ehr wuse das nunmher die ko. mat. darzu geneigt. Sollichs hath sich der Erzbischoff v. Cant. auch vornemen lassen': ibid. fo. 35.
75 Ibid. fos 35–v.
76 '[N]ichts liebers wolte dan das Mag. Philippus bei s. mat. sein mochte, dan s. mat. wolte gerne das ein concordia in der religion gemacht': ibid. fo. 36v.
77 '[M]an solte auch so harth nicht sein das man in nichts weichen wolte, dan es mochte villeicht in etzliche artickeln etwas weit gegangen sein dar inn man one vorletzung weichen und nachgeben mochte': ibid. fo. 37.

League, Cromwell had made such a religious exchange once more a possibility.

In the following days the marriage negotiations moved quickly to a successful conclusion. A treaty of marriage, including Saxony in the inheritance provisions, was finalised on 6 October.[78] The Germans seem to have left England shortly afterwards. By 20 October they were at the Cleves capital Düsseldorf. Dolzig and Burchard carried on from there to Cassel, and after a brief halt, apparently to inform Philip of Hesse of developments, continued their journey to Saxony.[79]

The Diet of Arnstadt, October–November 1539

For most of the time the Saxon ambassadors had been away in England, the Schmalkaldic leadership had been engaged in rejecting the signals from England which had come through Bucer and Mont. However, even as John Frederick dismissed them, he recognised that the continuing good progress of the Anglo-Cleves negotiations meant that the Schmalkaldeners could not completely ignore Henry, however much they might like to. Thus, in the very same letter of 11 October to Philip of Hesse in which he rejected Bucer's intercession on behalf of the evangelicals, John Frederick added that the question of continued contact with England should be put to the full League at its next diet, scheduled to convene at Arnstadt in November.[80] In his reply of 13 October, Philip of Hesse agreed and said that he would direct the League members in his region to come prepared to examine and vote on the matter at the diet.[81]

About a week later Burchard and Dolzig arrived back in Saxony. They brought good tidings. Burchard wrote to Melanchthon reporting Cromwell's comment that only the conservative bishops' 'sophistry and clamour' had brought the Act of Six Articles to pass and that it would soon be abolished. He noted that it had been enacted 'at the instance especially of the bishops of

---

[78] *LP* xiv/2, 285–6. The treaty did not mention provisions for mutual defence and suchlike, which were the subject of a separate agreement in late January 1540. For further detail on the Anglo-Cleves marital negotiations between September and November see Bouterwek, 'Anna von Cleve' (1867), 370–6, and Müller, 'Beziehungen Heinrichs zu Anna von Cleve', 35–44.

[79] Prüser, *England und die Schmalkaldener*, 213.

[80] HStMar, PA 2582, fo. 212–v [Prüser, *England und die Schmalkaldener*, 335–6].

[81] HStMar, PA 2582, fos 205–7. Philip also included information on the imprisonment of Latimer and Shaxton under the Act of Six Articles, and suggested that if an embassy were to go to England it might seek to help them. On 15 October Philip wrote to Bucer to tell him of the discussions of the English question at Arnstadt: *BwP* i. 108. Bucer, realising that the revival of Anglo-Schmalkaldic relations for which he had worked through the autumn was now a possibility, replied on 27 October, thanking him and John Frederick for their willingness to consider contact with England: *BwP* i. 114–15. Two days later he wrote to Cranmer to tell him of the forthcoming discussions at Arnstadt: *LP* xiv/2, 413.

London and Winchester, of whom one is dead and the other excluded from the court and public business'.[82] He also mentioned the information he had received from Cromwell on 20 September:

> the king seems already displeased at the promulgation of the decree, and little favourable to those who have so astutely done this, in order to supplant Cromwell and the archbishop of Canterbury and the Chancellor, excellent men, and most friendly to the purer doctrine of the Gospel.[83]

Thus the conservative victory of the summer had miscarried, turning the

> wicked counsel upon the heads of its authors, for these excellent men are now in greater favour than ever, and the papistical faction[84] (it does not confess this name, but may truly be called so) has nowise obtained its hoped-for tyranny.[85]

Burchard also emphasised the hopes of the evangelical faction for the part the Cleves marriage would play in reversing the conservative advance and promoting the cause of reform: 'all good men have the highest hope in the coming marriage of the king and Anne, sister of the prince of Juliers, that not only that statute will be abrogated, but the true doctrine of religion received'.[86]

Such optimistic reports as this, combined with the ambassadors' letters from England, their report and the conclusion of the Anglo-Cleves marital alliance, had the effect of bringing a significant change in John Frederick's outlook. Writing to Philip of Hesse and enclosing a copy of the ambassadors' letter of 20 September on the situation in England,[87] he noted that

> Cromwell was delighted at their arrival, and there is good trust and hope that the king, insofar as the holy gospel and God's word are concerned, will be able to be brought back on to the right track. And although at the moment this is difficult to grant credence, should it be found in essentials to be true (which we still rather doubt, but which only time and experience will reveal): then in such a case one would have all the more reason to send a further embassy to England.[88]

---

82 *LP* xiv/2, 423 [CR iii. 600].
83 *LP* xiv/2, 423 [CR iii. 600–1].
84 CR iii. 601 [*LP* xiv/2, 423]: 'factio papistica'.
85 *LP* xiv/2, 423 [CR iii. 601].
86 Ibid.
87 HStMar, PA 2582, fos 230–4 (final version of letter), 239–40 (copy of letter from Dolzig and Burchard).
88 'Crumellus irer ankunftt hoch erfreuet auch des konigs halben von wegen des hailigen Evangelii und Gottes wort nach wol trost und hofnung das er widder auf die Rechte Bhan zu bringen vor handen sein solt. Und wiewol dorauf noch zur zeit nit sonders zustellen sein will, soltt es aber im grund also gelegen befunden werden, darfur wirs doch nit achtenn mugen, welchs aber die zeit und erfarung wirdet geben: so wirdet man uf solchenn vhal zu weiterer schickung in Engeland dest mher ursach haben': ibid. fo. 234.

As this news and other reports on the successful conclusion of the Anglo-Cleves marital alliance reached Hesse, Philip began to perform one of his characteristically mercurial about-faces. Before long he had reached the conclusion that an alliance between England and the League was both desirable and a very strong probability. On 2 November he wrote to the League members in his region to inform them that they should send delegates to Arnstadt appropriately instructed to discuss the English question. He went on to review the recent promising developments in Anglo-Schmalkaldic relations, and said that an embassy should be sent to England, since it was now likely that 'the king of England will join with us in a convenient confederation'.[89] His growing enthusiasm is clear to see in the instructions for his delegates to Arnstadt. His first draft, dated 5 November, stated that if it were agreed to send an embassy to England, neither Melanchthon nor Bucer should go, since the task could be done equally well by other men.[90] However, by the next day he was writing to John Frederick, arguing in favour of an embassy to England and saying that, in fact, 'one should let Philip go to him'.[91] The final version of his instructions, dated 14 November, developed that position even more fully, stating that 'a considerable embassy, also including Melanchthon, should be sent to England, and should negotiate first an agreement in religion and then a binding league'.[92]

John Frederick, meanwhile, was himself becoming increasingly aware that the practical consequences of an Anglo-Cleves marital alliance meant that he would have to be willing to countenance the possibility of an embassy from the League to England. This is clearly apparent in the instructions he issued to his delegates to Arnstadt.[93] Although directing that the adverse opinion of the Wittenberg divines on religious contact with England should be relayed to the diet, he also instructed Burchard to declare the more optimistic impressions of English religious affairs that he and Dolzig had gained during their visit to England with the Cleves delegation. He noted that if 'it is considered good that a further despatch be made to England by the whole League, then we shall not stand in the way'.[94] Instead, if it was decided to send an embassy, he directed his delegates to discuss its personnel, its conditions of despatch and what it should seek to achieve in England. As to the possible advantages of such an embassy, John Frederick suggested that

---

89 '[K]ön. würde zu Engelland mit uns, diesem tail, in bequeme confederation einlassen': HStMar, PA 522, fos 27–8 [PC ii. 635, cited in Prüser, *England und die Schmalkaldener*, 219].

90 HStMar, PA 520, fo. 11v.

91 '[M]an im den Philippum wolt zukommen lassen': HStMar, PA 2583, fo. 8v.

92 '[E]yn statlich potschaft und auch Philippum mit hinein in Engellandt schicke, erstlich zu vergleichunge der religion, darnach uf entliche puntnus zu handlen': HStMar, PA 522, fo. 57 [cited in Prüser, *England und die Schmalkaldener*, 220].

93 TStWei, Reg. H. 248/249, no. 108, vol. 1, fos 53v–4v (English section only; entire instructions at fos 28–59).

94 '[F]ur guet ansehen das ain weitere schickunge in Engellandt solt zuthun sein, von aller stende wegen, so solle es uns auch nit zu wider sein': ibid. fo. 53v.

'through it the king might be held in the hand, and in religious matters be brought onto the earlier and right track'.[95]

The instructions for the Strassburg delegates were predictably positive. They were to recommend the despatch of an embassy, or at the very least a letter, to England, with a view to achieving the abrogation of the Act of Six Articles and the freeing of those who had been imprisoned under it. An alliance on purely political grounds was to be recommended only if the League would have a financial advantage over England.[96]

On 21 November 1539 the League gathered at Arnstadt. Reports from Dolzig, Burchard and the Wittenberg theologians were heard. In the light of these the diet discussed whether the League should send a delegation to England to accompany the Cleves party as it conveyed Anne to her wedding. At the conclusion the matter was put to the vote. The duke of Lüneberg's men voted in favour, referring to the positive aspects of the report from Dolzig and Burchard and the opportunity to seek the abrogation of the Act of Six Articles. Württemberg voted similarly. Strassburg agreed, suggesting that instructions be written immediately and Dolzig and Burchard be sent in the next couple of days. Frankfurt voted with Strassburg. Esslingen, Goslar and Hamburg agreed to support the majority decision. Bremen, Magdeburg and Braunschweig agreed to follow Hesse and Saxony. The only dissenting votes came from Augsburg and Ulm (which latter also had powers to vote against an embassy on behalf of Isny, Kempten, Memmingen, Heilbronn, Biberach and Reutlingen). The Hessian and Saxon delegates went into conference at this stage, and returned with provisional instructions for an embassy to England, led by Dolzig and Burchard, which were discussed and approved by a majority of the diet on 22 November.[97]

The conclusion to the diet recorded the aims of the embassy to England in general terms. It was suggested that it should seek information and intelligence on the state and progress of Protestantism in England, and in particular whether the Act of Six Articles and the associated persecution of English evangelicals looked likely to be revoked. Dolzig and Burchard would then report back to the League at the next diet. Only if their impressions were

---

[95] '[S]olt gleichwol der konigk, dardurch an der handt behalten, und der Religion halben uff vorige und die rechte Bhan bracht werden': ibid., fo. 54.

[96] PC ii. 641.

[97] This account of the voting and discussions derives from two sources: a tallying and description of the delegates' votes in TStWei, Reg. H. 248/249, no. 108, vol. 5, fos 57–62; and a report by Philip's delegates on the voting and decision dated 21 November in HStMar, PA 520, fos 30–1 [Prüser, England und die Schmalkaldener, 336–8]. The delegates of Duke Henry of Saxony came without instructions to discuss the embassy to England. Delegates did not attend from the margrave of Brandenburg, from Constance, Halle, Göttingen, Hannover or Einbeck.

satisfactory and there seemed to be a resurgence of Protestantism in England would a major embassy led by Melanchthon follow.[98]

The instructions for Burchard and Dolzig were more specific, providing detail on how these general aims should be pursued.[99] Neatly summed up in the heading, 'Investigation and inquiry in England through the king's foremost councillors and servants who are inclined towards the Christian religion, and in particular through lord Cromwell', the ambassadors' principal task was to contact and seek information from the evangelical faction.[100] A number of specific tasks was then listed. The ambassadors were to make a special effort to find out from the evangelicals how likely it was that the Act of Six Articles would be revoked, and to see if Latimer and Shaxton were still suffering under the act. They were to ask Cromwell for advice on 'how he thinks that matters between the king and the Christian league of the German nation with respect to religion might be brought to a good agreement'.[101] If Cromwell were to ask for the despatch of a major embassy including Philip Melanchthon, the ambassadors should say that unless Henry accepted the Confession of Augsburg such an embassy would be a waste of time and only lead to unfortunate results. The ambassadors should ask Cromwell to report to Henry the League's conditions for the despatch of a major embassy. If the king still thought it should be sent then they should ask him to suspend the Act of Six Articles until it arrived. Evidently conscious of the difficulties which had emerged during the theological contests of 1538, the instructions directed the ambassadors to ask that any committee selected to discuss theology with a delegation from the League should exclude theologians sympathetic to Rome, since their presence would make any prospect of agreement unlikely. Finally they were to raise with Cromwell the question of military assistance, specifically his proposal of late May 1539 that a sum of money for the use of the League or England might be deposited at an agreed location. If the associated question of reciprocity were raised by the king, he should be told that this could only be granted once a full agreement on religion had been reached. All Cromwell's answers were to be reported back to John Frederick and Philip.

98   TStWei, Reg. H. 248/249, no. 108, vol. 1, fos 3v–4, 26v (draft), 73–v, 102v (copy); HStMar, PA 520, fos 76v–7, 106–v (copy).
99   TStWei, Reg. H. 260, 111, vol. 2, fos 86–9 (copy), 90–5 (copy); HStMar, PA 522, fos 63–6 (copy).
100 'Erforschung und Erkundigung in Engellandt bei den furnembsten rethen und dienern des konigs so der Christlichen religion geneigt haben und in sonderheit bey dem hern Crumello': TStWei, Reg. H. 260, 111, vol. 2, fos 86 (copy), 91 (copy); HStMar, PA 522, fo. 63 (copy).
101 '[W]ie er doch meynte das die sache zwischen ko. wirde und den Christlichen Stenden Deutscher Nation der religion halben zu eyner gutten vergleichung solte zupringen sein': TStWei, Reg. H. 260, 111, vol. 2, fos 86v (copy), 91v (copy); HStMar, PA 522, fo. 64 (copy).

Henry VIII and Anne of Cleves, November 1539–February 1540

On 22 November Dolzig and Burchard departed for Cleves to join the wedding party for the journey to England.[102] The ambassadors seem to have reached Cleves quickly, and on 26 November set out from Düsseldorf with Anne and her entourage. The Germans made their way through the Low Countries and France, and were received at Calais in mid-December. Bad weather kept them there longer than planned, but in late December the winds and tides combined to allow them to make the crossing. On 27 December 1539 Anne took her first steps on English soil at Deal.[103]

As the Germans prepared to make their way from the south coast up to London, the victory finally appeared to be Cromwell's. Even after the disaster of the Act of Six Articles, he had persisted with the policy of seeking to use the Germans to support the reformist policy aims of the evangelical faction. Though the efforts directed through Bucer and Mont had come to nothing, the carefully nurtured marital alliance with Cleves looked set to provide the springboard by means of which Cromwell and the evangelicals could over-leap the conservatives at the court, in the council and in the Church. But not only would the Cleves marriage secure a place of unchallenged primacy for the evangelicals in the central areas of political life. It would also prepare the ground for an alliance with the Schmalkaldic League; and that would lay the foundations for a thoroughgoing reformation of the Church.

But suddenly, the grand scheme turned sour. For if Henry and Anne had looked perfect together on paper and portrait panel, in the flesh it was imme-diately clear that they had been horribly mismatched. On New Year's day Henry came face-to-face with Anne at Rochester for the first time. From the very beginning he found her deeply unattractive, his face revealing a deep 'discontentment and misliking of her person'.[104] No less appalled than Henry was Cromwell, who had confidently stayed behind at Greenwich to await the king's return from Rochester. When he approached Henry upon his return and asked him how he found Anne, he was shocked to receive the tart retort, 'nothing as well as she was spoken of', and the observation that had he known before what he knew now, 'she should not have come within this realm'.[105]

---

102 Prüser, *England und die Schmalkaldener*, 224–5. The day after their departure, the diet received news of checks on travellers through the Low Countries. A letter was therefore im-mediately written to Philip of Hesse, requesting him to intercept Burchard and Dolzig and relieve them of their instructions, so that any inspection would reveal 'no practices against the house of Burgundy or the emperor' ('keinen practicken widder das haus Burgundi oder k. ma.': HStMar, PA 520, fo. 34v). The instructions appear to have been sent on later by post.

103 For the journey to, and reception in, England see Bouterwek, 'Anna von Cleve' (1867), 376–84, 410–13; Müller, 'Beziehungen Heinrichs zu Anna von Cleve', 44–7; Warnicke, *Marrying of Anne of Cleves*, 114–54.

104 Strype, *Ecclesiastical memorials*, i/2, 457.

105 Burnet, *History of the Reformation*, iv. 425.

It is probably unlikely that so politically astute a man as Cromwell forced or even persuaded Henry into marrying Anne after the disastrous meeting at Rochester. Though Henry desperately looked for an avenue of escape by asking for an investigation into the question of Anne's possible marital pre-contract, once this way out was closed to him he realised himself that the foreign situation allowed him no choice but to go through with the marriage. France and the empire once more appeared to be on the verge of forming an alliance to launch a crusade against England; in such a position Henry could not afford to risk an open rebuff to Anne and her family. As he glumly confided to Cromwell, the only reason for marrying Anne was to avoid 'making a ruffle in the world: that is to mean, to drive her brother into the hands of the emperor and the French king's hands, being now together'.[106]

Thus at eight o'clock in the morning of 6 January 1540, Henry and Anne were married by Archbishop Cranmer at Greenwich Palace. The wedding ceremony was conducted smoothly, and the lavish celebrations which followed went off in great style, running through the day and into the evening. All this, however, was but a prelude to the moment of reckoning for Henry and Anne, and when they retired to the bedchamber that night the festivities stopped. Though Henry did his best, he found himself unable to stir that great body of his to any degree of activity. When Cromwell put his head into the king's privy chamber the following morning and asked Henry how he now liked his queen, he received the solemn reply, 'as ye know, I liked her before not well, but now I like her much worse. For I have felt her belly, and her breasts, and thereby, as I can judge, she should be no maid; which struck me so to the heart when I felt them, that I had neither will nor courage to proceed any further in other matters.'[107]

In spite of the unpropitious beginning, Cromwell sought to develop England's relations with the League through the Schmalkaldic ambassadors.[108] However, he had to proceed with care. It was at this time that the minister made perhaps his most candid extant comment on his religious

---

106 Ibid. iv. 426.

107 Ibid. iv. 427. Cromwell's evidence is discussed in Warnicke, *Marrying of Anne of Cleves*, 137–9, 164–7. Warnicke argues that Henry was unable to consummate the marriage for 'psychogenic' reasons: he was rendered impotent by his suspicion that Anne's physical attributes indicated that she had previously been married to Duke Francis of Lorraine.

108 On 7 January the two Saxons were joined by the Hessian diplomat Ludwig von Baumbach, whom Philip had sent to convey to Henry certain information he had received concerning the emperor's aggressive intentions towards England. Von Baumbach would return to Germany after only a couple of weeks. During his stay in England he joined the Saxon ambassadors in some of their discussions with Henry and Cromwell. What follows will make some use of von Baumbach's account of those discussions, printed in Merriman, *Life and letters of Thomas Cromwell*, i. 272–7 (since the information Baumbach carried was top secret and had to be taken through imperial territories, his written instructions were a cover: they referred innocuously to the Protestants' concern about the Act of Six Articles, saying that even though the Protestants understood that it had not been applied with full rigour, they wanted Henry not to undertake anything contrary to the Gospel, and hoped

beliefs, telling the German ambassadors that 'he sees our opinions in matters of the faith, but the world standing now as it does, whatever his lord the king holds, so too will he hold'.[109] Two remarks may be made in relation to this comment. The first concerns the opening clause: the admission of Cromwell's concurrence with the faith of the Lutheran ambassadors should be noted as further evidence for the view that Cromwell inclined towards a Lutheran form of Protestantism. The second concerns the interpretation of the comment by Geoffrey Elton, who cited it as evidence of the fact that although Cromwell accepted a form of Protestantism, he would not pursue a religious path contrary to the king's.[110] This is certainly true to some extent: Cromwell would never join any open opposition to official religious policy. However, the inference that Cromwell was the king's faithful and disinterested servant in religious matters must be resisted. The reason for this may be seen by considering an aspect of the comment which has not before been sufficiently emphasised: chronology. Cromwell made this remark on 10 January 1540.[111] That is to say, ten days after Henry's disastrous meeting with Anne at Rochester, four days after their wedding, and just three days after Henry's revelations as to how Anne had terrorised him so in the nuptial bed. Given such a chronology, the words, 'the world standing now as it does', take on a special meaning. Cromwell was in trouble, and he knew it. His comment should not be construed as implying undying adherence to the king's religious beliefs. Rather, it should be seen as indicating that in the current circumstances his insidious methods of working within the government and shaping from the inside the regime's religious policy would have to be pursued with greater care. Cromwell continued to accept the League's Lutheran beliefs and would continue to promote them; but for now he intended to exercise greater caution than he had before in leading the king in religious affairs – at the least, that is, until such time that the world was not 'standing now as it does'.

Certainly, the minister continued to assure the ambassadors of his efforts on behalf of Protestantism. As they would report:

> Cromwell, who has the most influence about the king – indeed, who might as well be king himself – said that he has up to now held back the parliament and the execution of its decree, for he is very favourable to the gospel.[112]

---

that he would not let the considerable negotiations of the past lapse through inaction: Prüser, *England und die Schmalkaldener*, 237–8).

109 '[E]r siehe unser maynunge den glauben betreffen aber wie die weldt iczt stehet wesz sich sin her der konnig halte desz wolle er sich auch halten': Merriman, *Life and letters of Thomas Cromwell*, i. 279.

110 See, for example, Elton, *Studies*, i. 206, and *England under the Tudors*, 151. See also the comment in Bernard, 'Making of religious policy', 344–5.

111 Not 1538, as in Elton, *Reform and Reformation*, 171.

112 'Crumellus, der bei dem könig am meisten gehört, ja könig selber sei, der hab inen gesagt, das er soliche parlament und die exequution des decrets bisher ufgehalten, dan er sei

And in seeking to help the cause of the Gospel, he and his friends continued to push what by now can only be described as the classical evangelical policy:

> Cromwell and others have considered it useful and good that the League send a major embassy there and with it Philip Melanchthon; it should serve well the affairs of God's glory and the promotion of his holy word. And such a despatch should take place before the month of April, for in April there will be a parliament. There will also be no lack of a special provision allowing one to speak against the decree, which is otherwise strongly forbidden; he, Cromwell, will see to that.[113]

At the foot of the ambassadors' account this policy was noted again: Cromwell once more approached the ambassadors and 'begged [them] to promote the embassy'.[114]

As their instructions had made clear, however, the League would only send such an embassy if the ambassadors found the religious situation in England to have improved and if the king agreed to the conditions of a Schmalkaldic alliance with England. Once the ambassadors entered into discussions with the king it became obvious that there were difficulties. Although the ambassadors appear to have followed Cromwell's advice before their first audience with the king not to 'speak with him too severely, so that his majesty is not raised to anger and impatience',[115] Henry and the Germans were unable to reach the sort of agreement which would have paved the way for the major delegation to conclude an alliance which Cromwell and the evangelicals sought. On religion, Henry remained adamant that the League could not dictate terms, but that there should be concession on both sides:

> the king spoke to them himself, saying that he had been sufficiently advised by his learned men that ours have gone too far with regard to priestly marriage, communion in both kinds and the private mass. And although his learned men might err, so might ours also err. Indeed, he said, we will see that ours err

---

seer wol am evangelio': PC iii. 32 (report of the Strassburg delegates on the English ambassadors' account presented to the Schmalkaldic diet at Schmalkalden in March 1540).

113 '[E]s hab Crumellum und andere für nutz und gut angesehen, das man von disen stenden ain treffenliche potschaft hinein und mit denen dominum Philippum Melanchton ordnet; solt der sachen zur eer gottes und furderung seins h. worts hoch dienstlich sein, und das solche schickung sover möglich ante tempus aprilis geschehe, dan im aprillen soll aber ain parlament werden. an genugsamer vergleitung – damit man auch wider das decret reden dörf, das doch sonst hoch verpoten sei – soll es nit mangeln; er Crumellus wölls versehen': ibid.

114 '[D]ie schigkhung zu fördern gebetten': citation from the original of the ambassadors account in A. Stern, 'Heinrich VIII. von England und der Schmalkaldische Bund, 1540', *Forschungen zur deutschen Geschichte* x (1870), 500. Stern also provides some useful additional detail on the ambassadors' activities in England in early 1540.

115 '[N]icht zu hart myt s. mayestät reden wolten etc. da myt s. mayestät nicht zue ungenaden und ungedulden erregt werde': Merriman, *Life and letters of Thomas Cromwell*, i. 279.

in many respects: in sum, he holds his view to be justified, and desires that he or his be written to on these and other essential articles and our reasoning be demonstrated.[116]

Though with these comments Henry clearly defended the Act of Six Articles, he did not mean to reject the possibility of an alliance in matters of the faith. He went on to note that 'we are of one opinion in the principal matters of the faith; justification and the most essential points'.[117] In the light of this considerable common ground, he suggested that England and the League should seek to establish an alliance. He also proposed that 'an understanding be made with the League not only in religious matters, but also in all external temporal matters',[118] going on to say that 'he marvels that the League is only united in religious matters, for it will not be attacked in the name of religion but under another pretext'.[119]

Cromwell also did what he could to move the ambassadors towards a compromise. He advised entering into an alliance first and then working out the remaining religious differences.[120] He also noted that if 'one could negotiate a partially satisfactory agreement, his lord the king would not neglect to put down a considerable sum of money to which the League could have access in times of emergency'.[121] The ambassadors, however, were unresponsive. They refused to be drawn, saying that they had no powers to negotiate on such matters. The most they could say was that the League stood only for the defence of religion and that it could not be extended for other purposes.[122]

The Schmalkaldic ambassadors returned to Germany in February, having stuck by their refusal to enter into negotiations on an alliance, or even to commit the League to sending a major embassy to England. They undertook

---

116 '[D]er könig hab selbs aigner person mit inen geredt, er sei von seinen gelerten sovil, das die unsern in denen puncten die priesteree, die communion sub utraque specie und die privatmessen belangend ze weit gangen. wiewol die seinen möchten irren, so mögen aber die unsern auch irren. und sonderlich sag er, wir werden sehen, das wir in vil stucken irren: in summa, er halt sein opinion für gerecht und beger, man soll ime oder den seinen von disen und andern notwendigen artikeln schreiben, unsere grund anzaigen': PC iii. 32 (report of the Strassburg delegates: see n. 112).
117 '[W]ir seien im haupthandl in der rechten glaubenssachen der justification und den notwendigsten puncten ains': ibid.
118 '[M]it disen stenden nit allain in religion sonder allen auch eusserlichen prophansachen ein verständnuss ze machen': ibid.
119 '[E]s neme ine wunder, das dise stend sich nur in religionssachen zusamen verainigen, dan man werd sie nit im namen der religion angreifen sonder under aim andern schein': ibid.
120 Von Baumbach's account in Merriman, *Life and letters of Thomas Cromwell*, i. 279.
121 '[M]an ain wenig zu guter vergleichung handlen könnt, es wurde bei seinem hern dem konig an erlegung einer namhaften summa gelts, so disen stenden in nöten zu gutem kommen köndt, nit mangel haben': PC iii. 32–3 (report of the Strassburg delegates: see n. 112).
122 Ibid. iii. 33. See also von Baumbach's account in Merriman, *Life and letters of Thomas Cromwell*, i. 279–80.

only to inform the League of their findings and pass on its determinations to Henry forthwith. The relationship with Germany so carefully reconstructed by Cromwell since the parliamentary setback of the summer had in the course of just a few weeks lost its promise of victory and now appeared to be foundering.

The Diet of Schmalkalden, February–May 1540

Dolzig and Burchard left England at the end of January and arrived back in Germany in the second week of February.[123] In accordance with their instructions, they reported to the next League diet, which was convened at Schmalkalden at the beginning of March. They delivered their report on 7 March. On the negative side, they noted that the religious situation in England still left a lot to be desired, with Latimer and Shaxton still in prison, the marriage of the priesthood still forbidden (and many clergymen therefore hiding their wives) and the king unwilling to give way on holy communion and the private mass. On the positive side, however, they reported the more conciliatory of Henry's comments and the encouraging attitude of Cromwell and his fellow evangelicals.[124]

But the League remained unwilling to go along with the evangelical faction's pleas for a major theological embassy and the conclusion of an alliance of mutual defence. Though Martin Bucer wrote to Philip on 11 March to encourage an agreement with England on the limited political terms which the king desired, his was a lone voice.[125] The League, still influenced by the truce agreed with the emperor under the Frankfurt Interim, had decided to adhere to the policy of caution in relations with England.

On 15 April the diet finalised its closing statement.[126] The findings of Dolzig and Burchard were reviewed, and it was noted that although the Act of Six Articles remained in force, there was good reason to think that Henry might be willing to reconsider the disputed articles. But it was decided that before the League went any further with Henry it must ascertain his position on these articles: the League's theologians should prepare a tract explaining its position on the disputed doctrinal questions. Henry should also be offered a further doctrinal discussion in Germany between his theologians and some

123 Prüser, England und die Schmalkaldener, 246 n. 1.
124 PC iii. 32–4. Stern, 'Heinrich und der Schmalkaldische Bund', 498–502; Prüser, England und die Schmalkaldener, 248–9.
125 BwP i. 146. Bucer pointed to the friendship between Charles and Francis, and speculated on the possibility of a coalition of France, the empire, the papacy and Scotland being offset by one of England, Cleves, Denmark and the League.
126 TStWei, Reg. H. 295, no. 121, vol. 4, fos 62v–5v (relevant section taken from copy of closing statement); HStMar, PA 538, fos 61–2v (copy of relevant section of closing statement enclosed in letter of delegates to Philip, 16 Mar., fos 55–8); Stern, 'Heinrich und der Schmalkaldische Bund', 505–6.

from the League. When these had been satisfactorily concluded, a final follow-up round could take place in England.[127] The diet noted that Henry's
response to this would enable an assessment to be made of the prospects for a
religious agreement with England. As to the king's interest in an alliance with
the League not only on religious grounds but also political, he was to be
informed that at this stage such an arrangement seemed unlikely. The most
the king should be told was that if an agreement were to be reached on theological matters then a further understanding might be achieved.

By the time the closing statement was finally agreed, the tract to which it
referred was ready. It was a standard statement of Protestant doctrine on the
mass, communion in both kinds, clerical marriage and vows, making no
concessions whatsoever to the king's views.[128] It was accompanied by a letter
dated 12 April, written nominally by John Frederick (the drafts show that it
was actually written by Melanchthon) which restated the Germans' belief in
their doctrine on the abuses and referred Henry to the tract on this question
which had been included for him to consider. The letter also mentioned the
suggestion of a theological conference, first in Germany and then in England.
In closing, it showed little enthusiasm for Henry's interest in an all embracing
alliance, saying that the League comprehended no causes other than religion,
and that without the agreement of all members of the League neither John
Frederick nor Philip could enter into a wider understanding.[129]

These messages were badly timed and reinforced Henry's growing irritation with the Germans. He was rapidly losing patience with all things
German, as his unsuitable marriage to Anne of Cleves and the constant
demands and unwillingness to compromise of the League drove him to question his pro-German policy of recent years and those who had counselled it.
Of the tract on the abuses, the French ambassador Marillac reported on 21
May that

> the duke of Saxony and other German lords of his league have sent this king a
> printed pamphlet of the articles decided upon in their diets, with an invitation
> to adopt them; but it is thought their request will have little effect, and it is
> even said publicly that the said pamphlet contains several erroneous doc-
> trines.[130]

The letter which accompanied the tract fared little better. Henry's reply of 1
June reflected his impatience. He complained at the attitude of the Germans

---

127 TStWei, Reg. H. 295, no. 121, vol. 4, fos 63v–4 (relevant section taken from copy of
closing statement); HStMar, PA 538, fo. 61v (copy section of closing statement: see n. 126);
Stern, 'Heinrich und der Schmalkaldische Bund', 506.
128 TStWei, Reg. H. 165, no. 78 ii, fos 1–13 (German copy), 14–34 (Latin draft in
Melanchthon's hand) [LP xv. 310]; Prüser, England und die Schmalkaldener, 253–4.
129 CR iii. 1006–9 [LP xv. 310 (placed a little too early in March), 509.i (correctly placed
on 12 April)].
130 LP xv. 697.

to England's religious legislation and asked for those who criticised his religion in Germany to be punished. He said that although he had not yet read the tract sent to him, he would give a final answer at a theological conference. In closing, he complained that such a conference, which he had so long sought, had not already taken place in England.[131]

Cranmer received a letter from John Frederick around the same time. This, though not extant, seems to have criticised Henry, for Cranmer took pains in his reply of 10 May to emphasise all that Henry had done for the reformed religion in England, pointing out that he had expelled the papacy, idolatry and monasticism. As for the League's tract, he said that he had not yet heard of it, but trusted Henry would reply when ready. Finally, perhaps sensing Henry's growing discontent with the Germans' continued importuning, he warned them not to harangue the king so, explaining that he was very learned and might become offended.[132]

The collapse of Anglo-Schmalkaldic relations, March–July 1540

In the weeks and months which followed the wedding, the king's marriage deteriorated steadily.[133] Though Henry continued to sleep with Anne from night to night, that was all he did. He would come to bed in the evening, kiss her and take her by the hand, say 'good night, sweet heart', and promptly fall asleep; in the morning he would kiss her again, bid her 'farewell, darling', and depart. For her part, Anne remained blissfully unaware of what was going on. When asked some months later by a group of gossiping ladies at the court whether she was still a virgin, she innocently reproached them, 'how can I be a maid, and sleep every night with the king?' When one of the ladies observed that 'there must be more than that', Anne proceeded to describe Henry's bedchamber performances and asked, 'is this not enough?' In the awkward silence which followed the worldly-wise countess of Rutland spoke up: 'madam', she assured Anne, 'there must be more than this, or it will be long before we have a duke of York'.[134]

Yet if Anne could continue happily in her innocence, able to tell her ladies-in-waiting that 'I am contented with this, for I know no more', Henry found the lack of a sexual dimension to the marriage intolerable.[135] To his closest physician, Dr Butts, he protested his own virility, assuring him that

---

131 TStWei, Reg. H. 313, no. 128, fos 18–21 (Latin final version), 24–8 (German trans.) [Seckendorf, *Historie des Lutherthums*, 1903–4].

132 TStWei, Reg. H. 313, no. 128, fos 22–3 (Latin final version), 29–32 (German trans.) [Seckendorf, *Historie des Lutherthums*, 1904–5].

133 The references in this and the following paragraph are taken from the printed version of the divorce depositions in Strype, *Ecclesiastical memorials*.

134 Ibid. i/2, 462. For doubts about this evidence see Warnicke, *Marrying of Anne of Cleves*, 234–6.

135 Strype, *Ecclesiastical memorials*, i/2, 462.

since the wedding he had had two wet dreams and thought himself able 'to do the act with others but not with her'.[136] The problem was Anne's physical attributes: Henry told his doctors that he 'found her body in such a sort disordered and indisposed to excite and provoke any lust'; that he had a 'misliking of her body for the hanging of her breasts and the looseness of her flesh'; that he found her loathsome and could not 'overcome that loathsomeness, nor in her company be provoked or steered in that act'.[137]

Before long Henry's dissatisfaction with the marriage was common knowledge. It was also soon clear that Cromwell had been badly weakened by it. This was a perfect opportunity for those conservative opponents whom the minister had beaten down in the late summer of 1539 and one they were quick to grasp. In the early months of 1540 they began to re-group under the joint leadership of Stephen Gardiner and the duke of Norfolk. Now plans began to be made for a renewed campaign against the minister, conducted on two fronts.[138] First, they set out to subvert the Cleves marriage. Then they set about overthrowing Cromwell directly. Their instrument was the seductive Catherine Howard, niece of the duke of Norfolk. Under the supervision of the conservatives, Catherine was placed in the king's presence, and there she went to work. Before long, Henry had been hooked. The attack on Cromwell began to come out into the open; soon a vicious faction fight was in progress. An early sign of the developing battle came when Stephen Gardiner, preaching at St Paul's Cross, was publicly attacked by Robert Barnes; when the dispute was brought to Henry's attention at Easter he decided in favour of the bishop and had the Lutheran put in the Tower.[139] Also around this time the religious powder keg that was Calais blew, in the form of a report on radicalism in the Pale and the failure of Cromwell and Cranmer to act with the requisite alacrity against it.[140] By 10 April Marillac was reporting back to France that the Barnes affair was just a symptom of a wider set of reverses for the evangelicals: Cromwell and Cranmer 'do not know where they are', he told the constable, adding that 'Cromwell is tottering' and that the king was

---

[136] Ibid., i/2, 461.

[137] Ibid.

[138] The assertion that a conservative faction led by Gardiner and Norfolk campaigned to overthrow Cromwell is in line with traditional historiography, and is supported by evidence, principally from the French ambassador. That Gardiner's involvement was central has been disputed in Redworth, Gardiner, 105–29, where Cromwell's fall is presented as a diplomatic event. According to this view, the king wished to realign his diplomatic position, breaking his links with the Germans and joining with the emperor, and calculated that such a shift would be most expediently effected by removing Cromwell. It will by now be clear that I prefer to see principle at the heart of things: Cromwell was attacked because his conservative opponents detested and felt threatened by his Protestant beliefs.

[139] LP xv. 306, 485. The Barnes affair is reviewed in Redworth, Gardiner, 109–15. See also Brigden, London and the Reformation, 309–12.

[140] See Brigden, 'Thomas Cromwell and the "brethren" ', 47; MacCulloch, Cranmer, 262.

about to restore to the council the conservative bishops Gardiner, Tunstall and Clerk.[141]

Cromwell fought back, and with some success. Two weeks later Marillac reported to the constable that Cromwell had been promoted to the earldom of Essex and to the position of lord great chamberlain, and 'is in as much credit with his master as ever he was'.[142] In May, he managed to turn the Calais situation to his advantage, using the defection of Lord Lisle's chaplains to secure the Deputy's arrest for treason. This was followed towards the end of the month by the arrest of the two conservative court theologians Richard Sampson and Nicholas Wilson, who followed Lisle to the Tower, also accused of treason. On 1 June Marillac wrote to the constable that

> a trustworthy personage says he heard from Cromwell that there were still five bishops who ought to be treated thus; whose names, however, cannot yet be learnt unless they are those who lately shook the credit of 'maistre Cramvel', so that he was very near coming to grief. Things are brought to such a pass that either Cromwell's party or that of the bishop of Winchester must succumb.[143]

Though Marillac also noted that 'both are in great authority and favour of the king their master', Cromwell's evangelical faction now appeared to have the advantage. Cranmer had been appointed to preach in Gardiner's place at St Paul's Cross, and Barnes and Latimer appeared to be on the verge of being returned to liberty. The same day, Marillac wrote to Francis that

> the rest of the bishops are in great trouble, some for fear of being found guilty of the same deed [as that attributed to Sampson and Wilson], and some for the differences they have upon some religious questions, as each party to establish what they maintain would destroy those who sustain the contrary.[144]

All this seems to suggest that Cromwell, desperately fighting to survive the failures of his German policy, was threatening a genuine holocaust of conservative opponents at the court, in the council and in the Church.

It was most probably the gravity of this threat which explains the next move. Desperate to escape the blade Cromwell was sharpening for them, his opponents seized upon an audacious way out. They decided to accuse the minister of treason before the king. This step finally forced the issue. Now Henry had to intervene and pass judgement. The charges made against Cromwell were much too serious to ignore; either the accusers or the accused must be put down. But whom to choose? It was a close run thing, but Cromwell's promotion of the Cleves marriage, his long advocacy of Anglo-Schmalkaldic relations and the untrue but plausible taint of partiality

[141] *LP* xv. 486.
[142] *LP* xv. 567.
[143] *LP* xv. 737.
[144] *LP* xv. 736.

towards extremists in Calais had diminished the king's trust in him and laid him open to accusations of religious radicalism. After due consideration of the charges before him, Henry turned against Cromwell. On 10 June the minister was arrested at the council board and thrown in the Tower.

The reasons for Cromwell's arrest have been obscured by historians. It has generally been assumed that the litany of charges in Cromwell's parliamentary attainder was precisely the same as those brought to Henry in the first place. In fact, the majority of those charges emerged later on, when Cromwell was for all practical purposes unable to defend himself. Once Cromwell was behind bars, anything could be alleged against him and in the event almost anything was. Most of the charges in his attainder actually have nothing to do with the original reasons for his arrest and are therefore substantially irrelevant to his fall. To identify the original charges, it is necessary to look at the strictly contemporary evidence.[145]

There were, in fact, just two inter-related reasons. On the day of his arrest, the council wrote to Wallop in France, telling him to explain to Francis that Cromwell had been arrested because he had

> not only [1.] been counterworking the king's aims for the settlement of religion, but [2.] said that if the king and all the realm varied from his opinions he would withstand them, and that he hoped in another year or two to bring things to that frame that the king could not resist it.[146]

Cromwell's Schmalkaldic policy gave these accusations the necessary ring of truth. Marillac wrote on the day of the minister's arrest that Henry had sent a gentleman from the court to tell him that 'Cromwell, as attached to the German Lutherans', had favoured the new religion against the old, and was determined to see it triumph before all opposition, including the king's.[147] Cromwell's Schmalkaldic policy also provided the evidence with which his accusers were finally able to bury him. The day following his arrest, Cromwell's longstanding secret involvement with the Schmalkaldic League was revealed, and this evidence removed any last vestiges of doubt Henry might have had about the charges against him. Marillac reported that Cromwell's house had been searched on 11 June, and that there

---

[145] This very important distinction was first drawn by Glyn Redworth in his *Gardiner*, 122–3. For the classic account of Cromwell's fall see Elton, *Studies*, i. 189–230. See also Warnicke, *Marrying of Anne of Cleves*, 187–228, for the argument that Cromwell fell not because of factional infighting, but because he had interfered in the king's marital affairs by advising Anne to make herself more attractive to Henry, had leaked private information on the state of the marriage to the earl of Rutland (in violation of the privy chamber ordinance of secrecy in the Eltham ordinances), and was associated with the sorcery that Henry believed was responsible for his inability to consummate the marriage.

[146] *LP* xv. 765. The abstract is an accurate reduction of the full version in PRO, SP 1/160, fos 181–4 [*StP* viii. 349–50].

[147] *LP* xv. 766.

were found several letters he wrote to or received from the Lutheran lords of Germany. Cannot learn what they contained except that this king was thereby so exasperated against him that he would no longer hear him spoken of, but rather desired to abolish all memory of him as the greatest wretch ever born in England.[148]

What were the incriminating papers in Cromwell's Schmalkaldic file? Materials connected with the first secret intimations made to the League in 1534? Luther's letter to Cromwell of 1536? Correspondence associated with Theabold's undercover mission of 1537 perhaps? Even communications with respect to Mont's private messages to Philip of Hesse in 1538? Or were the papers related to the covert passing of information to Martin Bucer in mid-1539? They might have been all or none of these; it is impossible to know, for the records were not preserved. Nevertheless, the existence and the incriminating nature of the evidence to which Marillac alluded should not be doubted: where Cromwell and the League of Schmalkalden were concerned there was an abundance of muck to be raked.

The two charges which first put Cromwell behind bars were not only credible because of Cromwell's involvement with the Schmalkaldic League, they were also essentially true. This is especially so of the first charge: throughout the decade Cromwell had been pursuing, within the foreign policy parameters set by the king, a clandestine religious agenda, and, as his comments to the Saxon delegation of September 1539 show, from the summer of that year he had been working to prevent the implementation of the Act of Six Articles. Even the second charge has an element of truth: Cromwell had, after all, been seeking to use relations with the League to shape circumstances so that Henry would be swept along with the tide of reformed doctrine. The only aspect of the charge which should be resisted is that which implies that Cromwell would actually have forced the king to go along with continued reform. Cromwell's plan was always to work with rather than against the king; never to attempt to bludgeon the king into reform, but to create circumstances – conferences and alliances with the German Lutherans, for example – which would encourage Henry down a reformist path.

Quite apart from the plausibility of the charges against Cromwell, one can understand from the very circumstances of the time why Henry, when compelled to choose between the accusers and the accused, chose in favour of the conservatives. They, on the one hand, had brought into his life an enchanting nymphette and, having been kept from power for so long, they had the tempting attraction of the new and untried. On the other hand, Cromwell's advocacy of closer alignment with the League had brought Henry only pain. Since 1535 the Germans had consistently refused to accept Henry's invitations to send Melanchthon to England as the leader of a major theological delegation. They had stubbornly refused to offer mutually benefi-

[148] *LP* xv. 804.

cial alliance conditions. They had insisted throughout that Henry accept all aspects of their doctrine. They had impugned loudly any theological deviation on the king's part, and ignored his interest in a religious compromise. Finally, as if to heap insult upon injury, they had sent him an unattractive wife and refused to consider thoroughgoing involvement in an alliance in the aftermath of the marriage. In the light of all this it is not difficult to see why the king, forced to decide between Cromwell and his opponents, elected to believe the charges against the man whose theologically orientated foreign policy had brought him to such a sorry pass.

One can feel some sympathy for Cromwell. There were certainly grounds for believing that the policy he had pursued as faction leader might have been successful. Henry had always been interested in theological discussions with the Germans, and in political alliance with them as well. Had the Schmalkaldeners proceeded with the evangelising sensibilities of a Bucer, they might have helped achieve a comprehensive Reformation in England. Instead they had throughout shown little interest in serious engagement with Henry in religious matters. Even where political questions such as mutual aid were concerned they had shown little enthusiasm for diplomatic cooperation with England. Cromwell's mistake was not that he sought to use the Schmalkaldeners as an instrument of faction for the cause of the Gospel; it was that he persisted in doing so beyond the point when their unsuitability for the task should have been apparent.

It was a mistake which cost him his life. Once his Schmalkaldic file had been discovered and shown to the king, Henry was prepared to believe anything alleged about him. Now the floodgates opened. The ludicrous charge of sacramentarianism was followed by a catalogue of others formulated while Cromwell was unable to defend himself. The evidence was duly reviewed and accepted by parliament. On 28 July Cromwell was led out onto Tower Hill to suffer the axeman's stroke.

As Cromwell was languishing in the Tower, his enemies began to encourage Henry to dispose of the Cleves marriage once and for all. With the foreign policy situation improving, Henry agreed that he could safely discard Anne, and made plans to take Catherine as his fifth queen. Anne was devastated when she received the news in early July that Henry was considering leaving her. To her ambassador, she insisted that the king was the man whom she had married, 'and whom she therefore considers to be her true lord and husband'.[149] Her protests continued, wrote the ambassador back to Germany, with 'such tears and bitter cries that they would have made a heart of stone feel compassion'.[150] However, by this time events had gone too far for Anne

---

[149] '[U]nd do hielt sie In für Iren eelich hern und man': W. Bouterwek, 'Anna von Cleve: Gemahlin Heinrichs VIII, Königs von England', *Zeitschrift des Bergischen Geschichtsvereins* vi (1869), 173 (letter from Karl Harst to the duke of Cleves, London, 10 July 1540).
[150] '[S]olches weynes und bitter schreyes thut sie, das es ein steinen hertz mochte erbarmen': ibid.

to able to change anything by weeping: within a week, convocation had met and annulled her marriage, and she had been put away to live the rest of her life as an obscure, if well-endowed, spinster.[151]

In the early summer of 1540, Anglo-Schmalkaldic relations quickly degenerated. In June intelligence began to arrive in Germany of a wave of persecutions of Protestants in England.[152] In July came the complete break. Henry's divorce from Anne of Cleves and the humiliation that implied for her German relatives were bad enough. But then came the execution of Cromwell and the burning at Smithfield as heretics of a number of other Protestants, including Wittenberg's most beloved Englishman, Robert Barnes. These developments outraged the League; the Schmalkaldeners immediately renounced any interest in further contact with England, and by the autumn of 1540 relations between England and the League of Schmalkalden had completely collapsed.

---

151 Anne's experiences in England from her arrival in late 1539 to her death on 16 July 1557 are reviewed in Müller, 'Beziehungen Heinrichs zu Anna von Cleve', 46–98, and Bouterwek, 'Anna von Cleve' (1869), 97–180.
152 See, for example, the three reports printed in Prüser, *England und die Schmalkaldener*, 341–2.

6

Diplomatic Standstill and Stagnation, 1540–1547

Hiatus, July 1540–August 1544

After the excitement of the 1530s, Anglo-Schmalkaldic relations during the 1540s are something of an anti-climax. There are no more religious conferences; no more instances of close royal involvement; no more major ambassadorial exchanges; no more dramatic factional disputes. Rather, there is a series of disconnected diplomatic efforts, which ultimately achieve and mean relatively little. Nevertheless, a brief discussion of this period allows for an appraisal of relations between England and Protestant Germany over the whole life of the League from 1531 to 1547; moreover, the very discontinuity of interest in diplomacy during the 1540s – like the early 1530s – helps to throw into higher relief the distinctiveness of the ideologically motivated period of Anglo-Schmalkaldic relations between 1534 and 1540.

In the years following the breakdown of Anglo-Schmalkaldic relations in the summer of 1540, few efforts were made to revive diplomatic contacts. For the Germans' part, not only was there the outrage at the turn of events in England in mid-1540, but the problems caused by Philip of Hesse's bigamous marriage in the same year and the League's efforts at internal consolidation, signalled by its crushing of Duke Henry of Braunschweig-Wolfenbüttel and the institution of a Reformation in his territories in 1542. These developments caused the League to turn away from foreign entanglements and concentrate on domestic matters.[1] In England, meanwhile, Cromwell's erstwhile opponents dominated the king's counsels from mid-1540, their position consolidated by the marriage of the king to Catherine Howard that same year and the development of a pro-imperial, anti-French foreign policy, with a war against Scotland commencing in 1542 and an Anglo-imperial campaign in France underway in July the following year. As the decade wore on, however, the conservative ascendancy began to wane. An early sign was a change in the king's marital arrangements: the execution of Catherine Howard in early 1542 was followed in June of the following year by his marriage to Catherine Parr, a woman with strong Protestant sympathies. The evangelical presence at court soon became more powerful. If still lacking a single-minded leader of

---

[1] The bigamy episode is dealt with fully in Rockwell, *Doppelehe Philipps von Hessen*. For the League's German policy in the early 1540s see Brady, 'Schmalkaldic League', 171–2.

the calibre of Thomas Cromwell, by mid-1544 the evangelicals were beginning to present a challenge to the conservative dominance of the early 1540s. Then, just as the evangelicals were dragging themselves back into contention as a political force, there was a further blow to the conservative position. During 1544 England's pro-imperial foreign policy, which had been championed by Stephen Gardiner, began to falter. As the Anglo-imperial offensive against France fell to pieces in the summer of 1544 and Charles signed the peace of Crépy with Francis behind Henry's back on 18 September 1544, the conservatives who had counselled that the king ally himself with Charles against Francis found themselves drifting out of the king's favour.[2] Certainly, they still held sway in England, but their grasp on the reins of power was loosening and the strength was rising of those evangelicals who might be inclined to support the idea of a resumption of relations with the Schmalkaldic League. With the hardening of papal plans to summon a general council to Trent and the pressing need for allies against France in the wake of the imperial withdrawal from the campaign against the French, the circumstances were becoming favourable for someone prepared to take the initiative and push for a renewal of Anglo-Schmalkaldic relations. In the late summer of 1544, such a man stepped forward.

Anglo-Schmalkaldic relations renewed, August 1544–August 1545

The man who grasped the opportunity to re-open contact between England and the Schmalkaldic League was England's perennial German diplomat, Christopher Mont. Since the fall of Cromwell, Mont had been lying low in Germany. Though he continued to provide Henry with intelligence and received a living from the king, he does not appear to have felt sufficiently secure to return to England. Instead, he spent most of his time after 1540 in Speyer, providing Henry with intelligence on a part-time basis while reading for a doctorate in the civil law at the Protestant university in the city.

Mont completed his studies in 1544. It was in the period following this that he began his return to the more vigorous diplomatic activity which had characterised his service in the 1530s. He knew that the time was right for a renewal of Anglo-Schmalkaldic relations. He was as well aware as any other European political observer that the Anglo-imperial war effort against France was flagging,[3] and knew that failure, coming after the Parr marriage, was yet another blow to the conservative faction. In August 1544 Mont made his first soundings in a letter to William Paget. In this he hinted that he would be

---

[2] Redworth, *Gardiner*, 208–22.
[3] In September he was one of the first to advise Henry of Charles's unilateral negotiation of peace with Francis: *LP* xix/2, 199.

interested in helping to revive Anglo-German relations.[4] There was, however, no response. This was not the Cromwellian heyday of the 1530s, and there was no one in England prepared to seize the opportunity to develop relations with the League. Thus Mont decided to take the matter in his own hands, and to work independently from Germany to engineer an *rapprochement*. To this end, he decided to use the good offices of the German who in the late 1530s had showed himself the most interested in developing contact with England and in advancing the English Reformation: Martin Bucer.

From September 1544 through to early 1545, Mont and Bucer combined to press the case for a revival of diplomatic relations in both England and Germany. In Germany, Bucer worked through Philip of Hesse, pointing out in letters to the landgrave the decline in the fortunes of the conservative faction in England, the poor state of England's relations with France and the utility of a common Anglo-Schmalkaldic policy on the forthcoming general council for both England and the League.[5] His entreaties were not fruitful. Although Philip of Hesse was receptive, he was unable to gain the support of John Frederick, who refused to have any contact with the king of England, going so far as to refer to him in one letter as that 'crazy man'.[6] Mont had greater success with William Paget in England. Like Bucer, he cited the potential efficacy of a common policy on the general council; he also emphasised England's need for allies in view of the recent peace between Charles and Francis.[7] His letters persuaded Paget to take the matter up with the king; this he did to such good effect that in January 1545 a decision was taken to despatch an embassy from England to Germany to investigate once more the possibility of an Anglo-Schmalkaldic alliance.[8]

On 26 January money and instructions were issued at Greenwich to

---

4 *LP* xix/2, 81. Mont offered his active service in Germany, asking Paget to recommend how he might do more to warrant the king's kindness.

5 Correspondence in December between Bucer and Philip: *BwP* ii. 267–8, 273–5, 279–80.

6 Philip to Gregor Brück, John Frederick's chancellor, 22 Dec. 1544, HStMar, PA 2628, fos 135–8; Philip to Bucer, 22 Jan. 1545 (explaining that John Frederick did not want any contact with Henry and enclosing John Frederick's letter to Philip, Torgau, 12 Jan. 1545), *BwP* ii. 283; HStMar, PA 2629, fos 97–100 (final version) [*BwP* ii. 283–5, n. 1] (John Frederick had referred to Henry as a 'vorruchten manne': HStMar, PA 2629, fo. 97 [*BwP* ii. 283, n. 1]); Bucer's letter to Philip of 8 Feb., expressing regret at John Frederick attitude: *BwP* ii. 289.

7 Paget to Petre (on Mont's proposals for an alliance), PRO, SP 1/195, fo. 41 [*LP* xix/2, 582]; correspondence between Paget and Mont, PRO, SP 1/195, fo. 69 [*StP* x. 187–8; *LP* xix/2, 596].

8 Petre and Wriothesley to Paget, directing him to tell Mont to investigate the possibility of an alliance in Germany, PRO, SP 1/195, fos 112–13 [*StP* x. 188–9; *LP* xix/2, 614]; Mont to Henry, 14 Dec., on the possibility of a revival of Anglo-Schmalkaldic relations, PRO, SP 1/195, fos 229–30 [*StP* x. 232–4; *LP* xix/2, 746]; Mont to Henry, 5 Jan., on Philip of Hesse's interest in reviving diplomatic contact with England, PRO, SP 1/197, fos 30–1 [*StP* x. 239–41; *LP* xx/1, 28]. See also Mont to Paget on the negative attitude of the duke of Saxony, *LP* xx/1, 212.

Catherine Parr's secretary, Walter Bucler,[9] who was instructed to meet Mont at Speyer and go directly to the landgrave. The two men were to begin their discussions with Philip by proposing that an alliance be concluded as expeditiously as possible. Because of the speed required, only England, Denmark, Bremen, Lübeck and Hesse should be included: if the other members of the Schmalkaldic League were to be involved, time-consuming negotiations would be needed. The alliance should be offensive and defensive. It was suggested that the ambassadors should be sent from Hesse to Denmark immediately, and thence to England. No great ceremony need be observed. Interest in an alliance was clearly sincere. Not only was the greatest haste encouraged, but it was suggested that the men sent to England should have full powers, since anything less than a quick settlement would be of little use to either England or Protestant Germany. As far as religion was concerned, rising evangelical influence and interest were balanced by an awareness of the League's past intransigence: the ambassadors were to emphasise Henry's religiosity, but say that the last embassy to go to England stuck so stubbornly to its religious principles that its demands became quite unreasonable. Subsequent communications from Germany, however, had shown rather more moderation and it was to be hoped that this would be the spirit in which any further discussions would be conducted. The ambassadors were to point out that since England and the League had a common enemy in the pope, they were likely to concur on a general alliance; if such an alliance could be concluded, a further conference on matters of religion would follow, which would undoubtedly produce an agreement.[10]

Bucler appears to have set off in early February. He first wrote from the continent on 10 February, providing Henry with a report on the state of

9 For finance see John Williams, treasurer of the Augmentations, assigning diet money etc. to Bucler and Mont, 26 Jan., PRO, SP 1/197, fos 133–4 [LP xx/1, 89]; for instructions see PRO, SP 1/197, fos 150–74 [StP x. 278–83; LP xx/1, 91]. Another set of instructions is shown at PRO, SP 1/197, fos 135–49 [StP x. 222–7; LP xx/1, 90]. The actions of the ambassadors, however, indicate that these were not followed; they appear to have been an earlier set which were superseded by PRO, SP 1/197, fos 150–74, after further discussion between the king and council.

10 The instructions covered two further matters, proposals which Mont had reported to Henry in his letter of 5 January 1545 (see n. 8 above: LP xx/1, 28), but which were not pursued at any great length by the ambassadors. One was the proposal Philip of Hesse had made for a marriage between the Princess Mary and Duke Adolphus of Holstein (brother to Christian of Denmark), the other an offer of mercenaries. The instructions noted that the alliance was the main proposal, the others peripheral. The marital interest disappeared from sight within a few weeks. The question of mercenary recruitment in general is not a concern of this study, as competition between Francis and Henry in 1544/1546 to recruit mercenaries in Germany (a contest which France usually won) did not involve the Schmalkaldic League as such, but rather individual German noblemen and private mercenary captains such as Reiffenberg. It is discussed fully in D. L. Potter, 'The international mercenary market in the sixteenth century: Anglo-French competition in Germany, 1543–50', EHR cxi (1996), 24–58.

affairs in Antwerp.[11] Two days later he was in Brussels and then seems to have met up with Mont at Speyer in late February.[12] But the embassy met with little success. Philip of Hesse gave his blessing to an alliance which would provide for a common policy on security matters and on the Council of Trent, and the League put together a proposal at a diet summoned to Worms in May 1545. However, throughout the summer, John Frederick continued to refuse to commit himself to an understanding with England.[13] The duke's chief reservation was not only Henry's past conduct, but his fear of retaliation from Charles if he entered into an alliance with England.[14] Matters dragged on without resolution into the autumn and early winter.[15]

Eventually, on 6 November 1545, the privy council wrote to Bucler and Mont, informing them that Henry wanted Bucler to be sent back to England. They were instructed to tell Philip that the matter they had come to negotiate had been so dragged out that they were being recalled; there seemed to be no interest on the Protestant side in concluding any sort of an alliance. If the German Protestants wished to take the matter further, they should send

11 *LP* xx/1, 172.

12 *LP* xx/1, 183–4.

13 See Philip's initial response to the ambassadors, conveyed to Henry in a letter of 12 Mar. 1545, PRO, SP 1/199, fos 11–14 (cipher), 15–20 (decipher) [*StP* x. 338–44; *LP* xx/1, 350]; Henry's response, 30 Mar., PRO, SP 1/199, fos 129–35 [*StP* x. 379–81; *LP* xx/1, 451]; Philip's instructions to his delegates at Worms to advocate an alliance with England, HStMar, PA 729, fos 19–20; Bucer to Philip in support of an alliance with England, 12 Apr., *BwP* ii. 334; Bucler and Mont, 6 May, on the early progress of the negotiations at Worms, PRO, SP 1/200, fos 177–80 [*StP* x. 420–5; *LP* xx/1, 667]; privy council to Bucler and Mont, 12 May, PRO, SP 1/201, fos 22–5 [*StP* x. 433–4; *LP* xx/1, 715]; Bucler and Mont to Henry on the progress of the negotiations at Worms, 25 May, PRO, SP 1/201, fos 132–3 (heavily ciphered), 134–6 (decipher) [*StP* x. 441–4; *LP* xx/1, 808]; Hessian delegates to Philip on the writing of a provisional alliance document, 24, 28 May, HStMar, PA 729, fos 184–7, 211–14. See also PC iii. 606–7. The alliance proposal, known as the 'Capita', is HStMar, PA 729, fos 215–18 (copy); PA 736, fos 331–6 (copy). For Bucler and Mont to England on their unsuccessful efforts to elicit a final decision from the Germans, see *LP* xx/1, 870, 965–7, 1047–8, 1092, 1135, 1137, 1205, 1227, 1243, 1250–1. On 2 July Bucler and Mont wrote to Philip of Hesse seeking a final decision: HStMar, PA 1801, fos 99–102 (German text by Mont; signed by Bucler and Mont). Philip replied on 7 July, saying that he would do what he could with his own men to get a final decision. *LP* xx/1, 1138. The same day he wrote to his delegates to urge greater haste in getting an answer: HStMar, PA 730, fos 55–6.

14 The correspondence recording John Frederick's objections is printed in A. Hasenclever, 'Neue Aktenstücke zur Friedensvermittlung der Schmalkaldener zwischen Frankreich und England im Jahre 1545', *Zeitschrift für die Geschichte des Oberrheins* xx (1905), 225–8. See also the letter from John Frederick to Philip in late June on his reservations about doing business with Henry: HStMar, PA 2635, fos 10–13.

15 On 5 August Bucler and Mont sent a Latin copy of the 'Capita' to England: *LP* xx/2, 46.ii. (Versions also exist in HStMar, PA 736, fos 337–42 [German copy; only a few verbal differences from the 'Capita'], 342–6 [Latin copy].) They enclosed letters to Paget, apologising for the delays: *LP* xx/2, 47–8. Further letters from Bucler and Mont to England in September, seeking a response are at *LP* xx/2, 310, 381–3.

men with appropriate powers to England immediately.[16] As Paget later wrote to Mont, he and Bucler had been sent to seek the League's friendship, and 'could get but a sleeveless answer. And yet, in calling Mr Bucler home, the king did not utterly renounce the former practice; but looks for them to send to him next if they mean anything with him'.[17]

As in the 1530s, the Schmalkaldeners had let pass an opportunity both to gain a powerful ally and to support the accelerating swing towards the evangelicals in England. Within a year, as the imperial troops streamed out of the south and bore down on the armies of the League, it would be something which the Schmalkaldeners would have cause to regret.

Schmalkaldic peace mediation of the Anglo-French War, March 1545–February 1546

Although efforts to establish an Anglo-Schmalkaldic alliance receded during the middle months of 1545, diplomatic relations in general between England and the League did not cease altogether. In fact quite the opposite was the case, as during the summer and autumn a parallel Schmalkaldic diplomatic initiative emerged to replace the fading proposals for an alliance. Centred around efforts by the League of Schmalkalden to mediate an end to the war between England and France, it was dominating the diplomacy of both England and the League by the closing months of 1545. The background to this venture stretched back to the beginning of the year. After Bucler and Mont met at Speyer, they had travelled to Cassel to meet Philip of Hesse. On 6 March he mentioned to them that it would please him to see England and France at peace again.[18] On 3 April the matter was raised again, this time in a letter from Bucler and Mont to Paget and Petre. The ambassadors said that they had spoken with some man who had expressed a wish to see an honourable peace arranged between England and France. The ambassadors said that they had not yet mentioned this to Henry, but only to Paget and Petre, because it appeared more like a matter to be mentioned to counsellors rather to be directly raised with the king. Paget and Petre, they said in closing, would know better what to do, for they knew the minds of influential men better than Mont or Bucler.[19]

There appears, however, to have been no reaction to this from England. And though there were some murmurings at Worms about peace between

---

[16] *LP* xx/1, 736.

[17] *LP* xxi/1, 272.

[18] *LP* xx/1, 350. He claimed, rather disingenuously, that he only wanted to see England and France at peace again so that greater resistance to the Turk could be organised.

[19] PRO, SP 1/199, fo. 182 [*StP* x. 385; *LP* xx/1, 487].

England and France during May,[20] in Germany too the matter seems to have lost some momentum. Not, however, for long, for it was clear to virtually the whole of the League that while England and France were at war with one another, Charles, making more threatening noises by the day towards the Schmalkaldeners, would be free to contemplate action against the German Protestants. Thus German interest in mediating an Anglo-French peace soon resurfaced.

During July there was a flurry of activity in Hesse and Strassburg directed towards securing support for the despatch of a Schmalkaldic team to England and France to mediate.[21] In the following month it became clear that this had been successful: in early August proposals to send embassies to England and France were agreed and finalised.[22] The Schmalkaldic committee at Worms produced a memorandum which appointed four ambassadors: Ludwig von Baumbach and Johann Sleidan were to go to England; Hans Bruno and Christopher von Vennigen to France. The document went on to explain that they were going to England and France in order to negotiate a truce, which would then be followed by further discussions to finalise a peace treaty.[23] Their instructions were much the same as the memorandum, and indeed were probably based upon it.[24] An additional document provided a summary: the ambassadors were to arrange for an exchange of information between England and France; to attempt to establish a truce for one year, or at least until Easter 1546; to suggest that the outstanding disputes over Boulogne and the payment of the French pension be dealt with by a sequestration to the League until Henry and Francis could agree on a settlement; and to arrange a

[20] For example HStMar, PA 729, fos 154–9: letter dated 18 May from Philip's delegates speaking of hopes that England and France might conclude a treaty.
[21] See, for example, Jakob Sturm of Strassburg to Mont outlining the peace proposal, 11 July 1545, *LP* xx/2, 1170; Bucer to Philip of Hesse advocating a peace embassy, 12 July, *BwP* ii. 354–5; Bucler and Mont to Henry and Paget on the peace proposal, 16 July, *LP* xx/1, 1205–7. For Mont's advocacy in Germany see *BwP* ii. 357; *LP* xx/1, 1229. See also report from Philip's ambassadors on interest among the delegates at Worms in a peace embassy, HStMar, PA 730, fos 247–52; corroborative report by Jakob Sturm, *PC* iii. 618–19; letter from John Frederick to Philip setting out his reservations, 24 July, HStMar, PA 2635, fo. 159; Philip's reply, stating his intention to support the proposals, 30 July, HStMar, PA 2635, fos 162–9.
[22] Philip to his delegates at Worms, telling them that he wanted the mediation embassies to proceed, HStMar, PA 730, fos 324–5; similar letter telling them to go ahead with all haste, 1 Aug., fo. 326; Philip to Bucer saying he wanted the peace mediation to proceed, 1 Aug., *BwP* ii. 358; Paget to Bucler and Mont saying that Henry wanted the mediation to go ahead, 24 July, *LP* xx/1, 1262. In early August, Francis similarly accepted in principle the Schmalkaldic offer of mediation: *PC* iii. 624–5. For the Hessian delegates' report on discussions as to staffing of the embassy see HStMar, PA 730, fos 250–1.
[23] HStMar, PA 735 (unfolioed); PA 736, fos 348–9 (copy), 350–2 (draft) [partially printed in Hasenclever, 'Neue Aktenstücke', 228–9; *Sleidans Briefwechsel*, ed. H. Baumgarten, Strassburg 1881, 86].
[24] HStMar, PA 736, fos 679–82 (copy), 685 (fragment) [Hasenclever, 'Neue Aktenstücke', 229–31].

place and time for an agreement to be reached. Otherwise, the ambassadors were to act in accordance with their discretion and good sense.[25]

The four ambassadors met in late August and departed early the next month. They travelled together to Amiens, where they separated on 12 September. Baumbach and Sleidan arrived at the English court at Windsor on 19 September, bearing letters with six seals, including those of Hesse, Württemberg and Saxony.[26] The negotiations soon moved to France. As a result of the work of the Schmalkaldic ambassadors there, Francis I sent word that Henry should despatch an embassy to Ardres to treat for peace. Baumbach and Sleidan left for France in October, and were reunited with Bruno and Vennigen; in November they were joined by the English representatives, William Paget and Cuthbert Tunstall.[27] On 26 November the peace talks began.[28]

They soon began to run into intractable problems. The main points of difficulty were whether a peace between England and Scotland should be comprehended in a peace between England and France, whether the French should have Boulogne back and the question of the French pension.[29] Before long there was an impasse. On 11 December Paget presented the king's final demands to the French representatives. These included an undertaking to resume payment of the pension, to forfeit Guisnes and Boulogne and to pay war reparations. When these demands were rejected the negotiations began to deteriorate irretrievably.[30] Early in January 1546 they broke down completely, and the Schmalkaldic ambassadors returned to Germany. On 6 February Sleidan and Bruno wrote to Paget and assured him of the Protestants' regret at the outcome of the negotiations, Bruno adding that the Protestants would remain neutral in the war between England and France and

25 HStMar, PA 730, fos 677–8 [Hasenclever, 'Neue Aktenstücke', 231–3].

26 LP xx/2, 421. Letter from the imperial ambassador to Charles. The ambassadors' financial accounts verify the arrival date at Windsor: A. Hasenclever, Die Politik der Schmalkaldener, vor Ausbruch des schmalkaldischen Krieges, Berlin 1901, 72–3.

27 Ibid. See also Johann Sturm in France to Jakob Sturm in Strassburg, reporting on the progress of the negotiations there, 21 Sept. and 10 Oct., PC iii. 635–9, 652–5. For the negotiations at the French court see also D. L. Potter, 'Diplomacy in the mid-sixteenth century: England and France, 1536–1550', unpubl. PhD diss. Cambridge 1973, 121–6. On the moving of the negotiations to France see Sleidans Briefwechsel, 88; LP xx/1, 647–9, 651–2, 675, 810, 836; Hasenclever, Politik der Schmalkaldener, 78–9; PC iii. 660–1, 667–71; Potter, 'Diplomacy in the mid-sixteenth century', 124–5.

28 Meanwhile an Anglo-French truce had been arranged by the Germans for the duration of the talks: PC iii. 673–4. While these were going on under Schmalkaldic mediation, the emperor was mediating peace talks at Brussels between an English delegation led by Gardiner and a French delegation under the French admiral. These talks are summarised in Potter, 'Diplomacy in the mid-sixteenth century', 118–19 n. 3.

29 LP xx/2, 972–3. See Johann Sturm's detailed report to Jakob Sturm dated 10 December and the French king's answer to the proposal: PC iii. 679–89.

30 For a detailed discussion of the Anglo-French negotiations at Ardres see Hasenclever, Politik der Schmalkaldener, 81–93, and Potter, 'Diplomacy in the mid-sixteenth century', 126–36.

that they hoped as much as ever to help establish peace between the two. On 10 February Mont conveyed similar sentiments from the Protestants to Henry and Paget.[31]

Yet if the Germans put a brave face on the outcome, they were in no doubt that they had failed and that they could contribute little further. When the ambassadors arrived back in Germany, they reported to a Schmalkaldic diet in Frankfurt. Though they noted that many of the French and English wanted the League to continue with its efforts,[32] the report made clear that the negotiations had collapsed completely.[33] In the light of this bleak intelligence, in the weeks and months which followed the Schmalkaldeners' interest in bringing about an Anglo-French peace petered out.[34]

Though it must have been disheartening for the Schmalkaldic ambassadors to see the peace talks collapse before their eyes, there is little they could have done: the blame for this diplomatic breakdown rested entirely with the English (and, of course, the French).[35] Moreover, the Schmalkaldic efforts had not been entirely without success. By getting England and France to the negotiating table the Germans had at least been able to facilitate a breaking of the ice between the two countries. This in itself might have contributed to the fact that as the ambassadors returned to Germany, the war between England and France did not have much longer to run. Though Henry consented to a major offensive against the French in March 1546, this disintegrated almost as quickly as it had begun. By May the English and French delegations were again around the negotiating table (though this time without the mediation of the Schmalkaldic League). Finally, on 6 June, at Guisnes, the details were settled and peace was made between England and France.[36] The fact that this happened within six months of the Schmalkaldic mediation probably indicates that the Schmalkaldeners were more successful in their efforts to help end the Anglo-French war than they or anybody else at the time appreciated.[37]

---

[31] LP xxi/1, 173, 180–1, 191–2.

[32] PC iii. 711.

[33] HStMar, PA 849, fos 122–31.

[34] Though some subsequent traces of interest remained (for example, PC iv. 70–1), they were few and far between.

[35] Indeed, on 2 December 1545, Paget reported to Henry that without the Germans' help the negotiations would long before have fallen through: LP xx/2, 917.

[36] The final months of the Anglo-French war and the making of the peace are analysed in Potter, 'Diplomacy in the mid-sixteenth century', 136–61, and summarised in his 'Foreign policy', 132.

[37] The Germans had also been able to renew diplomatic connections with England at a variety of levels. Johann Sleidan offered to send Henry a copy of the history of the Reformation he was planning to publish. On a more practical level, in a letter towards the end of 1545, Henry ordered Paget to seek to have the German ambassador, Hans Bruno, brought into the king's service and given a pension: LP xx/2, 1037. Henry's command was probably a response to a number of earlier reports from Paget indicating Bruno's qualities and friendliness towards England (for example, LP xx/1, 1014). A memo by the king's council around

Last efforts at agreement, February 1546–April 1547

Though interest in an Anglo-Schmalkaldic alliance which Mont and Bucler had investigated in 1545 receded during the second half of the year as the peace negotiations took over as the chief diplomatic concern, it did not disappear completely. At the Schmalkaldic diet in Frankfurt which convened in December 1545, a belated discussion of the alliance negotiations from earlier in the year took place at the behest of the Hessian delegates.[38] Nevertheless, substantial progress continued to be elusive. Although the conclusion to the diet's discussions early in 1546 noted that it would be useful for England and the League to stand together against a general council,[39] the League remained unwilling to make any decisive or formal commitment to seek an alliance with England. And although England made some efforts through the opening months of 1546 to investigate the possibility of an Anglo-Schmalkaldic alliance, little subsequent progress was made.[40] The impression was that, with the exception of Philip of Hesse, the League had little serious interest in an alliance. By May, even William Paget was writing of his despair of ever achieving anything through diplomatic activity in Germany.[41]

In the summer, however, all this changed, as Charles decided that the time of reckoning had arrived for the Schmalkaldic League. In the course of imperial diets at Worms in March 1546 and Regensburg from April to July 1546, Charles made preparations with the papacy and his Catholic subjects for a major campaign against it. He declared war at Regensburg in July, justifying his action by reference to the invasion of Braunschweig-Wolfenbüttel by Hesse and Saxony in 1542. Suddenly, the members of the League understood the need for external friends, and in the wake of the Anglo-French peace treaty at Guisnes in June, plans quickly began to be made for appeals for help from Francis and Henry.[42]

In early July, as the League received its first hints of Charles's intentions, preparations for an embassy to Henry began. John Frederick wrote to Philip on 5 July and, his former reluctance to do business with Henry gone, urged that Johann Sturm and Hans Bruno be sent to England with all possible haste.[43] On 15 July he wrote again, repeating the need for great speed, and

the same time was also favourable towards Protestant Germany. It mentioned a pension for Bruno and that the Protestants should be told that they might be useful in later peace negotiations, even though it now looked unlikely that they would be called upon: *LP* xx/2, 1036.
[38] *PC* iii. 712.
[39] HStMar, PA 847, fos 293v–4.
[40] *LP* xxi/1, 272, 278, 385, 423–4, 475–6, 580, 796–8, 1129.
[41] *LP* xxi/1, 831.
[42] The background to, and development of, France's involvement in the Schmalkaldic War is examined in D. L. Potter, 'Foreign policy in the age of the Reformation: French involvement in the Schmalkaldic War, 1544–1547', *HJ* xx (1977), 525–44.
[43] HStMar, PA 2653, fos 72–4.

saying that the embassy should seek to obtain financial support from the king.[44] This was repeated in the instructions for Sturm and Bruno. They also asked Henry to return those German mercenaries whom he had employed against Francis and suggested that in the light of the Anglo-French peace treaty perhaps England and France would consider a common policy to help the League.[45]

The ambassadors arrived in England in August.[46] On 30 August Henry gave them an answer. He offered a pension of 12,000 florins to the landgrave, in return for which the landgrave would serve Henry alone, take no other pension, furnish Henry with soldiers and agree to supply Henry's enemies with none. The king then went on to say that he would be willing to enter an alliance with the Protestants against 'all men and for all causes'. For this purpose he asked the League to send ambassadors to England as soon as possible. He proposed that he would be the alliance's leader and that he would have more votes than the other members, since he would have to provide more than them. In a throwback to the Anglo-Schmalkaldic heyday of the 1530s, he also suggested that a theological conference be convened in England between his theologians and some of the League's. The Protestants should send a list of possible participants to England and from that list Henry would select between four and six participants.[47]

Armed with these proposals, Sturm and Bruno made their way back to Germany. They reported to an emergency League diet at Ulm in late

---

[44] HStMar, PA 2654, fos 7–13.

[45] HStMar, PA 896, fos 30–7. As Bruno and Sturm left for England, Mont did what he could to help, writing to Henry and Paget on 15 July about Charles's aggression. In the letter to Paget he entered a special plea for granting some aid to the League: *LP* xxi/1, 1285–6.

[46] Charles V had anticipated that the Germans would seek Henry's help, and instructed his ambassador in London to keep a close eye on developments. When the Germans arrived in England, the council ensured that the ambassador was misinformed as to their purpose, being told that they were only in England for discussions related to the peace mediation of the previous winter; Gardiner and Paget added that they thought it would be regrettable if Charles were to be defeated in Germany: *LP* xxi/1, 1110, 1463, 1481; xxi/2, 27, 34.

[47] *LP* xxi/1, 1526. The positive reception which Henry gave to the Schmalkaldic ambassadors in August and just before his death is dismissed as mere diplomatic calculation in Smith, 'Protestant triumph', 1237–64 (Smith's view is largely accepted in Scarisbrick, *Henry VIII*, 466–9). It is argued that Henry was simply encouraging the Germans in their fight against Charles and had no genuine interest in a religiously based alliance with them (pp. 1258–9). This forms part of a general theory that Henry in fact did not lean towards Protestantism in the last years of his reign as was suggested in Foxe, *Acts and monuments*, v. 562–4, 690–2. This study cannot accept this argument, in particular or in general. Though wider European diplomacy always played a part in Henry's calculations, the growing interest in political and religious diplomacy with the League should be seen within the context of Henry's growing sympathy for Protestant theology from the mid-1540s onwards (it is not within the scope of this book to examine Henry's move towards Protestantism towards the end of his life, but it broadly adheres to the views in Starkey, *Personalities and politics*, 151–3 and, of course, Foxe, *Acts and monuments*). German evidence suggests that Foxe, *Acts and monuments*, v. 692, was accurate when he described Henry as pledging his support to the German Protestants near the end of his life (see p. 215 below).

September. After hearing from Bruno, the delegates concluded that Henry was well inclined towards the Protestants. They agreed to accept his proposals for a religious conference and suggested that ambassadors be sent to England to conclude an four-year alliance of mutual defence. On 2 October John Frederick and Philip wrote in agreement from their battlefield camp near Nordlingen. It is a measure of the seriousness of the situation facing the Schmalkaldeners that John Frederick, who not long before had ridiculed the idea of an alliance with the 'crazy man' Henry, now heartily supported an additional proposal that the Anglo-Schmalkaldic alliance should last a full twelve years.[48] Yet even in these difficult circumstances, the League proved unable to act expeditiously and decisively. Discussions dragged on through October and November.[49] In November, it was finally agreed that the English offer of an alliance needed further explanation and posed difficulties on the question of mutual aid; to iron out these problems another embassy would have to be sent to England.[50] It was subsequently proposed, and agreed, that on its way it should negotiate with Francis and that it should be composed of Franz Burchard, Nicholas Lersener (a Hessian nobleman) and Strassburg's Johann Sturm. It was to ask for soldiers and money to be sent to Germany as soon as possible. It should also ask Henry to mount an immediate attack on Charles. Yet in spite of these forthright proposals, the characteristic Schmalkaldic caution remained: the ambassadors' powers were only to close an alliance with Henry and Francis up to the point of ratification.[51]

In December the embassy left for France. When the privy council received information that it was on its way through France in late December, it instructed the English ambassador there to ensure that it first enter into an alliance with the French king, in case Francis should 'slip to the emperor'.[52] Francis saw things similarly. Lersener's account shows that in an audience which Francis granted the Germans on 24 December, the French king said that he would only enter an alliance with the League if Henry would do the same.[53] With this promising beginning made, the ambassadors travelled from the French court to England to seek Henry's agreement. On 10 January Burchard wrote to John Frederick from London. The embassy had recently

---

48 HStMar, PA 916, fos 60–5.
49 See, for example, the correspondence between Strassburg and its delegates at Ulm in October and November: PC iv. 452–4, 465, 486–8. It appears that during this time an English herald named Somerset arrived in Germany, conveying an offer almost exactly the same as that made to the German ambassadors by Henry on 30 August: ibid. 452–4.
50 PC iv. 465.
51 HStMar, PA 916, fos 154–9. The ambassadors also took a separate letter from John Frederick and Philip, which thanked Henry for the response he had given to Bruno and Sturm, and asked him to enter into an alliance with the League: PA 921, fos 2–4 [German, followed by Latin copy].
52 LP xxi/2, 619.
53 HStMar, PA 921, fos 31–4. A letter from Burchard to Jakob Sturm of the same date and a further letter of 29 December conveyed similar sentiments: PC iv. 531–2, 544–5, 545 n. 1.

been joined by Bruno.[54] He reported that they hoped to have an audience soon with Henry, who, although he had been weak for some time, had with God's help recently improved. The signs of success were good: the duke of Norfolk, 'who was the greatest papist and persecutor of the gospel',[55] and his son had recently been imprisoned, and Henry had reputedly authorised the despatch of an embassy to Denmark to defend the Gospel. Burchard believed that they would have a good answer, and promised to write when they had had an audience with Henry.[56]

That audience never took place. On 6 February Burchard wrote to Jakob Sturm that Henry had died on 28 January and had been succeeded by his only son. He reported, nevertheless, that the new king and his regency council appeared to be very favourable to the Gospel, and that already 'Winchester is excluded from all counsels'.[57] Moreover, it appeared likely that the new regime would grant the League money and that within a few days a comprehensive agreement would be reached.[58] But if Burchard was correct in his observations on the sea change in English politics, he was overly optimistic in thinking that the result of the swing in favour of the English evangelicals would mean instant aid for the Schmalkaldic League. As Lersener later explained, though the outlook had been promising

on 28 January, the king died. For this reason the ambassadors were kept waiting until 2 March. Then the appointed men, that is to say the protector and the other councillors, explained that the late king had decided not to abandon the League, but to enter into an alliance with it etc. But since he had passed away, they can perform in the same way as the king, and do not want to go ahead because the present king is a minor, the kingdom is not yet stable, and

---

[54] The evidence in this and the following paragraph will suggest that John Foxe was reliably informed when, in demonstrating Henry's growing sympathy for Protestantism towards the end of his life, he followed his famous evidence of Henry's observation to the French ambassador that he was thinking of abolishing the private mass with a second piece of evidence (*Acts and monuments*, v. 692): 'The other cause which leadeth me thereunto is also of equal credit, grounded upon the declaration of the king's own mouth after that time, more near unto his death, unto Bruno, ambassador of John Frederick, duke of Saxony [*sic*: Bruno was from Metz, and had been sent on behalf of the League, probably as an appointee of Strassburg or Hesse]: unto the which ambassador of Saxony the king gave this answer openly, that if the quarrel of the duke of Saxony were nothing else against the emperor, but for religion, he should stand to it strongly, and he would take his part, willing him not to doubt or fear. And so with this answer he dismissed the ambassador unto the duke, openly in the hearing of these four sufficient witnesses, as the lord Seymour earl of Hertford, lord Lisle then admiral, the earl of Bedford lord privy seal, the lord Paget.'

[55] '[W]elcher der grost Bapist und verfolger des Evangelii gewesen ist': HStMar, PA 2569, fo. 29.

[56] Ibid. fos 29–30.

[57] 'Wintoniensis prorsus ab omni consilio exclusus est': PC iv. 598.

[58] PC iv. 598–9.

the ambassadors' powers are not valid but have expired through the king's death.[59]

The ambassadors were told that if they returned to Germany for valid powers, England would by then be ready to enter into an alliance with France and the Schmalkaldic League. A sympathetic letter of 4 March, from Edward VI, reiterated that if the ambassadors would return with valid powers there would be no obstacle to concluding an Anglo-French-Schmalkaldic alliance.[60] With these decisions in hand, the ambassadors decided to return to Germany.

On the way back they stopped in France to discuss the alliance question once more with Francis. On 25 March Francis told the Germans that he would send ambassadors to England forthwith to negotiate on the nature and extent of Anglo-French aid for the Protestants. Upon receiving this answer the Germans resumed their journey to Germany to urge that ambassadors with new powers to negotiate and conclude the proposed alliance be sent to England and France as soon as possible.[61]

It was too late. During March and April the fortunes of the League's numerically superior army in the battles with Charles's experienced Spanish troops declined. On 24 April 1547 at Mühlberg, by the river Elbe, the League suffered a decisive defeat. Soon afterwards its forces surrendered, and John Frederick and Philip submitted as the emperor's prisoners. This brought to an end the Schmalkaldic League, and hence the history of Anglo-Schmalkaldic relations.

---

[59] '[A]uf den 28 Januarii ist der kunig gestorben. Derhalben die gesandten auffgehalten worden bis auf den 2.tn Marcii. Do haben die verordneten namlich der protector und die andern Regenten angezaigt wie der kunig seligen genzlichen bei sich beschlossen disse stende nit zuverlassen besonder sich mit inen in buntnuss zu begeben etc. Dweil er aber vorscheiden kunten sie dero gestalt als der kunig thun mogen und wollen nit furt schreitten auss ursachen das der itzige kunig unmundig, das kunigreich noch nicht stabilirt, der gesanten mandata nicht genugsam sondern expirirt durch des kunigs sterben': HStMar, PA 921, fos 32r–v [PC iv. 684].
[60] HStMar, PA 921, fo. 30 (signed by Edward and Somerset).
[61] HStMar, PA 921, fos 31–4 [PC iv. 683–5]. The account, dated 18 April, went on to note that new powers would also be needed for France, in the light of the subsequent death of Francis. The ongoing hope that the new regime in England would uphold the Gospel is reflected in an anonymous letter from Strassburg dated 9 March 1547: PC iv. 644–5. On 18 March Burchard wrote to Jakob Sturm from Amiens of the good hope of concluding an alliance in London with England and France: PC iv. 653.

Conclusion

The orthodox view of Anglo-Schmalkaldic diplomacy was formulated in the nineteenth century, when it seemed that the world could be measured and mastered by mechanical means. According to this view, England and the League were a dependent part of a greater trigonometrical system in which Henry, Charles and Francis ordered their diplomatic actions in perfect accordance with the relative inclinations and movements of their counterparts. This work has offered a different interpretation. It has sought to move the history of Anglo-Schmalkaldic relations away from the nineteenth-century obsession with mechanical order and structure, and to put it back where it belongs: in the sixteenth century. In that world, talk of modern, secular-minded Euro-politicking is out of place, and it becomes clear that although the wider European political scene was part of the backdrop to Anglo-Schmalkaldic diplomacy, it did not determine the direction of relations between England and the League. Rather, the course of Anglo-Schmalkaldic diplomacy was dominated by the particular influences which the religious preoccupations of the time wrought upon it.

And so I have drawn the main lines of this history. The king was interested in the Schmalkaldeners not merely for their political usefulness but also as a consultative source to help establish his new Church and as possible co-religionists; Thomas Cromwell and the evangelicals believed that an Anglo-Schmalkaldic alliance would benefit their cause and therefore encouraged the king to develop relations with the League; the English conservatives realised that an alliance with the League would endanger their position and so sought to undermine efforts to achieve an agreement with the Germans. Given the interest in Anglo-Schmalkaldic relations shown by the king and the reformers, an alliance between England and the League might have appeared likely. But the Germans, and especially those of the rigidly Lutheran east, were constrained by theological principle and the threatening presence of Charles V. Their insistence on English adherence to the letter of the Confession of Augsburg, their refusal to send a major embassy to England headed by Melanchthon, their rejection of a reciprocating military alliance – all played into the hands of the defenders of orthodoxy. The Schmalkaldeners' 1538 embassy threw into relief five articles of theological dispute which, after the unhelpful visit of the minor Schmalkaldic legation of May 1539, the king was persuaded by the conservatives to settle in parliament along the particular lines which he had come to consider correct. These formed the backbone of the conservative reaction of mid-1539, the Act of Six Articles. Though the evangelicals subsequently fought back, the Schmalkaldeners' diplomatic freedom of action was limited by the truce they had agreed with Charles V in April 1539 (the Frankfurt Interim); their consequent prevarications through late 1539 and early 1540 wore down the king's patience and his goodwill towards the Germans. The Cleves marriage was the last straw. Once it failed Cromwell was left without a leg to stand on and the field was open for the conservatives to poison the king's mind against both the minister and the Germans. A climactic faction fight followed. Cromwell fell, Barnes was burned and Anne discarded; relations between England and the League collapsed, never again to be as close as during the 1530s.

Anglo-Schmalkaldic diplomacy took place within, indeed was a part of, a larger contest over religion; and that religious contest was conducted through the medium of faction politics. Thus it was, essentially, the course of English faction politics which played the chief part in deciding the outcome of Anglo-Schmalkaldic relations. In the historiography of Henry's reign faction has occupied a central place from the beginning, ever since the original historian of the English Reformation, John Foxe, wrote of

> how variable the state of religion stood in these days. . . . Even as the king was ruled and gave ear sometimes to one, sometimes to another, so one while it went forward, at another season as much backward, and sometimes clean altered and changed for a season, according as they could prevail, who were about the king.[1]

A factional view of the Reformation was first challenged in the early twentieth century by A. F. Pollard, who in his great biography of Henry laid stress on the independent decision-making capacity of the king. Pollard's views were later developed by J. J. Scarisbrick in his groundbreaking study of the reign and more recently have been taken further in a number of articles by G. W. Bernard which have depicted Henry as a kind of absolute monarch, independent of influence from the political world he inhabited.[2]

Yet perhaps there is a middle ground, distinct from the rigid alternatives of a king-or-faction (or, for that matter, king-or-minister) dichotomy. For its part, this study has placed faction at the heart of affairs. It has proposed an historiographical synthesis in which a powerful, strong-minded monarch co-exists with rival factions actively competing for his ear.[3] In this model, the king's indecision on a given issue is the key starting point: it is accepted that once Henry was set on a specific policy or course of action, faction was to all

---

[1] Foxe, *Acts and monuments*, v. 260. Those who have in one measure or another adhered to Foxe's interpretative scheme include Sir Geoffrey Elton, A. G. Dickens and Eric Ives. See Bernard, 'The making of religious policy', 321–2, for an account of these views; the article as a whole offers a criticism of the factional view of Henrician politics. See Warnicke, *Marrying of Anne of Cleves*, 192–5, for support for Bernard's interpretation.
[2] Pollard, *Henry VIII*; Scarisbrick, *Henry VIII*; Bernard, 'The making of religious policy', 321–49.
[3] See Gunn, 'Structures of politics', 89–90, for a similar 'have our cake and eat it' approach to faction and the king.

intents and purposes irrelevant. Had Henry known from the early 1530s exactly what he wanted in the religious sphere there would have been no religiously-based faction politics. However, in the second half of the reign the king was a seeker; and in pursuing his search for the truth he wanted to listen to the advice of those around him, not to mention those from more distant shores who had already broken with Rome. This is not to say that until he had reached a final decision Henry was prey to whatever clever theological words he had heard last. For example, he had reservations about Lutheran doctrine on the abuses as early as 1535 and, in spite of a variety of persuasions from German and English evangelicals alike, he maintained these throughout the remainder of the decade. Still, if he had certain inclinations, they were not set in stone: he wanted them submitted to proper theological examination. Moreover, it would be unwise to dismiss Henry's interest in theological disputation as mere diplomatic posturing: witness Henry's behaviour in the summer of 1538, when he could easily have directed Cuthbert Tunstall to compose a scholarly rejection of Lutheran doctrine on the abuses and simply have appended the royal signature to it; instead he threw himself into researching and writing a reply to the Lutherans which not only stands as a significant example of his theological literacy but impresses as the work of a man with a passionate involvement in the issues. We will never know whether Philip Melanchthon would have been able to overcome Henry's objections to Lutheranism in a face-to-face disputation (my own speculation is that Master Philip might have had some success on confession and perhaps even justification, but would have made little headway with communion in both kinds, priestly marriage or, most critically, private masses). Be that as it may, when English evangelicals pleaded for Melanchthon to be sent to England, they did so in the knowledge that Henry was genuinely interested in discussing the theological questions involved and was open to persuasion. The point of departure for this study has been that the place of Anglo-Schmalkaldic relations in English politics was a function of Henry's interest in consulting with the League on the direction of his Church. It was, above all, royal interest in the League's religious principles that transformed Anglo-Schmalkaldic relations from a mere diplomatic episode to an important feature of English domestic politics.

Yet if this study has rejected the historiographical excesses of a do-nothing king helplessly swaying amid a storm of faction, it can have no truck with the other extreme which posits a sort of Henrician absolutism. Yes, Henry was the initiator, manager and final arbiter of political activity, but as long as he remained undecided on the great ideological question of his reign, factional conflict was rife. It is sometimes suggested that the evidence for this conflict is tainted because it comes from diplomatic sources which are credulous and superficial in their understanding of English politics and prone to represent all they see in partisan terms. As it happens, this study has only on one occasion made extensive use of the sort of diplomatic evidence most disliked by those historians who downplay the relevance of faction: that which comes from resident ambassadors (here in Marillac's correspondence on the fall of Thomas Cromwell).[4] Nevertheless, a word should be said in support of the reliability of those diplomatic records which have formed the evidential basis of the factional view of politics which has been developed here. Firstly, it should be noted that much of the diplomatic evidence presented in this study has had independent corroboration. For example, in September 1539 Martin Bucer claimed that in spite of the fervent requests of certain English evangelicals, the Schmalkaldic delegation of the previous year had prematurely concluded its theological negotiations in London and returned home. This claim is corroborated by independent evidence from August 1538, both in the form of correspondence between Cromwell and Cranmer, and letters from the ambassadors themselves to their masters in Germany. Or consider the evidence of September 1539, when the Saxon ambassadors to England reported that Cromwell had explained to them that the Act of Six Articles had been introduced by some conservative bishops during his illness. This is independently corroborated by letters from Cromwell to the king in the previous April, a number of which explained that he had a tertian fever and so could not attend at the court, and one of which cited a letter from Philip Melanchthon against some English bishops who were currently agitating in support of the abuses. There is also the evidence of 1540, when the resident French ambassador, Marillac, claimed that Henry had turned irrevocably against Cromwell after the discovery of a Schmalkaldic file in the minister's house. This both independently corroborates and is corroborated by numerous letters and papers during the period from 1533 to 1540, all of which betray the extent of Cromwell's secret involvement in Germany during the time of his ministry. Still more important than such instances of independent corroboration, is the weight and the consistency of the evidence which this study has produced. Never mind that much of the contemporary German material is violently partisan: as with the early English Protestant historians, it is the very crudity of the Germans' anti-Catholicism which makes it so easy to compensate for their biases. Once one strips away the judgements of who was good and who was bad, there stands revealed an evidential store which,

---

[4] Though the point cannot be pursued here, I do not accept the view that even resident ambassadors' reports are in some way inherently inferior as evidence. The following comments in E. W. Ives, 'Stress, faction and ideology in early-Tudor England', *HJ* xxxiv (1991), 196, are noteworthy: 'Diplomatic reports are the main, often the only, contemporary source for politics and the court. If they are unreliable, there is little can be said on the topic. It is not that ambassadors' letters merit automatic credence, but that the only way to elucidate Henrician politics at all is to engage critically with each letter in detail, not discount them *a priori*.' For a wider attack on an alleged general theory which asserts that certain categories of evidence are intrinsically superior to others see D. R. Starkey, 'Tudor government: the facts?', *HJ* xxxi (1988), 929. See also Gunn, 'Structures of politics', 64–7, for discussion of diplomatic evidence and what it can tell historians about faction politics. Warnicke, *Marrying of Anne of Cleves*, 187–8, 206, expresses doubts about the reliability of resident ambassadors' evidence.

for the 1530s, tells a consistent and detailed story of faction politicking. Certainly, any one or two of the instances of factional intrigue cited from 1533 to 1540 could, in isolation, be dismissed as aberrations, but the body of evidence as a whole cannot be so easily wished away.

Thus, to one side of the king stood a group of 'English councillors and distinguished people who favour the gospel'. So spoke the 1534 Schmalkaldic Diet of Nuremberg; and in subsequent years many more references were made to such a group, whether in Chancellor Brück's 1536 talk of the 'many honest bishops and others in England who are heartily inclined to these matters [of the gospel], and who promote the same well', or in Bucer's allusion in 1537 to men 'united' in a common 'purpose and undertaking', or in other references to 'fine learned men, who teach pure and true' (Mykonius in 1538), to 'excellent men, and most friendly to the purer doctrine of the gospel' (Burchard in 1539), to 'pious Christians' (Bucer in 1539), to 'the king's foremost counsellors and servants who are inclined to the Christian religion' (the Arnstadt diet in 1539), to the 'kindhearted', 'good men', 'dear people', and so on. What has emerged most clearly from this study, then, is that this collection of elite politicians was, first and foremost, a religious association. It was held together, not by personal jealousies or lust for power, but principally by a common interest in establishing Protestantism in England: this is why it has been called here the evangelical faction. This is also why the group was so interested in the League: the evangelical faction wanted 'an embassy with articles etc.' to be despatched from Germany in order that 'the gospel might be brought into England' (so the 1534 Nuremberg diet); for an embassy to be 'sent to England where it might promote the gospel' (Theabold in 1537); for the Schmalkaldeners to 'despatch a considerable embassy to England and with true devotion look after the religion and the pious Christians there' (Bucer in 1539); for England and the League to be brought together, and thus 'the true doctrine of religion received' (Burchard in 1539). The evangelicals promoted relations with the League not merely because it made good diplomatic sense to do so, but because the League was Protestant, and it was therefore thought that an alliance with it would help the evangelical faction in its efforts to establish reform in England.

A number of individuals have emerged as leading lights in the evangelical faction, among them Thomas Cranmer, Edward Foxe, Thomas Audley, Robert Barnes and Christopher Mont. However one name before all others has stood out: Thomas Cromwell. This study has suggested that Cromwell led the evangelicals both in the pursuit of their general aim of establishing a reformed Church and in the particular policy of seeking to realise that aim by promoting relations with the League. Such a portrayal is at odds with some modern scholarship. In particular, it runs counter to the picture of Cromwell drawn by Sir Geoffrey Elton. For Elton, Cromwell was the architect of a revolution in the government of England, a man whose primary purpose and achievement were to reform the way in which the country was run by means of a systematic overhaul of the organs of government. In support of Elton's thesis, it should be acknowledged that a glance through the state papers does suggest a Cromwell busily intent on reforming the machinery and practice of government: letters and papers abound from the minister and his office dealing with a wide range of administrative, bureaucratic and financial concerns. Elton's thesis is also in keeping with the famous portrait by Holbein, which most obviously depicts the tireless administrator, ready at his desk, inkpots and pen to hand, a letter opened before him and various papers scattered about.[5]

One may however ask whether such a view of Cromwell touches upon the essence of the man. For if Cromwell dealt with a wide range of matters and introduced many administrative reforms in the course of his ministry, it can be argued that these were simply the product of the demands of his job and the singular circumstances of the first years of the English Reformation. Moreover, as a new man of low birth, following in the steps of the flamboyant Wolsey, he probably judged it prudent to cultivate the image of an honest, austere, bureaucratic plodder, selflessly serving king and commonwealth. None of this, it should be noted, is to accept Bernard's description of the minister as a hard-working civil servant without an original idea in his head: it is hard to see how Bernard's Cromwell could have made a single enemy in the 1530s, let alone manage the feat of being executed.[6] Rather, it is to argue that it was behind Cromwell's workaday ministerial duties, behind his public face, that his real concerns were to be found; that he had special interests: that an hour spent adjudicating a land dispute, or even creating new financial agencies or streamlining the secretariat or council, was not so important to him as five minutes spent plotting the translation and distribution of the Bible, or scheming Taverner's translation of the Confession of Augsburg, or engineering the appointment of evangelicals to the episcopate, or, indeed, crafting closer contacts with the German Protestants. Perhaps there is in that painting by Holbein a more appropriate symbolism: in the book before Cromwell, its spine judiciously turned from the public view; and still more in the folded paper clutched in the minister's left hand, held most closely of all, its contents yet hidden from the official gaze.

This study has suggested that it was Cromwell's unofficial religious agenda which truly defined the man. Not only was he the chief advocate of a Protestant alliance with the Germans, by his own admission to Philip of Hesse in 1538 one who would not 'neglect any occasion, nor such offices as I possess, with which to strengthen and establish such friendship daily with a strong bond', or, as Burchard noted the same year, a man 'most favourably

---

5 This is the essence of Elton's position on Cromwell. It did, however, undergo considerable development over forty years. Probably the best (and certainly the most entertaining) account of that development is Christopher Haigh's, 'Religion', *Transactions of the Royal Historical Society* 6th ser. vii (1997), 281–99. See also Bernard, 'Elton's Cromwell', 587–607.
6 Bernard, 'Elton's Cromwell', 587–607, and 'The making of religious policy', 329–47.

inclined and affectionate towards the affairs of the Christian religion and the German nation', or as Marillac pointedly wrote after the minister's arrest, 'attached to the German Lutherans'. He was also recognised as the pre-eminent advocate of Protestantism. In 1536 Martin Luther, replying to a complimentary letter from Cromwell, declared his joy at the 'earnestness' of the minister's 'goodwill in the cause of Christ', and in view of that earnest goodwill his especial pleasure at 'your authority in the entire kingdom and about the king, with which you can do much'. As the 1540 Schmalkaldic ambassadors observed, Cromwell was the man with 'the most influence about the king – indeed who might as well be king himself . . . [and who] is very favourable to the gospel'. Thus when Cranmer wrote to continental reformers in 1537 of Cromwell, he spoke not of the administrator or remaker of government. Rather, he eulogised the man 'who has done more than all others together in whatever has hitherto been effected respecting the reformation of religion and of the clergy'. Here, surely, is the real Cromwell. The man his contemporaries recognised; the man the first historians of the Reformation depicted. Cromwell was a faction politician for whom religion was a primary motivation; a man who pursued a Protestant alliance with the League with such unrelenting singlemindedness that in the end it contributed materially to his death. In the final analysis, this study can only stand in support of the traditional view that Cromwell's greatness, his historical significance, rests in his religious work; in the central role he played as the leader of the evangelicals in introducing Protestantism to the English nation.

To the king's other side stood the conservatives. About the conservative faction this study has had much less to say. Nevertheless, in such references as Theabold's report of 'those whose spiritual inclination is to the papacy', Burchard's 1539 identification of the 'opponents of the gospel', his subsequent reference to the 'papistical faction', and his observation that the conservatives were 'very frightened at our arrival', the essentials have emerged. The conservatives were men of equal but opposite religious commitment to the reformers. They saw from early on the dangers which alliance with the League would spell for their cause, and so did their best to spoil efforts to achieve an Anglo-Schmalkaldic agreement. Again this study supports the essentials of the historical tradition: led by such capable figures as Gardiner ('the evil bishop of Winchester'), Norfolk ('the greatest persecutor of the gospel'), Stokesley ('an evil old papist and sophist') and Tunstall (only dexterous Durham dodged such invective), the conservatives were men whose actions were guided by religious principle; men who devoted their lives from the 1530s to resisting the advance of religious reform.

And so, king and faction have come to be seen as symbiotic aspects of high politics in the Henrician Reformation. One cannot help but recall Cranmer's words in 1537, when he spoke of how the king was wont to consult on theological matters first with one side of the religious divide and then with 'some one else of an entirely opposite way of thinking'; only when he had made himself 'master of their opinions, and sufficiently ascertained both what they

commend and what they find fault with' would he declare 'his own judgement respecting the same points'. Henry knew that differences of religious
opinion existed around him. Far from simply putting up with it or trying to
suppress it, he used this conflict as part of the decision-making process.
Perhaps Henry would have been attracted by the prospect of unfettered auto-
cratic power, but his awareness of the history of the previous century must
have told him that venturing on the momentous changes of the 1530s as an
absolute monarch would be fraught with danger: faction was a means by
which the king could interact with and consult the political nation in the
early Reformation. That said, this was no virtuoso prince smoothly managing
the factions he had let loose around him; for once Henry had made clear his
willingness to listen to both sides of the religious divide before passing judgement, the stakes were high and the contests quickly became commensurately
sharp. There is considerable evidence that the factional contests of the 1530s
generated high risk political behaviour. Factional intrigue could take place
behind the king's back: the discussions at the Diet of Nuremberg in 1534 on
the evangelicals' pro-Schmalkaldic advocacy 'though unknown to the king';
Thomas Theabold's secret mission to Germany of 1537; the instruction that
Foxe's involvement in Theabold's mission be kept from Henry 'for in these
matters the king is not to be joked with'; the private instructions for Mont in
1538; the secret messenger to Bucer in 1539; and German reports of Cromwell's efforts to prevent the implementation of the Act of Six Articles.
Factional conflict became increasingly dangerous: in 1537 it was necessary to
keep Foxe's name secret 'so that he does not come into any danger with his
lord the king'; in 1539 Philip Melanchthon wrote to Cranmer of 'the
dangerous conflicts in which he [Cranmer] is engaged'. And, of course,
factional conflict became more and more violent, as demonstrated by Cromwell's comment to Burchard that the Act of Six Articles was introduced 'by
the opponents of the gospel, because they wanted to extirpate the lord of
Canterbury, the Chancellor and lord Cromwell'; by Cromwell's imprisoning
of Sampson and Wilson; by Marillac's observation that 'either Cromwell's
party or that of the bishop of Winchester must succumb' for 'each party to establish what they maintain would destroy those who sustain the contrary';
and, most vividly, by the bloody end to Cromwell's life. Certainly, the king
retained ultimate control of the competing parties throughout; but once he
declared open the question of the religious direction of his realm, the prospect of a new Jerusalem, whether happy or otherwise, would be the spur to all
manner of political action.

At the outset of this work, I suggested that its broad thematic concern would
be to illustrate by way of a specific case study of foreign policy the inter-
relationship between religion and politics during the Henrician Reformation.
I believe that the exposition of faction politics presented here has helped to
illumine this inter-relationship. The contention that Anglo-Schmalkaldic
relations were determined by the course of a religiously-based factional

conflict supports the view that the Reformation brought a new dimension to the relationship between English religion and politics. The faction politics of the Henrician Reformation were unprecedented in that they were based on a conflict over ideas which were regarded by the protagonists as eternal truths. There had been faction politics before in English history. But faction had never before been based on ideology. Faction had previously formed on the basis of practical matters: whether to go to war with France or not; whether to increase certain taxes; whether to augment the power of a particular noble. Now ideology, the ideology of religion, entered the stage for the first time as the essential determinant of political allegiance and behaviour. Henceforth, the shape and major conflicts of English and British politics would be defined by religious and later secular ideology; much more than anything else, it is the birth of ideology as the fundamental dynamic of the political culture of England which makes the Henrician Reformation truly a time of epochal change. A Tudor revolution indeed, but in politics not in government.[7]

This new inter-relationship between religion and politics, in which the two effectively merged, thus creating ideological politics conducted through the medium of faction, explains why relations with the League of Schmalkalden were so important in England: diplomacy with the League, like faction itself, was ideological. That is why England engaged in such in-depth diplomacy with what was little more than a rag-bag collection of minor princes and provinces. It is why diplomacy with the League went forward when the reformers and reform were in favour, and went backward when the conservatives and reaction held sway. It is why the king took such a close interest in England's German diplomacy; and it is why the king's men were prepared to fight, connive, lie and die over relations with the League of Schmalkalden.

---

[7]   See, however, John Watts, 'Ideas, principles and politics', in A. J. Pollard (ed.), *The Wars of the Roses*, London 1995, 110–33, for the persuasive argument, all the more compelling for being developed on the apparently unpromising ground of the Wars of the Roses, that political conflict before the Reformation still had to take ideology into account. I am grateful to Steven Gunn for suggesting that I think about the ideological aspects of such pre-Reformation issues as Henry II's dispute with Thomas Becket. The large claim I essay here does not rule out ideology before the Reformation, but suggests that it was only from the sixteenth century that political conflict actually began to be predicated on long-term ideological difference, as opposed to the pre-Reformation period in which ideology merely exercised short-term, discrete and discontinuous influences on politics. See D. R. Kelley, *The beginning of ideology: consciousness and society in the French Reformation*, Cambridge 1981.

Bibliography

Unpublished primary sources

Cambridge, Corpus Christi College
Parker Library Manuscripts: MS 109

London, British Library
MS Add. 25114
MSS Cotton Caligula E.ii; Cleopatra E.v; Cleopatra E.vi; Cleopatra E.vi, vol. 2;
  Titus B.i; Vitellius B.xiii; Vitellius B.xiv; Vitellius B.xxi
MSS Harleian 6148, 6989
MS Royal 7.c.xvi

London, Public Record Office
State papers, Henry VIII: SP 1/78, 79, 80, 82, 85, 94, 96, 99, 123, 125, 126, 129,
  130, 133, 134, 135, 136, 137, 139, 142, 155, 160, 195, 197, 199, 200, 201
State papers, Theological Tracts: SP 6/2; 3; 6
Exchequer, Treasurer of the Receipt, Manuscript Books: E 36/143

Marburg, Hessisches Staatsarchiv
Politisches Archiv Philipps von Hessen: PA 269, 279, 282, 293, 295, 409, 437,
  439, 440, 443, 445, 455, 469, 520, 522, 538, 729, 730, 735, 736, 847, 849, 896,
  916, 921, 1452, 1799, 1800, 1801, 1809, 2065, 2546, 2547, 2556, 2561, 2562,
  2563, 2565, 2566, 2569, 2572, 2574, 2575, 2578, 2581, 2582, 2583, 2628,
  2629, 2635, 2653, 2654

Munich, Bayerisches Hauptstaatsarchiv
Kurbayern Äußeres Archiv MSS 2087, 2089

Weimar, Thüringisches Staatsarchiv
Registrande H, Schmalkaldische Bund: Reg. H 40, 51, 53, 59, 76, 91, 105, 106,
  107, 114, 115, 120/2; p. 137, no. 64; p. 146, no. 70; p. 165, no. 78 i; p. 165, no.
  78 ii; p. 191, no. 88; p. 198, no. 91; p. 207, no. 94; p. 248/249, no. 108, vol. 1;
  p. 248/249, no. 108, vol. 5; p. 260, no. 111; p. 260, no. 111, vol. 1; p. 260, no.
  111, vol. 2; p. 282, no. 118; p. 295, no. 121, vol. 4; p. 313, no. 128
Registrande N, Religiöse Sachen: Reg. N 736

Published primary sources

Briefwechsel Landgraf Philipps des Grossmüthigen von Hessen mit Bucer, ed. M. Lenz,
  Leipzig 1880–7
Calendar of state papers, Spanish, ed. G. Bergenroth, P. de Gayangos and M. A. S.
  Hume, London 1862–95

Calendar of state papers, Venetian, ed. R. Brown, C. Bentinck and H. Brown, London 1864–98

Corpus reformatorum, ed. C. G. Bretschneider, Halle 1834–60

Der Briefwechsel des Friedrich Myconius (1524–1546), ed. H.-U. Delius, Tübingen 1960

Die Beschlüsse der oberdeutschen schmalkaldischen Städtetage, 1530–1536, ed. E. Fabian, Tübingen 1959–60

Die schmalkaldischen Bundesabschiede 1530–1536, ed. E. Fabian, Tübingen 1958

Die Wittenberger Artikel von 1536, ed. G. Mentz, Leipzig 1905

Disputationen in den Jahren 1535–1545 an der Universität Wittenberg gehalten, ed. P. Drews, Göttingen 1895

Documents of the English Reformation, ed. G. Bray, Cambridge 1994

'Epistolae reformatorum', ed. N. Linde, *Zeitschrift für Kirchengeschichte* v (1877), 164–6

Formularies of faith, ed. C. Lloyd, Oxford 1856

Letters and papers, foreign and domestic, of the reign of Henry VIII, 1509–47, ed. J. S. Brewer, J. Gairdner and R. H. Brodie, London 1862–1910

Letters of Stephen Gardiner, ed. J. A. Muller, Cambridge 1933

Lisle letters, ed. M. St Clare Byrne, London 1981

Miscellaneous writings and letters of Thomas Cranmer, ed. J. E. Cox, Cambridge 1846

'Neue Aktenstücke zur Friedensvermittlung der Schmalkaldener zwischen Frankreich und England im Jahre 1545', ed. A. Hasenclever, *Zeitschrift für die Geschichte des Oberrheins* xx (1905), 224–51

Original letters relative to the English Reformation, ed. H. robinson, Cambridge 1846

Politische Correspondenz der Stadt Strassburg im Zeitalter der Reformation, ed. H. Virck and O. Winckelmann, Strassburg 1892–8

Politisches Archiv des Landgrafen Philipp des Grossmütigen von Hessen, ed. W. Heinemeyer and F. Küch, Leipzig–Marburg 1904–59

Records of the Reformation, ed. N. Pocock, Oxford 1870

Sleidans Briefwechsel, ed. H. Baumgarten, Strassburg 1881

State papers published under the authority of His Majesty's Commission, of King Henry VIII, London 1830–52

Weimarer Ausgabe der Werke D.M. Luthers, Abteilung Briefe, Weimar 1930–48

Secondary sources

Bacon, F. and F. Godwin, *The history of the reigns of Henry the seventh, Henry the eighth, Edward the sixth and Queen Mary*, London 1676

Beckingsale, B. W., *Thomas Cromwell: Tudor minister*, London 1978

Bedouelle, G. and P. Le Gal (eds), *Le 'Divorce' du roi Henry VIII*, Geneva 1987

Bernard, G. W., 'Elton's Cromwell', *History* lxxxiii (1998), 587–607

——— 'The making of religious policy, 1533–1546: Henry VIII and the search for the middle way', *HJ* xli (1998), 321–49

Blunt, J. H., *The Reformation of the Church of England*, London 1878

Bouterwek, W., 'Anna von Cleve: Gemahlin Heinrichs VIII., Königs von England', *Zeitschrift des Bergischen Geschichtsvereins* iv (1867), 337–413; vi (1869), 97–180

Brady, T. A., 'Phases and strategies of the Schmalkaldic League: a perspective after 450 years', *Archiv für Reformationsgeschichte* lxxiv (1983), 162–81

Brandi, K., *Kaiser Karl V*, Munich 1937

Brigden, S., 'Thomas Cromwell and the "brethren" ', in Cross, Loades and Scarisbrick, *Law and government*, 31–49

———— *London and the Reformation*, Oxford 1989

Brooks, P. N., *Thomas Cranmer's doctrine of the eucharist: an essay in historical development*, London 1965

Burnet, G., *History of the Reformation of the Church of England*, ed. N. Pocock, Oxford 1865

Cameron, E., *The European Reformation*, Oxford 1991

Clark, F., *Eucharistic sacrifice and the Reformation*, Oxford 1967

Coleman, C. and D. R. Starkey (eds), *Revolution reassessed: revisions in the history of Tudor government and administration*, Oxford 1986

Collier, J., *An ecclesiastical history of Great Britain*, London 1852

Cross, C., *Church and people, 1450–1660*, London 1976

———— D. Loades and J. J. Scarisbrick (eds), *Law and government under the Tudors: essays presented to Sir Geoffrey Elton, Regius Professor of Modern History in the University of Cambridge, on the occasion of his retirement*, Cambridge 1988

Davies, C. S. L., *Peace, print and Protestantism, 1450–1558*, London 1976

Delius, H. U., 'Königlicher Supremat oder evangelische Reformation der Kirche: Heinrich VIII. von England und die Wittenberger, 1531–1540', *Wissenshaftliche Zeitschrift der Ernst-Moritz-Arndt-Universität Greifswald, gesellschafts- und sprachwissenschaftliche Reihe* xx (1971), 283–91.

Dickens, A. G., *Thomas Cromwell and the English Reformation*, London 1959

———— *The English Reformation*, London 1964

Dixon, R. W., *History of the Church of England from the abolition of the Roman jurisdiction*, London 1884–1902

Dodd, C., *Church history of England*, London 1889

Doernberg, E., *Henry VIII and Luther*, London 1961

Doran, S., *England and Europe in the sixteenth century*, Basingstoke 1999

———— and G. Richardson (eds), *Tudor foreign policy*, London forthcoming

Drews, P., *Disputationen in den Jahren 1535–1545 an der Universität Wittenberg gehalten*, Göttingen 1895

Dugmore, C. W., *The mass and the English reformers*, London 1958

Dülfer, K. D., *Die Packschen Händel*, Marburg 1958

Eells, H., *Martin Bucer*, New Haven 1931

Elton, G. R., *The Tudor revolution in government: administrative changes in the reign of Henry VIII*, Cambridge 1953

———— *The Tudor constitution: documents and commentary*, Cambridge 1960

———— *Reformation Europe, 1517–1559*, London 1963

———— *Policy and police: the enforcement of the Reformation in the age of Thomas Cromwell*, Cambridge 1972

———— *Reform and renewal: Thomas Cromwell and the common weal*, Cambridge 1972

———— *England under the Tudors*, 2nd edn, London 1974

———— *Studies in Tudor and Stuart politics and government, I: Tudor politics/Tudor government; II: Parliament/political thought; III: Papers and reviews, 1973–1981*, Cambridge 1974–83

―――― *Reform and Reformation*, London 1977

―――― (ed.), *The new Cambridge modern history*, II: *The Reformation, 1520–1559*, 2nd edn, Cambridge 1990

Fabian, E., *Die Entstehung des Schmalkaldischen Bundes und seiner Verfassung*, Tübingen 1962

Figgis, J., *The divine right of kings*, Cambridge 1914

Fines, J., *A biographical register of early English Protestants and others opposed to the Roman Catholic Church*, Abingdon 1985

Fisher, H. A. L., *The political history of England, 1485–1547*, London 1906

Fox, A. G. and J. A. Guy, *Reassessing the Henrician age: humanism, politics and reform, 1500–1550*, Oxford 1986

Foxe, J., *Acts and monuments*, ed. G. Townsend, London 1843–9

Froude, J. A., *History of England from the fall of Wolsey to the defeat of the Spanish armada*, London 1870–5

Fuchs, W. P., *Das Zeitalter der Reformation*, Munich 1973

Fuller, T., *The church history of Britain*, Oxford 1845

Gairdner, J., *The English Church in the sixteenth century from the accession of Henry VIII to the death of Mary*, London 1902

―――― *Lollardy and the Reformation in England*, London 1908–13

Gammon, S. R., *Statesman and schemer: William, first Lord Paget, Tudor minister*, Newton Abbot 1973

Grafton, R., *Grafton's chronicle*, London 1809

Gunn, S. J., 'The structures of politics in early Tudor England', *Transactions of the Royal Historical Society* 6th ser. v (1995), 59–90

Guy, J. A., *Tudor England*, Oxford 1988

Haigh, C., 'The recent historiography of the English Reformation', *HJ* xxv (1982), 995–1007

―――― 'Religion', *Transactions of the Royal Historical Society* 6th ser. vii (1997), 281–99

Hall, E., *Hall's chronicle*, London 1809

Hardwick, C., *A history of the articles of religion*, Cambridge 1859

Hasenclever, A., *Die Politik der Schmalkaldener vor Ausbruch des schmalkaldischen Krieges*, Berlin 1901

Herbert, E., *The life and raigne of King Henry the Eighth*, London 1649

Heylyn, P., *Ecclesia restaurata: the history of the Reformation of the Church of England*, London 1674

Hildebrandt, E., 'Christopher Mont, Anglo-German diplomat', *Sixteenth Century Journal* xv (1984), 263–87

Holborn, H., *A modern history of Germany: the Reformation*, London 1965

Holinshed, R., *Holinshed's chronicles of England, Scotland and Ireland*, London 1808

Hook, W. F., *Lives of the archbishops of Canterbury*, London 1860–75

Hopf, C., *Martin Bucer and the English Reformation*, Oxford 1946

Hughes, P., *The Reformation in England*, London 1963

―――― and J. F. Larkin (eds), *Tudor royal proclamations*, New Haven 1964–9

Ives, E. W., *Anne Boleyn*, London 1986

―――― *Faction in Tudor England*, London 1986

―――― 'Stress, faction and ideology in early-Tudor England', *HJ* xxxiv (1991), 193–202

—— 'Henry VIII: the political perspective', in MacCulloch, *Reign of Henry VIII*, 29–31

Jacobs, H. E., *The Lutheran movement in England*, Philadelphia 1891

Jenkyns, H., *The remains of Thomas Cranmer*, Oxford 1833

Kelley, D. R., *The beginning of ideology: consciousness and society in the French Reformation*, Cambridge 1981.

Kelly, H. A., *The matrimonial trials of Henry VIII*, Stanford, CA 1976

Kidd, B. J., *The later medieval doctrine of the eucharistic sacrifice*, London 1898

Knecht, R. J., *Francis I*, Cambridge 1982

Koenigsberger, H. G., *The Habsburgs and Europe, 1516–1660*, New York 1971

Kouri, E. I. and T. Scott (eds), *Politics and society in Reformation Europe: essays for Sir Geoffrey Elton on his sixty-fifth birthday*, London 1987

Kreider, A., *English chantries: the road to dissolution*, London 1979

Lehmberg, S. E., 'Supremacy and vicegerency: a re-examination', *EHR* lxxxi (1966), 225–35

—— *The later parliaments of Henry VIII, 1536–1547*, Cambridge 1977

Lingard, J., *A history of England from the first invasion of the Romans*, London 1823–31

Loades, D. M., *Politics and the nation, 1450–1660: obedience, reistance and public order*, London 1979

Logan, F. D., 'Thomas Cromwell and the vicegerency in spirituals: a revisitation', *EHR* ciii (1988), 658–67

MacCulloch, D., 'Henry VIII and the reform of the Church', in MacCulloch, *Reign of Henry VIII*, 159–80

—— 'The religion of Henry VIII', in Starkey, *European court*, 160–2.

—— *Thomas Cranmer: a life*, New Haven 1996

—— (ed.), *The reign of Henry VIII: politics, policy and piety*, London 1995

MacGrath, A., *Reformation thought: an introduction*, Oxford 1988

Mackie, J. D., *The earlier Tudors, 1485–1558*, Oxford 1952

Mattingly, G., *Renaissance diplomacy*, London 1955

Maynard-Smith, H., *Henry VIII and the Reformation*, London 1963

Mentz, G., *Johann Friedrich der Grossmütige, 1503–1554*, Jena 1903–8

Merriman, R. B., *Life and letters of Thomas Cromwell*, Oxford 1902

Messenger, E. C., *The Reformation, the mass, and the priesthood*, London 1936

Möller, W., *Andreas Osiander: Leben und ausgewählte Schriften*, Elberfeld 1870

Muller, J. A., *Stephen Gardiner and the Tudor reaction*, London 1926

Murphy, V. M., 'The literature and propaganda of Henry VIII's first divorce', in MacCulloch, *Reign of Henry VIII*, 135–58

Mykonius, F., *Historia reformationis*, Leipzig 1718

Nicholson, G., 'The Act of Appeals and the English Reformation', in Cross, Loades and Scarisbrick, *Law and government*, 19–30

Parker, T. M., *The English Reformation to 1558*, London 1950

Peters, H. and H. Lahrkamp, 'Zwei Bildnisse Heinrichs VIII. auf Schenkungsurkunden für Anna von Kleve', *Düsseldorfer Jahrbuch* xlviii (1956), 293–309.

Pollard, A. F., *Thomas Cranmer and the English Reformation, 1489–1556*, London 1926

—— *Henry VIII*, London 1902

Pollard, A. J. (ed.), *The Wars of the Roses*, London 1995

Potter, D. L., 'Foreign policy in the age of the Reformation: French involvement in the Schmalkaldic War, 1544–1547', *HJ* xx (1977), 525–44

—— 'Foreign policy', in MacCulloch, *Reign of Henry VIII*, 101–34

—— 'The international mercenary market in the sixteenth century: Anglo-French competition in Germany, 1543–50', *EHR* cxi (1996), 24–58

Powicke, F. M., *The Reformation in England*, London 1941

Prüser, F., *England und die Schmalkaldener, 1535–1540*, Leipzig 1929

Redworth, G., 'A study in the formulation of policy: the genesis and evolution of the Act of Six Articles', *Journal of Ecclesiastical History* xxxvii (1986), 42–67

—— 'Whatever happened to the English Reformation?', *History Today* xxxvii (October 1987), 29–36

—— *In defence of the Church Catholic: the life of Stephen Gardiner*, Oxford 1990

Rex, R. A. W., 'The English campaign against Luther in the 1520s', *Transactions of the Royal Historical Society* 5th ser. xxxiv (1989), 85–106

—— *Henry VIII and the English Reformation*, Basingstoke 1993

Ridley, J. G., *Thomas Cranmer*, Oxford 1962

Rockwell, W. W., *Die Doppelehe des Landgrafen Philipp von Hessen*, Marburg 1904

Rupp, E. G., *Studies in the making of the English Protestant tradition*, Cambridge 1947

Russell, C., *Unrevolutionary England, 1603–1642*, London 1990

Scarisbrick, J. J., *Henry VIII*, London 1968

Scheible, H., *Das Widerstandsrecht als Problem der deutschen Protestanten, 1523–1546*, Gütersloh 1969

Scherffig, P., *Friedrich Mekum von Lichtenfels*, Leipzig 1909

Seckendorf, V. L. von, *Historie des Lutherthums*, trans. E. Frick, Leipzig 1714

Sleidan, J., *A famouse cronicle of oure time, called Sleidanes commentaries, concerning the state of religion and common wealth, during the raigne of the Emperour Charles the Fift*, trans. J. Daye, London 1560

—— *The general history of the Reformation of the Church*, trans. E. Bohun, London 1689

Smith, H. M., *Henry VIII and the Reformation*, London 1962

Smith, L. B., *Tudor prelates and politics, 1536–1558*, Princeton 1953

—— 'Henry VIII and the Protestant triumph', *American Historical Review* lxxi (1965–6), 1237–64

—— *Henry VIII: the mask of royalty*, London 1971

Smith, P., 'Luther and Henry VIII', *EHR* xxv (1910), 656–69

—— 'German opinion of the divorce of Henry VIII', *EHR* xxvii (1912), 671–81

—— 'Englishmen at Wittenberg', *EHR* xxxvi (1921), 422–33

Smithen, F. J., *Continental Protestantism and the English Reformation*, London 1927

Soames, H., *The history of the Reformation of the Church of England*, London 1826–8

Speed, J., *The history of Great Britaine under the conquests of the Romans, Saxons, Danes and Normans*, London 1650

Starkey, D. R., 'From feud to faction: English politics ca. 1450–1550', *History Today* xxxii (November 1982), 16–22.

—— *The reign of Henry VIII: personalities and politics*, London 1985

—— 'Intimacy and innovation: the rise of the privy chamber, 1485–1547', in Starkey, *English court*, 71–118

———— 'Privy secrets: Henry VIII and the lords of the council', *History Today* xxxvii (August 1987), 23–31

———— 'Tudor government: the facts?', *HJ* xxxi (1988), 921–31

———— and S. Wabuda, 'Acton Court and the progress of 1535', in Starkey, *European court*

———— (ed.) *Henry VIII: a European court in England*, London 1991

———— D. A. L. Morgan, John Murphy, Pam Wright, Neil Cuddy and Kevin Sharpe (eds), *The English court: from the Wars of the Roses to the Civil War*, London 1987

Stern, A., 'Heinrich VIII. von England und der Schmalkaldische Bund, 1540', *Forschungen zur deutschen Geschichte* x (1870), 489–507.

Stone, D., *A history of the doctrine of the holy eucharist*, London 1909

Stowe, J., *Annales*, London 1631

Strauss, G. (ed.), *Pre-reformation Germany*, London 1972

Strype, J., *Ecclesiastical memorials, relating chiefly to religion, and the Reformation of it, and the emergencies of the Church of England, under King Henry VIII, King Edward VI, and Queen Mary I*, Oxford 1822

Sturge, C., *Cuthbert Tunstal*, London 1938

Tjernagel, N. S., *Henry VIII and the Lutherans*, St Louis 1965

Vergil, P., *The Anglica historia of Polydore Vergil*, ed. D. Hays, London 1950

Waitz, G., *Lübeck unter Jürgen Wullenwever und die Europäische Politik*, Berlin 1855–6

Walther, W., *Heinrich VIII. von England und Luther*, Leipzig 1908

Ward, P. J., 'The politics of religion: Thomas Cromwell and the Reformation in Calais, 1534–40', *Journal of Religious History* xvii (1992), 152–71

Warnicke, R. M., *The marrying of Anne of Cleves: royal protocol in early modern England*, Cambridge 2000

Wernham, R. B., *Before the armada: the growth of English foreign policy, 1485–1588*, London 1966

Williamson, J. A., *The Tudor age*, London 1964, 158–9.

Wriothesley, C., *A chronicle of England during the reigns of the Tudors, from 1485 to 1559: by Charles Wriothesley*, ed. W. D. Hamilton, London 1875

Wurm, C. F., *Die politischen Beziehungen Heinrichs VIII. zu Markus Meyer und Jürgen Wullenwever*, Hamburg 1852

Unpublished dissertations

Lange, P., 'Die englisch-deutschen Beziehungen 1531 bis 1535 mit besonderer Berücksichtigung der Politik Philipps von Hessen', DPhil. diss. Marburg 1924

McEntegart, R., 'England and the League of Schmalkalden, 1531–1547: faction, foreign policy and the English Reformation', PhD diss. London 1992

Meyer, A. O., 'Die englische Diplomatie in Deutschland zur Zeit Eduards VI. und Mariens', Breslau 1900

Müller. A., 'Die Beziehungen Heinrichs VIII. zu Anna von Cleve', DPhil. diss. Tübingen 1907

Murphy, V. M., 'The debate over Henry VIII's first divorce: an analysis of the contemporary treatises', PhD diss. Cambridge 1984

Neville, P. A., 'Richard Pynson, king's printer (1506–1529): printing and propaganda in early Tudor England', PhD diss. London 1990

Potter, D. L., 'Diplomacy in the mid-sixteenth century: England and France, 1536–1550', PhD diss. Cambridge 1973

Singer, P., 'Beziehungen der Schmalkaldischen Bundes zu England im Jahre 1539', DPhil. diss. Greifswald 1901

Ward, P. J., 'Thomas Cromwell and Calais, 1530–40', BA diss. Armidale, NSW 1988

Index